The Collected Courses of the Academy
Series Editors: Professor Grái
Fordham Law
Professor Bruno de Witte,
Professor Marise Cremona, and
Professor Francesco Francioni,
European University Institute,
Florence
Assistant Editor: Anny Bremner, *European University*
Institute, Florence

VOLUME XVI/2
Confronting Global Terrorism

The Collected Courses of the Academy of European Law
Edited by Professor Marise Cremona, Professor Gráinne de Búrca,
Professor Bruno de Witte, and Professor Franceso Francioni
Assistant Editor: Anny Bremner

This series brings together the Collected Courses of the
Academy of European Law in Florence. The Academy's mission is to
produce scholarly analyses which are at the cutting edge of the two
fields in which it works: European Union law and human rights law.
A 'general course' is given each year in each field, by a
distinguished scholar and/or practitioner, who either examines the
field as a whole through a particular thematic, conceptual, or
philosophical lens, or who looks at a particular theme in the context
of the overall body of law in the field. The Academy also publishes
each year a volume of collected essays with a specific theme in each
of the two fields.

Confronting Global Terrorism And American NEO-Conservatism

*The Framework of a Liberal
Grand Strategy*

TOM FARER

OXFORD
UNIVERSITY PRESS

OXFORD
UNIVERSITY PRESS

Great Clarendon Street, Oxford ox2 6DP

Oxford University Press is a department of the University of Oxford.
It furthers the University's objective of excellence in research, scholarship,
and education by publishing worldwide in

Oxford New York

Auckland Cape Town Dar es Salaam Hong Kong Karachi
Kuala Lumpur Madrid Melbourne Mexico City Nairobi
New Delhi Shanghai Taipei Toronto

With offices in

Argentina Austria Brazil Chile Czech Republic France Greece
Guatemala Hungary Italy Japan Poland Portugal Singapore
South Korea Switzerland Thailand Turkey Ukraine Vietnam

Oxford is a registered trade mark of Oxford University Press
in the UK and in certain other countries

Published in the United States
by Oxford University Press Inc., New York

British Library Cataloguing in Publication Data

Data available

Library of Congress Cataloging in Publication Data

Data available

Typeset by Newgen Imaging Systems (P) Ltd., Chennai, India
Printed in Great Britain
on acid-free paper by
Biddles Ltd., King's Lynn

ISBN 978–0–19–953472–2
ISBN 978–0–19–953473–9 (Pbk.)

1 3 5 7 9 10 8 6 4 2

Dedication

To the next generations: Paola, Miriam, Dima, Linus,
Jean-Louis, and Renan,
with love

Acknowledgements

The only thing certain about any acknowledgment is that it will inadvertently omit mention of some persons who deserve to be included. For as the artist Whistler famously noted during his cross-examination in the libel action he brought against a critic, every work is in some sense the product of our entire life and all the people who have been consequential in it. That said, every author plows ahead because respect must be paid to the people and institutions that have played an immediate and conspicuous role in the process culminating in a book.

I start appropriately with the directors of the Academy of European Law at the European University Institute in Fiesole, Professors Marise Cremona, Bruno de Witte and my principal interlocutor among them, Professor Francesco Francioni. These days the dean of a professional school in a private university is a de facto CEO wrestling with the academic equivalent of marketing, product enhancement and innovation, human resource management, budgeting, and the other tasks that have always fallen to managers in the private sector, tasks that can easily consume one's waking hours, if not one's minor dreams. It is easy to intend to remain a contributor through scholarship to the discourse of public policy; it is harder to execute that intention. Without the flattering invitation to deliver the General Course, I might still be wandering in the realm of intention.

Beyond stiffening my will, the directors opened to me the sensual pleasure of a week above Florence and the intellectual one of exchanging ideas with a truly challenging group of "students," many of them, of course, are professionals in one or another precinct of human rights law. To every one of them who pressed me in class to sharpen my thoughts, indeed to every one who remained awake for two hours in the high heat of late June not long after Florentine lunches (which appeared to be all of them, but never trust the lecturer on such a point), I acknowledge my appreciation. I must also acknowledge the Academy's Administrative Director, Anny Bremner, and its Publications Officer, Barbara Ciomei, who guided me through the final steps in the transformation of my lectures into this book.

Without the assistance of my research assistants—Cate Conley, King-in Marshall, Chris Winningham, and Joel Pruce—I would still be transforming. My debt to all of them is large. I also want to acknowledge one of my students at the Academy, Sabine Park, both for her close and critical reading of my chapter on communal conflict and for her assistance in designing the cover of this book. The carving out of time to complete this little work required all the ingenuity of my Assistant at the Graduate School of International Studies, Joanne Evilsizer, whose unfailing good humor disarms me as it does everyone else she encounters.

Finally, I want to acknowledge the inestimable assistance rendered to me in this matter as in all others by my life's companion, my dearest friend, my wife Mika who expresses in her way of living in the world all of the values I profess more, I fear, than I practice.

Denver, Colorado

11 February 2007

Foreword

A word of advice to the general reader

This is a book written for the general reader concerned with the great contemporary challenges to national and human security. However, it is also a work directed to specialists and students studying international law, human rights, and international relations in an era marked by transnational terrorism and the proliferation of weapons of mass destruction. The latter expect and require a level of technical legal and policy detail which the general reader does not need and may find distracting from the book's main line of analysis and argument. Particularly in sections of Chapter 3 and, arguably, in Chapter 2 as well, the level of detail could turn the general reader's canter into a diversionary slog. To be sure, the more technical details may become more interesting and useful after one sees the overall thrust of the book. In that case, of course, one can backtrack. My advice, then, is to read as follows: Chapter 1; the short section of Chapter 2 that precedes "The Original Understanding" and then the last section on "The Liberal Case for Conserving Normative Restraint"; in Chapter 3, I would read the very short introduction preceding the section on "Standards" and then jump to the last two sections beginning with "Liberal Values and the Temptation to Torture." After that I might jump to Chapter 6 and only after finishing it go back to Chapters 4 and 5, but that would depend on time and taste.

Tom Farer

27 April 2007

Contents

1

Introduction: Liberalism, Human Rights, Terrorism and Neo-Conservatism

Most war movies have been about heroes, our heroes, and individual differences among the enemies were irrelevant, since their villainy could be taken for granted. In fact, showing individual character, or indeed any recognizable human qualities, would be a hindrance, since it would inject the murderousness of our own heroes with a moral ambiguity that we would not wish to see. The whole point of feel-good propaganda is that the enemy has no personality; he is monolithic and thus inhuman. (Ian Buruma)

The terrorist attack launched on American soil by Islamic *jihadists* in September 2001 and the first stage of the American-led response demolished the facile optimism that had marked the pronouncements of many scholars, publicists and political elites, particularly in the triumphant West, after the fall of the Berlin Wall.[1] Rather than ending in the triumph of the ideas and values associated with liberal capitalist democracy,[2] history appeared to lurch forward violently into a new era of deadly conflict in which, once again, irreconcilable ideas and values far more than material national interests propelled the antagonists. It was as if there had erupted out of the clear field for liberalism, envisioned by many in the aftermath of Communism's collapse, a furious alternative vision of the good society and the moral life, one far more alien than communism which, after all, had stemmed, however eccentrically, from the same Enlightenment and humanist roots as liberalism itself.

As presented by the Administration of President George W Bush, the conflict is strictly between *jihadist* Islam—which, to give him his due, the President

---

[1] See, eg, Francis Fukuyama, *The End of History and the Last Man* (New York: Free Press, 1992), 283: "The post-historical world is one in which the desire for comfortable self-preservation has been elevated over the desire to risk one's life in a battle for pure prestige, and in which universal and rational recognition has replaced the struggle for domination." To be fair, he added the caveat that, "Outside the Islamic world, there appears to be a general consensus that accepts liberal democracy's claims to be the most rational form of government, that is, the state that realizes most fully either rational desire or rational recognition," 211–12. Even then, however, there were some far-sighted pessimists. See, eg, Lawrence Freedman, "Order and Disorder in the New World," *Foreign Affairs*, 71(1) (1991), 20–37: "Certainly, if the 'new world order' is supposed to mean the triumph of liberalism and free markets, the rule of international law and an era of peace and prosperity, then the performance will be found wanting against the ideal."
[2] See Francis Fukuyama, "The End of History?", *National Interest*, 3 (1989), 3–18.

sought to distinguish from the Islamic religion and its adherents as a whole[3]—
and liberal (or at least capitalist) democracy. To the President, if we take him at
his word, this conflict, like the preceding one against the Soviet Union, is an
ideological battle of world-historical dimension. However that may be, in most
other respects it is nothing like the Cold War or any other war in memory, hot or
cold. For on the one side you have a highly organized society, the United States,
enjoying a military power imbalance against other states unparalleled in world
history,[4] and, on the other side, you have...well, what exactly? Not a state. Not
even an organization, if one thinks in terms of some entity with vertical lines of
authority and responsibility. Rather, in Al Qaeda we seem to have a shifting cluster
of self-starting grouplets, in loose association, answerable finally to themselves,
drawing inspiration, perhaps, from the iconic personality of Osama bin Laden,
bonded by a particular interpretation of the Islamic faith, by a narrative of redeem-
able humiliation, and by a perceived enemy.[5] Having no authoritative leader, the
phenomenon is immune to decapitation. Having no territorial base, it is immune
to deterrence, for there is nowhere to send the deterring promise of massive
retaliation and there are no critical capital investments at risk. Being nowhere, it
could be anywhere. And out of all proportion to the numbers of its "troops," it has
managed to make Western Governments and peoples, particularly those of the
United States, see it as a powerful threat to their security. This is understandable.
For Al Qaeda and its ideological offspring have arrived, not by chance, coincident
with the integration of national economies into a global economic order vitally
dependent on transportation and communications networks vulnerable to
catastrophic attack by militants able to access the very instrumentalities and
technologies that have made integration possible.

This view of the struggle with terrorism is not limited to the Bush Administration. It echoes in the mass media and through most of respectable American

---

[3] In an address to the Joint Session of Congress and the American People on 20 September 2001,
<http://www.whitehouse.gov/news/releases/2001/09/20010920–8.html>, accessed 20 July 2006,
President George W. Bush addressed Muslims directly: "We respect your faith. It's practiced freely
by many millions of Americans, and by millions more in countries that America counts as friends.
Its teachings are good and peaceful, and those who commit evil in the name of Allah blaspheme
the name of Allah. The terrorists are traitors to their own faith, trying, in effect, to hijack Islam
itself." He had previously shared similar remarks in a 17 September 2001 address to the Islamic
Center of Washington, DC, <http://www.whitehouse.gov/news/releases/2001/09/20010917–11.
html>, accessed 20 July 2006, saying, "The face of terror is not the true faith of Islam. That's not
what Islam is all about. Islam is peace. These terrorists don't represent peace. They represent evil
and war."
[4] See, eg, Paul Kennedy, "The Eagle has Landed," *The Financial Times*, 2 February 2002.
[5] See Thomas Powers, "Bringing 'Em On," Review of Daniel Benjamin and Steven Simon, "The
Next Attack: The Failure of the War on Terror and a Strategy for Getting it Right," *New York
Times*, 25 December 2005. Simon and Benjamin describe the Jundullah ("Army of God") as a
prime example of the new, decentralized, self-starting groups, typically composed of the educated
middle class and inspired by Al Qaeda's ideology, 30–1. Regarding the appeal of Al Qaeda to
European Muslims and its ideological community, see "The Enemy Within," *Economist*, 16 July
2005, 24–6.

society and can be heard, although with many more discordant notes, in other Western countries.[6] But like all popular narratives, it is selective and to that extent offers only a partial truth. Al Qaeda's worldview is irredeemably hostile to liberal values[7] and difficult to reconcile with the ethos of post-industrial, consumption-oriented capitalism and hence to its quotidian manifestations. And of course it is also true that, given the vulnerability of infrastructure in the advanced industrial countries and the ever-widening diffusion of the knowledge required to produce weapons of mass destruction, the Al Qaeda network constitutes a very real material danger to Western societies and also to more-or-less secular, modernizing regimes in every country where Muslims are a significant proportion of the national population. And because global interdependence readily transmits shocks in one country to many others, the danger to human security is literally global in scope.

The popular narrative is a bit partial, however, in ignoring not so much the existence as the relevance to the conflict, seen as an ideological as well as a material one, of militant Christian and Jewish groups within the West, *jihadists* in their own right, that share Al Qaeda's hostility to the liberal culture of tolerance, skepticism and individualism and yearn, like their bearded counterparts, for a restoration of traditional hierarchies, restraints, and uncontestable beliefs.[8] Strongly represented now in the Republican Party and the Bush Administration

---

[6] See, eg, British Prime Minister Tony Blair's statement on 21 July 2005, <http://www.number10. gov.uk/output/Page7858.asp>, accessed 21 July 2006, following the London 7/7 bombings: "We will show, by our spirit and dignity, and by our quiet but true strength that there is in the British people, that our values will long outlast theirs." Jacques Chirac echoed similar sentiments during a 22 September 2003 United Nations Conference, "Against Terrorism—For Humanity," <http://www. ambafrance-us.org/news/statmnts/2003/chirac_terrorism_NY092203.asp>, accessed 21 July 2005: "It will take time to overcome terrorism, and relentless efforts on the part of the entire international community. We must close ranks against the forces of hatred arrayed across the world and bound together by underground networks that exploit modern technologies, finding shelter in countries that are either complicit or powerless, in alliance with drug traffickers and mafia gangs." Finally, see also Spanish Prime Minister Jose Maria Aznar, "Seven Theses on Today's Terrorism," address at Georgetown University on 21 September 2004, <http://www3.georgetown.edu/president/aznar/ inauguraladdress.html>, accessed 21 July 2005: "The war against terror can only succeed if we are finally able to eliminate the deeper root of its existence: hate of modernity and Western values, a feeling that circulates throughout the Middle East with particular virulence."

[7] See generally, Paul Berman, *Terror and Liberalism* (New York: Norton Publishing, 2003); Olivier Roy, *Globalized Islam: The Search for a New Umma* (New York: Columbia University Press, 2004); and Gilles Kepel, *The War for Muslim Minds: Islam and the West* (Cambridge, Mass.: Harvard University Press, 2004).

[8] On Jewish fundamentalism see Robert Friedman, *Zealots for Zion: Inside Israel's West Bank Settlement Movement* (New York: Random House, 1992); Ian Lustick, *For the Land and the Lord: Jewish Fundamentalism in Israel* (New York: Council on Foreign Relations, 1988); and Ehud Sprinzak, *The Ascendance of Israel's Radical Right* (New York: Oxford University Press, 1991). On militant fundamental Christianity, see, eg, Nicholas Kristof, "Jesus and Jihad," *New York Times*, 17 July 2004, 13; and Thomas Franck, *What's the Matter with Kansas: How Conservatives Won the Heart of America* (New York: Metropolitan Books, 2004). For an example of Christian fundamentalist thought, see Pat Robertson, *The Ten Offenses* (Nashville: Integrity Publishers, 2004). A recent example of American theocratic thinking is Dinesh D'Souza, *The Enemy at Home: The Cultural Left and Its Responsibility for 9/11* (New York: Doubleday 2006).

and increasingly influential in the mass media,[9] they seem likely to affect the tactics and strategies by means of which the United States wages its struggle with militant Islam both at home and abroad. At a minimum, although these Western *jihadists* are committed to moral clarity, their own struggles to dominate political and cultural life in the West (to be sure, struggles that are seen by them as defensive in character, responding to a notionally aggressive secular humanism)[10] reduce the moral clarity of the West's position, without softening the sense of engagement in an apocalyptic conflict. On the contrary, by their passions and beliefs—their sense of the *other* as moral filth—they intensify that sense.

It is not simply the physical and psychological security of Western peoples that is threatened. In addition, the liberties and the norms and institutions embodying and protecting those liberties, norms and institutions painfully constructed over the bloody millennia of Western history, are also at risk precisely because of the insecurities stemming from the threat of catastrophic terrorism. Civil liberties have never thrived in menacing times. Threatened peoples tend to endow the authorities with extraordinary powers to make them safe, an endowment invariably accepted. In Republican Rome the concentration of extraordinary power was formalized in the Senate's appointment of a temporary "Dictator" with, as the title implies, almost unlimited power to commit mayhem for the public good.[11] Most modern constitutions, as well as human rights treaties, authorize declarations of emergency and coincident suspension of many liberties. But they set substantive and, by implication at least, temporal limits to executive discretion, thus working to reconcile demands for protection with the preservation of rights deemed basic for the survival of liberal democratic government and also with prevention of

[9] See, eg, Linda Kintz and Julia Lesage (eds), *Media, Culture, and the Religious Right* (Minneapolis: University of Minnesota Press, 1998).

[10] See, eg, Pat Robertson, *Courting Disaster: How the Supreme Court is Usurping the Power of Congress and the People* (Nashville: Integrity Publishers, 2004); and Ann Coulter, *Slander: Liberal Lies About the American Right* (New York: Crown Press, 2002). The phenomenon is also discussed in Thomas Frank, *What's the Matter with Kansas?* (New York: Metropolitan Books, 2004). Christmas is often used as a focal point for airing religious grievances against secularism. See, eg, Fox News anchor John Gibson, *The War on Christmas: How the Liberal Plot to Ban the Sacred Holiday is Worse Than You Thought* (New York: Sentinel, 2005). In 2004, fellow Fox News anchor Bill O'Reilly ran a segment in the "Talking Points," portion of his program entitled, "Christmas Under Siege," which became a regular feature in 2005. Bill O'Reilly, "Christmas Under Siege: The Big Picture," *Fox News* [website], published online 24 December 2004, <http://www.foxnews.com/story/0,2933,140742,00.html>, accessed 20 July 2006: "Now most people, of course, love Christmas and want to keep its traditions, but the secular movement has influence in the media, among some judges and politicians. Americans will lose their country if they don't begin to take action."

[11] See Clinton Rossiter, *Constitutional Dictatorship: Crisis Government in the Modern Democracies* (Princeton: Princeton University Press, 1948), 16, 23: "There did exist in ancient Rome a political phenomenon, the dictatorship, whereby in time of crisis an eminent citizen was called upon by the ordinary officials of a constitutional republic, and was temporarily granted absolute power over its whole life, not to subvert but to defend the republic, its constitution, and its independence... Once the Imperium had been conferred upon him, the dictator became as absolute a ruler as could well be imagined, with the only formal limitation being the six-month term of office."

irremediable injury to the innocent. However, even democratic leaders may find restraint galling and, with or without popular invitation, may and have decided for themselves what values to sacrifice on the altar of "necessity."[12]

Collision between the executors of a self-proclaimed counter-terror "war" and the norms embodied in human rights treaties and the humanitarian laws of war (and in most modern constitutions) is inevitable, since the norms are, above all, restraints on the exercise of power. Even when fought for, theoretically negotiable ends between groups of recognizably similar people, asymmetric wars, whether the "weaker" antagonist is a conventionally armed rural guerrilla movement or a network of urban militants, press hard against normative restraint. When ends are seen as non-negotiable and opponents as Satanic, restraints readily appear, in the words of former White House Counsel, Albert Gonzalez, as "quaint,"[13] the relics of another time, appropriate, if at all, to different conflicts, conflicts (in the words of the nineteenth-century imperial powers) between "civilized" peoples and states.[14]

The 9/11 atrocity and the ensuing war on terrorism, if "war" it is, have managed to link, with all the intimacy of scar tissue from a single wound, a cluster of policy issues that were previously more loosely connected. The proper definition of and response to terrorism; the universality of human rights and the limits of sovereignty; the proper interpretation and application of humanitarian law; the legitimate use of force; the treatment of minorities (particularly illiberal minorities within western states); the authority and modes of interpreting international law: each subject has had its own literature and savants, its moral, legal and public policy discourse, and its scholarly writings. They have overlapped and penetrated each other, to be sure, but with nothing like their present state of integration. As the war has more firmly integrated these subjects, it has coincidentally clarified

[12] See, eg, Michael Ignatieff, *The Lesser Evil: Political Ethics in an Age of Terror* (Princeton: Princeton University Press, 2004). An example of the sacrifice of liberal values in the name of "national emergency" is the internment of Japanese-Americans during the Second World War. See Roger Daniels, Sandra C Taylor, and Harry HL Kitano (eds), *Japanese Americans: From Relocation to Redress* (Seattle: University of Washington Press, 1991); and Wendy Ng, *Japanese American Internment During World War II: A History and Reference Guide* (Westport, CT: Greenwood Press, 2002).

[13] See Gonzales' memo to President Bush on 25 January 2002, "Decision Re: Application of the Geneva Convention on Prisoners of War to the Conflict with Al Qaeda and the Taliban," <http://msnbc.msn.com/id/4999148/site/newsweek/>, accessed 26 July 2006: "In my judgment, this new paradigm renders obsolete Geneva's strict limitations on questioning of enemy prisoners and renders quaint some of its provisions."

[14] See, eg, John Stuart Mill, "A Few Words on Non-Intervention," *Collected Works of John Stuart Mill: Essays on Equality, Law, and Education, XXI*, John M Robson (ed) (Toronto: University of Toronto Press, 1984), 118–19: "To characterize any conduct whatever towards a barbarous people as a violation of the law of nations, only shows that he who so speaks has never considered the subject...The only moral laws for the relation between a civilized and a barbarous government, are the universal rules of morality between man and man." For a history of international law and colonialism, see, eg, Martti Koskenniemi, *The Gentle Civilizer of Nations: The Rise and Fall of International Law 1870–1960* (New York: Cambridge University Press, 2001); and Anthony Anghie, *Imperialism, Sovereignty and the Making of International Law* (New York: Cambridge University Press, 2004).

and heightened if not envenomed the normative and epistemological debates that have marked them in the past.

My concern in this brief study is to sketch the contours of a counter-terror strategy informed by liberal values. In doing so, I need to engage, albeit at varying length, with all of the subjects enumerated above. Engagement with them implies involvement in the debates they have inspired, a prospect from which I do not shrink. To those debates, I will bring the values and premises which lend some measure of coherence, I hope, to my work over the years and to my life, assuming it makes any sense at all.

1. Liberalism

The term "liberalism" encompasses a sufficiently diverse set of views about the good society and the ethical life, as well as policies for best expressing them, that it can be misleading, whether invoked to admire or abuse, unless the user explains in some detail what ideas, values and policies are implied. In using the term liberal, I do not pretend to fix the term for all who parade under the banner, much less to summarize magisterially a centuries-old discourse about premises, epistemology, values and policies that could by itself furnish a library.[15] It is intended primarily to locate me, to give me a reasonably clear and stable normative position from which to view and assess the cluster of issues crowded into the arena of counter-terrorist policy. At the same time, the conception of liberalism that I deploy does, I think, capture a way of seeing and being in the world that unites many critics of certain salient features of post-9/11 American foreign policy.

Liberalism, as I interpret it, stems at one level from the normative premise that the good society is one that enables each individual to shape continuously a personal identity and a life plan in light of her or his understanding of the meaning and value and possibilities of human existence.[16] We can see in that premise both a canonical statement about what it means to be truly or most fully human—the human being as creator of meaning out of the mute raw materials and experiences of life—and a prudential recipe for maintaining a relatively stable and largely voluntary association of people organized as a political community. In either or

---

[15] See, eg, John Rawls, *Political Liberalism* (New York: Columbia University Press, 2005); Ronald Dworkin, *Taking Rights Seriously* (Cambridge, Mass.: Harvard University Press, 1977); Ronald Dworkin, *Law's Empire* (Cambridge, Mass.: Belknap, 1986); and Michael Walzer, *Spheres of Justice* (New York: Basic Books, 1983). Cf. Michael J Sandel, *Liberalism and the Limits of Justice* (Cambridge, UK: Cambridge University Press, 1982).
[16] Will Kymlicka, *Liberalism, Community, and Culture* (Oxford, UK: Oxford University Press, 1989), 10: "Many liberal philosophers have argued for tolerance because it provides the best conditions under which people can make informed and rational judgments about the value of different pursuits. Respect for the liberty of others is predicated not on our inability to criticize preferences, but precisely on the role of freedom in securing the conditions under which we can best make such judgments."

both forms, it implies a state that restrains itself from endorsing any particular substantive vision of the good (other, of course, than the more procedural vision that is liberalism)[17] and employs its coercive power to protect individuals from interference by others in their quest for meaning. In other words, each person is entitled to the widest zone of freedom compatible with the like exercise of freedom by other members of the society *and* with the shared need to sustain a community, a political culture, and a state able to protect individual freedom and to foster some base-line equality of life chances.[18]

But liberalism has a still deeper root, namely the belief that the ultimate meaning of life is unknowable[19] at least in the sense that it is not susceptible to common apprehension. We are left, then, not with a grand design to which all right-thinking people will conform their lives, but only with competing convictions about the nature of the design, some more widely shared than others, or the conviction that there is no primordial design, only designs constituted by the shared creativity of clusters of believers. If there is no ascertainable grand design, no transcendent consciousness or will, no indisputable direction for life on which all people can theoretically agree, whether guided by right reason or by revelation, then, given the human need for community, we are faced with two alternatives. One is perpetual struggle among groups, each seeking to impose by all available means its vision of the good. The other, the liberal alternative, is agreement to organize communal life on the basis of mutual acceptance of divergent beliefs. It was just such an agreement among the leaders of the Western states, following the calamitous wars of religion in the early to middle part of the seventeenth century, which produced the system of public international law that still helps to structure the relations of states.[20]

As I have already suggested, however, liberalism is not simply a pragmatic of survival, a less dangerous way than tyranny of escaping the Hobbesian dilemma. If that were all it is, liberalism would be a dry account of everyday life, hardly comparable to the operative narratives of the Abrahamic or pagan faiths. But that is not all it is. Liberalism has its own high drama, except its tragic hero is the Promethean individual, creator of meanings and things, illuminator of reality through the application of reason, restless searcher if only for what George Bernard Shaw, speaking of metaphysics, described as the black cat in an unlit cellar who is, in fact, not there.

---

[17] Charles Larmore, "The Moral Basis of Political Liberalism," *Journal of Philosophy*, 96(12) (1999), 600: "Liberal thinkers have concluded that political association should no longer undertake to express and foster a conception of the ultimate ends of human existence. Instead, it must seek its principles in a minimal morality, which reasonable people can share despite their expectably divergent religious and ethical convictions."

[18] See Amartya Sen, *Inequality Reexamined* (Cambridge, Mass.: Harvard University Press, 1992).

[19] See Michael Sandel, *Liberalism and the Limits of Justice*, 175: "Where neither nature nor cosmos supplies a meaningful order to be grasped or apprehended, it falls to human subjects to constitute meaning on their own."

[20] See Daniel Philpott, *Revolutions in Sovereignty: How Ideas Shaped Modern International Relations* (Princeton: Princeton University Press, 2001).

Though they are center stage, individuals don't stand alone. Unlike their hypertrophied libertarian relatives, liberals understands that individuals can survive and create only within schemes of cooperation and that without a legacy of meanings deposited by preceding occupants of the communities into which they are born, individuals would be overwhelmed by the roaring buzzing confusion of unmediated life.[21] Community being the essential medium within which the individual strives, liberalism has to be more than a norm of mutual non-interference. It cannot be a mere guardian of the frontiers between persons, a declaration of rights limited only by the negative duty not to interfere with the lonely exercise by others of the same rights.

A community is not a cluster of guarded compounds linked by the juxtaposition of their barbed wire walls. A community has common spaces and public goods and rules for allocating responsibility to fund and maintain them. If it is liberal, the community's members will participate in the creation, application and change of those rules. But decisions need not be unanimous. And they are binding. Thus liberalism inhibits perfect freedom in order to produce community and public goods. But because it is liberal, not only must the individual have a fair chance to shape the rules for allocating responsibilities, in addition those responsibilities must be fairly allocated according to widely endorsed principles of fairness and there are limits beyond which the community cannot intrude on the individual's freedom. In short, liberalism, as I conceive it, contains within itself a tension between individual rights and communal interests but with a refutable presumption in favor of individual rights and a core zone where individual rights trump communal interests.[22]

At this juncture, I want to make a further point about the implications of a liberal political philosophy. The individual rather than the community being at the center of its normative concerns, the community being only an essential means to the realization of individual ends, liberalism has a cosmopolitan character. The persons having a hard core of irreducible rights are all persons, not just those that belong to your ethnic or national community. Expressed today in the various international human rights covenants, this idea of universal rights has a long pedigree[23] which includes, of course, one of the founding documents of the United States: "We hold these truths to be self evident. That all men are created equal and are endowed by their creator with certain inalienable rights."

Since the French Revolution, the idea that all people have a common core of rights has been a principal line of demarcation between liberals and conservatives.

---

[21] Cf. William Kymlicka, *Liberalism, Community, and Culture* (Oxford: Oxford University Press, 1989).

[22] See Ronald Dworkin, *Sovereign Virtue: The Theory and Practice of Equality* (Cambridge: Harvard University Press, 2001); and Dworkin, *Taking Rights Seriously* (Cambridge: Harvard University Press, 1978).

[23] See Micheline Ishay, *The History of Human Rights: From Ancient Times to the Globalization Era* (Berkeley: University of California Press, 2004).

I know nothing of universal rights, said Edmund Burke, parliamentary scourge of the French Revolution, I know only of the rights of Englishmen.[24] But liberalism's inherently cosmopolitan spirit has not precluded parochial attachments in practice. Given the self-regarding character of most electorates most of the time, England's Liberal Party could hardly have dominated British politics for the half-century preceding the First World War if it had treated the material interests of the British electorate as having no greater claim on its concern than those of Frenchmen or the dependent peoples of the British Empire.

Liberals' privileging of their own national community is not simply a pragmatic compromise of principle in the name of partisan political survival. It is, rather, another corollary of the human need for community to which I referred above. Communities, as Benedict Anderson has famously taught us,[25] are imagined by their members. To this point in human history only a few extraordinary people have been able to imagine and to identify with a universal community. Despite their adherence to a faith with universal aspirations, most Christians and Muslims still appear to limit their primary loyalty to national and sub-national communities or at best to the community of their faith. Communities, above all national ones, define themselves at least as much by who they are not as by who they are. The notion of a borderless community sounds to almost everyone as a contradiction in terms.

Borders by their nature privilege the community members within them in the first place by limiting entry of new people and by limiting to varying degrees the participation in governance of outsiders, including people allowed to enter for an indefinite period of time to fill important societal roles.[26] If community members relinquish these basic privileges to some more encompassing organization, they have already begun to imagine themselves part of the larger entity. And as the locus of privilege-allocation shifts toward that larger entity (an entity like the European Union), so will people's primary loyalties, albeit with a lag, possibly a long lag, resulting from the inertial force of habit, interest, entrenched narratives, and received sentiments. If, as I have already argued, individuals depend on the community for survival and for the intellectual resources that allow them to

[24] My paraphrase of *Reflections on the Revolution in France*, Frank M Turner (ed), (New Haven: Yale University Press, 2003), 28: "In the famous law of the 3rd of Charles I, called the Petition of Right, the parliament says to the king, 'Your subjects have inherited this freedom, claiming their franchises not on abstract principles "as the rights of men"' but as the rights of Englishmen, and as a patrimony derived from their forefathers."

[25] Benedict Anderson, *Imagined Communities: Reflections on the Origin and Spread of Nationalism* (London: Verso, 1983).

[26] An overview of EU member state voting rights compared with traditional immigration countries can be found in Harald Waldruch's work "National Europe Centre Paper No. 73: Electoral Rights for Foreign Nationals: A Comparative Overview of Regulations in 36 Countries," *The Challenges of Immigration and Integration in the European Union and Australia*, University of Sydney, 18–20 February 2003. See also, Randall Hansen, "Citizenship and Integration in Europe," in *Toward Assimilation and Citizenship: Immigrants in Liberal Nation-States*, Christian Joppke and Ewa Morawska (eds), (New York: Palgrave Macmillan, 2003).

develop life plans and ideas about the meaning of life and the nature of a good society, and if communities are bound by their nature to privilege their members, then such privileging would seem to be implicit in, rather than a compromise or even corruption of, liberal principles.

Privileging community members, moreover, can be seen as a necessary incident of respect for individual freedom. For that freedom includes developing life plans that cannot be executed other than through willed and stable association with other individuals. Respect for individualism, in other words, must include respect for the contractual arrangements, in a more general sense the schemes of cooperation, into which individuals choose to enter or, if born into them, to remain. Of course the force of this argument depends on the freedom of individuals to transfer their loyalties from one community to another, something they may wish to do as changes occur in their conceptions of what constitutes a good society or how they should live their lives.

Cosmopolitan liberalism is not, then, incompatible with national and other sub-universal attachments. The political theorist, Anthony Appiah, refers to liberal nationalism as "grounded Liberalism."[27] But how nationalist can liberalism be and still retain its cosmopolitan temper without which it ceases to be liberal? In trying to answer that question, I have found helpful Richard Miller's homely analogy. As a parent, I have an obligation to rescue my child, if I see her drowning. Do I have the same obligation in the case of a stranger's child? Miller says respect for the view that every person should have equal access to certain fundamental values, beginning with life, requires an affirmative answer, at least where I can save the child without undue risk to myself or my child. But I do not have to buy the stranger's child a present on her birthday just because I always buy one for my own.[28] Applied to the relations of communities including nation-states, Miller's analogy proposes at a minimum that liberal communities cannot seize advantages that compromise the basic interests of other peoples and still regard themselves as liberal. A stronger implication is that where, at modest cost to itself and certainly without compromising basic interests, a liberal community can prevent a devastating assault on another people's vital interests, it should. This question of the limits of community self-privileging will recur in this volume.

---

[27] Anthony Appiah, *The Ethics of Identity* (Princeton: Princeton University Press, 2005), 246: "It is because humans live best on a smaller scale that liberal cosmopolitans should acknowledge the ethical salience of not just the state, but the county, the town, the street, the business, the craft, the profession, the family as communities, as circles among the many circles narrower than the human horizon that are appropriate spheres of moral concern. They should, in short, endorse the right of others to live in democratic states, with the rich possibilities of association within and across their borders, states of which they can be patriotic citizens. And as cosmopolitans, they can claim that right for themselves."

[28] Richard Miller, "Cosmopolitan Respect and Patriotic Concern," *Philosophy and Public Affairs*, 27(3) (1998), 207.

2. Human Rights

"Man is born free," Jean Jacques Rosseau announced more than two centuries ago, "but everywhere he is in chains."[29] "All human rights are universal [and] indivisible," delegates to the 1993 World Conference on Human Rights announced sonorously in their final consensus Declaration;[30] perhaps because most of them lacked the French instinct for irony they did not add that those rights are violated on the same universal scale.[31] They did, however, manage to imply as much by calling for continuing efforts and new measures of defense and promotion.

Like the whole body of international legal norms of which they form a part, the claim of human rights to be authoritative, to be binding in a moral and psychological as well as a formal sense, is shadowed by the ubiquity of their disregard. But non-trivial violations of officially declared rules is a feature of all legal systems, even those with powerful and pervasive means of enforcement, as someone like me, who has been violently deprived of his watch and wallet in more than one of America's great cities, can personally attest. A New York City policeman once informed me, in the wake of an encounter with delinquency, that of the tens of thousands of assaults and burglaries that occur in the Big Apple every year, he and his colleagues managed to clear about 2 per cent. Yet New Yorkers, generally not the most gullible of people, continue to believe that the laws against robbery and burglary and other declared felonies and misdemeanors are authoritative. And therefore, law being the product of inter-subjective understandings about which norms are binding, they are.

Can the same be said of international law? Is it too supported by a widespread sense that there is an obligation to obey its prescriptions and an expectation that in general the relevant actors will comply?[32] As far as I know, the comprehensive

---

[29] Jean-Jacques Rousseau, *On The Social Contract*, Drew Silver (ed), (Mineola, NY: Dover, 2003), 102.

[30] *Vienna Declaration and Program of Action*, World Conference on Human Rights, Vienna, 14–25 June 1993, UN Doc No. A/Conf.157/24.

[31] This tragic reality is recorded annually by, among other institutions, Amnesty International, Human Rights Watch, and the US Department of State. For 2005, see Amnesty International, *Amnesty International Report 2006: The State of the World's Human Rights* (London: Amnesty International Publications, 2006); Human Rights Watch, *Human Rights Watch World Report 2006: Events of 2005* (New York: Human Rights Watch, 2006); and United States Department of State, *2005 Country Reports on Human Rights Practices* [website], <http://www.state.gov/g/drl/rls/hrrpt/2005>, accessed 20 July 2006.

[32] See Louis Henkin, *How Nations Behave: Law and Foreign Policy* (New York: Praeger, 1968), 32: "More or less consciously, more or less willingly, all governments give up the freedom of anarchy and accept international law in principle as the price of membership in international society and of having relations with other nations. For that reason, too, they accept basic traditional international law." See also ibid, 42: "[T]he daily sober loyalty of nations to the law and their obligations is hardly noted. It is probably the case that almost all nations observe almost all principles of international law and almost all of their obligations almost all of the time." But see Richard Goldstone, "How International Law Strengthens New Democracies," in *Promoting Democracy through International*

empirical inquiries that might support a confident answer to those linked questions have not been made. So in affirming or disclaiming the binding character of international law or some particular part of it like human rights, we rely on *objective* indications of the *subjective* state of the governing elites and the rapidly growing number of non-governmental actors whose behavior international law regulates. With inevitable circularity, we rely, that is, on the degree to which their behavior and the behavior of the institutions they control or strongly influence are generally consistent with the norms these same elites have declared binding. For in this decentralized legal system, the principal subjects of law are also for the most part its creators, appliers, enforcers, and its agents of change.

The large overlap between the identity of persons and institutions making, applying, enforcing, and changing the law and the persons and institutions seeming to violate it is a principal source of international law's appearance of debility in the eyes of the general public and even of those members of the legal profession concerned exclusively with domestic legal matters.[33] But where official behavior conforms to international norms under conditions in which non-compliance might serve short-term interests, then that very overlap of identities can be cited as evidence of international law's effective authority. Even where there is non-compliance, if officials make strenuous efforts to conceal the true facts or to wrap their delinquencies in legal language, they implicitly testify to the power of the norm they are evading as an influence on public opinion and as a vehicle for expressing interests which, in the generality of cases, the delinquents share with officials of other countries. I assume, for instance, that one of the reasons the Bush Administration tried to make a legal case for the invasion of Iraq,[34] or at least to narrow the precedent it might be establishing, was a desire to maintain to the extent possible the UN Charter ban on the aggressive use of force.

Turning from international law generally to the subset of human rights, in what condition do we find its current authority? Decidedly divisible, it seems fair to say despite Vienna's contrary claim. Since the Administration of Ronald

---

Law: Second Report of the Empire and Democracy Project, Andrew Kuper (ed), (New York: Carnegie Council on Ethics and International Affairs, 2004), 15: "The rule of law is the assurance that leaders will be judged by the same laws that apply to all citizens and that those laws will apply to the wealthy as well as the poor, to the powerful as well as the weak. It is that same rule of law that is so needed and so missed in the international community ... [r]espect for international law is not possible when the wide perception is that international law is intended to be a constraint on the activities of poor nations and does not apply to the wealthy and powerful nations. This widely held and growing perception is fed by the resistance of wealthy nations who do not wish to be bound by international conventions. The most visible, but by no means the only, example is the United States—as is evident from its opposition to the International Criminal Court and to the Kyoto Protocol on global warming."

[33] But some scholars argue that it is a positive strength, see, eg, Myres McDougal and Florentino Feliciano (eds), *Law and Minimum World Public Order: The Legal Regulation of International Coercion* (New Haven: Yale University Press, 1961), esp. ch 1.

[34] The US case for invasion can be found in UN Doc. No. S/2003/215 (2003). For humanitarian arguments, see, eg, Thomas Cushman (ed), *A Matter of Principle: Humanitarian Arguments for War in Iraq* (Berkeley: University of California Press, 2005).

Reagan, the United States has rejected the very idea of economic, social, and cultural rights.[35] A number of Islamic States openly discriminate in their treatment of women in ways that are very difficult to square with the language of the International Covenants and the Universal Declaration,[36] much less the Convention on the elimination of Discrimination Against Women.[37] In addition, those states, like Iran and Saudi Arabia, which enforce some version of *Sharia*, interfere with the free exercise of religious belief by criminalizing conversion to other faiths and by precluding evangelical activities.[38] Moreover, states that carry weight in international relations, notably China and Saudi Arabia, dismiss any supposed human right to democracy,[39] despite the language of Article 25 of the Covenant on Civil and Political Rights which proclaims a right "to take part in the conduct of public affairs, directly or through freely chosen representatives" and a right "to vote and to be elected at genuine periodic elections which shall be by universal and equal suffrage and shall be held by secret ballot, guaranteeing the free expression of the will of the electors." Construing similar language in the Inter-American Convention on Human Rights, the Inter-American Commission on Human Rights concluded several decades ago that governments could comply only if they were electoral democracies.[40]

[35] See, eg, Richard Schiffer, then Assistant Secretary for Human Rights and Humanitarian Affairs, "US commemorates 40th anniversary of the Universal Declaration of Human Rights," remarks at White House ceremony, 8 December 1988, <http://www.findarticles.com/p/articles/mi_m1079/is_n2144_v89/ai_7537759/pg_1>, accessed 25 July 2006: "The United States has been very dissatisfied when the United Nations has departed from its original purposes, particularly in regard to the promotion and protection of basic human rights. The past 25 years have seen a tendency to redefine human rights to include a new category of 'social and economic rights,' such as the right to education, the right to food, or the right to housing... The United States sees these socioeconomic 'rights' as the goals of sound policy rather than as true human rights." See also Paula Dobriansky, then Deputy Assistant Secretary for Human Rights and Humanitarian Affairs, address before the Council of Young Political Leaders on 3 June 1988, "US Human Rights Policy: An Overview," <http://www.findarticles.com/p/articles/mi_m1079/is_n2139_v88/ai_6876354>, accessed 25 July 2006.

[36] *The International Bill of Human Rights* consists of the *Universal Declaration of Human Rights* (art 1), adopted by GA Res. 217A (III), 10 December 1948; *International Covenant on Economic, Social and Cultural Rights*, adopted and opened for signature, ratification and accession by GA Res. 2200A (XXI), 16 December 1966 with entry into force 3 January 1976, in accordance with art 27; and *International Covenant on Civil and Political Rights*, adopted and opened for signature, ratification and accession by GA Res. 2200A (XXI), 16 December 1966 with entry into force on 23 March 1976, in accordance with art 49.

[37] *Convention on the Elimination of All Forms of Discrimination against Women*, adopted and opened for signature, ratification and accession by GA Res. 34/180 on 18 December 1979 with entry into force 3 September 1981, in accordance with art 27(1).

[38] See Jacob Gershman, "Saudis Arrest Christians for Spreading 'Poison,'" *New York Sun*, 2 May 2005.

[39] See Tom J Farer, "The Promotion of Democracy: International Law and Norms," in Edward Newman and Roland Rich (eds), *The UN Role in Promoting Democracy: Between Ideals and Reality* (New York: United Nations University Press, 2004), 38–9.

[40] See The Annual Report for The Inter-American Commission on Human Rights (IACHR) of the Organization of American States (OAS) (1979–80), 151.

Laws and unconcealed practices in many countries concerning the limits of free speech and association also disregard plausible interpretations of the relevant Covenant language. Until 2002, however, at least two bodies of human rights norms did appear to command broad official support and not only in the realm of rhetoric. One concerned the right not to experience discrimination on racial or ethnic grounds. The other concerned personal security rights, above all protection from summary execution, torture and other cruel and inhuman and degrading treatment, and conviction and/or punishment without due process of law. Among the governments of leading states, China has for years been even more ardent than the United States in resisting under sovereignty's banner external appreciation of its internal behavior.[41] In 1997, on the occasion of my first visit to China, I met with the President of a prominent government think tank. Although it was not on our carefully negotiated agenda, the question of human rights arose in the context of a tour of issues troubling Sino-American relations. "Of course," he began dismissively, "we have different views of this matter reflecting our different cultures." He seemed to anticipate agreement.

"There are differences," I replied, "that might be attributed to different historical experiences. Every country, for instance, imposes some limits on speech and association. At this point China and the United States are, to be sure, at very different points on the continuum of limitation. And we clearly differ on how to construe the right to participate in government, which in principle we both accept." "But surely," I said, "we agree that no government has the right to summarily execute people, to torture them or to imprison them without a fair trial." "We do agree on that," he responded without apparent reluctance. "Then," I replied, "it seems fair to conclude that cultural differences, such as they are, do not affect our mutual recognition of rights to personal security." He did not demur.

Yet if the vitality of human rights and humanitarian law depended on widespread compliance, we would have to say that the law of personal security is moribund. For every one of the credible surveys of global human rights practices—those of Amnesty International, Human Rights Watch, even the American Department of State's annual review, which would normally be expected to ignore barbarism in any country Washington finds cooperative on geo-strategic issues—testifies that torture and other varieties and intensities of cruelty are still not anomalous.[42] But until 2001, virtually no government[43] publicly defended plans and practices irreconcilable

---

[41] Regarding the United States and its resistance to interference on matters such as capital punishment, see William A Schabas, *The Abolition of the Death Penalty in International Law* (Cambridge, UK: Cambridge University Press, 2002), 316. See, eg, AE Kent, *China, the United Nations, and Human Rights: The Limits of Compliance* (Philadelphia: University of Pennsylvania Press, 1999), 45–6.

[42] See, eg, <http://web.amnesty.org/report2005/sau-summary-eng>, accessed 20 August 2006 and <http://www.state.gov/g/drl/rls/hrrpt/2005/61698.htm>, accessed 20 August 2006. The full text of the State Department's 2005 *Country Reports on Human Rights Practices* is available at <http://www.state.gov/g/drl/rls/hrrpt/2005/index.htm>.

[43] With the arguable exception of Israel, which in 1987 established an official commission of inquiry to probe the charges against the interrogation methods of its internal security services.

with the minimum standards of behavior mandated by the International Covenant and by common Article 3 of the almost universally ratified Geneva Conventions of 1949[44] which prohibits even in the case of internal conflicts:

(a) violence to life and person, in particular murder... mutilation, cruel treatment and torture;...
(c) outrages upon personal dignity, in particular, humiliating and degrading treatment; and
(d) the passing of sentences and the carrying out of executions without previous judgment pronounced by a regularly constituted court affording all the judicial guarantees which are recognized as indispensable by civilized peoples.

As hypocrisy is the deference vice pays to virtue, according to the old epigram, so one can say that the mendacity of governments in denying the use of torture and other cruel means testifies to the compliance pull of the relevant norms which stems, I believe, from their ability to mobilize public revulsion, to prompt dissent within official circles, and to reflect concern even among officials authorizing torture in a particular set of circumstances about its more generalized application or its contribution to a general erosion of the rule of law. I will return to these issues in Chapter 3.

3. Terrorism

In the discourse of modern international politics, terrorism is one of those terms, self-determination is another, which has consistently eluded consensus definition despite ubiquitous use.[45] Perhaps as in the case of self-determination, its uncertain shape is a principal cause of its ubiquity. Imprecision of definition allows it to be summoned for service by each side in prominent conflicts.

Named after former Israeli Supreme Court Justice Moshe Landau, the Landau Commission concluded that "if the security services were confined to the methods of interrogation used in ordinary criminal investigations they would not be able to obtain the information needed to thwart hostile terrorist activity. The conclusion was that moderate force could be used when necessary in cases of 'hostile terrorist activity or political subversion that is illegal under the laws in Israel or in the territories.'" The Israeli State accepted the recommendation of the 1987 Landau Commission of Inquiry. See Eugene Cotran and Chibli Mallat (eds), *The Arab-Israeli Accords: Legal Perspectives* (Boston: Kluwer Law International, 1996), 89–90. However, the court later reversed some of the Commission's allowances. See *Flawed Defense: Torture and Ill-treatment in GSS Interrogations Following the Supreme Court Ruling 6 September 1999–6 September 2001*, Jerusalem, Israel, September 2001. See also <http://www.hrw.org/worldreport99/mideast/israel.html>, accessed 20 August 2006, for examples of Israel's infractions against the Geneva Conventions relative to the West Bank and Gaza Strip. See also Tom J Farer, "Israel's Unlawful Occupation," *Foreign Policy* Spring 1991, and discussion in chs 3 and 5.

[44] There are 194 states that are parties to the Geneva Convention of 1949 and their additional protocols. For a complete list, see <http://www.icrc.org/Web/eng/siteeng0.nsf/html/party_main_treaties>, accessed 11 March 2007.

[45] Charles Townshend, *Terrorism: A Very Short Introduction* (New York: Oxford University Press, 2002), 3–6.

To chart the competing uses of the "terrorist" label is to chart some of the key fault lines of nineteenth and twentieth-century politics, principally the ones between labor and capital before they negotiated the welfare state compromise, between the imperial powers of the West and the indigenous inhabitants of the territories they conquered, between democratic and autocratic regimes, between the post-Second World War US-led alliance of capitalist states and the Marxist bloc led by the Soviet Union and, for a time, China, and the contemporary one between liberals and religious authoritarians of various stripes.

Given the present connotations of the word "terror," the numerous persons whose historical knowledge does not extend much beyond yesterday's television news must assume that it has always been a label which rational actors would choose to evade. The fact, of course, is that in the years before the Second World War and during the war itself, some strategists trying to determine the optimal use of air power saw one of its functions as spreading terror among the enemy's civilian population in order to undermine war production or the morale of kin in the armed forces or to bring public pressure to bear on governments to sue for peace.[46] Indeed, once it became clear in the later stages of the war that bombing from reasonably safe heights was too inaccurate to have much direct effect on war production or even the movement of goods, the only justification, other than revenge, for deflecting massive resources to strategic bombing campaigns was the presumed indirect effect on the enemy's war-making capacity stemming from the terrorization no less than the decimation of the enemy's civilian population. Only with the arrival of atomic weapons did the Anglo-American alliance have the means to threaten the enemy political leadership directly, to threaten them with personal extinction.

Ambiguous feelings about strategies of terror did not originate in the desperate circumstances of the Second World War and did not expire with them. In the latter years of the nineteenth century, opponents of the absolutist rule of the Russian Czar sometimes assassinated high public officials (not always without collateral injury) as part of their effort to overthrow the regime.[47] While these acts were often labeled "terrorist" in nature, and while no government advocated them as a means of democratizing Russia, the more-or-less democratic states of Europe like the United Kingdom, France and Switzerland wrote a political-offence exception into all their extradition treaties[48] which in practice made these countries sanctuaries for members of violent Russian dissident organizations who managed to escape the czarist police.

---

[46] Ibid, 6–7. See also, Stewart Halsey Ross, *Strategic Bombing by the United States in World War II: The Myths and the Facts* (Jefferson, NC: McFarland & Co, 2003), 73, 203.

[47] Paul Berman, *Terror and Liberalism* (2003), 31–2. See also Andrew Sinclair, *An Anatomy of Terror: A History of Terrorism* (London: Pan Macmillan, 2003), 133, 136.

[48] See Victor V Ramraj, Michael Hor, and Kent Roach, *Global Anti-Terrorism Law and Policy* (Cambridge, UK: Cambridge University Press, 2005), 578. See also, Wybo P Heere, *From Government to Governance: The Growing Impact of Non-State Actors on the International and European Legal System* (Cambridge, UK: Cambridge University Press, 2004), 370.

The political-offence exception was officially justified not as a means of protecting terrorists or encouraging terrorism but as an incident of the organization of Europe into sovereign states. A corollary of sovereignty, it was argued, is non-involvement in the domestic politics of other states. The political-offence exception, according to governments insisting on its inclusion in extradition treaties, is no more than a declaration of non-interest or neutrality concerning each other's internal affairs.[49] Perhaps it was just that, the operational expression of a broad principal of non-intervention. But one suspects that it also reflected a certain ambivalence among liberal governments and electorates about violent efforts to overthrow a Czarist regime detested for its absolutist pretensions in an increasingly secular and democratic age. The means might be deplored, but not the end of removing the tyrant or forcing him to accept the restraints of a constitutional monarchy. Hence there was a certain sympathy for militants, even those using violence, against a regime that ruled on the basis of inheritance and God, backed by the whip and the sword.

The implied, hidden ambivalence about political violence in earlier decades morphed during the decolonization struggles that succeeded the Second World War into unambiguous and open defense of armed resistance to foreign domination or regimes seen as legacies of Western colonial rule. In its initial form, the debate, for which the UN General Assembly was a principal forum, centered around the legitimacy of foreign military assistance of one kind or another, to "Liberation Movements."[50] While the United States was prepared, earlier than the European states with colonial legacies, to support calls for decolonization,[51] it opposed foreign military aid to such movements,[52] notionally on grounds that they violated the principle of non-intervention, but primarily because it assumed that the aid would come mainly from Communist China and the Soviet-Bloc and would go to anti-colonial parties with a Marxist orientation. In other words, the Cold War shaped US policy on this issue as on so many others.

Polarization over the question of the legitimacy of assistance to so-called Liberation Movements, with the Soviet-Bloc and Third World states on one side and most Western states on the other, replicated itself in the overlapping debate about whether the United Nations should develop a comprehensive treaty defining terrorism as an international crime. Attacks on international aviation initiated the effort to secure a treaty although other concerns, particularly attacks on persons enjoying diplomatic immunity, soon crowded in.

---

[49] See "The Evolution of the Political Offence Exception in an Age of Modern Political Violence," *Yale Journal of World Public Order*, 9(2) (Spring 1983), 315–41.

[50] See UNGA 20th Session, 1400th Plenary Meeting, 17 December 1965, A/L.478 and UNGA, 20th Session, 1405th Plenary Meeting, 20 December 1965, at 1, 20. See also UNGA Res. 2105(XX), *Implementation of the Declaration on the Granting of Independence to Colonial Countries and Peoples*, para 13, adopted 20 December 1965.

[51] See Gerhard L Weinberg, *A World at Arms: A Global History of World War II* (New York: Cambridge University Press, 1994), 726.

[52] The Department of State Bulletin, Vol. LXXII, No. 1873, 19 May 1975, 629.

All efforts to achieve agreement on a comprehensive treaty foundered on the inability of states to agree on a definition of terrorism.[53] In domestic legislation and other official tests of one kind or another, the United States defined terrorism in essence as violent attacks on civilians designed to achieve some political end.[54] However, in the context of a democratic state, the definition expanded to incorporate politically motivated violence of any kind, including attacks on military and police targets.[55] American officials have, moreover, labeled attacks on American armed forces, such as bombings of US military facilities in the Middle East and of the *USS Cole*, a warship, as terrorism.[56] But although in political rhetoric the United States has used the word elastically, in its counter-terrorist legal initiatives, it has emphasized attacks on civilians as the act's defining feature, denouncing them as a universally illegitimate means whatsoever their ends.

In doing so, it could draw moral support from international humanitarian law which forbids the use of cruel means by all parties, defenders no less than aggressors. In both cases, good ends cannot legitimate bad means. Their opponents refused to accept this absolute division of means and ends. National Liberation movements, Third World and Soviet-Bloc countries insisted, simply could not be labeled "terrorist," since their cause, uprooting colonial or alien domination, was authorized by recent evolution in international law, not merely by debatable moral norms.

Of course one could condemn terrorist methods without insisting that, whenever employed, they de-legitimate the group using them, converting it into an international outlaw. In practice even Western countries have not consistently equated the tactic and its users. Over decades, for example, the United States looked the other way while the Irish Republican Army successfully solicited financial backing from ethnic-Irish communities in the United States.[57] During the Central American wars of the 1980s, the Reagan Administration continued its support for

[53] United Nations, *Note by the Secretary-General—"A More Secure World: Our Shared Responsibility,"* Report of the Secretary-General's High-Level Panel on Threats, Challenges and Change, 59th Session, Agenda Item 55, page 3, New York, 2 December 2004.

[54] The US National Counterterrorism Center (NCTC) defines terrorism as "premeditated, politically-motivated violence perpetrated against noncombatant targets by sub-national groups or clandestine agents," see Title 22, Chapter 38 § 2656f of the Annual Country Reports on Terrorism.

[55] Although the US National Counter-terrorism Center defines victims of terrorist attacks as 'noncombatants', interpretation of the term is left open. The State Department, in conjunction with the NCTC, considers military, paramilitary, militia, police under military command and control, civilian police, military assets and diplomatic assets, including personnel, embassies, and consulates as noncombatant targets. For more information, see <http://www.state.gov/documents/organization/65489.pdf>, accessed 21 July 2006.

[56] In his autobiography, *My Life*, former President Bill Clinton describes the 1995 attack against US military complex Khobar Towers in Saudi Arabia and the 2000 attack against the *USS Cole* in Yemen as terrorist attacks or acts committed by terrorist organizations. See William Jefferson Clinton, *My Life* (New York: Random House, 2004), 1148 and 1487, respectively.

[57] Fraser Cameron, *US Foreign Policy After the Cold War: Global Hegemon or Reluctant Sheriff?* (New York: Routledge, 2002), 145.

opponents of Nicaragua's leftist government, the so-called "Contras," despite their attacks on the civilian population[58] and did nothing to shut off financial support for right-wing paramilitary death squads in El Salvador.[59] The cliché that one person's terrorist is another person's freedom fighter bore the weight of truth.

Despite their disagreement in the abstract, which stemmed partially from conflicting political sympathies, the United States and its opponents joined in outlawing behavior which was equally threatening to their common interests. Two early examples were attacks on civil aviation and on "protected persons," primarily diplomatic personnel. Ignoring the general question of whether the acts in question constituted terrorism, the treaties negotiated with respect to these problems[60] simply named the acts, declared them criminal, and required parties to prosecute or extradite, thereby nullifying to that extent the political-offence exception in most extradition treaties.

On their surface, the debates that accompanied the failed effort to secure a comprehensive treaty or at least a norm-asserting declaration of the General Assembly were a dialogue of the deaf. US representatives shouted that terrorism is indefensible, a crime against civilization. Third World representatives agreed and then added that national liberation movements are by their nature not terrorist organizations because they are engaged in just and legitimate struggles. Suppose both sides had tired of these clashing official mantras. Suppose beginning as early as the 1970s, they had decided to argue candidly. How then might the debate have sounded?

A. The Moral Economy of Terrorism in the Service of National Liberation

First let's consider the historical setting for the early debates over definition. The riptide of Western empire has receded and in most of what today we call with some geographical incoherence the Global South, indigenous figures run the former imperial administrative units now deemed sovereign states. Africa, however, is a partial exception. An intransigent authoritarian government in Portugal clings to Angola and Mozambique and wages brutal war against indigenous rebels. In the prosperous former British colony of Southern Rhodesia, a small white minority, having unilaterally declared independence from the United

---

[58] Max Hilaire, *International Law and the United States Military Intervention in the Western Hemisphere* (The Hague: Kluwer Law International, 1997), 97. See also <http://www.hrw.org/reports/1989/WR89/Nicaragu.htm>, para. 2, accessed 28 August 2006.

[59] See generally, Christopher Dickey, *With the Contras* (New York: Simon & Schuster, 1987).

[60] The 1973 UN Convention on the Prevention and Punishment of Crimes Against Internationally Protected Persons, including Diplomatic Agents (protects senior government officials and diplomats), Parties: 117; and the 1988 UN Protocol for the Suppression of Unlawful Acts of Violence at Airports Serving International Civil Aviation (extends and supplements the Montreal Convention on air safety), Parties: 113. See <http://untreaty.un.org/English/Terrorism.asp>, accessed 26 July 2006, for text, status and summaries of each respective anti-terrorist convention.

Kingdom, controls the government and economy quietly backed by conservative forces in Europe and the United States.[61] And in South Africa, the continent's richest country, a government openly committed to separation of the races and the permanent subordination of the non-white population, rules with all the comprehensive brutality available to a rich and technologically advanced state uninhibited, given its racist ideology, by moral anxiety.

Against this backdrop of brutal struggle, a frank statement of the case for terrorism as the United States sought to define it would have sounded something like the following. In struggles by repressed peoples against racist and colonial or other kinds of alien regimes, the deck is heavily stacked against the repressed. The distribution of armed force is profoundly asymmetrical. And, as a savage irony, the asymmetry often stems in some important measure from the very oppression the liberation struggle seeks to end.

In the contemporary world, the coercive power of sophisticated hegemonic groups is a function of their collective will to dominate backed by superior organization and military technology. In addition to enjoying incomparable military superiority, by virtue of being in control of a competent and well-financed state bureaucracy, such groups have at their disposal an elastic prison system (a gulag of one kind or another) to hold detainees in whatever conditions they deem efficacious. Colonial regimes and systems of repression based on race or ethnicity also have internal cohesion, an ideological justification of their domination, and a strong sense of separate identity, all of which loosen inhibitions on the will to repress and the means employed.

In the face of these huge advantages, the oppressed are equal or superior only in will and possibly cohesion, although the latter can be made problematical by the oppressor's ability to coerce and selectively reward and also to block communication within the oppressed group and between militants and their popular base. Asymmetries of power leave the oppressed with a very limited range of options. One is passive resistance exemplified by the Gandhian struggle to force the British out of India. The British case is frequently invoked, both by dedicated believers in its efficacy and by persons mainly determined to show that terrorism or even politically motivated violence in general is immoral in part because it is unnecessary. Why always this case? Well, perhaps because it is hard to think of another where it is at least arguable that passive resistance was mainly responsible for achieving liberation.[62]

Whether it was in fact the prime mover of Indian independence is certainly debatable. After all, Gandhi's effort began more than two decades before independence.[63] The British did not decide to leave India until the end of the Second World

---

[61] See Sidney Lemelle, *Imagining Home: Class, Culture, and Nationalism in the African Diaspora* (London: Verso, 1994), 257.

[62] But compare Louise Richardson, *What Terrorists Want* (New York: Random House, 2006), 17.

[63] See Manfred B Steger, *Judging Nonviolence: The Dispute Between Realists and Idealists* (New York: Routledge, 2003), 64.

War.[64] That war bankrupted Britain and made it dependent on the generosity of the United States for the recovery of its economic balance.[65] The United States, being a great liberal power in its commercial ascendancy, was hostile on grounds of principle and interest to empires with their attendant trading preferences. In addition, both in Europe and, most dramatically in Asia where Japan had thrashed British forces, the Second World War had stripped the British of the aura of invincibility, of the martial prestige, which they had cultivated in India and which had served them well there. Moreover, the ultimate victors in the Second World War had fought in the name of liberal values against the fascist powers, thereby strengthening the normative appeal of national self-determination, and aggravating the erosion of the authoritarian and hierarchical paradigm implicit in the colonial enterprise. It eroded not only in the colonies, but in the Metropoles themselves, and nowhere more strongly than in the United Kingdom.

In sum, by 1945, Britain lacked the financial means to impose its will on India in the event of a revolt. Moreover, its elite and its electorate probably lacked the will to try. British society fervently anticipated a peace dividend after the terrible rigors of a long war, the second in a quarter century, an anticipation evidenced by the electorate's overwhelming rejection of Winston Churchill and his Conservative Government in the first post-war election. Furthermore, a reasonable person could see within India a growing will to resist continued domination by an alien power. Popular rebellion, led by a large educated Indian elite, was on the horizon. It could be repressed only with the support of an Indian Army more likely to side with the rebels at that point than with the United Kingdom. Given all these elements, it is entirely reasonable to assume that the British Government would have moved preemptively to salvage its pride, so much of its prestige as survived, and its many economic connections with India by setting an early date for independence, even if passive resistance had never occurred and Mahatma Gandhi had ended his days as a lawyer, a political prisoner or the victim of violence in South Africa where he had gone as a young man and attempted, with limited and transient effect, to organize passive resistance.[66]

From the outset of Gandhi's campaign, the conditions for passive resistance to the British occupation of India were peculiarly favorable. In the first place, the British force-to-space ratio was very low and, such as it was, depended heavily on indigenous soldiers and police. Whitehall could not physically dominate the great bulk of this sub-continent. There was plenty of space to plot, hide, and organize in the event of repression. Moreover, the United Kingdom was not well-positioned to improve the force-to-space ratio. By the twentieth century,

---

[64] See Janice Hamilton, *Winston Churchill* (A&E Biography), (Minneapolis: Lerner Publishing Group, 2006), 56.

[65] See Robert Skidelsky, *John Maynard Keynes: 1883–1946: Economist, Philosopher, Statesman* (London: Penguin, 2003), 634, 756 and 785, respectively.

[66] See Carol Dommermuth-Costa, *Indira Gandhi: Daughter of India* (Minneapolis: Lerner Publications Company, 2002), 20.

Britain's surplus rural population generated by land enclosure, abundant in the first part of the nineteenth century,[67] had been largely absorbed into the modern industrial economy or had emigrated.[68] A large permanent increase in the British component of the armed forces and state officialdom would also have been financially challenging. Of course it could have been, and indeed was, accomplished for short periods by means of the statist economy maintained during the First and Second World Wars. But even on the dubious assumption that the British electorate would have borne such a burden in order to repress the Indian population, it is extraordinarily unlikely that imperialist ardor could long have survived the costs to the British economy of maintaining a very large occupation force indefinitely.

In addition, by the twentieth century, liberalism had become the United Kingdom's hegemonic ideology, as one would expect in a Protestant country where elite and mass had over time become dependent on free trade for their prosperity. Liberal ideology nourished the idea of self-determination and made brute repression of free speech and association seem morally illegitimate. The historical contingencies that had produced a regime of parliamentary democracy with its ideological corollary of self-rule also discouraged or inhibited—although, as the repression of indigenous rebellion in Kenya illustrates, they did not preclude recourse to—state terror.[69] Gandhi could invoke the values by which the British governed themselves.

Even British chauvinism and racism contributed paradoxically to the conditions favorable to passive resistance. For because the British were as nationalist as they were liberal, they could not adopt the cooptive strategy of offering Indians gradual entry into full British citizenship or even, in order to assuage the concerns of liberals in the United Kingdom, sketch this as a preferred long-term outcome. Democracy at home in combination with tyranny abroad is bound to produce extreme ethical dissonance. In addition, India was not white settler country. Home was still the United Kingdom for the British who lived there. So government policy was not hostage, as in certain eastern African countries, to a powerful and desperate community of transplants determined to remain yet able because of their skin color to marshal political support in the Metropole whose homely charms they wished by all means to avoid except as occasional visitors.

Review of many other cases of alien domination suggests the impracticability of passive resistance in most of them. Force-to-space ratios are invariably far superior, think of South Africa before the terminal stage of apartheid and Kosovo

---

[67] Britain's rural population steadily declined throughout the nineteenth century, beginning the century at 51 per cent of the population and ending at 23 per cent. See Manfred Görlach, *English in Nineteenth-Century England: An Introduction* (Cambridge, UK: Cambridge University Press, 1999), 4.

[68] Dudley Baines, *Migration in a Mature Economy: Emigration and Internal Migration in England and Wales 1861–1900* (Cambridge, UK: Cambridge University Press, 1985), 3–4, 46.

[69] Caroline Elkins, *Imperial Reckoning: The Untold Story of Britain's Gulag in Kenya* (New York: Henry Holt and Company, 2005), 50.

under Serbian domination or all of the countries occupied by Nazi Germany during the Second World War. Moreover, for a variety of reasons, the occupier or dominating group often feels free to employ intensely punitive means against resistance, passive or otherwise. Suppose, for instance, as in the South African and Israeli cases, it views the dominated population as posing an existential threat. Or suppose, as in the Kosovo case, and arguably on the West Bank, it literally has no use for the dominated people, so it can largely dispense with their cooperation.

For the point I am making let it suffice to say that, at least in some circumstances, passive resistance is not an option. What is even clearer in many cases of domination of one national community by another is the futility of attempting liberation through attacks on the police and armed forces of the ruling group. German occupiers found these to be mere pinpricks. Even with a source of arms in next door Albania, the Albanians of Kosovo had no practical hope of regaining respect for their human rights, much less provincial autonomy or independence, by hit-and-run attacks on Serb forces. The contemporary experience of the United States in Iraq is not a contrary precedent. Rather it illustrates what happens when an occupier, with limited and transient interests, willfully underestimates the size of the force it needs to deploy and is, fortunately, inhibited by its electorate, its self-image and, perhaps more importantly, its larger strategic purposes, from employing terror tactics such as mass ethnic cleansing or large-scale massacre.

Where a "people," to use the UN idiom, is experiencing alien domination and neither passive resistance nor attacks on police and military targets are credible means of liberation and neither the Security Council nor powerful states are disposed to assist them effectively, what then are its alternatives? Must it yield to the Melian dictum that the strong do what they will and the weak bear what they must?[70] Or, when it reasonably appears that attacks on non-military targets, for instance on administrators or simply on the civilian population of the dominant group, may move the occupier over time to negotiate a more equal relationship or a division of territory or simply to withdraw from occupied territories, may the subordinate people have recourse to such methods as a last resort?

In refusing to endorse a definition of terrorism that precluded this last resort, Third World states implicitly answered that question in the affirmative. But the liberal values embodied in the normative body of human rights require a negative, for they preclude treating any human being as a mere instrument, however useful doing so may be for the welfare of the majority. Human rights, in other words, signify a rejection of the Utilitarian ethic that in deciding what is morally permissible, we need ask only what will produce the greatest happiness for the greatest number of people (or even the most deserving among peoples). However, human rights may not immunize all civilians. It may immunize only

---

[70] Thucydides *The Peloponnesian War* (revised, with an introduction by TE Wick), (New York: Random House, 1983), 351.

those not involved directly in activities that themselves constitute violations of human rights.

Although unable to reach agreement on a general anti-terrorist convention, as I noted above, the generality of UN members were able to negotiate conventions focused on particular kinds of terrorist actions that threatened their common interest in, for instance, the security of international transportation and of diplomats.[71] And so the question of the definition of terrorism moved unobtrusively into the back rooms of global diplomacy while its pragmatic practitioners dealt with concrete and immediate problems on a piecemeal basis. And there it remained until rocketed back into the grand ballroom of diplomacy by the traumatic terrorist attacks of 11 September 2001 on the United States.

B. Renewing the Struggle for a General UN Convention on Terrorism

Against the backdrop of the fallen World Trade Center in New York and the subsequent decision of the United States to invade Iraq, without Security Council

---

[71] Because the targets of terrorism have changed over the decades, the World Body has reacted by adopting specific conventions against assets or persons believed to be in current or future danger of terrorist aggression. There are 12 UN anti-terrorist conventions in total: (1) Convention on Offences and Certain Other Acts Committed on Board Aircraft, signed at Tokyo on 14 September 1963 and deposited with the Secretary-General of the International Civil Aviation Organization; (2) Convention for the Suppression of Unlawful Seizure of Aircraft, signed at the Hague on 16 December 1970 and deposited with the Governments of the Russian Federation, the United Kingdom and the United States of America; (3) Convention for the Suppression of Unlawful Acts against the Safety of Civil Aviation, signed at Montreal on 23 September 1971 and deposited with the Governments of the Russian Federation, the United Kingdom and the United States of America; (4) Convention on the Prevention and Punishment of Crimes against Internationally Protected Persons, including Diplomatic Agents, adopted by the General Assembly of the United Nations on 14 December 1973; (5) International Convention against the Taking of Hostages, adopted by the General Assembly of the United Nations on 17 December 1979; (6) Convention on the Physical Protection of Nuclear Material, signed at Vienna on 3 March 1980 and deposited with the Director-General of the International Atomic Energy Agency; (7) Protocol on the Suppression of Unlawful Acts of Violence at Airports Serving International Civil Aviation, supplementary to the Convention for the Suppression of Unlawful Acts against the Safety of Civil Aviation, signed at Montreal on 24 February 1988 and deposited with the Governments of the Russian Federation, the United Kingdom and the United States of America and with the Secretary-General of the International Civil Aviation Organization; (8) Convention for the Suppression of Unlawful Acts against the Safety of Maritime Navigation, signed at Rome on 10 March 1988 and deposited with the Secretary-General of the International Maritime Organization; (9) Protocol for the Suppression of Unlawful Acts against the Safety of Fixed Platforms Located on the Continental Shelf, signed at Rome on 10 March 1988 and deposited with the Secretary-General of the International Maritime Organization; (10) Convention for the Marking of Plastic Explosives for the Purpose of Detection, signed at Montreal on 1 March 1991 and deposited with the Secretary-General of the International Civil Aviation Organization; (11) International Convention for the Suppression of Terrorist Bombings, adopted by the General Assembly of the United Nations on 15 December 1997; and finally, (12) International Convention for the Suppression of the Financing of Terrorism, adopted by the General Assembly of the United Nations on 9 December 1999. See <http://untreaty.un.org/English/Terrorism.asp>, accessed 26 July 2006, for text, status and summaries of each anti-terrorist convention.

authorization, in the name of counter-terrorism, UN Secretary General Kofi Annan invited 16 notables largely from the world of diplomacy, individually distinguished (to varying degrees) but also broadly representative of the UN membership, "to assess current threats to international peace and security; to evaluate how well our existing policies and institutions have done in addressing those threats; and to recommend ways of strengthening the United Nations to provide collective security for the Twenty-first Century."[72] Dubbed the "Secretary-General's High-Level Panel on Threats, Challenges and Change," its members worked and doubtlessly negotiated among themselves strenuously for roughly a year to produce its report: "A more secure world: Our shared responsibility."

For those who normally reach for a double espresso when asked to read a UN document, I bring reassurance. In 91 crisp, incisive pages, the Panel admirably executed its mandate. There is little in its wide-ranging assessments, evaluations and recommendations that could be described as "anodyne." That individuals personifying such diverse and often competitive national, regional, and institutional interests could agree on so sharp an indictment of the status quo and on such unequivocal and apparently consequential recommendations for change testifies, I think, to a widely shared sense (a) of the gravity of contemporary security threats unresponsive to unilateral action, and (b) of the inadequacy of global governance mechanisms, institutions but also norms, for meeting them.

Drawing heavily on the Panel's Report, the Secretary-General disseminated a Report to the Fall 2005 General Assembly sunnily entitled "In larger freedom: toward development, security and human rights for all."[73] It finds that the "United Nations' ability to develop a comprehensive strategy [against terrorism] has been constrained by the inability of Member States to agree on an anti-terrorism convention including a definition of terrorism. This prevents the United Nations from exerting its moral authority and from sending an unequivocal message that terrorism is never an acceptable tactic."[74] The Secretary-General's Report then draws a distinction between the normative regulation of state and non-state behavior. Regulation of the former with respect to the use of force has grown ever stronger, it declares, but regulation of the use of force by non-state actors has not kept pace. It is true, the Report notes, that "virtually all forms of terrorism are [currently] prohibited by one of 12 international counter-terrorism conventions, international customary law, the Geneva Conventions or the Rome Statutes." But while these scattered prohibitions are well known to lawyers and governments, they have nothing like the political and psychological impact of a single powerful

---

[72] United Nations, *Note by the Secretary-General—"A More Secure World: Our Shared Responsibility,"* Report of the Secretary-General's High-Level Panel on Threats, Challenges and Change, 59th Session, Agenda Item 55, New York, 2 December 2004, p 8.

[73] See < http://www.un.org/largerfreedom>, accessed 25 July 2006.

[74] United Nations, *Report of the Secretary-General—"In Larger Freedom: Toward Development, Security and Human Rights for All,"* 59th Session, Agenda Items 45 and 55, New York, 21 March 2005, p 51, para 157.

declaration of terrorism's gross criminality. Hence, "achieving a comprehensive convention on terrorism, including a clear definition, is a political imperative."[75]

As the Panel's Report states, the "search for an agreed definition usually stumbles on two issues. The first is the argument that any definition should include States' use of armed forces against civilians.... The second objection is that peoples under foreign occupation have a right to resistance and a definition of terrorism should not override this right. The right to resistance," the Report further states, "is contested by some. But it is not the central point: the central point is that there is nothing in the fact of occupation that justifies the targeting and killing of civilians."[76] The rigid civil-military distinction gets a little flabby along its edge in the next Panel paragraph which declares that "[a]ttacks that specifically target *innocent* civilians and non-combatants must be condemned clearly and unequivocally by all" (emphasis added). By implication, then, attacks on civilians will not be terrorism if the civilians are not 'innocent.' The criteria of non-innocence are not explicated at that or any other point. Moreover, the innocent/non-innocent distinction appears to disappear when the Panel finally sets out its consensus definition: It is "any action, in addition to actions already specified by the existing conventions on aspects of terrorism, the Geneva Conventions and Security Council Resolution 1566 (2004), that is intended to cause death or serious bodily harm to civilians or non-combatants [presumably soldiers rendered *hors de combat* by sickness or wounds or capture], *when the purpose of such act, by its nature or context, is to intimidate a population, or to compel a Government or an international organization to do or to abstain from doing any act*"[77] (emphasis added).

While omitting the innocent/non-innocent distinction with all of its ambiguity, the Panel with its reference to "purpose" added a different qualification to what could otherwise be the blunt statement that terrorism equals all politically motivated attacks on civilians and military non-combatants. To note these nuances is not, I would argue, indulging in idle academic word-parsing. The subtle omissions and additions to the Panel's several definitional statements hint at a jot of unease at least among some members, a possibly semi-conscious appreciation of the moral and instrumental complexities the Panel chooses not to address, perhaps in the interest of consensus. I think this becomes clear if we imagine acts of violence that might not satisfy the purpose clause and if we try to put flesh on the innocent/non-innocent distinction raised and then dropped.

Take first the case of the tyrant or the vicious Minister of the Interior. Friends, lovers, or family of persons killed by either of these paradigmatic figures might kill or maim them not for the purposes of intimidating the population or compelling a government act, but rather for the good old-fashioned sentiment of

---

[75] Ibid, para 159.
[76] Ibid, para 160.
[77] Ibid, p 52, para 164.

revenge. To be sure, assassination of some officials is covered by one or more of the specific conventions the Panel would incorporate by reference. But is it clear that any of them immunize the tyrant (at least where he is not nominally the head of state or has retired to his high-walled villa in Provence) or the Interior Minister or equivalent folk? I think not. And if revenge is the purpose, they would apparently remain unprotected by the comprehensive convention championed by the Panel and by the Secretary-General in his report.[78] That may not be a bad thing, although people can differ rather dramatically in their respective views of what constitutes tyranny. After all, following the recent Terri Schiavo case in the United States, where the Supreme Court and lesser courts, state and federal, refused to overrule a state judge's determination that the feeding tube that had prolonged for some 15 years the life of a tragically brain-dead woman could be removed, certain members of the US Congress and certain self-proclaimed leaders of people of faith referred furiously to judicial tyranny, and one even recalled with apparent sentimental glisten an epigram of the late Joseph Stalin to the effect that by eliminating people one efficiently eliminated the problems they create.[79]

Along with the instrumental difficulties arising from predictably divergent views of what constitutes tyranny, there is the moral conundrum of whether all killing without official sanction, other than in self-defense, should be deemed "summary execution" within the meaning or at least the spirit of the human rights conventions and customary law norms that preclude it. Since there is now in the practice of a few states considerable precedent for "targeted killing" of persons deemed "terrorists" and since these acts have not been uniformly condemned, it is hard to argue that the assassination of persons who have committed crimes against humanity carried out by individuals or paramilitary organizations ought to fall within the forbidden category of summary execution. Yet there is execution, in the sense that the target is dead and it is hard to describe the process as anything other than summary.

The now-you-see-it, now-you-don't distinction between innocent and non-innocent civilians may itself be an effort, or at least an instinct, to deny human rights violators the protective benefits of an anti-terrorism treaty. It may also reflect some unease with the flat statement that "there is nothing in the fact of occupation that justifies the targeting and killing of civilians." Suppose the civilians are armed and planted in occupied territory precisely for the purpose of assisting the authorities in subjugating or progressively cleansing the indigenous population? Suppose the implanted civilians can kill or maim the indigenous inhabitants with de facto impunity? Would the civilian administrator of such territories be "innocent" in the minds of the Panel? What about civilian

---

[78] Ibid, p 26, para 29.

[79] See Karen MacPherson, "Schiavo's Tube Out Despite Congress; GOP Aims to Return to D.C. to Act Monday," *Pittsburgh Post-Gazette*, 19 March 2005. See also, Jeffrey Rosen, "It's the Law, Not the Judge; But These Days the Bench Is the Hot Seat," *Washington Post*, 27 March 2005.

interrogators who employ torture or other cruel and inhuman measures? The Panel's report leaves us to guess what its members' views might be.

A final point worth noting about the definition of terrorism, one closely connected to the innocent/non-innocent distinction: It is unclear how the Panel would view the killing of police and soldiers by militants hoping to arouse support for a wide-scale insurgency whether through their heroism or by provoking the government to generalized repression. Clearly such killings are murders under national law. But their perpetrators seemingly are not terrorists under the Panel's definition. In the view of the United States and many other UN members, however, they most certainly are. To reiterate a point made above, the United States regards all acts of politically motivated violence against governments it deems democratic or at least friendly as terrorist in character.

Aside from self-interest, probably the most compelling justification for this position is essentially the following: Violence must always be the last resort of persons no less than states and must be in defense of vital interests. A democracy possesses multiple avenues for redress of grievances. Moreover, real democracies do not threaten the vital interests of individuals and groups, objectively considered, since those interests—for instance, freedom of association, conscience and religion, and due process, and equal protection of the law—are by definition protected. Those protections are available even to self-conscious minorities that are unable to form coalitions with other groups to advance non-vital interests. Grievances they may have, but they are not related to fundamental interests. That statement could not, of course, have been made in relation to the African-American population of the southern part of the United States until the mid-to-late 1960s. But it certainly can be made today in relation to the claims of Basque nationalists in Spain and Irish nationalists in Ulster. While the profusion of illiberal democracies makes this a not entirely unproblematic argument if made without reference to context, in general I find moral force in the proposed distinction between democratic and authoritarian regimes of one stripe or another.

The one signal error of the Panel and the Secretary-General in their joint approach to the problem of terrorism is their refusal to include violence by the state within the strictures of the anti-terrorism general convention they propose. In his report, Kofi Annan declares dismissively that "[i]t is time to set aside debates on so-called 'State terrorism.'" Why? Supposedly, echoing the Panel, because the "use of force by States is already thoroughly regulated under international law." But so, according to the Panel's Report, is terrorism by non-state actors. The purposes of the proposed convention, both Secretary-General and Panel agree, are political and moral, not legal. What matters is the psychological effect. To me there is here a transparent inconsistency in argument which probably stems from the effort to achieve consensus.

Whether a comprehensive treaty will have the powerful psychological effect imputed to it by Panel and Secretary-General is speculative. One reason for the belief that it will is the affective character of the words "terrorism" and "terrorist."

Why should that negative effect be reserved for non-governmental fanatics and mass killers? Surely it is unlikely to amend their convictions that they do the work of God or some other cause that seems to them an end able to justify any means. It may, however, influence governments to act with greater vigor to repress or at least to avoid any form of collaboration with non-state terrorists. But if governments and the officials who run them also can fall under the terrorist label, it is not implausible that in some cases and to some degree they will amend their behavior for two reasons. One is the internal risk of regime de-legitimation. The other is the risk of being sanctioned and shunned by other states and possibly arrested and punished when no longer in office. In short, the material effects are likely to be greater where state officials fall within the definition of terrorist than when private actors do.

For decades use of the word "terrorist" to describe regimes that kill, torture and disappear people in order to terrify the rest of the population has been commonplace. In effect, the Panel and the Secretary-General have sought to alter a powerful moral discourse. Although their general purposes are respectable, I believe that the homage they have paid to regimes objecting to that discourse is unnecessary. Excluding the terrorism of state organs from a comprehensive treaty on terrorism is a moral error.

4. Neo-Conservatism

A. Neo- and Realist Conservatives

Neo-conservatism arose in the 1970s in response to a number of developments both within the United States and beyond the country's borders. I am concerned here primarily with the latter. Consequential among them was hostility by the Third World majority in the General Assembly to Israeli policy or, as many saw it, to Israel itself and to US interests and values more generally. Hostility induced a reciprocal hostility toward the United Nations that spread beyond its traditional precincts on the far right of the American political spectrum to become one of the distinguishing features of neo-conservatism and electoral groups that resonate to its themes.

Two related developments hardened and deepened neo-conservative concern not simply about the United Nations as an institution, but about the wider culture, institutions, and norms of international relations. One stemmed from choices Israel made following its victory in the 1967 war. The government of the time took the fateful decision to annex East Jerusalem de facto, to suppress the development of representative political institutions in the occupied territory and to begin planting Jewish settlements in them. The seemingly permanent denial of political and many civil rights to the population of these territories[80] was so in

---

[80] See Tom J Farer, "Israel's Unlawful Occupation," *Foreign Policy* 82 (Spring 1991), 37–58.

conflict with liberal democratic values that it was bound over time to threaten the hitherto broad base of support for Israel among liberal elites in the West.

The 1973 Middle East war also helped, however indirectly, to shape the neo-conservative project. After the easy triumph of 1967, the early days of the 1973 war were frightening as Israeli forces suffered serious casualties and ultimately needed rapid re-supply from the United States. Although the war ended in another defeat for neighboring Arab states, it restored the sense of vulnerability that the triumph of 1967 had sharply reduced. In addition, the unprecedented show of Arab unity in withholding oil from the market, not solely to benefit oil-producing states, but also to advance political ends, conveyed a message, in the event misleading, of Israeli and Western vulnerability. Was there not a danger of Western countries forcing Israel to accommodate Arab demands, if the backing for Israel was only sentimental or moral? However, neo-conservatives reasoned, if Israel could appear as a strategic partner, a protector of Western or at least US interests in the Middle East, Israel would be safer. Is it merely coincidental that emphasis on Israel's strategic value[81] and disparagement of Arab regimes[82] is a prominent feature of the neo-conservative canon?

In order to grasp the world view of neo-conservatives, it helps to compare them with conservative realists like Henry Kissinger and James Baker, foreign policy stalwarts in the Administrations of Richard Nixon, Gerald Ford, Ronald Reagan, and George HW Bush. For figures like Kissinger and Baker, the purpose of statecraft is to advance US power and material interests in a dangerously competitive and structurally anarchic world; the promotion of democracy and the defense of human rights is incidental and will sometimes prove inconvenient and hence dispensable. One result of this worldview is a readiness to strike deals with regimes seemingly of any ideological stripe or level of brutality in the treatment of their own people so long as those deals appear to advance immediate, largely material, national interests. Another is a certain measure of restraint in the exercise of power because of the judgment that the United States should not slay dragons that have no capacity or incentive to threaten the country materially.

Jeanne Kirkpatrick, Ronald Reagan's first ambassador to the United Nations, and Elliott Abrams, who became Assistant Secretary of State for Human Rights and Humanitarian Affairs early in the Reagan Administration, epitomize the foreign policy views of neo-conservatives. For them, the *Realpolitik* statecraft of Kissinger and Baker is too limited in its goals and too restrained in its means. The United States, for them, is not simply a great power but also a cluster of ideals. And by a marvelous even divine coincidence, pursuit of those ideals can only enhance

---

[81] William Kristol, "It's Our War," *The Weekly Standard*, 24 July 2006; Robert Satloff, "The Rogues Strike Back: Iran, Syria, Hamas and Hezbollah vs. Israel," *The Weekly Standard*, 24 July 2006.

[82] Efraim Karsh, "Saddam and the Palestinians," *Commentary*, 1 December 2002, 56–60.

the country's power, wealth, and security. In praising Reagan as the defender of liberal values, Kirkpatrick enunciated the core vision of the neo-conservative.[83]

"Liberal" was not, however, a description that Reagan's first Secretary of State, General Alexander Haig, would have welcomed. Underscoring the differences between the defeated Democratic Administration of Jimmy Carter and Reagan's, Haig quickly announced that human rights was off the agenda. Suiting deed to word, he purged from the diplomatic corps those ambassadors most closely identified with Carter's human rights policies.

This remained the declared position of the Administration until, still early in his first term, President Reagan accepted Secretary of State Haig's resignation. Shortly thereafter, Elliot Abrams became Assistant Secretary for human rights and related issues. His accession roughly coincided with a sea change in Administration rhetoric.[84] Until Haig left, there was dissonance between the Reaganite characterization of the relationship with the Soviet Union—a struggle between the free world and the "evil empire"—and hostility to Carter's human rights legacy. After Haig, the rhetoric segued into harmony by equating the defense of human rights with the promotion of democracy, in practice defined narrowly in terms of elections that were not grossly fraudulent.[85] This was a conspicuous departure from Carter Administration policy that had been deeply concerned with torture and summary execution in the Third World, even when perpetrated by such dependable US clients as right-wing military governments in Latin America.[86]

The post-Haig State Department responded by minimizing, denying, or rationalizing delinquencies[87] and urging elections while opposing negotiated power-sharing arrangements in cases where massive human rights violations were entangled with civil wars between military governments and left-wing guerrillas.[88] Thus, policy incorporated the view announced by Kirkpatrick before

---

[83] Tom J Farer, "Interplay of Domestic Politics, Human Rights and US Foreign Policy," in *Wars on Terrorism and Iraq: Human Rights, Unilateralism, and US Foreign Policy*, Thomas G Weiss, Margaret E Crahan, and John Goering (eds), (New York: Routledge, 2004).

[84] See generally, Aryeh Neier, *Taking Liberties: Four Decades in the Struggle for Rights* (New York: Public Affairs Press, 2003), 169–221.

[85] See Aryeh Neier, "Human Rights in the Reagan Era: Acceptance in Principle," *Annals of the American Academy of Political and Social Science* (506), (November 1989), 31–40.

[86] For a thorough discussion on the Reagan administration's human rights policy in Latin America see Kathryn Sikkink, *Mixed Signals* (Ithaca, NY: Cornell University Press, 2004), 148–80.

[87] See, eg, Aryeh Neier, *Taking Liberties: Four Decades in the Struggle for Rights* (New York: Public Affairs, 2003), 209–16.

[88] In late 1980 four American Maryknoll nuns were killed by US-backed Salvadoran soldiers during the civil war against the Frente Farabundo Martí para la Liberación Nacional (FMLN). At the time, Kirkpatrick remarked, "they were not just nuns...they were political activists on behalf of the Frente"; Flora Lewis, "Keeping it Honest," *New York Times*, 27 March 1981, A27. Also notorious was the Administration's involvement in concealing the truth about the El Mozote massacre of December 1981, in which over 750 Salvadoran men, women, and children were killed by a US-trained unit of the Salvadoran Army. See Mark Danner, *The Massacre at El Mozote: A Parable of the Cold War* (New York: Vintage Books, 1994). See also Alan Riding, "Duarte's Strategy May Work Better in US than in Salvador," *New York Times*, 27 September 1981, E5.

the administration assumed office, namely a categorical hostility to regimes and movements of the Left.[89]

After Haig's departure, latent tensions between realists and neo-conservatives rarely surfaced conspicuously. Whatever the differences in motives—between the conservative aim of maintaining unchallenged US hegemony in the Western hemisphere or the additional neo-conservative one of maintaining ideological purity by pulverizing left-wing regimes and movements—both supported ruthless right-wing regimes in El Salvador and Guatemala and efforts to overthrow an authoritarian leftist one in Nicaragua. Conflicts over relations with Moscow lost their edge once Mikhail Gorbachev assumed control of the Soviet state and initiated multi-faceted policies that would, with astonishing speed, precipitate liquidation of Moscow's empire and then the dissolution of the Soviet Union. But once George HW Bush took office and put James Baker in charge of foreign policy, discord reemerged, particularly over the failure to use the occasion of the first Gulf War to eliminate Saddam Hussein while at the same time attempting to engineer a settlement of the Arab-Israeli dispute by ending the occupation begun in 1967.[90] Modest pressure on Israel for concessions to Palestinian nationalism, including for the first time in years a hint of material sanctions, evoked a furious assault from neo-conservatives even to the point of implying that Baker was a hidden anti-Semite.[91]

Beyond factional conflict over particular issues lay the broader difference of worldviews. In a seminal statement of neo-conservative goals for the post-Cold War era, Charles Krauthammer caught the policy community's eye with an article calling for full exploitation of the "unipolar moment."[92] Concretely the United States was to employ its unrivaled power to shape a world reflective of American values: Elected governments, and free markets. Neither the cautious democracy-promoting efforts of realists nor their strategy of positive engagement with the nominally communist regime in China came close to satisfying this vision. And so the neo-conservatives noisily nursed their dissatisfactions, seemingly as disappointed as right-wing Christian groups with an administration so plainly indifferent to the excited ambitions and cultural sensibilities of both factions.[93]

Whatever their sour disappointment with the first President Bush, it was as nothing to the fury and contempt evoked by William Jefferson Clinton, the incarnation of the detested counter-cultural life-style, and his First Lady, a feminist icon. Hardly friends of Clinton's easy virtue and broad tolerance, the

---

[89] Tom J Farer, "The Making of Reaganism," 28 (21 and 22) *New York Review of Books* (1982).

[90] William Safire, "Bush's Moral Crisis," *New York Times*, 1 April 2001, A17.

[91] This was primarily a result of the Administration's decision to temporarily suspend loan guarantees to Israel in order to halt expansion of Jewish settlements in the West Bank. For a neo-con account of the fallout, see Jay P Leftkowitz, "Does the Jewish Vote Count?" *Commentary* 111 (March 2001), 50–3.

[92] Charles Krauthammer, "The Unipolar Moment," *Foreign Affairs* 70 (Winter 1990–91), 23–33.

[93] See, eg, Michael Isikoff, "The Robertson Right and the Grandest Conspiracy," *Washington Post*, 11 October 1992, C3.

neo-conservatives were even more enraged by what they saw as the dissipation of US opportunity and power. Realist conservatives could make common cause with neo-conservatives and the religious Right, their sometime allies in the broad conservative coalition, because they disliked Clinton's stance on Humanitarian Intervention and state-building.

To the limited extent that the 2000 presidential campaign debates engaged foreign policy, George W Bush sounded the themes of the realists. On his watch, US troops would be used as soldiers not humanitarian hand-holders.[94] He would not waste the country's human and material resources on errant adventures in nation-building or to rescue feckless peoples. Asked what he would have done had he been faced with the Rwandan genocide, he replied that he would have encouraged UN action but not sent US troops.[95]

Presumably to propitiate the increasingly powerful right wing of his own party, he also criticized placing American forces under UN command, as had happened briefly in Somalia, a position Clinton himself seemed to have adopted after October 1993.[96] Beyond that, Bush actually mirrored Clinton's views when he was first a candidate for the Presidency by deploring his father's accommodationist behavior toward China and intimating that he would shift to a much cooler tone.[97] In brief, nothing in the rhetoric of George W Bush's campaign or in his selection of two apparently realist conservatives, Colin Powell and Condoleezza Rice, to be his top foreign policy advisors augured a major change in foreign policy. Still, given the number of neo-conservatives who were slated for important posts, the role of the Christian Right (now in close alliance with the neo-conservatives), the volatility of the Middle East, and the existence of

[94] While referring to Somalia during the 11 October 2000 Presidential Debate at Wake Forest University, Bush said, "I don't think our troops ought to be used for what's called nation-building. I think our troops ought to be used to fight and win war." The text is available at <http://www. issues2000.org/Archive/Wake_Forest_debate_Foreign_Policy.htm>; see also: Condoleezza Rice, "Promoting the National Interest," *Foreign Affairs* 79 (January–February 2000), 45–62.

[95] In a *Washington Post* article entitled "The Lesson of Rwanda" of 13 October 2000, Bush's response to the Clinton administration's inaction in Rwanda is described as follows: "...Mr. Bush does not even see a policy failure in the way America allowed the genocide to unfold. The Texas governor said his foreign policy would be based on national interest alone; he further suggested that events in sub-Saharan Africa seemed to him remote from US interests." This point is also made clear with reference to Somalia in the Presidential Debate at Wake Forest University on 11 October 2000. The text is available at <http://www.issues2000.org/Archive/Wake_Forest_debate_Foreign_Policy.htm>.

[96] Issuing a strong campaign promise, then-Governor Bush, in a speech at the Ronald Reagan Presidential Library on 19 November 1999, clearly declares "I will never place US troops under U.N. command." Full text of the transcript is available at <http://www.mtholyoke.edu/acad/intrel/bush/wspeech.htm>.

[97] When asked by the TV personality Larry King, "What international policy would you change immediately?" Bush's response was, "Our relationship with China. The President has called the relationship with China a strategic partnership. I believe our relationship needs to be redefined as competitors ... [W]e must make it clear to the Chinese that we don't appreciate any attempt to spread weapons of mass destruction around the world, that we don't appreciate any threats to our friends and allies in the Far East," *Larry King Live*, 15 February 2000, transcript available online at: <http://transcripts.cnn.com/TRANSCRIPTS/0002/15/lkl.00.html>.

Al Qaeda with its expressed determination to drive the United States out of the Middle East, it would not have taken clairvoyance to imagine circumstances that would open the door for a dramatic policy shift.

From its inauguration in January 2001 until 11 September 2001, the Bush Administration complied roughly with the expectations that the President had cultivated while he was a candidate. Even his curt dismissals of US participation in international treaty regimes like Kyoto, the International Criminal Court, and the supplemental enforcement protocol to the Biological Weapons Convention were consistent with his general approach to national security policy, although in this respect also consistent with the neo-conservative distaste for international legal commitments. Then the attacks on the World Trade Center and the Pentagon opened a world of risk previously envisioned only by some of the national security cognoscenti. Neo-conservatives alone had a grand strategy of response, one that in its very ambition and vision corresponded to the shock and fury of the US public and to its congenital sense that wars should end in glorious, transformative victory.

B. The Neo-conservative Project

Hegemony, as neo-conservatives argued in the 1990s, is not the mere possession of dominating power, but also the will to use it on behalf of a coherent project. In the Clinton years, hegemony was only latent. The catastrophe of September 2001 created the circumstances in which it could be made real.

Although there is not a single comprehensive statement of the neo-conservative project and its premises, out of the particular policies advocated by its high priests and house organs, as well as the thicket of argument surrounding them, project and premises materialize.[98] Having won the Third World War, conventionally called the "Cold War" although it had many hot incidents, we are now by dint of circumstance launched into a fourth. Like the second and third ones, it stems from a conflict of values, not of mere interests. It is a war between believers in free peoples and markets, on the one hand, and unbelievers, on the other; it is a war between democratic capitalism and its enemies. The former is expanding, not at the end of a bayonet but in response to the desire of people everywhere to receive it or at least its blessings. It expands, in other words, by pull and not push. And that expansion is coterminous with the expansion of individual freedom.

The expansion coincidentally threatens where it does not immediately demolish the practices, beliefs, and institutions that thrive only where freedom is alien and can be made to remain so. As the financial and cultural base of the expansion

[98] See, eg, Charles Krauthammer, "The Unipolar Moment" *Foreign Affairs* 70 (Winter 1990–91), 23–33; Mark Helprin "What Israel Must Do to Survive," *Commentary* 112 (November 2001), 25–8; see also Daniel Pipes, "Who is the Enemy?" *Commentary* 113 (January 2002), 21–7; Norman Podhoretz, "How to Win World War IV," *Commentary* 113 (February 2002), 19–29; Nicholas Lemann, "The Next World Order," *New Yorker*, 1 April 2002, 42–8.

(sometimes labeled "globalization"), the United States is the inevitable target for all those who, being threatened, resist. And since globalization is not a public policy but the summation of millions of private initiatives, the US government cannot erase the bull's eye from the nation's flank by any policy other than attempting to remake the country in the image of its enemies, a closed society. For political reasons, the government could not do that; for moral ones, it should not try even if the political obstacles were to diminish.

So war is our fate. A conventional war would be a minor affair for a country with such military power. But in the epoch of globalization, we must contend with asymmetrical war. Since the enemies of the open society cannot stand up to our armies, they turn to such soft targets as civilians and the infrastructure that supports them. Here our enemies find vast vulnerabilities springing from the very nature of our open society and the delicate systems of communication and movement and energy generation that sustain quotidian life. The destruction of the World Trade Center illustrated the lethal potential of asymmetrical war even when waged without benefit of weapons of mass destruction. With unconventional weapons in the mix, images of unspeakable catastrophe are summoned.

As the United States is the center of expanding laissez faire capitalist democracy, the Islamic world, particularly its Arab sector, is the center of violent opposition precisely because the dynamism, pluralism, and instrumental rationalism of liberal capitalism challenge deeply rooted social arrangements. And this challenge occurs against a backdrop of nearly a millennium of armed conflict between the West and the various Islamic polities on the southern side of the Mediterranean and, in recent centuries, a succession of devastating military defeats and political humiliations for the latter. Added to this dangerous mix is a strain of sacrificial violence in contemporary, if not original, Islamic thought which leads to the suicide bomber.[99]

What, then, is to be done? A first step is to seek out and destroy immediate threats and demonstrate that US power is now driven by an implacable will and a universal capacity to revenge every injury by inflicting greater ones. Being hated is not good; being hated without being at the same time feared is far worse. In destroying the Taliban regime and killing or incarcerating various Al Qaeda members, the first step was taken. Going after Saddam Hussein also would have demonstration value. For the Taliban were barely a regime, virtually unrecognized and not fully in control of the country they misruled. Destroying the long-established regime in Baghdad, one not credibly connected to 11 September, was a dramatic expansion of the anti-terrorist project, calculated to be a qualitatively more potent demonstration of Washington's will and power.

---

[99] Daniel Benjamin and Steven Simon, *The Age of Sacred Terror* (New York: Random House, 2002), 28; see also Jessica Stern, *Terror in the Name of God: Why Religious Militants Kill* (New York: The Library of Congress, 2003), 54; Bernard Lewis, "Roots of Muslim Rage," in Charles W Kegley Jr (ed), *The New Global Terrorism: Characteristics, Causes, Controls* (Upper Saddle River, NJ: Prentice Hall, 2003).

If one is to take neo-conservatives at their word, however, the overthrow of Saddam Hussein also created the conditions for installing a capitalist democracy in the once most formidable and technologically advanced country in the Arab world.[100] This too would be done in part for its hopefully contagious effects on the surrounding Arab states. This hope flows from a key, if not always clearly declared, premise of neo-conservative grand strategy: given the opportunity, ordinary people will prove to be *homo economicus*, rational maximizers of their material well-being. To serve its interests and theirs, the United States should provide the opportunity, as it provides the quintessential model: strict limits on state power; the rule of law including transparency of the public realm; an independent judiciary; extensive rights to private property associated with constitutional limits on the confiscatory power of the state; and free elections to sustain the rest.

The individual, being protected from depredations of the state, is thereby liberated to pursue material well-being. The ethic of consumption will trump all other ends. An electorate of economic strivers will disown projects that conscript their wealth; they will find dignity and meaning in the struggle to produce as well as sufficient pleasure in the satisfaction of their appetites. That is why liberal democracies do not war with each other. To be sure, fanatics immune to the ethic of material consumption will not altogether disappear. But they will no longer be able to multiply themselves so easily. And liberal democratic governments, driven by the coercive power of elections to mirror the interests of their electors, will cooperate with the United States to extirpate fanatics.

Neo-conservatives publicists did not rely exclusively on a contagion of democracy springing from the demonstration factor of Iraq. The evidence of freedom, peace, and affluence in Iraq, they claimed, will weaken from within the stagnant autocracies of surrounding Arab states like Syria and Saudi Arabia. Meanwhile the United States, with such of its industrialized allies as it can muster, will encourage them with positive and negative incentives to manage a transition to open societies for the benefit of the Arab people in general and for ours. And for Israel's too because citizens of open societies will no longer have grounds to rage at their fate—rage which today's Arab governments deflect to Israel first and then to the United States.[101]

C. Liberalism and Neo-conservatism: Destined to Duel

To the extent it has survived the sanguinary setback in Iraq, is this project the expression of a small minority of ideologically-driven politicians and policy intellectuals or does it now reflect a widespread, irresistible conception of American interests? After 11 September's demonstration of US vulnerability to asymmetrical warfare,

---

[100] Alan Murray, "Bush Officials Scramble to Push Democracy in Iraq," *Wall Street Journal*, 8 April 2003, A4; Lawrence Kaplan, "Regime Change," *New Republic* 228, 3 March 2003, 21–3.

[101] See Thomas Carothers, "Promoting Democracy and Fighting Terror," *Foreign Affairs* 82 (January/February 2003), 84–97.

the neo-conservative vision could draw support from traditional conservatives concerned primarily with maximizing the country's security and wealth, as well as those who *a priori* equate US and Israeli security interests. Should it not appeal as well to human rights activists and to the wider universe of centrists and liberals? Can one believe in the universality of human rights and not embrace a strategy that purports to merge realism and idealism in the cause of freedom? Apparently so. Most of the established organs and prominent advocates of liberalism and most of the leading figures and institutions in the American as well as the international human rights world have reacted along a spectrum ranging from intense skepticism through selective criticism to comprehensive hostility toward the Bush Administration's grand strategy.[102]

Is the hostility a merely visceral response to the conservative messenger? Or are there reasoned grounds, rooted in liberal values and the deep essence of human rights, for rejecting this message? Actually, taking the messengers' identity into account is entirely reasonable, part of the seasoned wisdom of everyday life. We do not entrust things that we value except to persons who have created grounds for trust. And there are essentially two reasons why we trust people. One is that they have a record of fulfilling their commitments, and the other is that we have common values. The latter is particularly important when the mission we are called upon to entrust to the messenger has as its very purpose the advancement of our values.

If our end is the broader realization of human rights, then there were and there remain substantial reasons to distrust the right-wing executors of contemporary foreign policy. As noted above, when George W Bush sought the presidency, he disowned use of the coercive power of the United States where the only potential gain in a given case would be protection of human rights. This was also the position of his then National Security Advisor.[103] But the case for skepticism does not rely simply on the place of human rights in the President's declared hierarchy of concerns. In addition, his Secretary of Defense had served as a special envoy to Saddam Hussein during the Reagan Administration, when it was assisting the dictator whose aggression against Iran had backfired to the point where, without extensive external support, he faced defeat.[104] It was during this period that Saddam Hussein employed chemical weapons against both the Iranians and the Kurdish population of Iraq without in any way compromising Washington's support for his regime.

[102] Stanley Hoffman, "The High and the Mighty: Bush's National Security Strategy and the New American Hubris," *American Prospect* 13(24), 13 January 2003, 24; see also Chip Pitts, "A Constitutional Disaster," *The Nation* 21 October 2005, available online at <http://www.thenation.com/doc/20051107/pitts> (accessed 10 March 2007).

[103] See, eg, Condoleezza Rice, "Promoting the National Interest," *Foreign Affairs* 79 (January/February 2000), 45–62.

[104] Christopher Dickey and Evan Thomas, with Mark Hosenball, Roy Gutman, and John Barry, "How Saddam Happened'" *Newsweek*, 3 September 2002, 34–40.

Many senior members of the current Administration served in the earlier Bush Administration when it stood idly by as Yugoslavia disintegrated and Serbia initiated mayhem in Croatia and Bosnia. To be fair, they do not have more to answer for morally than the Clinton Administration, which also wrung its hands as Slobodan Milosevic and his colleagues murdered their way around the Balkans and as Rwanda's slow-motion genocide took place.[105] But Clinton never promised us a no-holds-barred crusade for liberal democracy and did not ask the country to entrust him with wartime power to spread the American Way.[106]

One could, moreover, argue that, if we are going to ground skepticism on past words and performance, we need to disaggregate realist conservatives like Rumsfeld and Rice from neo-conservatives like former Deputy Secretary of Defense Paul Wolfowitz or the National Security Council's Elliott Abrams, or pundits like Charles Krauthammer.[107] Even if it is hard to credit the traditionalists with an epiphany in September 2001, have the neo-conservatives not been at least rhetorically consistent? Indeed, is not a declared commitment to Wilsonianism with fixed bayonets a defining feature of neo-conservatism?[108] Thus, the problem seems less one of the messenger's sincerity than it is of the humanitarian implications of the message itself.

A crusade for democracy, even full-blown liberal democracy, overlaps but is not synonymous with a crusade for human rights. Moral criteria for evaluating the exercise of power stretch into the remote past.[109] So does the idea of possessing rights in relationship to power holders. But the idea of rights held in common not just by all members of the same class, profession, guild, race, religion, or nation but by every human being simply by virtue of being human, now that is a modern idea. And just as it is not synonymous with liberal democracy, it is not synonymous with general human welfare.

As I noted earlier, a common conception of human rights is that they are categorical claims on human beings and institutions, primarily on governments to act or refrain from acting in ways injurious to those rights.[110] At least the so-called first generation of civil and political rights that have evoked the widest consensus about their imperative quality are focused on the individual, not the wider

---

[105] See Samantha Power, *A Problem from Hell: America and the Age of Genocide* (New York: Harper, 2002), chs 9 and 10.

[106] This was due mostly to Clinton's emphasis on domestic—especially economic—policy. David Halberstram, *War in a Time of Peace: Bush, Clinton and the Generals* (New York: Scribner, 2001), 158, 167–8.

[107] See, eg, Ramesh Ponnuru, "Getting to the Bottom of this 'Neo' Non-sense," *National Review*, 16 June 2003, 29–32; and Ramesh Ponnuru, "The Shadow Men," *The Economist*, 26 April 2003, 21–3.

[108] See, eg, Stanley Hoffman, "The High and the Mighty: Bush's National Security Strategy and the New American Hubris," *American Prospect*, 13(24) 13 January 2003, 24.

[109] See Micheline Ishay, *Human Rights Reader: Major Speeches, Essays and Documents from the Bible to the Present* (New York: Routledge, 1997).

[110] Jack Donnelly, *Universal Human Rights in Theory and Practice* (Ithaca, NY: Cornell University Press, 2002), 35.

community. More than that, you will recall, they are claims that the community cannot trump, claims that cannot be subordinated to some presumed general good which, while causing injury to a few, enhances the welfare of the many.

Actually, even in the case of civil and political rights, this is something of an overstatement in the sense that, during periods of emergency, the community for its collective welfare can temporarily suspend the great majority of rights.[111] Many national constitutions so provide, as does the International Covenant on Civil and Political Rights.[112] But some cannot be abrogated under any circumstances. Among them are the right to life, the right not to be tortured, and the right not to be punished except as a result of a finding of guilt at the end of a fair trial.[113] It is conceivable that a good faith effort to implant liberal democracy throughout the Middle East and in other areas where it is largely absent, an effort carried out in part by war, armed subversion, assassination, and other instruments of coercive statecraft, might in the long course of history enhance human well-being beyond anything that could be achieved through such non-violent means as education, economic incentives, financial and technical assistance to democratic movements, and improving the welfare consequences of democracy so as to increase its attractions.

But even if we could be certain that human welfare would in the long term be better served by violent statecraft, if one were committed to the view that human rights are trumps, then one might still oppose a crusade for democracy. Taking of innocent lives is among the probable features of a violent crusade for whatever end. One particularly awful instance occurred during the invasion of Iraq, when a missile flying off course struck an apartment complex wiping out a child's immediate family, ripping off his arms, and crisping his body.[114] Since civilians were not targeted—on the contrary it appeared (at least before the insurgency began) that the US military made an unusual effort to minimize civilian casualties[115]—this child's horror was entirely within the boundaries of the humanitarian laws of war.[116] Moreover, given the Security Council resolutions violated by Saddam's regime, its chronic violations of human rights, and the loss

[111] For example, Chile's 1925 and 1980 constitutions permitted the suspension of certain rights under the Constitution during States of Emergency. Edward C Snyder, "The Dirty Legal War: Human Rights and the Rule of Law in Chile: 1973–1995," 2 *Tulsa J. Comp. & Int'l L.* 253 Spring 1995.
[112] International Covenant on Civil and Political Rights, GA Res. 00A (XXI) 21 UN GAOR Supp. (No. 16) at 5 UN Doc. A/6316 (1966), 999 UN T.S. 171 entered into force 3 March 1976, art 4.1.
[113] Ibid, art 4.2.
[114] Samia Nakhoul, "Boy Bomb Victim Struggles Against Despair," *Daily Mirror*, 8 April 2003.
[115] See George F Will, "Measured Audacity," *Newsweek* 14 April 2003, 66.
[116] The primary treaties of humanitarian law governing international armed conflict are the 1907 Hague Convention, the 1949 Geneva Conventions and the 1977 Additional Protocol 1 to the Geneva Conventions. Taken in concert, the provisions of these treaties require that military attacks must be directed at military targets and that the rules of necessity and proportionality be followed, but it does not mean that there cannot be civilian casualties. See Michael Bothe *et al*, *New Rules for Armed Conflict* (Dordrecht: Kluwer Law International, 1982), 304–5.

of life arising from Iraq's aggressions against Iran and Kuwait, a not entirely implausible Just War argument could be made in favor of the US-led invasion.[117] Nevertheless, pain and death inflicted predictably, albeit unintentionally, on the innocent rubs against the grain of human rights particularly in any war of choice rather than one of existential self-defense. And that would be the case whether the choice is made for the purpose of preserving US freedom of action or extending the incidence of democracy.

Because the one thing certain about armed intervention is the death and mutilation of the innocent,[118] and because core human rights are imperative claims by individuals not open to trumping by some supposed long-term general good, *a crusade to defend core human rights has built-in restraints that a crusade for the general expansion of democracy does not.* In the former case, we are constrained at least to balance the lives hopefully saved against those we will take in order to save them. But if democracy alone is the end, then as long as we are confident that some will survive to hold free and fair elections, civilian deaths are an acceptable cost. This may seem like an unfair *reductio ad absurdum*, carrying the logic of the neo-conservatives' position beyond the point that most of them would probably go. Yet in fact it is grounded in such experiences as the neo-conservative defense of state terrorism in El Salvador and Honduras and the at best toleration of terrorist methods employed by the anti-Sandinista insurgents in Nicaragua during the 1980s.[119]

Human rights concerns were a secondary justification for the invasion of Iraq. The Bush Administration defended it primarily on the grounds of national

---

[117] The White House claimed that Saddam Hussein repeatedly violated 16 UN Security Council resolutions designed to ensure that Iraq does not pose a threat to international peace and security. A list of those resolutions can be found in the White House briefing paper, "Iraq: A Decade of Deception and Defiance;" full text is available online at <http://www.whitehouse. gov/new/releases/2002/09/20020912.html>. See, eg, "Iraq: Witnesses Link Mass Graves to 1991 Repression," "The Graves of al-Mahawil: The Truth Uncovered," "Mass Graves Hide Horror of Iraqi Past," and "Human Rights Testimony on Prosecuting Iraqi War Crimes," all of which are available on the Human Rights Watch website at <http://humanrightswatch.org>. More than 1 million people were killed during the Iran-Iraq War. Dilip Hiro, *The Longest War* (New York: Routledge, 1991), 1. The US State Department reports that 1,000 Kuwaitis were killed during the Iraqi invasion and subsequent occupation in 1990–91. See <http://www.whitehouse.gov/ news/releases/2002/09/20020912.html>. The reader may also wish to compare the above with the "Special Report" published by the United States Institute of Peace after a December 2002 symposium to address the question, "Would an invasion of Iraq be a 'Just War?'" available at <http://www.usip.org/pubs/specialreports/sr98.pdf>.

[118] Stuart Taylor, Jr, "In the Wake of Invasion, Much Official Misinformation by US Comes to Light," *New York Times*, 6 November 1983, A20. The invasion of Panama resulted in the deaths of 300 Panamanians. Adam Issac Hasson, "Extraterritorial Jurisdiction and Sovereign Immunity on Trial: Noriega, Pinochet, and Milošević—Trends in Political Accountability and Transnational Criminal Law," *Boston College International and Comparative Law Review* 125 (Winter 2002), 125–58.

[119] For a discussion see Mark Danner, *El Mozote*; David K Shipler, "Senators Challenge Officials on Contras," *New York Times*, 6 February 1987, A3; Christopher Dickey, *With the Contras: A Reporter in the Wilds of Nicaragua* (New York: Simon & Schuster, 1987) and Marlene Dixon, *On Trial: Reagan's War Against Nicaragua* (San Francisco: Synthesis Publications, 1985).

security and of legitimate enforcement of Security Council resolutions.[120] Hence the occupation of Iraq may well not herald further wars against authoritarian regimes. But nothing in the premises and values of neo-conservatism precludes them. Neo-conservatives are prepared to make war not simply for the immediate purpose of installing elected governments, but also for the more general one of maintaining US hegemony indefinitely, a position now enshrined in the National Security Strategy Doctrine issued by the Government in September 2002. A hegemonic United States will assure, or is at least the best means of assuring, the long-term triumph of liberal democracy and hence the greater good of humanity, they argue.[121] Of course for traditional conservatives, hegemony needs no justification beyond the influence and wealth and presumably the security brought to one's own country. For them the tribal good does not have to be wrapped in the politically correct colors of the general good.

Is there any tension between the traditional realist and the neo-conservative worldviews? And if there is, should those who define the good in terms of the more effective defense and promotion of human rights prefer the triumph of the traditionalists or the crusaders? Some prominent traditionalists like former National Security Advisor Brent Scowcroft either supported without enthusiasm or opposed the Iraq war.[122] So did some academic "Realists."[123] In a state that for good reason feels the tide of history running against it, a state that feels geo-politically insecure, as Germany did when it ignited the First and Second World Wars, realists may be risk takers.[124] And few risks are consistently greater than the risk of war. But in a country like the United States—wealthy, cohesive, and without any rival in sight—realism generally operates as a restraint on military adventures. In terms of its implications for international order, neo-conservatism is a revolutionary doctrine being urged in the name of a state that, from a traditionalist perspective, should be the champion of the status quo.

The neo-conservative view, however, is that in light of the present conditions of international relations, broad freedom of action for the United States and the continuous deepening of global economic integration, both of which are deemed to serve humanitarian as well as national interests, require discretion to initiate preventive attacks on unfriendly states that develop weapons of mass destruction, particularly nuclear ones, even in cases where the states in question have credible grounds for feeling threatened by their neighbors or the United States and may

---

[120] David E Sanger, "Bush Sees 'Urgent Duty' to Pre-empt Attack by Iraq," *New York Times*, 8 October 2002, A1.

[121] See, eg, William Kristol and Robert Kagan, "Toward a Neo-Reaganite Foreign Policy," *Foreign Affairs* 75 (July–August 1996), 18–32.

[122] Henry Kissinger, "Phase II and Iraq," *Washington Post*, 13 January 2002, B7; Brent Scowcroft, "Don't attack Saddam," *Wall Street Journal*, 15 August 2002, A12.

[123] See, eg, John Mearsheimer and Stephen Walt, "An Unnecessary War," *Foreign Policy* (January–February 2003), 51–60.

[124] See generally, Gordon A Craig, *The Germans* (New York, 1991); William Shirer, *The Rise and Fall of the Third Reich* (New York, 1960).

therefore be seeking such weapons as a deterrent, as the only solid guarantee of their independence and territorial integrity. Neo-conservatives also believe that in order to address the terrorist threat, the United States must be free to exercise its police powers within but without the consent of other states. In other words, the United States needs to be free to arrest or kill persons believed to be planning attacks or conspiring to attack or to facilitate attacks on American persons or property abroad or within the United States.

A third means deemed necessary is the threat or use of force to press authoritarian regimes to morph into elected ones. Furthermore, in light of its furious opposition to proposed legislation setting limits to the methods US forces can use to interrogate prisoners[125] and in light, as well, of the methods that have been used to date obviously authorized at the highest levels of government,[126] the Bush Administration also deems it necessary for world order to violate if not the prohibition on torture, as it very narrowly defines it, then at least on cruel, inhuman, and degrading treatment that are contained in the Geneva Conventions of 1949, the Torture Convention, and the International Covenant on Civil and Political Rights.[127]

All in all, it seems fair to describe these various felt needs as so inconsistent with widely held but not universal views about sovereignty, intervention, and human rights as to merit the description "revolutionary" rather than "conservative."[128] In any event, they have predictably led to policies that are incompatible with the conservation much less the enhancement of liberal ends.

---

[125] As noted in Noah Feldman's piece entitled "Who Can Check the President?" in the *New York Times Magazine* of 8 January 2006, "A memo from the Department of Justice to the White House counsel dated Aug. 1, 2002, argued that any attempt to apply Congress's anti-torture law 'in a manner that interferes with the president's direction of such core war matters as detention and interrogation of enemy combatants thus would be unconstitutional.'"

[126] Writing in *The New Yorker* on 14 February 2005, Jane Mayer exposed the practice of extraordinary rendition utilized by the Bush administration in the war on terror. In her piece "Outsourcing Torture" she quotes Vice President Dick Cheney who, "reflecting the new outlook," argued, on "Meet the Press", that the government needed to "work through, sort of, the dark side". Cheney went on, "A lot of what needs to be done here will have to be done quietly, without any discussion, using sources and methods that are available to our intelligence agencies, if we're going to be successful. That's the world these folks operate in. And so it's going to be vital for us to use any means at our disposal, basically, to achieve our objective.".

[127] The United States has ratified the International Covenant on Civil and Political Rights; the Convention against Torture and other Cruel, Inhuman or Degrading Treatment or Punishment; the International Convention on the Elimination of All Forms of Racial Discrimination; and the Convention on the Prevention and Punishment of the Crime of Genocide.

[128] See Tom J Farer, "The prospect for international law and order in the wake of Iraq (Agora: Future Implications of the Iraq Conflict)," *American Journal of International Law* 97(3) (July 2003), 621–8.

2

Legal and Legitimate Use of Force: In the Struggle against Transnational Terrorism Is the UN Charter Quaint?

With fire and sword the country round
Was wasted far and wide,
And many a childing mother then,
And new-born baby died;
But things like that, you know, must be
At every famous victory

They say it was a shocking sight
After the field was won;
For many thousand bodies here
Lay rotting in the sun
But things like that, you know, must be
After a famous victory

Robert Southey

In human history, pacifism has been a minority taste. Most people most of the time have believed in the utility of armed force and have found little difficulty in constructing justifications for its use. In the earliest days of their faith, when they were objects of persecution by the imperial authorities of Rome, Christians tended to be members of that pacifist minority. But once the Roman Emperor embraced the faith, implicitly promising to back it with secular force, recourse to arms began to seem less objectionable, a form of human behavior that might actually be laudable in the right circumstances. It waited only for the great Saint Augustine to define those circumstances and thus give to the West (albeit he was a North African) the doctrine of Just War.

Accepting, as I do, the belief that some wars can be just, there remains the brute fact that the only thing entirely predictable about war is that it will destroy things, among them innocent lives. What is also predictable is that when democracies wage war, the liberties of their citizens shrink. Hence defenders of human rights are bound to regard recourse to force as a threat to their values and therefore a measure calling for close scrutiny and objection to its use where less destructive methods are at hand or where violent means are reasonably likely to have a net adverse effect on humanitarian values.

Even before the 9/11 destruction of the World Trade Center, persons identified with the neo-conservative movement in the United States were disparaging international law's restraint on the use of force, both for its supposed failure to restrain bad nations, that is nations unfriendly to American projects and associates, and for the way it threatened to trammel the use of American power to make a better world. In the eyes of these neo-con publicists, international law is a kind of conspiracy of the bad and the weak to restrain the good and the strong.[1] And since the strong at this remarkable historical moment is preeminently the United States, a country dedicated to the advancement of liberty of the person and of trade, such restraint is inconsistent with the human no less than the national interest. The supposed imperatives of the post-9/11 "war" against terrorism serve only to heighten neo-con concern that the hordes of Lilliput will use the cords of law to hamper the just exercise of American might.

Coincidentally, a number of international lawyers, mostly from the United States, have argued that Charter norms purporting to regulate the use of force have become so inconsistent with state practice that they can no longer be deemed legally binding.[2] These Charter skeptics (as I call them) do not appear to be claiming that practice has modified the original interpretation of those norms.[3] Their claim rather is that practice has demonstrated the collapse of the inter-state consensus, assuming a real one ever existed, necessary to sustain the Charter's normative scheme. Although their focus has been on the norms explicitly connected to the use of force, implicitly they are dismissing the broader Charter principles of non-intervention and the sanctity of sovereignty from which the use of force norms stem.

Precisely what legal conclusions follow from their notionally empirical observation is unclear. One possible conclusion is that the question of when a state can employ force, overt or covert, has become entirely political in character. Hence,

---

[1] Jeane Kirkpatrick makes this point clearly: "foreign governments and their leaders, and more than a few activists here at home, seek to constrain and control American power by means of elaborate multilateral processes, global arrangements, and UN treaties that limit both our capacity to govern ourselves and act abroad.", quoted in John Fonte, "The Ideological War Within the West", *Foreign Policy Research Institute* 3(6) (May 2002); and, more recently, the Pentagon's 2005 National Defense Strategy echoed the same sentiment: "Our strength as a nation state will continue to be challenged by those who employ a strategy of the weak using international fora, judicial processes, and terrorism;" the text of the document is available through the US Department of Defense's website at <http://www.defenselink.mil/news/Apr2005/d20050408strategy.pdf>.

[2] See, eg, Michael Glennon, "The New Interventionism," *Foreign Affairs*, 78(3) (1999), 2–7.

[3] Michael Glennon posits the exhaustion of the Charter system of collective security in *Limits of Law, Prerogatives of Power: Interventionism after Kosovo* (New York: Palgrave Macmillan, 2001). Though disagreeing with Glennon's analysis and conclusions at almost every point, Thomas Franck seems to end with the conclusion that international law is temporarily overborne by the violent reassertion of raison d'etat and sees no early prospects for revival in "Break It, Don't Fake It," *Foreign Affairs*, 78(4) (1999), 116–18.

it is possible to condemn particular uses of force only on the grounds that they are immoral or imprudent. An alternative possibility is that certain broad legal prohibitions persist, in particular the preclusion of force where its only justification is to impose the value system of the aggressor or to increase its wealth and power.[4] Or, to put this arguably residual norm in slightly different terms, the use of force is legal whenever it can be plausibly characterized as a good faith, no-feasible-alternative defense of vital interests of the force initiator or as an action in defense of core Charter values like basic human rights.

1. The Original Understanding

Are these chroniclers of the supposed demise of the use of force regime telling a true story? If so, where can we go from here, and how do we get there? I approach those questions from the baseline of what I call "the original understanding," by which I mean the interpretation of Charter restraints on the use of force that enjoyed wide but by no means uniform support in the early post-Charter years within the community of academic international lawyers and among ministries of foreign affairs.[5]

At the birth of the United Nations, a majority of legal scholars and probably of governments subscribed to the view that taking into account the language and structure of the Charter, in particular Articles 2(4) and 51 in conjunction with Chapter VII as a whole, and taking account also of the document's negotiating history, it should be read as dividing the universe of cross-border military coercion and intervention into three categories.[6] Category 1 is self-defense against an armed attack. Category 2 is force (or the threat thereof) authorized by the Security Council under Chapter VII to prevent a threat to the peace, a breach of the peace or an act of aggression. The domain of the illegal is Category 3, call it the default category, which is occupied by every act of state-initiated or tolerated cross-border violence that does not fall into the first two categories. However, it was not long before states with the capacity to project force across frontiers began proposing additional categories, based in part on curious readings of the

---

[4] See Tom J Farer, "Human Rights in Law's Empire: The Jurisprudence War," *The American Journal of International Law*, 85(1) (1991), 117–27.

[5] For an early contrarian view see Julius Stone, *Legal Controls of International Conflict: A Treatise on the Dynamics of Disputes and War-Law* (London: Rinehart, 1954), 43.

[6] See, eg, Myres McDougal and Florentino Feliciano, *Law and Minimum World Public Order* (New Haven: Yale University Press, 1961), 126; Lassa Oppenheim, *International Law*, 8th edn (New York: Longmans, Green & Co, 1955), 154; art 2(i) of the Draft Code of Offenses against the Peace and Security of Mankind, Report of the International Law Commission, Third Sess. (1951), UN Doc. A/1858. But cf. Derek Bowett, *Self Defense in International Law* (New York: Praeger, 1958), 11–13; Tom J Farer, "Panama: Beyond the Charter Frame," *American Journal of International Law*, 84(2) (1990), 503–15 and "A Paradigm of Legitimate Intervention," in LF Damrosch (ed), *Enforcing Restraint: Collective Intervention in Internal Conflicts* (New York: Council on Foreign Relations Press, 1993), 85.

Charter that happened to legitimate their uses of force, or discovered unexpected elasticities in the existing ones, and they invariably found some scholars[7] who sympathized with their claims. What follows is a sketch of the areas of ambiguity and contention that marked the Cold War years.

(A) What Constitutes an "armed attack" for purposes of activating the right of individual and collective self-defense?

(1) Do activities short of launching troops, planes or missiles across a frontier, for instance giving material assistance to an insurgency in another state or a terrorist group, ever trigger the right of self-defense?

During the Cold War, primarily with respect to the guerrilla wars waged generally by communist-inspired or communist-aided movements against pro-American regimes in Latin America and Southeast Asia, the United States argued that where State A provided weapons or training or safe haven to opponents of the recognized government of State B, the latter and allied states could treat that assistance as an armed attack.[8] With one dissent (by chance the American judge) in the case brought by the Government of Nicaragua (represented by a formal Legal Advisor to the Department of State)[9] against the United States, The World Court rejected this claim insofar as it purported to justify US acts of war within Nicaragua.[10]

While the US Government refused to appear and argue the merits, on the grounds that the Court lacked jurisdiction,[11] in the forum of public opinion the Reagan Administration claimed that its own clandestine operations inside Nicaragua and its financing, arming and training of Nicaraguan insurgents were legitimate acts of collective self-defense in response to Nicaraguan aggression against the Government of El Salvador,[12] an ally under the Rio Treaty of Mutual Defense.[13] The acts deemed constitutive of that aggression were various forms of assistance to the indisputably independent Salvadoran insurgents.[14] This was

---

[7] See, eg, Julius Stone, *Legal Controls of International Conflict* (London: Rinehart, 1954), 43, 243, 297–8; cf. Bowett, *Self defense in International Law* (1958).

[8] Tom J Farer, "The Role of Regional Collective Security Arrangements," in T Weiss (ed), *Collective Security in a Changing World* (Boulder: Lynne Rienner, 1993), 153–88.

[9] Military and Paramilitary Activities in and Against Nicaragua (*Nicar. v US*), 1986 ICJ 14 (27 June).

[10] *Ibid.*

[11] Eric Effron, "State Department maintains world court lacks jurisdiction in matter; historic verdict," *The National Law Journal*, 10 December 1984, p 11, col 1; Kenneth Jost, "Reagan criticized for rejecting role of World Court: Nicaraguan complaint," *The Los Angeles Daily Journal*, 10 April 1984, p 1, col 2; Stuart Taylor Jr, "World Court's jurisdiction disputed in Nicaragua case," *Chicago Daily Law Bulletin*, 10 April 1984, p 3, col 2.

[12] Philip Taubman, "Releasing intelligence data: a 'no win situation'," *The New York Times*, 5 March 1982, A16; Philip Taubman, "US offers photos of bases to prove Nicaragua threat," *The New York Times*, 10 March 1982, A1.

[13] Inter-American Treaty of Reciprocal Assistance of 1947, signed at Rio de Janeiro on 2 September 1947, 21 UNTS 77.

[14] Philip Taubman, "El Salvador as 'domino'," *The New York Times*, 20 February 1982, 8.

not a new argument for the United States. It had earlier been marshaled against Cuba for its encouragement and support of insurgency in various Latin American countries[15] and against North Vietnam for its support of the insurgency in South Vietnam.[16] In retrospect, Vietnam was the stronger case for the argument, since it now appears that at least by the time the United States became openly involved in combat, Hanoi was exercising substantial if not total strategic control over the Vietcong.[17]

Composed as it is of mostly distinguished judges and scholars from the various world regions, the Court's opinions, at least when they are nearly unanimous, are the closest thing we have to authoritative interpretation of the Charter.

(2) At what point, if any, do activities that could reasonably be construed as preparations to launch an armed attack, justify preemption?

Perhaps because on a number of occasions during the Cold War, mechanical and electronic devices erroneously signaled the launch of nuclear missiles,[18] some have argued that preemption should never be allowed, that self-defense requires a prior and actual border crossing.[19] But efforts by the Soviet bloc at the UN to secure

---

[15] For a general view of US justifications of use of force, see Tom J Farer and Christopher C Joyner, "The United States and the Use of Force: Looking Back to See Ahead," *Transnational Law and Contemporary Problems*, 1(1) (1991).

[16] This view is implicit in the Government's contention that North Vietnam's support of the Vietcong constituted an "armed attack" against the Saigon regime. See the Memorandum of the State Department on "The Legality of US Participation in the Defense of Vietnam," submitted to the Senate Committee on Foreign Relations on 8 March 1966, reprinted in Richard A Falk, (ed), *The Vietnam War and International Law* (Princeton: Princeton University Press, 1968), 583.

[17] See, eg, Robert McNamara's account of retaliation against North Vietnam for its support of the Vietcong, beginning in 1964 with proposed air strikes and CIA support for South Vietnamese covert operations in North Vietnam in Robert S McNamara, *In Retrospect: The Tragedy and Lesson of Vietnam* (New York: Crown, 1995), 114, 130. See also Robert D Schulzinger, *A Time for War: The United States and Vietnam, 1941–1975* (Oxford, UK: Oxford University Press, 1999), 95–6, for an account of the creation of the Vietcong (the National Front for the Liberation of Vietnam) in December 1960.

[18] An account of an erroneous signal during the Carter administration can be found in Robert M Gates, *From the Shadows: The Ultimate Insider's Story of Five Presidents and How they Won the Cold War* (New York: Simon & Schuster, 1996), 114–15.

[19] Albrecht Randelzhofer, "Article 51 and the Inherent Right to Self-Defence", in Bruno Simma (ed), *The Charter of the United Nations: A Commentary* 2nd edn (New York: Oxford University Press, 2002), 677. See also the exchange among European and US international lawyers in J Delbrück (ed), *The Future of International Law Enforcement: New Scenarios, New Law?: Proceedings of an International Symposium of the Kiel Institute of International Law, March 25 to 27, 1992* (Berlin: Duncker & Humblot, 1993). Oscar Schachter, "In Defense of International Rules on the Use of Force," *University of Chicago Law Review*, 53 (1986), is an exemplary expression of this view. See also, "The Use of Armed Force in International Affairs: The Case of Panama," *Report of the Association of the Bar of New York City* (June 1992); Louis Henkin, "Force, Intervention and Neutrality in Contemporary International Law," *Proceedings of the American Society of International Law* (1963), 147, 149, 165; Philip Jessup, *A Modern Law of Nations* (New York: Macmillan, 1948), 166; Hans Kelsen, *The Law of the United Nations* (New York: Lawbook Exchange Ltd, 1950), 797–8; Josef Kunz, "Individual and Collective Self Defense in Article 51 of the Charter of the United Nations," *American Journal of International Law*, 41(4) (1947), 872, 878.

a definition of aggression focused exclusively on first recourse to force failed.[20] The more generally prevailing view seems to be that if the behavior of State A is such as to lead a reasonable government in State B to believe that an armed and substantial attack is imminent and cannot be averted by means other than force, State B may preempt.

Most scholars have regarded *imminence* as the key criterion. Without it, measures plausibly intended for defensive or, in the case of nuclear weapons, deterrent purposes could be construed, hypocritically or otherwise, by another, unfriendly state as preparations for an attack justifying a first strike. If, as President Bush appeared to declare after 9/11, the United States is prepared to strike states deemed unfriendly whenever they engage in behavior which could facilitate an attack in the indeterminate future, whether by the state itself or by terrorists it might enable,[21] we are back in the era of preventive wars, the kinds of wars urged in the late nineteenth and early twentieth centuries by German strategists fearing the future military superiority of the continental-sized powers, Russia and the United States.[22] These are wars to eradicate merely contingent risks, often risks not to survival, ie not to political independence and territorial integrity, but rather to regional superiority or even global hegemony. Remove the requirement of imminence and it becomes very difficult to distinguish aggression from self-defense.

(3) Can forms of coercion other than military ones constitute an armed attack?

Developing states have sometimes argued that economic ones threatening their political independence should be so regarded.[23] The United States seemed to imply the same during the Arab oil boycott following the 1973 Middle East War.[24] In the West, there was little if any scholarly support for this view and efforts by some Third-World states to include economic coercion in the definition of aggression failed.

(B) Does the Security Council have authority under the Charter to authorize coercive measures including use of force in cases (a) where the threat to international peace and security is not imminent or (b) the "threat" consists of massive violations of human rights within a country but with little immediate spillover effect to other states?

---

[20] UN Doc. No. A/AC77/L4 (1957).

[21] An overview of the relevant Security Council Resolutions—and of the overall "case" the United States was making—can be found in the text of the draft resolution offered up by the United States, Spain and the United Kingdom S/2003/215 (7 March 2003). See also WH Taft IV and TF Buchwald, "Preemption, Iraq, and International Law", *American Journal of International Law*, 97(1), 5–10.

[22] See Wolfgang J. Mommsen, *Imperial Germany 1867–1918* (London: Hodder Arnold, 1995).

[23] See Tom J Farer, "Political and Economic Coercion in Contemporary International Law," *The American Journal of International Law*, 79(2) (1985), 405–13.

[24] See Robert W Tucker, "Oil: The Issue of American Intervention," *Commentary*, 59(1) (1975), 21–31.

With respect to (a), two views once competed for dominance. Some commentators argued[25] that the Council was an organ with jurisdictional authority strictly limited by the language of the Charter and that the Charter's grant of authority under Chapter VII to deal coercively with "threats" had to be read in the light of Chapter VI authorizing the Council to employ non-coercive measures like mediation in cases where a situation could develop into a threat. In other words, the Charter itself distinguishes in so many words between immediate and potential or longer-term threats and gives the Council authority to employ force only in the former case. So while it has authority to employ force (or to authorize force by states acting as its proxy) at a somewhat earlier point than an individual state can under Article 51, that authority does not extend to cases where the threat is in so early a stage of incubation that its actualization is uncertain and there is opportunity to test the efficacy of means other than force.

In recent years I have seen little support for this view in Western academic circles, although it may well reflect the preferences of the Chinese and certain other governments in the Global South. While the Council may not have absolute discretion to define its authority, it has and in contemporary circumstances must have a very broad discretion to decide at what stage in the gestation of a threat it should intervene with coercive means of one form or another.

With respect to (b), the practice of the Council since the end of the Cold War seems to have resolved the once sharp dispute over its authority to authorize coercion to avert or mitigate catastrophes that occur mainly within one country. When in the 1970s it authorized[26] coercive measures against the minority racist regime in what was then Rhodesia (contemporary Zimbabwe), the Council was sharply criticized by some legal commentators[27] and initially the United Kingdom took the position that the matter was an internal concern.[28] Sanctions against South Africa in the 1980s also encountered some opposition on legal grounds. Since the Cold War, however, the Council has authorized intervention to restore democracy (Haiti),[29] to protect the delivery of humanitarian relief (Bosnia and Somalia),[30] and to end civil conflicts marked by massive violations of human

---

[25] See, eg, Kelsen, *The Law of the United Nations* (1951), 769–815.

[26] S/RES/232 (1966) and S/RES/221 (1966). See Myres S McDougal and W Michael Reisman, "Rhodesia and the United Nations: The Lawfulness of International Concern," *American Journal of International Law*, 62(1) (1968), 1–19.

[27] Dean Acheson so argued and was criticized by Myres S McDougal and W Michael Reisman in "Rhodesia and the United Nations: The Lawfulness of International Concern," *American Journal of International Law*, 62(1) (1968), 1–19.

[28] The Lusaka communiqué, based on agreement by leaders of an August 1979 Commonwealth, along with establishing the principle of majority rule and legal independence from Britain, was interpreted by British officials as precluding any intervention by the United Nations, see Henry Wiseman and Alastair M Taylor, *From Rhodesia to Zimbabwe: The Politics of Transition* (New York: Pergamon Press, 1981), 4.

[29] S/RES/940 (1994); see also David Malone, *Decision-making in the UN Security Council: The Case of Haiti, 1990–1997* (New York: Oxford University Press, 1998).

[30] S/RES/816 (1993) and S/RES/794 (1992), respectively.

rights (eg Liberia and Sierra Leone).[31] Practice has confirmed the breadth of the Council's power to act for the sake of human as well as national security.

(C) Can regional and sub-regional organizations authorize uses of force that would otherwise be illegal?[32]

Articles 52–54 (Chapter VIII) of the Charter recognize a possible role for such organizations particularly in helping to mediate festering hostility that, if left unattended, could lead to armed conflict.[33] It also recognizes them as possible instruments of the Security Council in dealing with Chapter VII situations.[34] But Article 54 states that any "enforcement action" by such organizations requires the approval of the Security Council.

During the Cold War, the United States argued (in relation to the Cuban Quarantine of 1962,[35] the intervention into the Dominican Republic in 1965[36] and the invasion of Grenada in 1982)[37] that the approval could be after the fact and implicit, a position most scholars and governments rejected.[38] More recently the United States has altered its position insofar as the Organization of American States (OAS) is concerned, insisting (most clearly in the case of Haiti) that enforcement measures require Security Council authorization.[39] But the first Economic Community of West African States (ECOWAS) intervention in Liberia,[40] although not authorized, was not criticized, much less condemned. A distinguished panel of experts established by the Swedish government found

---

[31] S/RES/1497 and S/RES/1509 in the case of Liberia; S/RES/1132 (1997), S/RES/1181 (1998), and S/RES/1245 (1999) in the case of Sierra Leone.

[32] See generally, Farer, "The Role of Regional Collective Security Arrangements" in *Collective Security in a Changing World* (1993), 153–88; Tom J Farer, "Law and War," in Cyril E Black and Richard A Falk (eds), *The Future of the International Legal Order* III (Princeton: Princeton University Press, 1971), 56–62.

[33] UN Charter art 53; UN Charter art 52, para 1; See also Farer, "Law and War" (1971).

[34] UN Charter art 52, paras 1–3 but see restrictions in art 53 para 1.

[35] See Abram Chayes, "Law and the Quarantine of Cuba," *Foreign Affairs*, 41(3) (1963), 550–7; Abram Chayes, *Cuban Missile Crisis* (New York: Oxford University Press, 1974); James G Blight and David Welch, *On the Brink: Americans and Soviets Re-examine the Cuban Missile Crisis* (New York: Farrar, Straus & Giroux, 1989); Raymond Garthoff, *Reflections on the Cuban Missile Crisis* rev. edn (Washington, DC: Brookings Institution Press, 1989). A rejection of the argument can be found in Organization of American States, *Sixteenth Meeting of Consultation of Ministers of Foreign Affairs* (San Jose, Costa Rica, 29 July 1975), Resolution I.

[36] See Abraham F Lowenthal, *The Dominican Intervention* (Cambridge, Mass.: Harvard University Press, 1972); Piero Gleijeses, *The Dominican Crisis: The 1965 Constitutionalist Revolution and American Intervention* (Baltimore: Johns Hopkins University Press, 1978); and Leonard Meeker, "The Dominican Situation in the Perspective of International Law," *Department of State Bulletin LIII* (1 July 1965), 60–2.

[37] UN General Assembly censure of the US interventions in Grenada and Panama can be found in A/RES/44/240 (1989).

[38] See Tom J Farer, "The Role of Regional Collective Security Arrangements," in *Collective Security in a Changing World* (1993).

[39] See David Malone, *Decision-making in the UN Security Council: The Case of Haiti, 1990–1997* (1998).

[40] Kenneth B Noble, "5 NATIONS MOVING TROOPS TO LIBERIA; West Africans Begin an Effort to End Civil War but One Rebel Vows to Resist," *The New York Times*, 11 August 1990,

NATO's intervention in the Kosovo conflict to be not consistent with the Charter and thus technically illegal but nevertheless "legitimate."[41] Whether NATO, originally a self-defense rather than regional organization, can be said to have evolved into the latter is open to dispute.

(D) Does military intervention at the request of a recognized government to assist it in repressing domestic opponents constitute a permitted use of force?

Some scholars and governments have argued that the prerogatives of sovereignty certainly include authorizing foreign intervention and that the recognized government is the agent of state sovereignty.[42] Others have said that in cases of large-scale civil war, an intervention even if invited by the recognized government violates the country's political independence and the universal right of self-determination and should be deemed illegal.[43]

(E) Are interventions, not authorized by the SC, undertaken to prevent or terminate crimes against humanity ever legal under the Charter?

In the early decades after the Charter's adoption, scholars and governments especially were reluctant to concede that the claims of humanity might trump the principle of non-intervention,[44] although at least in particular cases some seemed disposed to treat the circumstances as highly mitigating. The Kosovo Commission mentioned above based its finding of "legitimacy" largely on what it perceived as the imperative necessity of using force in order to abort massive ethnic cleansing initiated by the Belgrade Government against the Albanian population of Kosovo. Few would dispute that mass ethnic cleansing is a "crime against humanity," with genocidal potential. With respect to the question of law, it is significant that even in the presence of such a crime, coupled with action by an arguably "regional organization" (but not, to be sure against a *member* of the organization) and Security Council resolutions condemning the Government of former Yugoslavia for its treatment of the Albanian population and calling upon it to cease and desist,[45] a committee of experts with a strong collective commitment to the protection of human rights has found that action to be illegal under the Charter yet still "legitimate." Nevertheless, some leading, primarily US-based international law scholars, including ardent defenders of the United Nations and

---

A3; Kenneth B Noble, "Civil War in Liberia Threatening to Divide West African Neighbors; Liberian War Threatens to Split West Africans," *The New York Times*, 29 August 1990, A1.

[41] Independent International Commission on Kosovo, *Kosovo Report* (New York, 2001).

[42] A/59/2005 (2005).

[43] See Myres McDougal and Florentino Feliciano, *Law and Minimum World Public Order* (1961), 194n; for an earlier view see William E Hall *A Treatise on International Law*, 6th edn (Oxford, UK: Clarendon Press, 1909), 286.

[44] Ian Brownlie, *Principles of Public International Law*, 4th edn (Oxford, UK: Clarendon Press, 1990), 304–5 and 324; and Ian Brownlie, *International Law and the Use of Force by States* (Oxford, UK: Clarendon Press, 1963), 339–42.

[45] S/RES/1244 (1999).

the Charter-based legal order, have argued that Humanitarian Intervention is legal where the following criteria are satisfied:

- a massive crime against humanity is imminent or has begun to be executed;
- either there is no time for recourse to the Security Council, if the crime is to be averted or aborted before its completion, or action by the Security Council is blocked by a Permanent Member's exercise of its veto;
- the action is reported to the Security Council;
- the intervention is carried out in good faith and so as to minimize its consequences for the political independence of the target state;
- the intervention complies with the Humanitarian Law of War and is reasonably calculated to cause less harm to "innocent persons" than would occur if the crime against humanity were allowed to proceed.[46]

Scholars insisting on the legality of interventions satisfying the above criteria have emphasized the Charter's recognition of human rights along with national sovereignty as paired constitutional principles.[47] Even scholars from countries with a history of intense opposition to intervention of any kind now show some disposition to concede that in extraordinary circumstances, for example the onset of genocide, international action may be justified even if the Security Council does not authorize it. A number of Chinese scholars from influential think tanks have so conceded in a recent discussion,[48] but they insisted that circumstances must be so exceptional that they cannot be codified, a position echoing that of the leading English authority on the use of force, Ian Brownlie, who analogized Humanitarian Interventions to "mercy killings" in domestic law which are illegal but may be overlooked in extraordinary circumstances.[49] Efforts by the Axworthy Commission, supported by the Canadian Government, to promote agreement that the prerogatives of sovereignty are dependent in some measure on states meeting minimum obligations to their citizens[50] initially met a cool reception from the generality of governments,[51] implying that they preferred the Chinese approach.

---

[46] These views are reflected by virtually all authors in JL Holzgrefe and RO Keohane (eds), *Humanitarian Intervention: Ethical, Legal and Political Dilemmas* (Cambridge, UK: Cambridge University Press, 2002); but cf. Tom J Farer with Daniele Archibugi, Chris Brown, Neta C Crawford, Thomas G Weiss and Nicholas J Wheeler, "Round Table: Humanitarian Intervention after 9/11," *International Relations*, 19(2) (2005) 211–50.

[47] See, eg, Anthony D'Amato, "Agora: US Force in Panama: Defenders, Aggressors, or Human Rights Activists," *American Journal of International Law*, 84(2) (1990), 516–24; and W Michael Riesman, "Coercion and Self-Determination: Construing Charter Article 2(4)," *American Journal of International Law*, 74(3) (1984), 642–5; see also Fernando Teson, *Humanitarian Intervention: An Inquiry into Law and Morality* (Dobbs Ferry, NY: Transnational Publishers, 1988).

[48] Simon Chesterman, Tom Farer, and Timothy Sisk, "Competing Claims: Self-Determination, Security and the United Nations," *International Peace Academy Policy Brief*, April 2001.

[49] Ian Brownlie, *International Law and the Use of Force by States* (1963).

[50] International Commission on Intervention and State Sovereignty, *The Responsibility to Protect* (Ottawa, 2001).

[51] See S Neil Macfarlane, Jennifer Welsh, and Caroline Thielking, "The Responsibility to Protect: Assessing the Report of the International Commission on intervention and state sovereignty," *International Journal*, 57(4), 489–502.

The humanitarian arguments invoked by the United States and the United Kingdom in the case of Iraq, arguments increasingly emphasized when evidence of WMD programs failed to appear, are unusual in that they refer to conditions that were chronic rather than acute.[52] In fact, at the time of the invasion, violations of core human security rights appear to have been considerably less acute than during earlier periods when popular resistance to Saddam was more pronounced. The moral basis for distinguishing chronic violations of rights from acute ones, as most advocates of Humanitarian Intervention do, is problematical.[53] But failure to require a sudden spike in human rights violations as a condition of "Humanitarian Intervention" would exponentially increase the number of potential targets; at least a strong plurality of UN members would be at risk.

(F) Are interventions strictly to rescue nationals arbitrarily threatened with death or grave injury, whether by the government of another country or by private groups whom that government cannot or will not control, legal under the Charter?

Some scholars have long insisted that intervention as a last resort for the protection of threatened nationals falls under the right to self-defense.[54] They note that a state consists of a determinate territory and a population.[55] Attacks on either, they argue, are "armed attacks" within the meaning of Article 51 of the Charter. It is also argued that such brief interventions, proportional to the imperative necessity of extracting the threatened persons, should not be regarded as violations of either the territorial integrity or the political independence of the target state and hence not violations of Article 2, paragraph 4 of the Charter.[56] That argument rests implicitly on a view much like that of the Axworthy Commission, namely that by failing to meet their international legal obligations to protect the nationals of other states, states to that extent relinquish temporarily the full prerogatives of sovereignty.

(G) Are reprisals legal under the Charter?

In pre-Charter international legal practice, reprisals were punitive acts responding to some illegal act committed by another state.[57] They were deemed legitimate if

---

[52] Tony Blair's arguments, among others, are included in Thomas Cushman, (ed), *A Matter of Principle: Humanitarian Arguments for War in Iraq* (Berkeley: University of California Press, 2005). A rejection of American and British Administration humanitarian arguments can be found in Kenneth Roth, "War in Iraq: Not A Humanitarian Intervention," in *Human Rights Watch World Report 2004: Human Rights and Armed Conflict* (available online at <http://hrw.org/wr2k4/>), 13–36.

[53] Tom J Farer, "Human Rights in Law's Empire: The Jurisprudence War," *American Journal of International Law*, 85(1) (1991), 117–27.

[54] Charles C Hyde, *International Law, Chiefly as Interpreted and Applied by the United States* 2nd rev. edn (Boston: Fred B Rothman & Co, 1945), 649; William D Coplin, "International Law and Assumptions about the State System," *World Politics*, 17(4) (1965), 615–34 at 618; Bowett, *Self Defense in International Law* (1958), 104.

[55] Defined as, "a politically organized body of people usually occupying a definite territory; *especially*: one that is sovereign," in Merriam-Webster's Dictionary of Law (1996), s.v. "State."

[56] Bowett, *Self Defense in International Law* (1958), 94.

[57] Ibid, 11–13; see also Georg Schwarzenberger, "The Law of Armed Conflict," in *International Law as Applied by International Courts and Tribunals, Vol. II* (London: Sweet & Maxwell, 1968).

they were proportional to the delinquency that occasioned them. One of their recognized purposes was to deter a repetition of the delinquency. In relation to a reprisal carried out by the United Kingdom during the 1950s in what is today the Republic of Yemen, the Security Council declared reprisals to be illegal under the Charter in that they did not constitute acts of self-defense.[58] Self-defense presumed an ongoing attack. A one-off border incursion by forces of State A into State B could be resisted. But if State A's forces withdrew before State B could mount a response and appeared unlikely to make another incursion in the immediate future, then the opportunity for the exercise of self-defense rights had passed.[59] State B would thus have to pursue other remedies for any damage done to it from the incursion including, of course, an appeal to the Security Council on the grounds that the situation constitutes an ongoing "threat to the peace."

Distinguishing reprisal and legitimate self-defense can be difficult in the context of ongoing hostile relations between states marked by numerous "incidents." For instance, the bombing of Tripoli by the United States in the wake of the bombing of a night club in Berlin frequented by US military personnel and attributed to Libyan intelligence operatives was arguably a reprisal[60]; but the United States could have argued that the night club incident was only one in a line of Libyan-organized attacks on US installations and personnel and that these various incidents amounted cumulatively to an ongoing attack. Similarly, some Israeli incursions into neighboring Arab states could have been characterized as incidents in a single ongoing low-intensity armed conflict. However, Israel has an explicit doctrine of reprisal; it has not tried to characterize every incursion as an incident of an ongoing war.[61] Many of its reprisals have been ignored by the Security Council or action has been blocked by the United States.

It appears that the Security Council has become inured to reprisals, at least in the context of the Arab-Israeli context, and therefore takes note of them only where they risk igniting a general conflict or possibly where they are grossly disproportionate to the damage inflicted by the act held to justify reprisal or violate rights protected by the Humanitarian Law of War. It did not condemn the US missile attack on Iraq following the alleged attempt by Saddam Hussein to assassinate former President George HW Bush during a visit to Kuwait. Arguably that was a reprisal, although it might have been defended as mere enforcement of the terms of the cease fire that ended the first Gulf War.[62]

---

[58] S/RES/188 (1964); Tom J Farer, "Law and War," in CE Black and RA Falk (eds), *The Future of the International Legal Order: Conflict Management, Vol. 3* (Princeton: Princeton University Press, 1969), 15–78.

[59] Anthony C Arend, "International Law and the Preemptive Use of Military Force," *The Washington Quarterly*, 26(2) (2003), 89–103; Sean D Murphy, *Humanitarian Intervention: The United Nations in an Evolving World Order* (Philadelphia: University of Pennsylvania Press, 1996), 92.

[60] "Transcript of Address by Reagan on Libya," *The New York Times*, 15 April 1986, A10.

[61] The United Nations condemns Israel's reprisals in S/RES/101 (1953) and S/3139/Rev. 2.

[62] S/RES/687 (1991).

To help probe the distinction between acts justifying reprisal and acts of war, I offer the following hypothetical case. Suppose the attack on the World Trade Center and the Pentagon on 9/11 had been the first violent act against US persons or property by persons under the direction of Osama bin Laden and his associates and had been accompanied by a statement from bin Laden describing it as a single retaliation for crimes committed against the Arab people and declaring that the slate was clean, there had been an eye for an eye, and now co-existence was possible. If, without the benefit of a Security Council resolution recognizing the availability of the claim of self-defense under the circumstances, the United States had launched its campaign to overturn the Taliban regime and to destroy bin Laden's infrastructure in Afghanistan and to kill or capture bin Laden and his lieutenants, would that have been a reprisal or lawful action in self-defense under the Charter?

It is implausible that under those circumstances, the United States or any other nation that had experienced such a blow would have felt constrained either by the Charter or even by the pre-Charter doctrine to treat that blow as something other than an act of war. As an act of war, an aggression against the United States, it would presumably allow the United States to take all necessary measures consistent with the Humanitarian Law of War to capture or kill the perpetrators and to dismantle their organization and to wage war against any state that interfered in this effort. In other words, some acts of violence may be of such scope and intensity that states generally will regard them as acts of war even if it is unclear that they will be repeated.

(H) What limits does the Charter impose on the right of self-defense once it is triggered by an act of aggression?

The hypothetical case in (G) above warrants two further questions. One is whether, in a case where following a wanton act of aggression the aggressor withdraws from any territory it may have occupied and places its forces in a defensive posture and calls for negotiation or mediation of whatever dispute occasioned the aggression, the victim state can initiate a defensive war without Security Council authorization even though it can seek such authorization without further endangering itself. The second is whether a state exercising its right of self-defense by preparing to invade an aggressor or destroy its military capability through an assault by missiles and aircraft must desist in cases where the Security Council, acting pursuant to Chapter VII, authorizes less intense measures such as economic sanctions or a blockade to force the surrender of the persons authorizing and conducting the aggression or takes other action which the victim state deems insufficient. Neither the practice of states and of the Security Council under the Charter nor the opinions of international legal experts has provided entirely clear answers to either question.[63]

---

[63] Compare, for instance, Albrecht Randelzhofer, "Article 51 and the Inherent Right to Self-Defence", in Bruno Simma (ed), *The Charter of the United Nations: A Commentary* (2002), 677; Kelsen, *Principles*

2. The New Global Context and the Call for Loosened Restraints on the Use of Force

Authoritative norms pull relevant actors toward compliance. If they fail, their authority is hollow. Why do legal rules and principles have that pull in a legal system lacking centralized enforcement institutions? Principally because they express the stable interests identified by the main subjects of the norms either through processes of unhurried deliberation (as in the various stages of proposing, negotiating, and ratifying a treaty) or through the retrospective rationalization of a series of initially extemporized responses to concrete problems. Whether a single long deliberative process or the cumulation of initially improvised responses, the resulting norm encapsulates national interest contemplated in serenity. (For the neo-Realist, of course, what I call a process of identification, implying the ultimately subjective character of interests, is really the appreciation of objective interests, the rational recognition of a country's fate).[64]

It follows (from this statement of the probably obvious) that the adequacy of the Charter use-of-force norms is a function of whether they express the interests of today's main actors. Charter skeptics claim they do not, usually citing in support of that claim the changed structure and challenges of the contemporary international system. That changes have occurred is indisputable, but is it clear that they have correspondingly effected a change in core interests relating to the use of force?

A. Law and the Interests of Powerful States: 1945–89

Understanding from where we have come helps us to appreciate where we are. The Charter norms stemmed from a profound deliberative process within and among the major states. Either those states believed that the Charter use-of-force norms optimally served their interests or one or more of them was playing an elaborate strategic game, signaling an intention to comply while actually envisioning multiple contingencies in which it would evade the norms in order to secure goals inimical to the interests of other major states.

An intention to comply in all or most foreseeable circumstances implied general satisfaction with the allocation of power and security resulting from the Second World War. Of course, up to a point, satisfaction would be consistent with continued competition for incremental gains that could be secured without gross and blatant violations of the rules and that would not be seen as markers of a grand strategy to alter profoundly the allocation of power in the system.

---

of International Law (1966), 62, 64–87; and Myres S McDougal and Florentino P Feliciano, *Law and Minimum World Public Order: The Legal Regulation of International Coercion* (1961), 233–41.

[64] See arguments for and against in Robert Keohane (ed), *Neorealism and its Critics* (New York: Columbia University Press, 1986).

Revisionist historians of the Cold War see both the United States and the Soviet Union (with some laying greater emphasis on US moves)[65] placing markers even before the Charter's adoption. Their opponents cite Soviet moves—such as the reluctance to withdraw from northern Iran and the establishment of puppet regimes in Eastern Europe—culminating in toleration of if not active complicity in North Korea's invasion across the agreed line of demarcation between the northern and southern part of Korea—as the markers that properly persuaded US policy-makers of the Soviet Union's revolutionary intentions.

No purpose is served here by pursuing that debate over origins. The point I would reiterate, however, is that in the context of the time, the Charter norms made sense at least initially as instruments to protect the interests of the United States and the Soviet Union and of other consequential states, particularly the United Kingdom and France. The latter still enjoyed vast empires and Germany and Japan, the long-term threats to their empires, were under indefinite occupation and in ruins. The former two enjoyed dominant power and vast territories rich in natural resources. For all of them the only long-term risk apparent to an external observer would have seemed to be renewed aggressive moves by a resurgent Germany and Japan, since the resource and territorial limits, reinforced by militaristic cultures and internal strains, that had made the Axis Powers enemies of the status quo had not altered. Without recourse to force, they could not at some indeterminate future date significantly alter the post-war dispensation. The cultural transformation of these two countries (more clearly in the German than the Japanese case) together with their successful integration into a world trading system that made all resources available to those able to export added them to the original list of satisfied states.

Pacific serenity in foreign policy is not, of course, a corollary of satisfaction unless all relevant parties appear to each other as perfectly satisfied. If they feel threatened, satisfied states can be no less belligerent, interventionist, and preemptive than dissatisfied ones. Feeling threatened in some of its important if not quite in its core interests first by the Soviet Union and quickly thereafter by Communist China (initially viewed, however, as a mere tool of Moscow) and disposed to see virtually all left-wing movements outside the Soviet sphere as instruments of Soviet and Chinese grand strategy, the United States, like its opponents, quickly found the Charter norms unduly restraining.

The Cold War antagonists had a common problem, namely instability in the areas they regarded as "theirs." For the Soviet Union that initially meant Eastern Europe. For the United States, after opting for total military containment of the Soviet Union rather than George Kennan's proposal for military containment in

---

[65] For an overview of Cold War history and historic writing, see John Lewis Gaddis, *We Know Now: Rethinking Cold War History* (New York: Oxford University Press, 1998); and John Lewis Gaddis, *The Cold War: A New History* (New York: Penguin, 2005). The role of the atomic bomb in shaping US attitudes at Potsdam is discussed in Gar Alperovitz, *Atomic Diplomacy: Hiroshima and Potsdam* (New York: Simon & Schuster, 1965).

Europe and determined political containment elsewhere,[66] that meant just about the rest of the globe, ie Latin America and the Caribbean, the Middle East, Asia, and Africa. Thus it was natural for Americans to speak of the "loss" of China following Communist victory in that country's civil war and Stalin no doubt felt the same about Yugoslavia when Tito defected from the Eastern bloc. Unlike Rome at the height of its imperial ascendancy, neither Moscow nor Washington governed the areas outside their national boundaries about which they felt proprietary. Moscow worked through proxies that varied in their reliability, as well as their ability to exercise local control without the support of Soviet troops. Outside of Western Europe, the United States relied on a complex mix of proxies, influence and alliance with more-or-less genuinely independent local elites.

As even the most casual student of history appreciates, the Soviet Union's problem was that its proxies either had difficulty legitimating themselves (Poland, Hungary) or opted for autonomy (Yugoslavia, Albania, Romania). The United States' problem was the convulsive political, social, and economic forces cracking the traditional structure of authority and thus threatening to displace predictably friendly elites or the empires of NATO allies in what came to be called the "Third World." In other words, each faced a continuous threat of defection by states it regarded as belonging to its side of the Cold War divide.

The grand strategy mind-set ("everything is connected to everything else in a delicate balance of power, real and perceived") fueled the temptation to evade the Charter either for the purpose of aborting latent and incipient defections among friendly states or of seizing opportunities to foster defection from the other side. Where defection or threatened defection of a state deemed important occurred, the effort to prevent it could lead to direct confrontation between the parties in which the one dissatisfied with the status quo, ie the new alignment, had to threaten or take action, like the proxy invasion of Cuba, that could not be justified as self-defense under Article 51 of the Charter.

The roll call of Charter evasions by the Cold War gladiators hardly requires repeating except for those deaf to history, a not uncommon disorder these days. For the United States it would include Iran (clandestine 1953),[67] Guatemala (semi-clandestine 1954),[68] Bay of Pigs (1961),[69] Cuban Missile Crisis (1962),[70] the Congo (clandestine 1961–62),[71] Dominican Republic (1965),[72] Grenada

---

[66] See George Kennan's famous "X" article, "The Sources of Soviet Conduct," *Foreign Affairs*, 25(4) (1947), 566–82.

[67] See generally, Stephen Kinzer, *All the Shah's Men: An American Coup and the Roots of Middle East Terror* (Hoboken, NJ: Wiley, 2003).

[68] See generally, Stephen Kinzer and Stephen Schlesinger, *Bitter Fruit: the Untold Story of the American Coup in Guatemala* (Garden City, NY: Anchor, 1982).

[69] See generally, Theodore Sorensen, *Kennedy* (New York, 1965).

[70] See generally, Abram Chayes, *The Cuban Missile Crisis* (1974).

[71] See generally, David N Gibbs, *The Political Economy of Third World Intervention: Mines, Money and US Policy in the Congo Crisis* (Chicago: University of Chicago Press, 1991).

[72] See generally, Abraham Lowenthal, *The Dominican Intervention* (1972).

(1982),[73] and Iran (1980–85: support for Saddam Hussein's aggression).[74] Interventions in Central America in the 1980s[75] were more legally ambiguous even if, in my judgment, they were morally repulsive in that they failed to satisfy Just War criteria.

The Soviet roll call would include the ongoing repression of political independence in Poland at all times, East Germany (certainly during the early postwar years when the regime was very weak and which therefore required backup by Soviet occupation forces and intelligence operatives), Hungary (1956), Czechoslovakia (1968), and Afghanistan (1979).

Actions springing from the sometimes hot, sometimes cold war between Israel and its neighbors also battered the Charter's normative order. Israel perpetrated with impunity arguably the most serious violations, in particular, the seizure of the Sinai in collusion with the French and British in 1956, the siege of Beirut (the temporary occupation of the bit of south Lebanon from which Israel was episodically shelled could conceivably have been defended under Charter norms), Israel's air attack on Iraq's reactor, various reprisals which, moreover, did not always satisfy the pre-Charter criteria of proportionality and were not always directed at the delinquent actors,[76] and the annexation after 1967 (in part *de jure*, in part de facto) of territory in which the Palestinian people had and continue to have the right to exercise self-determination.[77] During the years they allowed their territory to be used for guerrilla incursions across the de facto frontiers established by Israel during its war of independence, neighboring Arab states were also guilty of battering Charter norms.

Were these deviations from the Charter's normative paradigm necessary or at least bound to seem necessary to governing elites in the United States, the Soviet Union and Israel? Were they, in other words, a function of Fate rather than choice? Even accepting (arguendo) the Realist assumption that elites will almost always use available force to resist any serious threat to the allocation of power, except, of course, where a policy of force will aggravate the threat, the answer is in large measure unclear.

The great Cold War debates within the United States, epitomized by the convulsive one over Vietnam, concerned three over-lapping strategic issues. One was whether the balance of power was deeply anchored and therefore could not be

---

[73] See generally, Hugh O'Shaughnessy, *Grenada: An Eyewitness Account of the US Invasion and the Caribbean History that Provoked it* (New York: Dodd Mead, 1985).

[74] See generally, Michael Dobbs, "US Had Key Role in Iraq Buildup," *Washington Post*, 30 December 2002. The article cites a National Security Decision Directive 1399 of 5 April 1984, in which the Reagan Administration states its intent to support Iraq in the war against Iran (parts of this Directive remain classified).

[75] See generally, Roger Burbach and Patricia Flynn, *The Politics of Intervention: The United States in Central America* (New York: Monthly Review Press, 1984).

[76] Richard A Falk, "The Beirut Raid and the International Law of Retaliation," *The American Journal of International Law*, 63(3) (1969), 415–43.

[77] S/RES/242 (1967); see my discussion in Chapter 5 below.

shifted by the defection of miscellaneous Third World states from the Western alliance system regardless of the role played by the Soviet Union in inducing defection. A second was whether a threatened change in regime or in the declared ideology of a hitherto pro-American regime necessarily augured defection. And a third was whether the use of force in some form, whether overt or covert, to prevent or reverse defection was presumptively efficient, that is positive in terms of cost-benefit analysis.

Kennanites like myself argued in favor of an affirmative answer to the first question and a negative answer to the others. From the fact that we lost the debate it does not follow that we were wrong about the objective interests of the United States. Nor does the ultimate withdrawal of Soviet forces from Eastern Europe and other reaches of the Empire followed by the Soviet Union's dissolution demonstrate that militarized 360 azimuth containment was the optimal means for enhancing Washington's power (along with the general welfare of American society) and debilitating Moscow. In an era of revolutionary technological advance, the Soviet system of political economy could not support the weight of its imperial burdens, burdens which would only have grown if the US Government had followed Kennan's advice and allowed a few more strategically weightless and miserably poor countries like Ethiopia to join the Soviet Bloc and suck more capital and manpower out of Moscow. And we were fortunate that the increasing strains on the system which might easily have brought a violent, primitive gambler like Hitler or Saddam Hussein to power in Moscow allowed an opening for the ascension of the rational, cautious reformist Gorbachev, a man who flinched from violence.

The advantages of paradigm violations by Israel are at least equally subject to strategic doubt. Today virtually no one finds virtue in the 1982 march to Beirut or even the long-term occupation of southern Lebanon. What about the continuing use of force in order to effect, in violation of the Charter, the partially *de jure*, partially de facto annexation of some of the territory secured in 1967 under circumstances that arguably made the initial use of force legitimate?[78] Have those actions served Israel's core interests? Obviously that has been a matter for furious debate within the Israeli political system, never mind among governments sympathetic to the core security interests of the Israeli state. In short, there is no basis for thinking of these actions as destined by the iron rule of national interest.

B. Law and the Interests of Powerful States after the Cold War: The Neo-conservative Project and the Use of Force

In the years immediately following the end of the Cold War, it became almost conventional among writers about international relations to celebrate a new

---

[78] But see John Quigley, *Palestine and Israel: A Challenge to Justice* (Durham, NC: Duke University Press 1990), 161–7.

or renewed coincidence between the Charter system and the interests of states both large and small. Experts tended to assume that the disappearance of those fracturing pressures exerted on the system by Cold War strategies would allow Charter norms and processes to operate much more effectively.[79] Restraints on the projection of power across frontiers would now plainly serve the interests of almost all states. Force would be needed largely to protect human security threatened by ethnic tensions and autocratic rulers unable to legitimate their regimes.

Ethnic conflicts and massacres would not touch the core interests of powerful states. For cultural, ideological, and domestic political reasons, the major Western states would sometimes be prepared to undertake mercy missions.[80] The Security Council would legitimate Humanitarian Interventions on a case-by-case basis. True, the Chinese and possibly the Russians might be uneasy about the precedents. But normally neither would have interests sufficient to justify blocking interventions remote from their core interests to which its main trading and investment partners in the West were committed. Encouraged in part by the 1992–93 Somali interventions, this expectation seemed confirmed by Security Council authorization of intervention in Haiti primarily to restore democratic government,[81] a purpose considerably more controversial than ending slaughter.

As I explained in Chapter 1, at no point in this brief era of good feeling did neo-conservatives share the generally happy view of things. But until the 9/11 cataclysm, they could not shape policy to their ends. That cataclysm created the political conditions in the United States for the active employment of hegemonic military power. And so in alliance with the President and a number of figures, most notably Vice-President Cheney and Secretary of Defense Rumsfeld, who had previously been thought of as no more than conventional right-wing realists, they launched American foreign policy onto uncharted seas with potentially grave consequences for the just renewed normative order.

The Charter's norms cannot be reconciled with the full range of measures the Bush Administration and its neo-conservative advisors have declared necessary for the protection of American interests which it equates with the interests of the West and, indeed, of all states other than a few evil ones. That being so, one might reasonably have expected the Administration to campaign for corresponding reforms in the international legal order. In fact, just as it has evinced little concern about the gap between its stated policies and hitherto conventional views of what international law allows, it has evinced little interest in reform.

This relative disinterest in normative reform is subject to several interpretations. One is that the Administration is generally happy with the inherited normative arrangements, but regards them as inapplicable to the United States, because it,

---

[79] Edward C Luck, "Making Peace," *Foreign Policy*, 89 (Winter 1992); Charles William Maynes, "Containing Ethnic Conflict," *Foreign Policy*, 90 (Spring 1993).

[80] See Tom J Farer, "Humanitarian Intervention before and after 9/11: Legality and Legitimacy," in *Humanitarian Intervention: Ethical, Legal and Political Dilemmas* (2002).

[81] S/RES/940 (1994).

not the Security Council, is the ultimate guarantor of international order. Of course this claim has no precedent in the history of modern international law dating back to the middle of the seventeenth century. But that history coincided with the balance of power and an effective monopoly of force by the major states. Today, Administration officials might argue, the system is dominated by a single power and all of the major states are threatened by non-state actors. The attribution of exceptional legal privileges to the hegemonic power acting in the general interest is as congruent with the real character of international relations as the Westphalian idea of the legal equality of all civilized states was congruent with the reality of international relations in the preceding era.

A second possible interpretation is that the dominant figures in the Bush Administration do not regard international law as law or as an element in international relations that needs to be taken seriously. To be sure, the President and the Secretaries of State and Defense occasionally defend one or another policy—for example, the invasion of Iraq and the treatment of detainees—as being consistent with international law.[82] Moreover, when accused of actions that clearly violate treaty law, like the kidnapping of persons in foreign countries or the rendition of suspected terrorists to torture regimes or the torture and cruel and inhuman treatment of detainees by agents of the United States itself, the Administration sometimes pays a kind of deference to law by claiming that senior officials did not authorize the behavior or that despite what appear on the surface to be violations—rendition to regimes known to torture habitually, for example—it has taken steps to assure that violations will not occur, or by refusing to acknowledge that the behavior occurred.[83]

That said, the fact remains that the Administration was ready and stated its readiness to invade Iraq without Security Council authorization[84] and then sent as its chief representative to the United Nations a lawyer who has written that international law is not law as we know it domestically, but rather a matter of political understandings adopted for the convenience of states and subject to unilateral change when such understandings prove inconvenient.[85] In addition, the President's Counsel, later the Attorney General, endorsed the view, frequently advocated by writers on the right, that international law cannot as a constitutional matter and should not be understood to limit the discretion of the President of

---

[82] On 25 January 2002, then-White House counsel Alberto Gonzalez wrote a memo to the President justifying the use of torture in the war on terror due to new circumstances that placed prisoners outside the scope of Geneva Convention protections. See David Savage and Richard Schmitt, "Administration Lawyers Ascribed Broad Powers to Bush on Torture," *Los Angeles Times*, 10 June 2004.

[83] See "Secretary Rice's Rendition," *The New York Times*, 7 December 2005.

[84] Two months prior to the invasion of Iraq, a documented meeting between Prime Minister Blair and President Bush demonstrates that the United States was intent on invading even without a further UN resolution and even if UN weapons inspectors failed to find WMD. See Richard Norton-Taylor, "Blair-Bush deal before Iraq war revealed in secret memo," *The Guardian*, 3 February 2006.

[85] "The World According to Bolton," *The New York Times*, 9 March 2005.

the United States, for to do so would be to diminish the nation's sovereignty, a view of sovereignty that reduces treaty law to the equivalent of mere political understandings.[86] Moreover, in claiming that the United States was not bound by the Torture Convention's preclusion of cruel and inhuman treatment[87] because the Congress had limited enabling legislation to torture, the Administration simply ignored the strictures on abusive behavior contained in the International Covenant on Civil and Political Rights to which the United States is a Party. And these are only illustrations of what could fairly be described as a dismissive or simply disinterested attitude toward normative restraint in matters of national security.

A third possible interpretation of the Administration's position is that it agrees with those writers who claim, as I noted at the beginning of this chapter, that violations of Charter norms have in their number and severity stripped those norms of binding character.[88] That being our present normative condition, the Administration is implicitly imposing a new, more flexible regime that allows responsible states like the United States to exercise effectively in the altered conditions of international relations their inherent right to self-defense.

Yet a fourth interpretation is that the Administration is simply clarifying in light of changed conditions the actions that states are entitled to take pursuant to the "inherent right to self defense" recognized by Article 51 of the Charter. The main problem with this interpretation, of course, is that Article 51, while recognizing the "inherent right," limits its exercise to cases of "armed attack" (hitherto construed to be ongoing or at least indisputably imminent) and, in any event, appears to require a state taking self-defense measures to report them to the Security Council with the understanding that the Council shall determine what further actions can be taken by the state in question or by any other state. Given the apparent reluctance of the Administration to submit its actions to final review by the Security Council, this fourth interpretation should probably be seen as a merely cosmetic version of the first, second, or third.

All in all, the Administration's view of international law bears an ironical resemblance to views exhibited by Willhelmine Germany around the turn of the twentieth century and thereafter in the practices of the Third Reich. When the US delegation to the Hague Peace Conferences proposed agreed limits on the use of force and the arbitration of inter-state disputes, the leader of the German delegation responded bluntly that Germany was not prepared to sacrifice its predominant influence on the European Continent which consisted of its

---

[86] Michiko Kakutani, "Presidential Architect of Designs for Power," *The New York Times*, 11 July 2006. This article is a review of a biography of Attorney General Alberto Gonzales by Bill Minutaglio entitled *The President's Counselor* (Rayo/HarperCollins, 2006).

[87] David Johnston and Neil A Lewis, "Bush's Counsel Sought Ruling About Torture," *The New York Times*, 5 January 2005.

[88] Michael Glennon, "The New Interventionism," *Foreign Affairs*, 78(3) (1999), 2–7.

ability to mobilize and employ force superior to that of any other state.[89] The German neo-conservative of his day, Heinrich von Treitschke, once thundered: "How can a puny neutral state like Belgium claim to be a center of international law? The shaping of law lies only with great powers."[90] In the same temper, an anonymous senior White House official said to a *New York Times* journalist objecting to some Administration statement as contrary to the facts: "We are not fact-dependent because we have the power to create the facts."[91]

C. The Neo-conservative Project and the Interests of the West

One cannot dismiss the claims of neo-conservatives merely by invoking parallels to the century-old views of German chauvinists and, after them, Nazi ideologues. It is at least conceivable that people with different ends may never-theless adopt the same means, the means in this instance being a repudiation of widely held views about international law and about appropriate restraints on the use of force. Differences in people's ends should be presumed to matter until it is shown that the differences are dissolved by the common means. As I noted earlier, neo-conservatives offer a more-or-less coherent diagnosis of non-state transnational violence and then prescribe treatment that happens not to fit within the Charter's normative framework for the use of force and the protection of sovereignty. Nor, I should add, is it congruent with long-established views on the means states may employ to maintain either internal or external security. However, on the presumption that international law must reflect the interests of its subjects, opponents of the neo-conservative approach to international law need to challenge its diagnosis of the threat to Western interests or the efficacy of its prescription for reducing it.

On the matter of diagnosis, the neo-conservative explanation of anti-Western terrorism may obscure its real causes. Is it incontestable, as neo-conservatives and their acolytes like President Bush assert, that Islamic terrorism is best under-stood as a pathological response to the paradigmatic freedom and affluence Western states enjoy within their own borders, contrasted with the intellectual and material poverty of much of the Islamic world, or, to similar effect, is a demented aspiration to restore Muslim power in all the areas where it once was exercised (ie from Spain all the way down the Mediterranean basin and then north to the gates of Vienna) or is a fanatical effort to exclude from the Islamic World the diffuse cultural forces seen to issue from within the West, although they may be nothing more than the manifestations of a global post-industrial, consumerist economy?

---

[89] Calvin DeArmond Davis, *The United States and the Second Hague Peace Conference* (Durham, NC: Duke University Press, 1975), 149–55, 280.

[90] Heinrich von Treitschke, *Politics* (New York: Harcourt, Brace and World, 1963), 297.

[91] See Ron Suskind, *One-percent Doctrine* (New York: Simon & Schuster, 2006).

Isn't there a more parsimonious, straightforward explanation, one that treats Muslim terrorist leaders as rational human beings defending tangible commonplace interests by awful means? The more straightforward although not necessarily the most accurate explanation, let's call it a not absurd hypothesis, is that Muslim terror is in significant measure a well-precedented response of indigenous forces to what they perceive as an alien exercise of political-military power within territories they perceive as theirs, a response not fundamentally different from, although to this point much more narrowly based than, the rebellions or attempted rebellions in countries like Algeria, Angola, South Africa, Southern Rhodesia, Kenya, and Vietnam and earlier in Ireland against imperial structures of domination. To be sure, alien power is exercised through or in collaboration with elements of the indigenous population, is often indirect and to a considerable extent hidden. This is not unusual in the annals of colonialism.

It does not appear to be a controversial proposition of fact that, by means of the various instruments of statecraft—open military intervention (eg Iraq, Lebanon), intervention by proxy (eg support for Saddam Hussein's invasion of Khomeini's Iran), subversion (eg the overthrow of the democratically elected Mossadegh Government in Iran), payments to accommodating chiefs (eg the annual subvention for the Mubarak regime in Egypt), the arming and equipping of military, police and intelligence personnel (eg Tunisia, Morocco, Saudi Arabia, Egypt)—the United States, like the British and French before it, exercises what could reasonably be perceived as imperial power in the Middle East. I offer this fact not to make a normative point. People will doubtless differ on whether, at the end of the day, imperial domination contributes more to the well-being of local peoples than it extracts in tolls for its efforts. I invoke the fact simply to suggest that Muslim terrorism may be attributable in large measure to tangible policies of domination and perceived exploitation as was Irish, Kikuyu, and Algerian terrorism, to name only three well-known cases.

What follows from this hypothesis is that, at least in theory, it might be possible to reduce the incidence of Islamic terrorism by a sharp withdrawal of the Western political, clandestine, and military presence in Islamic countries leaving indigenous forces to negotiate accommodations in some places and to submit their differences to the arbitration of force in others. Even assuming that terrorism directed at the West might thereby be reduced, it does not, of course, follow that a manifest contraction of the Western political-military presence undertaken for the stated purpose of altering a relationship conceded to have been imperial would best serve the interests either of the West or the majority of local peoples. The requisite cost-benefit analysis would be immensely complex and, in the end, highly uncertain which generally means that inertia prevails.

I have put the policy issue dichotomously. In fact there are many points between wholesale dismantling of the imperial presence that has prevailed since the end of the First World War and a policy marked by strict non-intervention in local affairs. A finite number of acts such as the withdrawal of Western troops from

Arab countries, the establishment of a sovereign albeit neutralized Palestinian state with a capital in East Jerusalem, an apology for the subversion of Iran's nascent democracy in 1953 (the elephant does not notice the squashed hen, but the hen's children remember), and a declared commitment to non-intervention in Middle-Eastern countries might alter significantly the apparent perception among many young Muslims all over the Islamic world that the West is at war with them.[92]

I reiterate that even if one concluded that a package of such acts might alter perceptions and thus reduce substantially the pool of *jihadi* recruits and sympathizers, the costs of the package might seem too high. My point, then, is simply this: neo-conservatives call for a dismantling of restraints on the use of force and on unilateral intervention in the face of irreducible enmity from a pathological foe. In fact, there are plausible grounds for believing that the enmity is reducible, because the foe has tangible, familiar interests which we might be able to accommodate partially through changes in public policy. On this hypothesis, then, the status quo is not our fate; rather, in some measure admittedly difficult to specify, it is our choice.

The choice thus far has been to intrude more violently into the Middle East and to associate the United States openly with Israel's goal of barring a Palestinian political presence in East Jerusalem and annexing a substantial part of the territories it has occupied since the 1967 war,[93] a goal that seems incompatible with a negotiated solution of the Palestinian-Israeli conflict and with important norms of international law including the Fourth Geneva Convention dealing with the treatment of people in occupied territories.[94]

The invasion and occupation of Iraq is to this point the principal illustration of that flight from the Charter norms that the successful containment of terrorism is alleged to require. The catastrophic terrorist attacks on Madrid and London appear to have been motivated by this instance of flight. Various observers of trends in the Islamic World, including the part expatriated to Europe, believe that the invasion of Iraq has facilitated the translation of Muslim anger[95] and alienation into recruits for terrorist organizations.[96] Moreover, the now well-documented and widely publicized recourse to torture and inhuman and degrading treatment of detainees in Afghanistan, Guantánamo, and Iraq,[97] Abu Ghraib being a well-precedented

---

[92] Daniel Benjamin and Steven Simon, *The Age of Sacred Terror* (2002), 148–50; Pew Global Attitudes Project, "America's Image Slips, But Allies Share US Concerns Over Iran, Hamas," Pew Research Center, 13 June 2006, <http://pewglobal.org/reports/display.php?ReportID=252>.

[93] See, Henry Siegman, "Sharon's Phony War," *The New York Review of Books*, 18 December 2003, 16–18.

[94] See Chapter 5 below; see also Ian Lustick, "Israeli State-Building in the West Bank and Gaza Strip: Theory and Practice," *International Organization* 41(1) (1987), 151–71.

[95] Daniel Benjamin and Steven Simon, *The Next Attack* (2005), 15.

[96] Ibid, 16.

[97] Consider the Amnesty International reports: "Beyond Abu Ghraib: Detention and Torture in Iraq" (6 March 2006), "Guantánamo: Lives torn apart—The impact of indefinite detention on detainees and their families" (6 February 2006), "Afghanistan: Amnesty International's campaign

response to the frustrations of battling a guerrilla insurgency,[98] are certain to have weakened the West's necessary effort to build a worldwide consensus against the use of brutal means for political ends which is the essence of terrorism.

To be sure, it is early days. Things may look different years from now. We might take the leisurely historical view recommended by Premier Zhou Enlai to Henry Kissinger when, responding to the latter's query about his assessment of the French Revolution's impact, he said it was too early to tell. Still, if proponents of radical normative change are felt to carry the burden of persuasion, it seems fair to conclude at this point: "Case not proven." There is, however, a case for codifying certain minor deviations from a literal reading of the Charter norms that still leave in place powerful restraints on unilateral recourse to force. I now turn to them.

3. The UN's Restatement of its Norms

In the wake of the flaring doubt about the future of the United Nations, sparked by the invasion of Iraq without Security Council sanction, Secretary General Kofi Annan invited 16 notables broadly representative of the UN membership "to assess current threats to international peace and security, to evaluate how well our existing policies and institutions have done in addressing those threats, and to recommend ways of strengthening the United Nations to provide collective security for the twenty-first century."[99] Not surprisingly, one focal point of this High-Level Panel's unusually candid report is the legal regulation of the use of force. On the one hand, and this was surprising, the Panel appears to reinforce the Charter skeptics by stating bluntly: "That all States should seek Security Council authorization to use force *is not a time-honored principle*"[100] (emphasis added). On the other hand, it immediately breaks with the skeptics, who either disparage legal regulation of force in a unipolar world or call for new norms that would provide much more space for the violent defense of interests deemed vital. For the Panel goes on to say, referring to the claimed obligation to seek Security Council authorization for the use of force, that "what is at stake is a relatively new emerging norm, one that is precious but not yet deeply rooted...for the first 44 years of the United Nations, member states often violated these rules and used military force literally hundreds of times...and Article 51 only rarely provided credible cover. Since the end of the Cold War, however, the yearning for an international system governed by the rule of law has grown."[101]

to stop torture and ill-treatment in the 'war on terror'" (1 May 2006). All reports are available online through <http://www.amnestyusa.org>.

[98] See Wade Sanders, "Predictable Atrocities? History Shows that Combat has Sad Consequences," *San Diego Union-Tribune*, 31 May 2006, B7.

[99] See the UN report of the High Level Panel on Threats, Challenges, and Change entitled, "A More Secure World: Our Shared Responsibility" 2 December 2004, vii.

[100] Ibid, para 82.

[101] Ibid, para 186.

These words imply that the Charter's use-of-force rules collapsed as a legal regime within a few years of their adoption in 1945, the Cold War being conventionally dated from 1949. But in contrast to today's rule skeptics, the Panel sees not an intensification of indifference to but rather a strengthened desire ("yearning") for legal restraint. Complementing that yearning, the Panel Report continues, is something approaching a negative consensus (with the United States as the main possible holdout) in opposition to the merely de facto restraints of a balance of power system or to a security system legislated and policed "by any single—even benignly motivated—superpower."[102] Moreover, the Report states that "expectations about...legal compliance" with the Charter constraints [essentially as initially construed] "are very much higher [today]."[103]

In his March 2005 Report prepared for the following Fall's Special General Assembly on UN reform, former Secretary-General Kofi Annan took a similar nuanced position, stating that the Charter "as it stands offers a good basis for the understanding [among states about the use of force] that we need."[104] That is rather less than a ringing affirmation that the Charter rules on the use of force are declarative of international law.

What light do the Panel and Secretary-General's Report cast on the current state of the original understanding? With respect to the right of self-defense, while recognizing that the potential for catastrophic attack by terrorists has sharply intensified threats to national and human security, the Panel nevertheless adheres to the original view that resort to force without Security Council authorization is unacceptable where a threat is not imminent.[105] For, if it is not imminent, then there is time to have recourse to the Council. To be sure, the Panel concedes, "[t]he Council's decisions have been less than consistent, less than persuasive and less than fully responsive to very real State and human security needs." The answer to the resulting dilemma for states that feel deeply threatened, the Panel argues, is not unilateral action but reform of the Council. However, that the Charter empowers the Council to authorize preventive (as distinguished from merely preemptive) action is clear to the Panel.

With respect to the authority of regional and sub-regional organizations, the Panel fails to resolve the present uncertainty or to clarify divergent practice. It merely says that the one exception other than self defense to the Charter's prohibition of the use of force in Article 2(4) is "military measures authorized by the Security Council under Chapter VII (*and by extension for* [sic] *regional organizations under Chapter VIII*) [emphasis added]."[106] The Secretary-General's

---

[102] Ibid.

[103] Ibid, para 196. (The view of the law implicit in the third section of the Report is plainly informed by contemporary jurisprudence which recognizes that law is a matter of degree, the degree of consensus about its existence and application in given issue areas).

[104] A/59/2005 (2005), para 123.

[105] Report of the Secretary-General's High-level Panel on Threats, Challenges and Change, "A More Secured World: Our Shared Responsibility," paras 193–8.

[106] Ibid, para 185.

Report, which to a considerable degree tracks the Panel's, deals at much greater length with the relationship between regional organizations and the United Nations, but it too fails to state unambiguously that such organizations do or do not have independent authorizing power.

What about the authority of the Security Council to legitimate the preventive use of force where it concludes a threat to the peace is merely incubating? The Panel seems fully in accord with those who find such authority in the Charter. Not only does it recognize Charter authority for preventive action, it suggests that the authority may be read more broadly today than in the past.[107] The Panel illustrates preventive action with the hypothesized case of a state that has expressed hostility to another state suddenly acquiring nuclear weapons-making capability. Even without evidence of any intention to use or to seek concessions by threatening to use that capability, the Council could, in the Panel members' view, find a threat to the peace and therefore act or authorize action pursuant to Chapter VII.[108]

As for the Council's authority to authorize preventive force where crimes against humanity are threatened, the Panel's answer is an unambiguous affirmative. The almost universally ratified Genocide Convention evidenced decades ago the broadly shared conviction that the principle of non-intervention declared in Article 2(7) of the Charter cannot be used to protect perpetrators of crimes against humanity. In other words, they can and should be considered threats to international security. Revealing of the Panel's temper in this respect and therefore of the sea change that has occurred in the perceptions and values of official elites is the Panel's equation of national and "human" security, a juxtaposition of concepts—indeed of words—rarely heard in official discourse before the end of the Cold War. The Panel reinforces its position by citing "growing recognition that the issue is not the 'right to intervene' of any state, but the 'responsibility to protect' of *every* state when it comes to people suffering from avoidable catastrophe—mass murder, rape, ethnic cleansing by forcible expulsion and terror, and deliberate starvation and exposure to disease."[109] States that either choose not to meet that responsibility or simply lack the capacity to protect temporarily lose to that extent the normal insulation of sovereignty. The Panel recognizes and endorses an "emerging norm of a collective international responsibility to protect."[110]

Does that responsibility extend to individual states where a Permanent Member's veto blocks action? Like the Swedish-Government-funded Kosovo Commission, the Panel distinguishes between the legal and the legitimate use of force; but unlike the Commission, which was considering the propriety of force unauthorized by the Council, it does so only with respect to Security Council action, and preventive action at that. Thus it again avoids the question of Humanitarian Intervention.

[107] Ibid, para 194.
[108] Ibid, para 188.
[109] Ibid, para 201.
[110] Ibid, paras 202–3.

When it first considers the legitimacy issue, the Panel appears to introduce a third criterion for evaluating Council action, namely "prudence," by stating "[q]uestions of legality apart, there will be issues of prudence, or legitimacy."[111] Could the report be saying that prudence is the essence of legitimacy? I think not, in part because when it again turns to the issue, this time for a more detailed discussion, the Panel appears to treat prudence simply as *one* of the tests of the legitimacy of a Council decision.[112]

I reach this conclusion by tracking the sequence of the Panel's arguments in this subsection on "The Question of Legitimacy." It begins with the assertion that the "effectiveness of the global collective security system … depends ultimately not only on the legality of decisions but also on the common perception of their legitimacy—their being made on solid evidentiary grounds, and for the right reasons, morally as well as legally [note the absence here of any reference to "prudence."]"[113] Then the Panel says: "in deciding whether or not to authorize the use of force, the Council should adopt and systematically address a set of agreed guidelines, going directly not to whether force *can* legally be used but whether, as a matter of good conscience and good sense, it *should* be.[114] Finally, in paragraph 207 it sets out five guidelines. Closely tracking the criteria for a Just War widely recognized by moralists from Aquinas to contemporary thinkers, they include *Balance of Consequences*: "Is there a reasonable chance of the military action being successful in meeting the threat in question, with the consequences of action not likely to be worse than the consequences of inaction?" This, the last of the five proposed criteria, approximates the classical Just War criterion of "prudence" or "reasonable judgment." In short, prudence is an element of legitimacy, not a separate criterion.

The Panel dealt only with what, in the light of the Kosovo intervention and the invasion of Iraq, reasonably appeared to it as the most consequential of the various use of force issues enumerated above. The issues it passed over are not Cold War relics. They will recur. However, if the Security Council becomes the linchpin of the collective security system, acting consistently and effectively to address all cases that substantially engage international and human security, then it will doubtless resolve case by case the issues ignored by the Panel as they arise.

One such case is the chronic violation of core human rights. Most proposed guidelines for legitimate Humanitarian Intervention have included what I have elsewhere called the "spike test,"[115] ie a dramatic increase in the breadth and possibly the severity of human rights violations as distinguished from the quotidian

---

[111] Ibid, para 195.
[112] Ibid, paras 204–9.
[113] Ibid, para 204.
[114] Ibid, para 205.
[115] "Round Table: Humanitarian Intervention after 9/11," *International Relations*, 19(2) (2005) 211–50.

torture, mutilation, arbitrary imprisonment, and murder that characterize many tyrannical regimes like that of the deposed Saddam Hussein. The distinction does not have immediate moral appeal. For it could insulate regimes like Saddam's that are so effective in terrorizing the population that, except where external conflict weakens the regime's grip, it can endure for years without meeting the spike test. Yet over time it may well ruin far more lives than a regime that at one moment in time satisfies the test, as the Milosevic regime seemed to at the time of NATO's Kosovo intervention. Be that as it may, the Panel's first criterion of legitimacy appears to adopt the spike test ("In the case of internal threats, does [the threatened harm] include genocide and other large-scale killing, ethnic cleansing or serious violations of international humanitarian law, actual or imminently apprehended?"). That test would have justified Security Council authorization of intervention in Iraq for Saddam's decimation of the Kurds during the Iran-Iraq War and indiscriminate massacre of members of the Shia faith in the south of Iraq after Desert Storm.

The Panel also failed to clarify what constitutes both "last resort" and "proportional means" or "military action of the minimum necessary to meet the threat" of crimes against humanity as legitimacy tests for any use of force to prevent them. There are interpretations of those two tests that are politically correct in the traditional UN context and there are interpretations that persons with at least a modest concern for human security should prefer. The "last-resort" test asks whether "every non-military option for meeting the threat in question [has] been explored, with reasonable grounds for believing that other measures will not succeed." From the perspective of human security, the better test is *whether early resort to military action is the most likely way of aborting the threat at least cost to the intended beneficiaries of the intervention.*

The "proportional means" test, as traditionally construed, inhibits the international community from the root-and-branch reordering of the target government and possibly the society that the very severity of the humanitarian emergency suggests may well be necessary in order to prevent its recurrence. In the traditional construction, the intervention was designed to halt genocidal or mass killing, have minimal impact on social and political structures, and end as soon as the killing had stopped and there was no prospect of its imminent renewal. Concern about long-term occupation and deep political and social restructuring may well be appropriate in the case of unilateral or coalition interventions, where humanitarian concern may cloak more parochial motives. Where the Security Council authorizes intervention that concern seems inapplicable.

Given the broadly representative character of the Panel and the generally distinguished qualifications of its members, it seems reasonable to take its report as persuasive evidence of a normative consensus that includes virtually all powerful countries (and, *a fortiori*, weak ones) other than the United States under the present Administration and, in light of its past behavior, presumably Israel. So construed, it is an unequivocal reaffirmation of the core elements of what I have identified as the original understanding. Hence the declared policies of the Bush Administration are as irreconcilable with what I take to be the present consensus about appropriate legal restraints as they are with the initial interpretations of the Charter by most scholars and governments. To persist in those interpretations risks casting the United States as a rogue state, a role not well calculated to enhance that broad measure of international cooperation required to contain the terrorist threat.

While a hostile consensus seems broad and clear with respect to preventive war and unauthorized intrusions, for instance to arrest or assassinate persons deemed to be terrorists, it attenuates beyond that core to a point that allows some play in the joints of the tri-partite division of force that a literal reading of the Charter appeared to achieve. In two areas of potential importance there remains dissensus or ambiguity.

One is the authority of regional and sub-regional organizations. As long as the veto of one Permanent Member can paralyze the Security Council, international security may be enhanced by offering a state some alternative to impotence, on the one hand, and, on the other, recourse to force which it unilaterally determines to be essential to its interests and consistent with the purposes and principles of the United Nations. But not all present or potential regional and sub-regional organizations are equally good forums for appraising state claims. One can imagine an organization so dominated by its most powerful member that its preferences will always rule. NATO, by contrast, with its rule of unanimity, its numbers, and the democratic accountability of its member governments, really can evaluate proposed interventions persuasively in terms of their justness, their prudence, their threat to international peace and security, and the risk to national or human security of not acting. It would no more have approved the invasion of Iraq than would the Security Council. Its approval and monitoring of the Kosovo intervention strengthened the claim that the intervention was "legitimate" even if not strictly consistent with the Charter.

What follows is that if the community of states is going to concede to regional bodies the authority to legitimate military action, the community must begin to distinguish among claimants to regional organization status by establishing criteria of recognition. It should also concede a conditional delegation of authority to such organizations only in the event that Security Council action is blocked by a veto rather than the inability to secure nine votes. Finally, a doctrine attributing authorizing power to regional organizations could be more easily reconciled with respect for the principle of sovereignty, if such power could be exercised only with respect to actions against member states. In their case, one can argue prior consent to the procedures whereby the organization acts. If the target is a non-member state, reconciliation is far more problematical.

The other issue of potential importance, particularly to liberals, is whether armed intervention to prevent crimes against humanity can ever be legitimate without Security Council authorization.[116] Strangers to our planet wandering through the pre-9/11 academic and think-tank conference circuit or the associated literature might easily have concluded that every Western government with the means to project force beyond its own frontiers was straining against the leash woven out of normative uncertainties, awaiting only their resolution before hurling itself into the humanitarian fray. But even before 9/11's universal refocusing of concern, once these observant strangers moved from the conference room to the world of action, or in this case more frequently inaction, what would they have seen? Surely nothing less than the repulsive marriage of noble rhetoric and heroic constraint that has characterized the behavior of the United States and other Western countries when faced with slaughter in places outside their perceived circle of national interests or slaughter conducted by regimes with which they find it convenient to fraternize.

That said, it remains true that from time to time in certain states, public opinion, aroused by the international human rights community, moves governments (particularly when by chance they are led by persons who in some measure share the public's passions) to contemplate Humanitarian Intervention. On the whole, the Security Council has not been a bar to action. Kosovo was, in this respect, exceptional. The Chinese have grumbled, being still uneasy about any precedent for intervention, sometimes the Russians too; but in the end they acquiesced even in the Haitian case where the main emphasis of the proposed intervention was on restoring a democratically elected regime rather than ending crimes against humanity.

Still, there was Kosovo. And if the United States had wanted to intervene in the Sudan to end the slaughter in Darfur, it might have faced a Chinese veto on behalf of its budding investment in that country's petroleum reserves. In short, the Council can be an obstacle to authentic Humanitarian Interventions as distinguished, for example, from the US-led invasion of Iraq at a time when human rights violations were probably at a lower level than when Saddam Hussein was enjoying US patronage.

Although there is not yet broad support among governments for formal recognition of what the Canadian Government was perhaps the first to call "the responsibility to protect,"[117] non-fulfillment of which could justify intervention, even Chinese policy intellectuals concede that in certain horrendous circumstances, intervention may be appropriate.[118] It is in any event likely that, at various points in the future, slaughter in one country or another will generate within the United States and some other nations a powerful interventionary impulse that

---

[116] See my discussion in JL Holzgrefe and RO Keohane (eds), *Humanitarian Intervention: Ethical, Legal and Political Dilemmas* (2002).

[117] International Commission on Intervention and State Sovereignty, *The Responsibility to Protect* (Ottawa, 2001).

[118] Simon Chesterman, Tom Farer, and Timothy Sisk, "Competing Claims: Self-Determination, Security and the United Nations," *International Peace Academy Policy Brief,* April 2001.

will confront the threat of veto from a Permanent Member or at least demands immediate action while the Council debates.

There are two ways of managing the prospective collisions between that impulse and the Charter norms. One is to do nothing, an approach dictated by the belief that the collisions will be so exceptional that they can be absorbed without much damage into the normative order. The other, which I favor, is to agree on a set of conditions for intervention without Security Council authorization. Agreement may at first be informal, a declaration by various governments to which some other governments may voice objection. Or it might assume the form of a declaratory resolution of the Security Council, which arguably is not subject to veto. My own judgment is that expectations of compliance with Charter norms on the use of force will be enhanced by a frank insistence on the part of states favoring Humanitarian Intervention in extreme circumstances that it is compatible with state practice under the Charter regime if it satisfies the following conditions:[119]

- As a threshold or triggering requirement, there must be imminent or ongoing and massive crimes against humanity or a failure to protect against grave threats to life stemming from natural or man-made disasters.
- All remedies short of force have been exhausted except (a) where timely and effective intervention requires immediate recourse to force, or (b) remedies short of force (like comprehensive economic sanctions) that might ultimately be effective are very likely to inflict more collateral damage to human welfare than armed intervention would.
- The intervention is conducted in compliance with international humanitarian law and collateral damage, is projected to be minor in comparison to the damage to the subject population that would predictably have occurred if the intervention had not proceeded.
- There must be a high probability that the use of force will achieve a positive humanitarian outcome.
- The intervening states (a) must report the intervention to the Security Council, (b) must lay before the Council a program for eliminating the threat to human rights that precipitated the intervention and for restoring indigenous authority once the triggering conditions are terminated, and (c) must request the Council to monitor their compliance with the program and assess their satisfaction of conditions 1–4.

I think these conditions will usefully structure debate within states contemplating intervention, within the wider international community, and within the Security Council.

---

[119] See discussion in Tom J Farer with Daniele Archibugi, Chris Brown, Neta C Crawford, Thomas G Weiss and Nicholas J Wheeler, "Round Table: Humanitarian Intervention after 9/11," *International Relations*, 19(2) (2005) 211–50.

4. The Liberal Case for Conserving Normative Restraint

There is nothing new about powerful states using all of the instruments of statecraft including brute force, not only to disable potential rivals and to protect against immediate threats to vital interests, but also to create an international environment that mirrors their values. This is particularly true of states with a strong sense of ideological mission. They view the reproduction of their domestic institutions and values as a good in itself. Moreover, despite the disconfirming record of Sino-Soviet or Sino-Vietnamese relations, they presume that mirror image regimes will be far more cooperative than those reflecting very different ideas about government and society. In recent history we have seen Marxist, Fascist, social democratic, and liberal capitalist regimes all trying to clone themselves, just as in the Middle Ages Catholic governments sought to reproduce Christian polities in the then pagan areas of Northwestern Europe.

As I noted earlier, the main premise of neo-conservative ideologues like Charles Krauthammer is that the employment of American hegemony to spread democracy, if necessary at the point of the bayonet, serves American interests no less than its values, incidentally serving the interests and values of all human beings other than the evil ones. Let me confess that I, too, believe that human security would be far better served in a world of liberal democratic states. I am not convinced, however, that the use of force in violation of substantive and procedural norms supported by the generality of states, or at least the leading states, much less in flagrant violation of human rights and humanitarian law, will advance the democratic cause. On the contrary, there are signs that, at least in the United States, it is beginning to erode those constraints on executive power that have long distinguished North Atlantic Democracy from illiberal formal democracies in Latin America and parts of Asia.

If, as sometimes appears to be the case, the call for looser restraints on the use of force is in the service of a violent crusade for laissez-faire democracy, it will surely go unanswered, for such a crusade will threaten the interests of many states, the United States included. Perhaps for that reason the call is usually made in more traditional and hence disarming terms. Loosened restraint is said to be necessary not for the indefinite reproduction of congenial regimes, but rather to protect conventional interests that all states share, above all the protection of their populations from catastrophic attack.

The main argument is now familiar: unlike states, terrorists (ie NGOs with bombs) cannot be deterred because they have few if any sunk assets and operate entirely in clandestinity. Hence they must be preempted, that is killed or captured wherever and whenever they surface. This preemptive action is an exercise of the inherent right to self-defense. Exercise cannot be limited by mandatory recourse to the Security Council in advance of any action. Consultation involves some delay, while the opportunity to strike the shadowy fast-moving enemies of civilization will often be fleeting. Moreover, in order to persuade other countries of the need for action, it would often be necessary to reveal fragile intelligence sources that could easily be compromised.

To be sure, these concerns are not trivial. Can they be taken sufficiently into account by means of an interpretation of the received normative order that leaves it essentially intact? The answer, I think, is "yes."

Take the case of Al Qaeda. For a number of years before 9/11, it had attacked US targets, including its embassies in Kenya and Tanzania and a vessel of its armed forces in Yemen. These attacks were part of a declared campaign against the US presence in the Middle East. Although not carried out by a state, the attacks and their broad aims were arguably analogous in certain respects to the waging of war and the United States could therefore exercise its right of self-defense under Article 51 of the Charter. But even assuming the force of the analogy, still the United States was obligated to bring the situation to the Security Council so that it could review the situation and determine what collective measures would best serve international peace and security.

However, since the analogue of an aggressive attack had occurred and was likely to recur at times and places of Al Qaeda's choosing, arguably the United States was not required to remain inert while the Council deliberated. If, for instance, its armed forces encountered Al Qaeda operatives aboard a ship on the high seas flying no national flag, it certainly was privileged to attack and destroy the ship or to seize the operatives. Moreover, if, as was the actual case, Osama bin Laden was ostentatiously using a country as his operations base, the United States could demand of its government that bin Laden be detained and the base shut down, so no further attacks could be made. Moreover, if that government were indisputably colluding with bin Laden or there was substantial reason to believe that the host government either could not or would not prevent bin Laden from quickly shifting to a new venue, the United States could attack bin Laden without any prior request. And in the event that the bin Laden host government attempted to repel this exercise of self-defense rights under the Charter, it too would be a legitimate target of US forces.

In short, the Government of the United States could reasonably have construed the Charter to allow an attack on Al Qaeda installations in Afghanistan, for instance after the Embassy bombings, once it had conclusive evidence that Al Qaeda had authorized the bombings and the Taliban, despite being presented with this evidence, had thereafter refused to detain Al Qaeda leaders and shut down their camps or there were substantial grounds for believing that they were unable to do so even if they wished to or were unwilling. However, unless it appeared that prior referral to the Council would allow Al Qaeda leaders to conceal themselves or launch a new attack on US property or personnel, the United States would have to seek Council authorization. In the event that the Council failed to act, then, assuming the conditions just specified, the United States could have attacked Al Qaeda's bases in Afghanistan. The Security Council's implied authorization of the US invasion of Afghanistan following 9/11[120] is consistent with this analysis of what the Charter allows.

What the Charter does not allow is unauthorized military action against allegedly terrorist organizations or individuals residing in a country able and willing to prevent use of its territory for attacks on other states. Thus if Osama bin Laden were suddenly discovered summering in Provence, the United States would not be entitled to lob onto his villa even the most intelligent of missiles or to drop in a few members of Delta Force without permission from the French Government which, in my hypothetical case, is perfectly unaware of his presence. Rather it would have to either secure permission from Paris or authorization from the Security Council. Is this an intolerable constraint on the protection of nations against transnational terrorism? Would it not be fair to say that disregard of the extant law in a case like this would end that cooperation between the intelligence services of France and the United States which the Bush Administration has lauded?[121] Surely legal constraint in this case reinforces or at the very least reflects the conditions of interstate cooperation essential for the counter-terrorist struggle.

What can be done under Charter norms where a group allegedly disposed to transnational terrorism is merely nascent? Let us hypothesize a case where US intelligence identifies an anti-American group and determines that it is beginning to plan attacks on American targets. Since most governments are today hostile to transnational terrorism and inclined to cooperate in its suppression, a word from Washington wrapped, perhaps, in a few incentives, should be sufficient to secure local steps to suppress the budding terrorists. But suppose the government is reluctant or unable to act because the alleged terrorists are members of an important ethnic constituency or are located in a remote part of the country where there is virtually no governmental presence. Then there are two possibilities. One is that the United States would obtain the other state's authorization to act in effect as its proxy. Obviously the rights of sovereignty allow one state to outsource a limited exercise of its police power to another. The other possibility is that it would seek authorization from the Security Council. Since all Permanent Members regard transnational terrorism, particularly Islamic terrorism, as a threat to their respective national interests, if the United States can offer persuasive intelligence of the group's aims, the Council is likely to exercise its now well-precedented authority to authorize preventive action. This may, admittedly, involve some risk to intelligence sources.

But what is the alternative? That the United States globally and lesser powers regionally should be free to lob missiles or troops into a country and kill or kidnap

---

[120] S/RES/1368 (2001).

[121] See "Help from France Key in Covert Actions" in *The Washington Post* on 3 July 2005, which describes the important alliance between French and US Intelligence Officials. The article states that "the rarely discussed Langley-Paris connection also belies the public portrayal of acrimony between the two countries that erupted over the invasion of Iraq."

its residents, often with collateral injury to persons conceded to be innocent, on the basis of such intelligence as each deems sufficiently reliable? The likely result of repeated violation of the territorial integrity of states is the progressive collapse of cooperation on a whole range of issues including non-proliferation. If states are thrown back on their own resources to guarantee their security, the incentive to find means for deterring intervention by more powerful actors will be multiplied. It is hard to think of means to that end other than the reputed possession of weapons of mass destruction.

The one other scenario often adduced by enthusiasts for preventive intervention is the imminent acquisition of nuclear weapons by a state not presently a member of the nuclear club. The High Level Panel Report addresses this case directly, hypothesizing an instance where a state suddenly acquires nuclear weapons-making capability. The Panel members' response is that even without evidence of any intention on the part of the acquiring state to use the weapons or to seek concessions by threatening use, the Council could find a threat to the peace and authorize enforcement measures. In doing so, the Council might well take into account legitimate fears of intervention on the part of the acquiring state and condition enforcement measures on the provision of pledges of non-intervention from states that have previously threatened it.

The nub of the matter, then, is that, properly construed, the Charter normative and institutional arrangements are consistent with the imperative interests of great states in the era of transnational terrorism. They are inconsistent only with the dangerous hegemonic delusions not of the United States as a society, but of the small but powerful clique embedded in the Bush Administration.

Neither conclusion is intended to celebrate the existing system of global governance. It is plainly inadequate to deal very effectively with the full range of threats to human security. There are, for instance, two dozen or more states governed by tyrants and kleptocrats unable or unwilling to provide their peoples with a minimum number of public goods and thereby killing them through the slower mechanisms of malnutrition and preventable disease. A more perfect system of governance would remove these mafias or reckless incompetents and place these states under trusteeships for the benefit of their peoples. It would also foster much greater interstate cooperation, including intrusive surveillance, to reduce the risk of pandemics, a risk more grave than bio-terrorism at this time. These examples could easily be multiplied. More effective governance will not occur unless and until the United States is prepared to institutionalize cooperation among the leading states. As long as the United States is ruled by men and women unwilling to acknowledge normative restraint on their discretion to employ force, effective governance will be a vision unfulfilled.

3

Cruelty and the National Interest: The Question of Legitimate Means

Dear Friends, I am so shocked by this information [that after three years at Guantánamo, her husband, Hadj Boudella, seized by US officials after the Bosnian Supreme Court had found charges against him of plotting terrorism to be unsubstantiated, had been determined by a US Military Combatant Status Review Tribunal to be an Enemy Combatant and therefore subject to indefinite detention] that it seems as if my blood froze in my veins. I can't breathe and I wish I was dead. I can't believe these things can happen, that they can come and take your husband away overnight and without reason, destroy your family, ruin your dreams… (Hadj Boudella's wife in a letter to his American lawyers)

Ernest Hemingway, the twentieth-century American novelist, once wrote that the true test of character is the ability to display grace under pressure.[1] Thus his interest in bullfighters and hunters of dangerous game. In the same vein one could say that the true test of a nation's humanistic culture's depth, if it claims to have such a culture, is how it reacts to serious national security challenges. Western countries generally, and the United States in particular, are now being tested. This chapter is my effort to assess how they are doing. Because of its enormous power, its unique capacity to project military force, to influence the world economy and, by its acts and omissions, to shape and to challenge international law and order, I will concentrate on the United States, but the analytic framework could be applied to any state.

I used the word "humanistic." What is it intended to imply? Early in the Spanish Civil War, rebel fascist troops seized the city of Salamanca with its ancient university whose rector was the enormously distinguished philosopher, Miguel Unamuno, by that time an old man but still at work in the groves of academe. Unamuno was generally regarded as a classical conservative, which is why the fascists had not removed him from office. Not long after the occupation, the faculty and selected members of the public came together at the University to celebrate some national holiday. The self-selected principal speaker was the one-armed fascist general, known for his savagery, who commanded the forces in Salamanca. At the conclusion of a furious address assaulting Marxism and

---

[1] Interview with Dorothy Parker, *The New Yorker*, 5(41) (30 November 1929).

atheism and promising to cleanse the country of these alien ideas and restore its Catholic heritage, the General glared at the audience, gave the fascist salute and screamed *"viva la muerte,"* which translates as "long live death" or, in the American idiom, "three cheers for death." His fascist supporters howled their approval and in the years that followed would suit their deeds to his words.

Then Unamuno, frail but resolute, walked to the podium. "I myself have been known for my irony," he said, "but the celebration of death in the name of life that you have just heard is an obscenity, a repudiation of the history and culture I have struggled to defend." Then, looking at the one-armed general, he added: "This terrible war has crippled and twisted the bodies of many men. But worse than that, it has crippled and twisted the spirit of some." He sat down. Later that day the fascists placed him under house arrest. He was too eminent, too distinguished a conservative simply to kill. He died shortly thereafter.[2]

For me the humanistic tradition is marked by a transcendent respect for human reason as a means of unending inquiry into the nature of the world and the right conduct of life, by a commitment to defend that search, by respect for knowledge and the layered cultural legacy that every civilization has produced, and by appreciation of the individual as searcher and creator of meanings. The tradition is by its nature cosmopolitan and regards violence and destruction as last resorts to preserve humanistic culture. It tolerates the warrior virtues and war itself only as means to that end; it does not exalt them. In our age it is formally expressed in international law and, particularly, in the normative body of human rights.[3]

We are now engaged in what the President of the United States has called a "war" against terrorism on behalf of human rights, democracy and the rule of law. The question is whether we are prepared to engage in the struggle against terrorism of global reach and catastrophic potential by means compatible with human rights, democracy and the rule of law. An associated question is whether thinking of our struggle as a war will enable us to act in ways consistent with our claimed values.

1. Standards and the Post-9/11 Setting

It ought to verge on cliché to say that human rights law along with the laws of armed conflict or international humanitarian law, as they are often summarily called, provide the operational standards by means of which we can test whether

---

[2] Hugh Thomas, *The Spanish Civil War: Revised Edition* (New York: Random House, 2001), 486–9.

[3] "Laws, formal treaties, the customs of civilized nations, the legitimacy of international institutions—these were the dross of the past, and Bush was plunging into the future. And, as he plunged, he had no idea, nobody in his administration seemed to have any idea, *that international law, human rights,… and humanitarianism had willy-nilly become the language of liberal democracy around the world* (emphasis added). Paul Berman, *Terror and Liberalism* (New York: WW Norton, 2003), 193.

the methods employed in the struggle with terrorist groups are compatible with our general values. And yet it is not hard to find a substantial body of recent legal writing on the conflicts in Afghanistan and Iraq and on other dimensions of the struggle that focuses exclusively on the Hague Regulations, the Geneva Conventions of 1949 and the 1977 Protocols Additional to them, as if the laws of war alone provided relevant criteria for assessment of what we are doing. Even so fine and balanced a scholar as Professor Adam Roberts has been guilty of this omission in some of his work.[4]

That it is a serious omission, a failure to bring all relevant legal criteria to bear on the issues, seems to me hardly worth disputing. After all, there is nothing in the history or language of the baseline legal statement of core human rights, the International Covenant on Civil and Political Rights,[5] on which to ground an argument that it was not intended to apply once armed conflict begins. Rather the contrary. By virtue of being about human rights, the Covenant purports to declare the rights of all individuals at all times in all places and the corresponding duties of states. What distinguishes the idea of human rights from earlier normative declarations concerning rights and human dignity is precisely its comprehensiveness in time and space. The rights adhere to people by virtue of their being born rather than being Englishmen or Christians or persons at different levels of the feudal hierarchy. Moreover, the Covenant takes explicit account of exigent circumstances, such as threats to public order and security, both in its statement of certain rights, like freedom of association, and in its provision for the suspension of the majority of its guarantees "in time of public emergency which threatens the life of the nation."[6] Few threats other than a major armed conflict and the looming danger of catastrophic attack could satisfy that standard.

Nor is there anything in the parallel but largely independent evolution of the law of human rights and the law of armed conflicts suggestive of an intention by state parties that the latter should utterly displace the former whenever armed conflict erupts. Humanitarian law is rightly seen as *lex specialis*, a body of law that brings the relative generalities of the Covenant to earth in an often very detailed form taking painstaking account of the peculiar circumstances of

---

[4] See, eg, "The Laws of War and the War on Terror," *International Law and the War on Terror. International Law Studies*, 79. Fred L Borch and Paul S Wilson (eds), (Newport: Naval War College, 2003), 175–230.

[5] International Covenant on Civil and Political Rights, GA Res. 2200A (XXI), 21 UN GAOR Supp. (No. 16) at 52, UN Doc A/6316 (1966).

[6] Ibid, at Pt 2, art 4(1): "In time of public emergency which threatens the life of the nation and the existence of which is officially proclaimed, the States Parties to the present Covenant may take measures derogating from their obligations under the present Covenant to the extent strictly required by the exigencies of the situation, provided that such measures are not inconsistent with their other obligations under international law and do not involve discrimination solely on the ground of race, colour, sex, language, religion or social origin."

armed conflict. What, for instance, if it is not a commandment to pacifism, does the right to life mean in a context defined by the efforts of organized groups to achieve their political ends by killing each other? The law of armed conflict provides a reasonably detailed answer. But with respect to matters where it does not provide a clearer, more detailed and precise answer than the Covenant or where, allegedly, it does not apply to certain persons, human beings are not relegated to a normative abyss where anything goes. Thus in the context of armed conflict, human rights law can be seen as a safety net assuring that no one lies beyond the reach of legal protection. Article 16 of the Covenant, which states that "Everyone shall have the right to recognition everywhere as a person before the law," nicely expresses this idea of human rights law as the ultimate defense against the law of the jungle.

Before turning to legal and ethical issues that the counter-terrorist struggle has generated thus far and to their principal contemporary venues: Afghanistan, Iraq, and Guantánamo, the latter a place insidiously rescued from the obscurity of a century-old naval coaling station, I want in all fairness to recall the setting in which the Bush Administration made the fateful decision to pursue its ends unconstrained by conventional interpretations of the applicable law. In the immediate aftermath of the 9/11 catastrophe, the Administration imperative was to avert further attacks, attacks which its leaders appeared genuinely to fear.[7] Certainly such fear had ample grounds and, as the Report of the 9/11 Commission implies,[8] the extraordinary thing is that it took the destruction of the Twin Towers to arouse and focus it on the Al Qaeda network. After all, President Bush and his colleagues preside over a country with immense borders on the land and sea sides, dependent as a global economic powerhouse on the largely uninhibited movement of people and goods across those borders and without an effective accounting system for citizens and documented aliens much less undocumented ones. Furthermore, as the previous Oklahoma City bombing had demonstrated, the country has a super-abundance of targets vulnerable to catastrophic attack by means easy to assemble from separately innocuous items like fertilizer and diesel oil. In addition, rather than being confronted with some ultimatum to do one thing or another within a certain period of time lest a second attack occur, the Administration faced a diffuse, apparently vengeful, hostility possibly bonded to the belief that a series of devastating blows would effect that generalized withdrawal from the Middle East that Osama bin Laden seemed to seek or would generate broad support for him among Arabs, a people humiliated by centuries of defeat and foreign domination.

---

[7]   Compare "By invitation: Harold Hongju Koh, 'Rights to Remember,'" *The Economist*, 1 November 2003, 24: "The American administration responded to the twin-towers tragedy with a sweeping new global strategy: an emerging 'Bush doctrine,' if you will. One element of this doctrine is what I call 'Achilles and his heel.' September 11th brought upon America, as once upon Achilles, a schizophrenic sense of both exceptional power and *exceptional vulnerability* (italics added). Never has a superpower seemed so powerful and so vulnerable at the same time."

[8]   *The 9–11 Commission Report: The Final Report of the National Commission on Terrorist Attacks upon the United States* (New York: WW Norton and Co, Inc, 2004).

From this perspective, it was imperative to act with extreme urgency to disrupt communications and logistics within the terrorist network, to force its members into a defensive crouch, and to incapacitate as many of them as possible in the shortest possible time. Osama bin Laden and associates had been a fixture on the radar screen of US intelligence agencies for at least a half dozen years. As Richard Clarke has testified, the counter-terror specialists within President Clinton's National Security Council security network regarded Al Qaeda as one of the major threats, possibly *the* major threat, to the internal security of the United States, regarded it as an organization with the will and the capacity to inflict catastrophic damage whether through conventional means or biological and chemical weapons.[9]

Given these concerns, stemming in large measure from attacks on US military and diplomatic assets, intelligence agencies had no doubt been tracking persons associated with Al Qaeda for years before 9/11.[10] Thousands of Muslims had passed through the Al Qaeda training facilities in Afghanistan during the war of national liberation against Soviet occupation and afterwards or had at least fought in units that bin Laden had helped to arm. Many had then dispersed to various parts of the world, including Europe and even the United States.[11] All of these thousands had at least rudimentary training in firearms and explosives and most, having left home and family to face the rigors and mortal dangers of war, first against the Soviets and then against local enemies of the Taliban regime, could be assumed to embrace the militant form of Islam then encouraged by Pakistan, which had controlled the flow of American aid to the insurgency, and personified by bin Laden and the Taliban. Their numbers, training, and ubiquity and the probable disposition of many to see the world in the same terms as bin Laden and to take if not orders in all cases than at least inspiration from him provided ample grounds for the sensation of a grave and immediate threat of more 9/11s.

While the United States and cooperating intelligence agencies must have had many names on their watch lists,[12] some of them identified by CIA agents

---

[9] *Testimony of Richard A Clarke Before the National Commission on Terrorist Attacks Upon the United States*, 24 March 2004, available at <http://www.9–11commission.gov/hearings/hearing8/clarke_statement.pdf>. See also *Against All Enemies: Inside America's War* (New York: Free Press, 2004).

[10] See, eg, Andrew Zajac, "Report Details FBI 9/11 Flubs." *The Chicago Tribune*, 10 June 2005, 19. Zajac summarizes a report by the Justice Department's Inspector General on why the CIA and the Justice Department at their highest levels failed to receive and synthesize data, available at lower levels, which would have alerted them and hence the President to the immediate risk of a 9/11-like occurrence. The Report notes, for instance, that CIA agents had detected the presence in January 2000, at a meeting of Al Qaeda militants in Malaysia, of one of the 9/11 terrorists and had determined that he had acquired a US passport. They did not pass the information along to the FBI.

[11] See, eg, Hal Bernton, *et al.*, "The Terrorist Within: The Story Behind One Man's Holy War Against America," *The Seattle Times*, 23 June–7 July 2002, available at <http://seattletimes.nwsource.com/news/nation-world/terroristwithin/about.html>. See also "Frontline: Inside the Terror Network," available at <http://www.pbs.org/wgbh/pages/frontline/shows/network>.

[12] Zajac, 19.

working with the Afghan resistance to the Soviets, given the thousands of persons who had passed through the conflicts in Afghanistan and the clandestine ways in which they had entered and left that country, the agencies could not have believed that they had identified more than a small fraction of the persons who might be prepared to carry out missions for Al Qaeda. Moreover, again in light of the numbers involved, many militants must have disappeared from intelligence radar screens after they had left Afghanistan. In addition, given the level of anger and frustration within the Arab world about its poverty, backwardness, and legacy of domination by Western countries led since the Second World War by the United States, the intelligence agencies and the White House were probably destined to assume that the Afghan-trained militants could co-opt to their cause thousands of young men and women from all over the Arab and wider Islamic world including disaffected persons living within the large immigrant communities of Western Europe and, possibly, the much smaller American one. In short, the circumstances provided the White House with immense incentives to round up and detain anyone in the United States who might be associated with Al Qaeda and to extract actionable intelligence from them and from persons in other countries detained by their security services. Hence the question of allowable interrogation methods had to have been on the Administration's mind virtually from the outset of its response to 9/11.[13]

2. Deconstructing the Laws of War

Debate over the application of the Geneva Conventions to the conflict in Afghanistan appears to have begun within weeks of 9/11. By 18 January 2002, the Department of Justice had already issued a formal legal opinion concluding that Geneva Convention III did not apply to Al Qaeda and that there were reasonable grounds for the President to conclude that it did not apply to the Taliban either.[14] Whereupon the President announced that Convention III would

---

[13] Alan Dershowitz, *Why Terrorism Works* (New Haven: Yale University Press, 2002), 134: "shortly after that watershed event [9/11], FBI agents began to leak stories suggesting that they might have to resort to torture to get some detainees, who were suspected of complicity in al Qaeda terrorism, to provide information necessary to prevent a recurrence."

[14] See especially, John C Yoo and Robert J Delahunty, *Memorandum for William J. Haynes II*, 9 January 2002, available at <http://www.msnbc.msn.com/id/5025040/site/newsweek>. See also Neil A Lewis, "Justice Memos Explained How to Skip Prisoners Rights," *The New York Times*, 21 May 2004, A10. The evolution of the Bush Administration's thinking regarding the status and treatment of captured Taliban and Al Qaeda forces is perhaps best illustrated by the memorandums and correspondence issued in the months after the 9/11 attacks. For an extensive collection of these documents, see generally Mark Danner, *Torture and Truth: America, Abu Ghraib, and the War on Terror* (New York: New York Review of Books, 2004); and Karen J Greenburg and Joshua L Dratel (eds), *The Torture Papers: The Road to Abu Ghraib* (Cambridge: Cambridge University Press, 2005).

not apply to either.[15] The State Department immediately sought reconsideration. In a Memorandum to the President dated only seven days later, the then White House Counsel Alberto Gonzalez, after summarizing the competing arguments, concluded that those made by the State Department were unpersuasive. In that memorandum, Mr Gonzalez, the future Attorney General of the United States, argued that the war against terrorism was a new kind of war, one placing a premium on, among other things, "the ability to quickly obtain information from captured terrorists."[16] He then added: "In my judgment, this new paradigm renders obsolete Geneva's strict limitations on questioning of enemy prisoners."[17]

Taking into account the enormous number and variety of that Department's responsibilities, it would strain credulity if someone suggested that the initial Justice Department memorandum or those written the following year specifically on the issue of torture, were spontaneously generated by mid-level officials. Rather reason and experience dictates the conclusion that the White House requested legal advice both to determine the limits imposed by acts of Congress and the risk of criminal liability particularly for persons not in a position to deny responsibility if they went outside statutory law and their actions became public.

Along with incapacitating potential terrorists and collecting operational intelligence, the highest priority in those early days was to strike directly at bin Laden and to terminate use of Afghanistan as a terrorist haven by replacing the country's de facto government. An invasion of Afghanistan would serve punitive purposes and might coincidentally disrupt the Al Qaeda network, disperse its leading figures and limit their communications with cadres and affiliates in other parts of the world. A decision must have been made at a very early point that the Administration could not achieve its goals in Afghanistan simply through clandestine support of the Taliban's internal opposition, the Northern Alliance.[18] There had to be open military intervention.

Not only was this operationally necessary, for three reasons it might well have seemed positively desirable. First, it would demonstrate the power of the United States and the will of a right-wing Republican Administration, unlike its Democratic predecessor, to use it ferociously. For years one article of the neo-conservative faith had been that President Bill Clinton was dissipating the advantages of hegemony, indeed was actively betraying the national interest, by failing to use force robustly.[19]

[15] See White House Press Secretary Ari Fleischer, Press Briefing at the White House, 7 February 2002, 1–2, available at <http://www.whitehouse.gov/news/releases/2002/02/20020207–6.html>.

[16] Alberto Gonzalez, *Memorandum to Pres. George W Bush*, 25 January 2002, 2, available at <http://news.lp.findlaw.com/hdocs/docs/torture/gnzls12502mem2gwb.html>.

[17] Ibid. But compare Anthony Lewis, "Making Torture Legal," *The New York Review of Books*, 51(12) (15 July 2004), 6. In assessing the interpretations of international law advocated by Gonzalez and his associates, Lewis notes: "There is a French phrase for betrayal of standards by intellectuals: *la trahison des clercs*. I think this is the lawyer's version: *la trahison des avocats*."

[18] See *The 9–11 Commission Report* at 330–4 on the evolution of Administration planning regarding Afghanistan following the 9/11 attacks.

[19] See George Packer, *The Assassins' Gate: America in Iraq* (New York: Farrar, Straus and Giroux, 2005), 14–38.

In particular, neo-conservatives believed that the problem of terrorism directed at US assets abroad was integrally related to a perception on the part of terrorist-supporting regimes and of terrorist organizations that public opinion in the United States and hence the US Government was casualty averse.

Secondly, senior figures in the Administration were keenly aware of public opinion polling data stretching back decades indicating that short and decisive military operations produced spikes in Presidential popularity which could probably be translated into support for domestic initiatives.[20] In this instance, however, the President had already achieved that spike simply by virtue of going to the Trade Center site, talking tough and announcing that the country was at war.[21] Actually going to war was likely to sustain his extraordinary approval ratings. As the President appears to have been keenly aware, his father's approval ratings had fallen gradually but in the end decisively once the Gulf War ended.[22] Actual war, precedent indicated, could serve a third purpose, namely maximizing Presidential power under the Constitution by inhibiting Congress or the Courts from questioning it.[23] In time of peace, for instance, a declared policy of holding aliens, much less citizens, without charge or trial for as long as the President deemed necessary or subjecting them to trial by Courts Martial or Military Commissions or turning detained persons over to governments likely to torture them was unlikely to survive a test in the federal courts as currently staffed. So war there was to be and for the professional military and presumably for the President's civilian legal advisors, as well, that meant engagement with the laws of war, in particular the Geneva Conventions.

One benefit from invoking the laws of war is the *laissez passer* they give for killing anyone who appears to be a combatant. Combatants are legitimate targets

---

[20] See especially, Richard Neustadt, *Presidential Power and the Modern Presidents* (New York: Free Press, 1990). See also Jon Mueller, *War, Presidents, and Public Opinion* (New York: John Wiley and Sons, 1973).

[21] *See* Frank Newport, "Bush Job Approval was 51% Immediately Before Tuesday's Attacks." *The Gallup Poll*, 12 September 2001, available at <http://poll.gallup.com/content/default. aspx?ci'4882&pg'1>. See also "American Psyche Reeling From Terror Attacks." The Pew Research Center for the People and the Press, 19 September 2001, available at <http://people-press. org/reports/display.php3?ReportID'3>. Per the Pew survey, Bush's approval ratings spiked to "historic heights" in the weeks after 9/11: eight-in-ten Americans claimed to approve of Bush's job performance, an increase of 51% in a few weeks. Per the survey, "this placed Bush's approval mark on par with the 84% rating his father received in March 1991, shortly after the US victory in the Persian Gulf War." More specifically, Bush received even higher ratings for his response to the 9/11 attacks; per the survey, "85% approve of his performance on that front."

[22] See generally, "On the Eve of '92: Fault Lines in the Electorate." The Pew Research Center for the People and the Press, 4 December 1991, available at <http://people-press.org/reports/display. php3?ReportID'19911204>.

[23] The accumulation and concentration of war powers by the Executive Branch over the past few decades has generated a wide range of debate, scholarship and commentary. For a strong criticism of this pattern, particularly under the Bush Administration, *see generally* Louis Fisher, *Presidential War Power*, 2nd edn (Lawrence, Kansas: University Press of Kansas, 2004). But compare David Mervin, "Demise of the War Clause." *Presidential Studies Quarterly*, 30(4), (2000), for an (pre-9/11) argument in favor of enhancing the scope and scale of Presidential war powers.

at all times and places, not simply on the battlefield or when fleeing therefrom. The fact that he is on leave sniffing roses in his garden does not immunize a commander from attack. Hence another advantage derived from simply folding Afghanistan into a generalized war against international terrorism, to the extent this description came to be widely accepted as reasonable, was that it could arguably legitimate targeted killing of Al Qaeda operatives all over the world, not simply in Western Asia.[24]

Of course, if the killing occurred within the borders of a state not manifestly complicit with Al Qaeda, and without permission from that state's government, that government might claim after the fact a violation of sovereignty, but at least the war paradigm would tend to nullify a parallel claim of gross violation of the right to life. Moreover, the United States might defend itself against the alleged breach of sovereignty by citing the Security Council Resolutions following 9/11 recognizing and authorizing exercise by the United States of self-defense rights under Article 51.[25] It could claim, in other words, that the resolutions, adopted pursuant to Chapter VII, implicitly licensed the United States to take all measures necessary for self-defense against a diffuse threat.[26] And that might include striking Al Qaeda functionaries immediately, wherever found, if delay occasioned by the effort to contact the relevant government and secure permission might allow the target to escape. A further advantage of the war paradigm, as previously suggested, is its power to justify detention without charge or trial for the duration of the conflict.[27] The conflict in Afghanistan itself promised to be short, but as the President and Secretary of Defense repeatedly declared, the war against terrorism could last for a generation or more.

---

[24] See, eg, David Johnston and David E Sanger, "Threats and Responses: Hunt for Suspects, Fatal Strike in Yemen was Based on Rules Set Out by Bush," *The New York Times*, 6 November 2002, A16. See also Philip B Heymann and Juliette N Kayyem, "Long-Term Legal Strategy Project for Preserving Security and Democratic Freedoms in the War on Terrorism," *Final Report of the Long-Term Legal Strategy Project* (Cambridge, MA: Belfer Center for Science and International Affairs), 16 November 2004, 62–70. But compare Daniel Byman, "Do Targeted Killings Work?" *Foreign Affairs*, 85(2) (March/April 2006).

[25] See S/RES/1368 (2001), S/RES/1373 (2001), S/RES/1377 (2001), S/RES/1378 (2001). Resolutions and Decisions of the Security Council, 1 January 2001 to 31 July 2002. UN Document Symbol: S/INF/57. Call Number S (01)/R3. Publication Date: 2003.

[26] Charter of the United Nations, ch VII, art 51. Article 51 states, in part: "Nothing in the present Charter shall impair the inherent right of individual or collective self-defence if an armed attack occurs against a Member of the United Nations, until the Security Council has taken measures necessary to maintain international peace and security." See also Yoram Dinstein, "Jus Ad Bellum Aspects of the 'War on Terrorism'," in Wybo P Heere (ed), *Terrorism and the Military: International Legal Implications* (The Hague: TMC Asser Press, 2003), 13–22: "What gives rise to the rightful invocation of self-defense is only (and exclusively) an armed attack. All the same, once an armed attack is unleashed the victim state is allowed by Article 51 to take forcible action (without seeking the prior approval of the Security Council)."

[27] See Avril McDonald, "Terrorism, Counter-Terrorism and the Jus in Bello." *Terrorism and International Law: Challenges and Responses*, Meeting at the International Institute for Humanitarian Law, 30 May–1 June and 24–26 September 2002, 68.

The main disadvantage in invoking the humanitarian law of war is, as the former White House Counsel noted, its detailed safeguards for prisoners of war.[28] The Bush Administration must have hoped to capture and interrogate those members of Al Qaeda who survived the fighting. Senior Taliban commanders might also have information useful for foiling planned actions and rolling up the Al Qaeda global network. Geneva law does not incorporate anything like the American Miranda rule[29] which requires police to inform criminal suspects of their right to remain silent and to have appointed counsel and also requires them to cease interrogating a suspect who, having been informed of his rights, requests a lawyer. Interrogation can begin again after the lawyer appears, but in the normal course defense lawyers counsel silence at least until suspect and lawyer have had a chance to develop a defensive strategy.

Military interrogators can ask POWs all the questions that occur to them, but Article 17 of the Third Geneva Convention ties the hands of coercion by stating that "[n]o physical or mental torture, nor any other form of coercion, may be inflicted on prisoners of war to secure from them information of any kind whatever." And just in case that is not clear enough, it adds: "Prisoners of war who refuse to answer may not be threatened, insulted, or exposed to unpleasant or disadvantageous treatment of any kind." In addition, Article 21 limits more subtle forms of coercion by declaring that "prisoners of war may not be held in close confinement (eg in cells) except where necessary to safeguard their health." Naturally there is an exception where prisoners are properly subjected to penal and disciplinary sanctions, as would be the case if they had attacked guards or fellow inmates or attempted to escape. Article 25 goes still further and requires that POWs be quartered "under conditions as favorable as those for the forces of the Detaining Power who are billeted in the same area."

Other articles spelling out obligations concerning the provision of medical services, food, clothing, opportunities for physical exercise, and contact with the outside world through letters to loved ones also assure that the conditions of detention are not such as to pressure militant detainees into providing the authorities with intelligence. Overall the Geneva-mandated POW regime is far less severe than the regime for common criminals in most prisons, certainly less severe than prisons in the United States[30] other than those set aside primarily for wealthy non-violent felons biding their time before returning to the wars of capital accumulation. Nor is it possible to evade the regime by transferring detainees to

---

[28] See generally, 1949 Geneva Convention III Relative to the Treatment of Prisoners of War [hereinafter GC III]. See also Silvia Borreli, "The Treatment of Terrorist Suspects Captured Abroad: Human Rights and Humanitarian Law," in Silvia Borreli (ed), *Enforcing International Law Norms Against Terrorism* (Oxford: Hart Publishing, 2004), 39–61.

[29] See *Miranda v Arizona*, 384 US 436, 86 S.Ct. 1602 (1966).

[30] See, eg, Jamie Fellner, "Prisoner Abuse: How Different are US Prisons?" *Human Rights Watch*, 14 May 2004, available at <http://hrw.org/english/docs/2004/05/14/usdom8583.htm>. For a European perspective, see, for instance, Bernard-Henri Lévy, *American Vertigo: Traveling in the Footsteps of Tocqueville* (New York: Random House, 2006), 23–5, 85–8, and 150–3.

the custody of governments less punctilious about observing the commandments of Geneva III. Article 12 precludes transfer to any state's authority unless the transferring state "has satisfied itself of the willingness and ability of the [receiving state] to apply the convention."

As far as one can tell, the chronology of Bush Administration responses to this dilemma was essentially as follows. Its first reaction was to declare that the Geneva Conventions did not apply to the conflict in Afghanistan because the Taliban was not a government but rather a mere faction and therefore its troops were not members of the armed forces of a High Contracting Party, to use the language of the Convention.[31] The previously mentioned Justice Department memorandum suggested, moreover, that the President could conclude that Afghanistan was a "failed state," ie that there had been a complete collapse of legitimate authority.[32] As a matter of general international law, the claim that the Taliban leaders did not constitute the government of Afghanistan was a hard position to maintain persuasively in a legal order in which historically the de facto authorities had generally been deemed to embody sovereignty for most purposes. In September of 2001 and for several years previously, the Taliban had controlled all but a small fraction of the country.[33] Moreover, it enjoyed formal recognition by Pakistan, Saudi Arabia, and the United Arab Emirates.[34]

A second difficulty for the Administration, assuming it sought a free hand in dealing with members of Al Qaeda and the Taliban, arose from Article 2 of Geneva IV, which deals with the protection of civilians.[35] It provides that "The Convention shall ... apply to all cases of partial or total occupation of the territory of a High Contracting Party" (Afghanistan was such a party). If, as the semi-official steward of the Conventions, the widely respected International Committee of the Red Cross, has concluded, all persons in occupied territory are either civilians or POWs, then if the Taliban soldiers and officials were not the latter, they were the former and that meant, according to Article 27 of the Fourth Convention, that "they are entitled to respect for their persons," that "they shall at all times be humanely treated, and shall be protected especially against all acts of violence or

[31] See footnote 15 above, at 1.
[32] Ibid, at 1: "Afghanistan was a failed state because the Taliban did not exercise full control over the territory and people, was not recognized by the international community, and was not capable of fulfilling its international obligations." But compare William H Taft, *Memorandum to John C. Yoo*, 11 January 2002, 4, available at <http://www.nytimes.com/packages/html/politics/20040608_DOC.pdf> [hereinafter the Taft Memo]: "neither the United States nor any other country has viewed Afghanistan at any point as ceasing to be a State. Neither the United States nor any other State has viewed it as ceasing to be a party to international agreements. The fact that the United States did not recognize the Taliban as the government of Afghanistan is completely irrelevant."
[33] For a concise overview of the creation and evolution of the Taliban, *see generally* "Afghanistan—Crisis of Impunity: The Role of Pakistan, Russia and Iran in Fueling the Civil War," *Human Rights Watch*, 13(3) (July 2001).
[34] Ibid, 16.
[35] 1949 Geneva Convention IV Relative to the Protection of Civilian Persons in Time of War [hereinafter GC IV].

threats thereof and against insults and public curiosity." As if that were not enough protection, the Fourth Convention Four doubles up along the lines of the Third. Article 32 state that "The High Contracting Parties specifically agree that each of them is prohibited from taking any measure of such a character as to cause the physical suffering... of protected persons in their hands. This prohibition applies not only to murder, torture, [and] corporal punishment... but also to any other measure of brutality whether applied by civilian or military agents."

In one respect, the Fourth Convention looked to be a harder legal nut to crack for the administration's purposes even than the Third, because unlike the latter, it precluded "individual or mass forcible transfers, as well as deportations of protected persons from occupied territory to the territory of the Occupying Power or to that of any other country, occupied or not, . . . regardless of motive." The only exception allowed is movement of people who get in the way of military operations under circumstances where moving them elsewhere in the territory is impossible. But persons so moved must be "transferred back...as soon as hostilities in the area in question have ceased." It is clear from the overall language of the Article that merely having conflict going on, as it still is, in some part of Afghanistan, for instance in a remote area near the Pakistan border, would not justify keeping civilians from returning to an area of the country where the ongoing conflict would not threaten their well being.

Worse yet, from the Administration's perspective, the Fourth Convention appears applicable to Al Qaeda members no less than native Afghanis. For Article 4 defines Protected Persons not as citizens or permanent residents of the occupied territory, but simply as "those who, at a given moment and in any manner whatsoever, find themselves, in case of a conflict or occupation, in the hands of a Party to the conflict or Occupying Power of which they are not nationals."

Faced with these obstacles to its ends, the Bush Administrations had two conceivable means for circumventing them. One, the one they actually chose, was to reject the ICRC dichotomy and insist that in addition to POWs, protected by the Third Convention, and civilians, protected by the Fourth, in any given conflict there may be a third category of persons: these are people who are not civilians, because they were organized combatants, but neither are they POWs because they do not satisfy the Third Convention's criteria of eligibility for POW status. Those are the criteria, the Administration claimed, set out in Article 4, paragraph A(2), namely being commanded by a person responsible for his subordinates, having a fixed distinctive sign recognizable at a distance, carrying arms openly, and conducting operations in accordance with the laws and customs of war.

Now you do not have to peruse Article 4 very carefully to detect some difficulty with this claim. The difficulty stems from the fact that the Article lists various categories of persons qualifying for POW status and the enumerated criteria apply syntactically only to persons in category 2. Category 1 consists of "Members of the armed forces of a Party to the conflict as well as members of militias or volunteer corps forming part of such armed forces." Category 2, by contrast, incorporates

"Members of other militias and members of other volunteer corps, including those of organized resistance movements, belonging to a Party to the conflict and operating in or outside their own territory, even if this territory is occupied."

Standing behind the dry lawyer's language, of course, is the profound humanitarian purpose of minimizing suffering, in part by trying to wall off the civilian population from all the killing, in part by insisting on humane treatment of combatants rendered harmless by virtue of wounds, sickness or capture. The two purposes can sometimes cross. In order to protect civilians, the laws of war try to facilitate identification of who is fighting and is therefore dangerous and who is not. If combatants attempt to blend into the general population while continuing to fight, their opponents will soon find it too dangerous to attempt to discriminate between them and the sea of humanity in which they lurk. But if the need to discriminate leads to criteria or at least interpretations of criteria tending to deprive sick, wounded, and captured combatants of POW status, those no longer dangerous ex-combatants may not survive the fury induced by the desperate passions of war.

It could be argued, and supporters of the Bush Administration have indeed argued,[36] that although the four criteria listed above appear to apply only in the case of category two persons, the appearance is deceptive. The criteria are not made explicitly applicable to members of the regular armed forces, so the argument goes, because the drafters naturally assumed that such forces, virtually by definition, would satisfy them, ie would wear distinctive uniforms, carry arms openly, and be members of hierarchically organized units integrated into armed forces that in general comply with the laws and customs of war. Resistance movements, conversely, might be expected in the generality of cases not to comply with the criteria. In particular, they were likely to conduct operations clandestinely and attempt to use the civilian population as a kind of camouflage. Thus what paragraph 2 attempted to do was provide them with incentives to act like regular army units and thereby to protect the civilian population by distinguishing themselves from it.

While not entirely without persuasive force, the argument is far from conclusive and as further elaborated by lawyers inside the Administration it became not stronger but frailer. The units of a regular army engaged in large-scale combat, armed with rockets and cannon, are pretty easy to distinguish from the general population whether or not they wear uniforms. Thus, in the case of regular forces, the deep instrumental goal of achieving visible differentiation from the civilian

---

[36] See, eg, James Terry, "Al Qaeda and Taliban Detainees: An Examination of Legal Rights and Appropriate Treatment," in Fred L Borch and Paul S Wilson (eds), *Terrorism and the Military: International Legal Implications* (Newport, Rhode Island: Naval War College, 2003), 441–54. See also David B Rivkin, Jr and Lee A Casey, "Unleashing the Dogs of War," *The National Interest*, 73 (Fall 2003), 57–69. Rivkin and Casey assert that "many who have promoted a 'lawful' status for irregular combatants have done so in an effort to bring them 'within the system,' in the hope that, once privileged, guerrillas would behave better in their own operations. It has not, unfortunately, worked out that way."

population does not require full compliance with the four criteria. Uniforms are costly and may not be as well adapted to environmental conditions as traditional dress. Is POW status to be denied to regular units fighting openly simply because the authorities had decided to spend money on arms rather than clothes? Is it consistent with the values behind humanitarian law that such regular forces be subject to trial and punishment for fighting at the direction of the constituted authorities of their state? That could be the result of the denial of POW status. After all, only regular combatants, only combatants that can qualify for POW status, are immunized from punishment for killing their opponents.[37]

Ironically, the interpretation of Article 4 proposed by the Bush Administration and its defenders would result in POW protection being denied regular forces for failing to wear uniforms or some other distinctive sign like, I suppose, some sort of warlike headgear, perhaps something with a nice long spike on it or a skull or a great horse-tail plume such as one sees warriors wearing on ancient Greek pots, while what the French call the *levée en masse* and what Article 4 describes as "inhabitants of a non-occupied territory, who on the approach of the enemy spontaneously take up arms, without having had time to form themselves into regular armed units" are able to obtain POW status as long as they do nothing more than what Taliban and Al Qaeda forces did at the time of the US-led invasion, namely to carry arms openly. Well, they must, in fact, do one thing more, which is to "respect the laws and customs of war." So if, for example, they habitually slaughter all the troops they capture, they do not qualify.

Should at least these two criteria be read into paragraph 1 of Article 4, so they would apply to regular units of the armed forces? Not necessarily. Again I note the distinction between regular forces, under most circumstances easily differentiated from the general population, and little clusters of peasants or militant urban youths rising spontaneously to defend their turf that probably will not be readily distinguishable to an invading force from their more passive or at least cautious neighbors.

But would it not serve the purposes of humanitarian law if we at least insisted that regular units comply with the laws and customs of war if they hope to obtain POW status? Not necessarily. In a large-scale conflict, some individuals and possibly whole units on each side may commit grave breaches, giving no quarter, killing prisoners when they become burdensome, or torturing them for information or pleasure. Determining whether the delinquencies of some units should be imputed to all can be a complicated question, one unlikely to be resolved in favor of the captured in the middle of a bloody war. Arguably more humane outcomes will result from a bright-line rule that imputes POW status to all regular forces and then with due deliberation the captors can single out for prosecution

---

[37] See Jordan J Paust, "Detention and Due Process Under International Law," *Terrorism and the Military*, Heere (ed), 187–8: "members of the armed forces of the Taliban (and perhaps members of Al Qaeda units attached to the Taliban) would have combat immunity for otherwise lawful acts of warfare."

those individuals who have committed grave breaches, for they are most certainly not immunized by POW status from severe punishment.

If the Convention is read literally, that is if it is read as I have proposed, then on the further assumption that the Taliban was the de facto government of Afghanistan at the time the United States intervened, all members of the armed forces of the Taliban captured before a new government was formed should have received POW status. And arguably so should residents of other countries fighting alongside the Taliban troops, the so-called Al Qaeda forces, if they were operationally integrated into the Taliban army battling with United States and Northern Alliance troops. On that factual assumption, they would fall within the Article 4, paragraph 1 sub-category of a "volunteer corps forming part of [the Party's] armed forces." If the actual degree of operational integration was unclear for individuals if not for entire units, as I think it was, then under Article 5 of the Third Convention, the United States was obligated insofar as foreign fighters were concerned to place the POW issue before what the Convention calls a "competent tribunal" which would then determine, presumably on a case-by-case basis (since some foreigners may have been integrated while others may have fought in units that took their orders entirely from the Al Qaeda leaders and constituted, in effect, a separate albeit allied force).

In the event foreign combatants were not integrated, then they would indeed fall in category two of Article 4 and therefore would be properly denied POW status if, as it appears from the published facts, they did not satisfy each of the four criteria the Bush Administration applied to the Taliban and Al Qaeda alike. During the Vietnam War, the United States had frequently employed Article 5 military tribunals to resolve POW-status issues.[38] They were not employed in Afghanistan or, initially, in Guantánamo when some persons in Afghanistan were transferred there. But following the decision of the US Supreme Court in *Hamdi v United States*[39] rejecting the Bush Administration's claim that persons held in Guantánamo were beyond the reach of the American Constitution and outside the jurisdiction of US courts, the Administration established a cursory procedure for conducting status reviews of Guantánamo detainees which, it claimed, could substitute for habeas corpus review and should be so regarded by the federal courts. I will have more to say below about this procedure.

Despite the very arguable legal differences between Taliban and Al Qaeda forces, initially the Bush Administration treated them as legally indistinguishable and uniformly ineligible for POW treatment. Article 5 status determinations were

---

[38] The *Taft Memo*, 22–5. Note that at the time of the 9/11 attacks, the US military continued to utilize art 5 Tribunals for determining POW-status; this practice was abandoned *after* 9/11 because of conflicting and confusing directives issued by the Bush Administration. See US Army, *Operational Law Handbook*, International and Operational Law Department, The Judge Advocate General's School, US Army, Charlottesville, Virginia, 15 June 2001, 16. See also "DoD Enemy POW Detainee Program," DoD Directive 3115.09, 3 November 2005, available at <http://www.cdi.org/news/law/DoD-Directive-3115_09.pdf >.

[39] 542 US 507 (2004).

unnecessary, Administration officials insisted, because the status issue was not in doubt.[40] Among the reasons cited for the supposedly indisputable ineligibility of the Taliban was that, like Al Qaeda, they had failed to conduct their operations in accordance with the laws and customs of war.[41] But the evidence cited in support of that proposition was Al Qaeda's destruction of the World Trade Center. Now if a hugely destructive act perpetrated by a non-governmental organization can, consistent with generally held views about international law, be deemed an act of war, then the denial of POW status to Al Qaeda members does not seem unreasonable; for it seems fair to presume that members of Al Qaeda knew the organization was prepared to employ for its ends indiscriminate attacks on civilian targets. What is somewhat more debatable is whether the Taliban armed forces as a whole should be deemed either to have colluded in or endorsed the terror attack.

When it received the US demand following 9/11 to surrender bin Laden, the regime had asked for proof that he had ordered the attack, implying that if such proof were forthcoming, they would then feel justified in turning him over.[42] That would seem to have been an acknowledgment of the criminality rather than an endorsement of the attack. In light of the assistance, bin Laden, along with the United States, had rendered to the Afghan resistance in the struggle against the Soviet occupation[43] and his subsequent financial and military assistance to the Taliban in its efforts to take over the country,[44] the Taliban might have allowed bin Laden to use the country as a haven not to express support for his jihad against the United States, but rather out of a sense of obligation for services previously rendered and a sense of need for continuing financial and military support. These possible motives were irrelevant to the question of whether the United States was entitled to intervene militarily following the failure of the Taliban to extradite bin Laden and to incarcerate or expel his entire organization. I, myself, believe it was so entitled. They are relevant, however, to the question of whether for purposes of POW status determination, the Taliban were contaminated by Al Qaeda's targeting of civilians.

I referred earlier to the Bush Administration having two options for evading the grant of POW status to Taliban and Al Qaeda combatants or, alternatively, recognizing them as civilians in Occupied Territory and hence protected by the Fourth Convention. The second option for the Bush Administration was to say as little as possible about the Conventions and avoid acts that would be widely seen

---

[40] See especially Jay S Bybee, *Memorandum for Alberto R. Gonzalez, Re: Status of Taliban Forces Under Article 4 of the Third Geneva Convention of 1949*, 7 February 2002, available at <http://www. washingtonpost.com/wp-srv/nation/documents/012202bybee.pdf>. See also Danner, 96–104.

[41] Ibid, at 3–5. But compare the *Taft Memo*, 20–1.

[42] See, eg, John F Burns, "A Nation Challenged: Last Chance; Taliban Refuse Quick Decision over bin Laden," *The New York Times*, 18 September 2001, A1.

[43] See generally, Michael Griffin, *Reaping the Whirlwind: Afghanistan, Al Qa'ida and the Holy War* (London: Pluto Press, 2003).

[44] See generally, Amalendu Misra, *Afghanistan: The Labyrinth of Violence* (Cambridge, UK: Polity Press, 2004).

as flagrant violations pending the establishment of a friendly, widely recognized government in Kabul. If, at that point, Al Qaeda and Taliban units still survived in remote parts of the country, the United States and its new partner in Kabul could argue either that the conflict was an internal one governed by the minimalist provisions of Common Article 3 of the Geneva Conventions which has no provision for POW status or, better yet, that the level of conflict was so low that it did not cross even the Article 3 threshold to become an armed conflict not of an international character.[45] In other words, the holdout units of the Taliban and Al Qaeda would be treated as if they were mere bandits, a criminal element to be handled through domestic policing activities. Geneva Law would not then inhibit, for instance, the transfer of prisoners by the government of the sovereign nation of Afghanistan to such places as its good friends in the District of Columbia might suggest including an old naval coaling station in Cuba. It might do so on the grounds that Afghanistan lacked a functioning judicial system and/or a prison system that remotely satisfied the implied requirements of the Covenant on Civil and Political Rights, particularly if they were construed to coincide with the UN Declaration on Minimum Conditions of Detention. "Only by transferring these poor detainees to detention centers established by our well organized and affluent American friends," the government in Kabul might have said, "can we comply, as we wish to, with human rights standards." In addition, some persons could be quietly renditioned to other countries with long experience in inducing the initially mute to speak.

But this option had tactical as well as its own legal problems. The tactical one was the imperative of collecting operational intelligence as quickly as possible in a protected environment ideally organized to that end and far from scrutiny by journalists and other nuisances like the presumably over-sensitive employees of international humanitarian NGOs who for purposes of helping in the restoration of a semblance of order in Afghanistan were useful. They would not be needed in Guantánamo. It is now well established that very coercive interrogations were conducted in Afghanistan by US personnel, including CIA agents, private contractors and, possibly, military intelligence.[46] It is now conceded that a number of deaths resulted from the rigor of these inquiries.[47]

But brute force alone could not compete in efficacy, one assumes, with force applied in conditions of total isolation and utter strangeness, conditions where the authorities enjoyed complete control over every moment of life and could at an instant shift prisoners from conditions of physical and mental agony to rather

[45] See generally, Tom J Farer, "Humanitarian Law and Armed Conflicts: Toward the Definition of International Armed Conflict," *Columbia Law Review*, 71(1) (January 1971).

[46] See generally, "'Enduring Freedom-Abuses' by US Forces in Afghanistan," *Human Rights Watch*, 16(3) (March 2004). See also Douglas Jehl and Tim Golden, "C.I.A. is Likely to Avoid Charges in Most Prisoner Deaths," *The New York Times*, 23 October 2005, A6.

[47] "Enduring Freedom," 43–4. See also Carlotta Gall, "US Military Investigating Death of Afghan in Custody," *The New York Times*, 4 March 2003, A14.

pleasant ones and then back again. Moreover, there were hundreds of persons whom the United States wanted to interrogate, not mere dozens. So the Defense Department and other agencies would have presumably balked at suggestions that they move no one until there was a friendly recognized government in Kabul. Moreover, that government might not be entirely compliant. For it would be eager to use carrots as well as sticks to legitimize itself. Sending dozens perhaps hundreds of Afghani nationals abroad at the request of the United States, appearing, in other words, as a mere instrument deployed by the United States to work its will, might not seem to any Afghan government to serve its interests.

The legal problem was that the level of conflict with Taliban and Al Qaeda supporters might remain for some time at a sufficiently high level that denying the applicability of Common Article 3 of the Geneva Conventions on the theory that there was no continuing armed conflict would not have passed the global laugh test. Conceding that it did apply would be inhibiting in light of the following language:

In the case of an armed conflict not of an international character...the following acts are and shall remain prohibited at any time and in any place whatsoever with respect to [persons taking no active part in the hostilities, including members of armed forces who have laid down their arms and those placed hors de combat by sickness, wounds, detention or any other cause] (a) violence to life and person, in particular murder of all kinds, mutilation, cruel treatment and torture;...(c) outrages upon personal dignity, in particular, humiliating and degrading treatment and (d) the passing of sentences and the carrying out of executions without previous judgment pronounced by a regularly constituted court affording all the judicial guarantees which are recognized as indispensable by civilized peoples.

We may never know, but perhaps it appeared to persons in the Justice Department, the Pentagon or the National Security Council, or all three, that they stood on firmer ground by sticking with their initial position which was, you will recall, that Al Qaeda and Taliban fighters fell into the category of "unlawful combatant" and therefore enjoyed none of the protections offered by the Third and the Fourth Conventions respectively to POWs and Civilians in Occupied Territory. Had I been present at the very high level meetings where these matters must have been discussed at some point, I would have argued that assuming there are persons who do not fall into either the POW or the civilian-in-occupied-territory categories, they are still beneficiaries of the Article 3 prohibitions. And while those prohibitions do not prevent transfer of persons to other countries, they do preclude application of the whole repertory of techniques designed to subvert interrogated persons' egos, indeed their capacity to remain agents of their own will. For what no honest person could possibly argue is that Article 3 is limited in its relevance to civil conflicts, a view of the matter subsequently endorsed by the US Supreme Court in *Hamdan v Rumsfeld*.[48]

[48] 126 S. Ct. 2749 (2006).

3. Liberal Values and the Temptation to Torture

There can be no legitimate dispute about the proposition that Article 3 is a summary of the core elements of the Conventions, the elements designed to inject a minimum of humanity into the awful business of war, the elements without which war becomes a struggle among rabid beasts. In 1949 most states were unwilling to treat persons who took up arms against the constituted authorities as prisoners-of-war.[49] They wanted the option of treating them as criminals. Article 3 summarizes what minimal part of the Four Conventions they were willing to accept as inhibiting their choice of means. This minimum did not come from beyond the rest of the Four Conventions; it clearly came from the Conventions themselves. It is striking, and suggestive of how basic are the Article 3 prohibitions, how inseparable they are from the essence of the Geneva Conventions, that they correspond so closely to the substance of the idea of Crimes Against Humanity[50] as the activator of legitimate intervention and international criminal liability, concepts that have ripped holes in the definition of national sovereignty that prevailed at least until the end of the Second World War and the Nuremberg Trials.

From what the public record reveals to this point, it appears that international human rights law penetrated Bush Administration consciousness barely if at all, with one exception, namely the Torture Convention[51] and probably that Convention only because, unlike other human rights treaties, it had been indisputably integrated into domestic law by an act of Congress.[52] The seeming indifference to other human rights agreements including the fountainhead Civil and Political Rights Covenant was consistent with the President's later decision

---

[49] See Michael Bothe, *et al.*, *New Rules for Victims of Armed Conflicts* (The Hague: Martinus Nijhoff Publishers, 1982), 2–10. See also Elizabeth Chadwick, *Self-Determination, Terrorism and the International Humanitarian Law of Armed Conflict* (The Hague: Martinus Nijhoff Publishers, 1997), 80–5.

[50] Donald W Wells, *War Crimes and Laws of War*, 2nd edn (Lanham, Maryland: University Press of America, 1984), 114; quoting from "Nuremberg Trial Proceedings Vol.1: Charter of the International Military Tribunal." Section II, art 6, 8 August 1945, available at <http://www.yale.edu/lawweb/avalon/imt/proc/imtconst.htm>. Article 6 defines "Crimes Against Humanity" as: "namely, murder, extermination, enslavement, deportation, and other inhumane acts committed against any civilian population, before or during the war; or persecutions on political, racial or religious grounds in execution of or in connection with any crime within the jurisdiction of the Tribunal, whether or not in violation of the domestic law of the country where perpetrated."

[51] Convention Against Torture and Other Cruel, Inhuman or Degrading Treatment or Punishment. GA Res. 39/46, Annex, 39 GAOR UN Supp. No. 51, UN Doc. A/39/51 (1984). The Convention was introduced on 10 December 1984, and entered into force on 26 June 1987. See also generally, Nigel S Rodley, *The Treatment of Prisoners Under International Law*, 2nd edn (Oxford: Oxford University Press, 1999).

[52] See S EN. EXEC. RPT. 101–30, Resolution of Advice and Consent to Ratification (1990). See also Michael John Garcia, ACRS Report RL32438. UN Convention Against Torture (CAT): "Overview and Application to Interrogation Techniques," *Congressional Research Service—The Library of Congress*, 16 June 2004, available at <www.fas.org/irp/crs/RL32438.pdf>.

to appoint as the principal US representative at the United Nations a man who has declared that international agreements, although purporting to be constitutive of law, are actually no more than political understandings.[53] It of course follows from this view that compliance or non-compliance is entirely a matter of national interest calculation and dishonoring such commitments carries with it no moral stain. More importantly, it is consistent with a view commonplace on the American Right to the effect that international law in the age of American hegemony is little more than a stratagem of weaker states to constrain American power.[54]

In relevant part, the Convention Against Torture and Other Cruel, Inhuman or Degrading Treatment or Punishment defines "torture" as:

> any act by which severe pain or suffering, whether physical or mental, is intentionally inflicted on a person for such purposes as obtaining from him or a third person information or a confession … when such pain or suffering is inflicted by or at the instigation of or with the consent or acquiescence of a public official or other person acting in an official capacity.[55]

Consistent with the human rights Covenant, it provides that "No exceptional circumstances whatsoever, whether a state of war or a threat of war, internal political instability or any other public emergency, may be invoked as a justification of torture."[56] And it forecloses the evasive practice of rendition of persons to other jurisdictions by prohibiting extradition of a person "to another State where there are substantial grounds for believing that he would be in danger of being subjected to torture."[57] Also strikingly relevant is Article 11's requirement that "Each State Party shall keep under systematic review interrogation rules, instructions, methods and practices as well as arrangements for the custody and treatment of persons subjected to any form of arrest, detention or imprisonment in any territory under its jurisdiction, with a view to preventing any cases of torture." While not defining acts of cruel, inhuman, and degrading treatment which do not amount to torture, the Treaty says that all of the provisions in it relating to torture are also intended to cover such acts.

---

[53] John R Bolton, "US Isn't Legally Obligated to Pay the UN" *The Wall Street Journal*, 17 November 1997, A27. See also Bolton, "The Risks and Weaknesses of the International Criminal Court from America's Perspective," *Law and Contemporary Problems*, 64(1) (Winter 2001).

[54] James P Lucier, "Just What is a War Criminal?" *Insight on the News*, 2 August 1999, 3, quoting John Bolton: "It is a big mistake for us to grant any validity to international law even when it may seem in our short-term interest to do so—because, over the long term, the goal of those who think that international law really means anything are those who want to constrict the United States." See also generally, Tom J Farer, "Human Rights and the Neo-Conservative Project: What's Not to Like?" *Human Rights and Human Welfare—Working Papers*, Graduate School of International Studies, University of Denver, 4 May 2004, available at <http://www.du.edu/gsis/hrhw/working/2004/20-farer-2004.pdf>.

[55] Convention Against Torture, art 1.

[56] Ibid, art 2, para 2.

[57] Ibid, art 3.

The US criminal statute executing this Treaty deals only with torture. The State Department Legal Advisor at the time of the legislation attributes the omission from the statute of any reference to cruel, inhuman and degrading acts to the reservation relating to such methods filed by the United States at the time it ratified the Torture Convention.[58] Pursuant to the reservation, for purposes of US obligations under the treaty, those acts shall be defined by decisions of US Courts interpreting the Eighth Amendment to the US Constitution, which prohibits cruel and unusual punishment. Violations of the Eighth Amendment in itself or as made applicable to the individual states by the Fourteenth Amendment of the Constitution, were already subject to civil and criminal penalties. The Administration of the time wanted to avoid being bound by expansive notions of cruel, inhuman, and degrading behavior that might evolve through the practice of other states and render illegal behavior otherwise allowed under US law.[59]

The first formal statement of the Bush Administration's interpretation of the Torture Convention as incorporated into American law is contained in a memorandum addressed to the President's Counsel by the Department of Justice. It defines torture as:

Physical pain . . . equivalent in intensity to the pain accompanying serious physical injury, such as organ failure, impairment of bodily functions, or even death. For purely mental pain or suffering to amount to torture . . . it must result in significant psychological harm of significant duration, e.g. last for months or even years. [In sum], we conclude that the statute, taken as a whole, makes plain that it prohibits only extreme acts.[60]

Furthermore, according to the memorandum, insofar as criminal liability is concerned, officials are vulnerable only if it could be shown that they intended to inflict severe pain.[61] For conviction, it would not be sufficient that the officials acted "knowing that severe pain or suffering was reasonably likely [to result],"

[58] See generally, Abraham D Sofaer, "Letter to Senator Patrick Leahy," 21 January 2005, 2, available at <http://www.humanrightsfirst.org/us_law/etn/pdf/sofaer-leahy-cat-art16–093005.pdf>.

[59] Ibid, 2–3.

[60] See Jay S Bybee, *Re: Standards of Conduct for Interrogation under 18 US C 2340–2340A*, 1 August 2002, 2–3, available at <http://www.washingtonpost.com/wpsrv/nation/documents/dojinterrogationmemo20020801.pdf>. But compare Jerome Slater, "Should We Try to Regulate and Control Torture?" *Political Science Quarterly*, 121(2) (Summer, 2006), 195: "after severe criticism, the Justice Department formally retreated from the Bybee memorandum in late 2004; the Bush Administration now officially accepts that any 'severe' physical and mental pain and suffering constitutes torture and is therefore prohibited by US as well as international law."

[61] Bybee, *Re: Standards of Conduct for Interrogation under 18 US C 2340–2340A*, 39–46. Bybee devotes considerable time to the issue of "avoiding liability" for sanctioning highly aggressive interrogation techniques that, arguably, constitute torture: "we believe that under current circumstances, certain justification defenses might be available that would potentially eliminate criminal liability. Standard criminal law defense of necessity and self-defense could justify interrogation methods needed to elicit information to prevent a direct and imminent threat to the United States and its citizens." See also Jane Mayer, "A Deadly Interrogation: Can the CIA Legally Kill a Prisoner?" *The New Yorker*, 14 November 2005, 46. According to Mayer, "a source familiar with the memo's origins, who declined to speak on the record said it 'was written as an immunity, a blank check'."

for in that event they would have acted only with general intent rather than the specific intent called for by the statute. Under this construction such tactics as the removal of teeth by means of hammers and the extraction of finger and toe nails might be found merely cruel and inhuman in that they were not akin to acts producing organ failure or the impairment of bodily functions and therefore could be presumed not to cause the threshold intensity of pain. After all, as long as some teeth remain, a chap can eat; indeed with implants he can ultimately be as good as new, after a time. As for feet without nails, they can still be made to walk, however painfully.

From credible press reports, it is apparent that most military lawyers strongly opposed the conclusions of the memorandum, in part because they in effect licensed behavior clearly prohibited by the rules and regulations of the US armed forces.[62] When the memorandum was leaked to the press, it became the subject of widespread denunciation by human rights and civil liberties groups, by leading newspapers and by many independent legal experts. The Administration has denied ever acting on the basis of the definition of torture contained in the memorandum[63] and it has since nominally repudiated the definition's narrowness,[64] although it has never specified where it wants the line to be drawn and opposed the legislation that lay down binding limits on interrogation.[65] Nor has it repudiated perhaps the most controversial aspect of the memorandum, namely its claim that in time of war, the President as Commander-in-Chief under the Constitution can override Acts of Congress and international law and treaties incorporated by Congress into US law if, in his or her judgment, that is necessary for the effective prosecution of the conflict.[66]

---

[62] See Lisa Hajjar, "An Army of Lawyers: JAGs and Radicals Join Forces." *The Nation*, 281(22) (26 December 2005), 41. See also Charlie Savage and Bryan Bender, "Policy Rift Seen on Detainees," *The Boston Globe*, 24 June 2004, A1.

[63] *See* Kames G Lakely, " 'Values' Guided Bush Torture Ban," *The Washington Post*, 23 June 2004, A01. See also George W Bush, *Memorandum on the Humane Treatment of al Qaeda and Taliban Detainees*, 7 February 2002, available at <http://www.gwu.edu/~nsarchiv/NSAEBB/NSAEBB127/02.02.07.pdf>.

[64] *See* Bybee, *Re: Standards of Conduct for Interrogation under 18 US C 2340–2340A*; and *Re: Status of Taliban Forces Under Article 4 of the Third Geneva Convention of 1949*. But compare especially the Taft Memo. In his recently published book *War by Other Means: An Insider's Account of the War on Terror* (New York: Atlantic Monthly Press 2006), Yoo writes that the second memorandum, notionally repudiating the first (written largely by Yoo) was an "'exercise in political image-making'... [which] included a footnote to say that all interrogation methods that earlier opinions had said were legal were still legal." See Michiko Kakutani's review, "An Insider's Account of the War on Terror," *New York Times*, 31 October 2006, E1.

[65] See "Global Agenda: Bush Arm-Twisted Into a Torture Ban," *The Economist*, 16 December 2005. But compare Charlie Savage, "Bush Could Bypass New Torture Ban," *The Boston Globe*, 4 January 2006, A1.

[66] See generally, John Yoo, *The Powers of War and Peace: The Constitution and Foreign Affairs After 9/11* (Chicago: University of Chicago Press, 2005). See also Joel Whitney, "The Devils Advocate: An Interview with John Yoo," *Guernica Magazine*, December 2005, available at <http://www.guernicamag.com/interviews/102/the_devils_advocate/>.

In large measure, the President himself has stuck to his original script, insisting that persons captured in Afghanistan are not POWs but have been, in general, humanely treated and will continue to be so treated, consistent, however, with military necessity.[67] The positions of the Defense Department and the American armed forces have been more fluid. However, on 6 September 2006, the Department in effect repudiated several tactics of interrogation hitherto employed by specifically forbidding US troops from using forced nudity, hooding, stress positions, military dogs, and water-boarding to elicit information from detainees.[68] The new interrogation policies were incorporated in a revised Army field manual. The manual and the related Pentagon directive stated that US forces must adhere to the standards of the Geneva Convention's Common Article 3 and that its standards would apply to unlawful combatants including persons linked to non-state organizations like Al Qaeda. "The new policies also eliminate the...practice of hiding detainees—sometimes call 'ghosting'—and requires anyone operating in a Defense Department facility to follow the...new regulations."[69] On the same day, President Bush announced that, on the one hand, he was transferring to Guantánamo 14 top-level terrorism suspects from the secret prisons where they had been held, and, on the other, that the CIA's use of secret prisons around the globe needed to continue.[70]

Since the exposure of conditions in Abu Ghraib and subsequent revelations of deaths under interrogation in Afghanistan itself, together with other associated embarrassments, the Secretary of Defense and the Joint Chiefs of Staff have launched a number of inquiries into practices in the field which, taken collectively, confirm what the authors of the various reports, in most cases serving officers, themselves describe as indefensible behavior.[71] The so-called Schlesinger inquiry[72] conducted by a group led by former Secretary of Defense James Schlesinger, concluded, among other things, that as of the time of the report, there had been 28

[67] See, eg, "President Hosts United States—European Union Summit," *The White House*, 20 June 2005, available at <http://www.whitehouse.gov/news/releases/2005/06/20050620–19.html>. But compare "Amnesty International Report 2005," *Amnesty International*, 25 May 2005, available at <http://web.amnesty.org/report2005/index-eng>.

[68] Josh White, "New Rules of Interrogation Forbid Use of Harsh Tactics," *Washington Post*, 7 September 2006, 1.

[69] Ibid.

[70] Ibid.

[71] See, eg, LTG Anthony R Jones and MG George R Fay, "AR 15–6: Investigation of the Abu Ghraib Prison and the 205th Military Intelligence Brigade," 23 August 2004, available at <http://www.defenselink.mil/news/Aug2004/d20040825fay.pdf> [hereinafter the Jones-Fay Report].

[72] "Final Report of the Independent Panel to Review DoD Detention Operations," *Independent Panel to Review DoD Detention Operations*, August, 2004, available at <http://www.defenselink.mil/news/Aug2004/d20040824finalreport.pdf> [hereinafter the Schlesinger Report]. But compare "Getting to Ground Truth: Investigating US Abuses in the 'War on Terror'," *Human Rights First*, September, 2004, available at <http://www.humanrightsfirst.org/us_law/PDF/detainees/Getting_to_Ground_Truth_090804.pdf>. The report criticizes the Schlesinger Report (and other official investigations), claiming several critical "gaps" exist in the methodology used and conclusions reached, thus preventing a full understanding of what went wrong and who is to blame.

deaths among detainees, that 23 were still under investigation, and five had been determined to have resulted from abuse by US personnel during interrogations. Anonymous sources within the US Government have stated that agents of the Federal Bureau of Investigation, the institution closest in character to European domestic intelligence agencies, were deeply disturbed by the practices they observed in Guantánamo.[73] The ICRC, breaking with its practice of avoiding public comment in order to maintain access to detainees, has expressed public concern about practices in Guantánamo, Afghanistan, and Iraq and about the failure of the United States to register with it a significant number of detainees who have therefore been in an entirely unsupervised limbo.[74] The exact number of persons not registered with the ICRC is unknown. It is believed that they are held in various places around Afghanistan, in the Persian Gulf, on the remote Indian Ocean island of Diego Garcia, and possibly in one or more Central Asian countries.[75] At one point, unregistered persons were held in Iraq also.[76] Whether that remains the case is not known. Nor is it known how many persons have been turned over to governments generally conceded to use torture for purposes of interrogation.

The lack of clear guidelines was seen as one source of the delinquencies the various reports identify.[77] None of the reports consider the possible command responsibility of the Joint Chiefs of Staff, the Secretary of Defense, or the President. All the guidelines including the most recent revisions thereof apply to Defense Department personnel. Those guiding CIA interrogators remain confidential.[78]

---

[73] See, eg, Dan Eggen and R Jeffrey Smith, "FBI Agents Allege Abuse of Detainees at Guantánamo Bay." *The Washington Post*, 4 December 2001, A1. See also FBI records regarding torture at Guantánamo obtained by the ACLU per the FOIA, available at <http://www.aclu.org/torturefoia/released/052505/>.

[74] See Neil A Lewis, "Red Cross Finds Detainee Abuse at Guantánamo," *The New York Times*, 30 November 2004, A1. But compare "News Transcript: Special Defense Department Briefing on the International Committee of The Red Cross's Report on Detainees," *United States Department of Defense*, 16 July 2004, available at <http://www.defenselink.mil/transcripts/2004/tr20040716–1005.html>.

[75] See, eg, "Global Agenda: So, What's All the Fuss?" *The Economist*, 17 December 2005. See also Jane Meyer, "The Outsourcing of Torture," *The New Yorker*, 14 February 2005, 106.

[76] See, eg, Josh White, "Army Documents Shed Light on CIA 'Ghosting,'" *The Washington Times*, 24 March 2005, A15. See also David Morgan, "Pentagon Moves to Bar CIA 'Ghost' Detainees." *Reuters*, 28 April 2005, available at <http://www.abc.net.au/news/newsitems/200504/s1355978.htm>.

[77] Mayer, "A Deadly Interrogation," 47: "As a result of these contradictory mandates from Washington, the rules of engagement at Abu Ghraib became increasingly muddy, and the tactics grew increasingly ad hoc. Jeffrey H. Smith, former general-counsel of the CIA told me, 'Abu Ghraib has its roots at the top. I think this uncertainty about who was and who was not covered by the Geneva Conventions, and all this talk that they're all terrorists, bred the climate in which this kind of abuse takes place.'"

[78] Ibid, 47. Mayer discusses the confusion at Abu Ghraib over proper interrogation methods caused by having CIA operatives working side-by-side with military personnel, but following different, usually unknown, rules and regulations. See also "ACLU Challenges CIA Refusal to Admit Existence of Presidential Order on Detention Facilities Abroad,"

In order to give some flavor of what has been going on, let me cite verbatim from the internal Defense Department Report conducted by serving generals Anthony Jones and George Fay.

In October 2003, DETAINEE-07, reported alleged multiple incidents of physical abuse while in Abu Ghraib... He was interrogated on 8, 21 and 29 October; 4 and 23 November and 5 December. Detainee-07's claims of physical abuse (hitting) started on his first day of arrival. He was left naked in his cell for extended periods, cuffed in his cell in stressful positions ('High cuffed'), left with a bag over his head for extended periods, and denied bedding or blankets. Detainee-07 described being made to bark like a dog, being forced to crawl on his stomach while MPs spit and urinated on him, and being struck causing unconsciousness.
On another occasion DETAINEE-07 was forced to lie down while Military Police jumped onto his back and legs. He was beaten with a broom and a chemical light was broken and poured over his body... a police stick was used to sodomize [him] ... [He was hit in the ear and cut, requiring stitches.] The high cuffing, a standard stress position, led to the skin of his hand splitting and oozing pus.[79]

After describing this treatment, the report reviews the evidence and concludes that "it is highly probable DETAINEE-07's allegations are true."[80] You will note that this occurred in Iraq, not Guantánamo, in Iraq where according to official policy, the Geneva Conventions were applicable from the outset of the invasion.[81]

In government documents and testimony and in the discourse of intelligence professionals a distinction is frequently drawn between what is conceded to be torture and lesser coercive methods which, depending on the speaker or organization, are called such things as "highly coercive interrogation," "counter resistance strategies," or in the words of the former Director of the CIA, former Congressman Porter Goss, "professional interrogation techniques."[82] More colloquially they are described as "torture lite".[83] Among the techniques listed by Director Goss as falling in the category of "professional interrogation techniques"

American Civil Liberties Union, 12 December 2002, available at <http://www.aclu.org/natsec/emergpowers/22610prs20051212.html>.

[79] Jones-Fay Report, 74–5.

[80] Ibid, 75.

[81] See, eg, Eric Schmitt and Carolyn Marshall, "In Secret Unit's 'Black Room,' a Grim Portrait of US Abuse," *The New York Times*, 19 March 2006, 1. Schmitt and Marshall uncovered similar abuses occurring at Camp Zama, also in Baghdad, from the summer of 2003 to the summer of 2004. See also Human Rights Watch, "Leadership Failure: Firsthand Accounts of Torture of Iraqi Detainees by the US Army's 82nd Airborne Division," *Human Rights Watch*, 17(3) (September 2005), available at <http://www.hrw.org/reports/2005/us0905/>.

[82] See "CIA Whitewashing Torture: Statements by Goss Contradict US Law and Practice," *Human Rights Watch*, 21 November 2005, available at <http://hrw.org/english/docs/2005/11/21/usdom12069.htm>. But compare Deborah Pearlstein, "Laws of Gravity: When the Law Sanctions Torture-Lite, the Real Thing Always Follows," *The American Prospect, Online Edition*, 24 February 2005, available at <http://www.prospect.org/web/page.ww?section'root&name'ViewWeb&articleId'9239>.

[83] Mayer, "A Deadly Interrogation," 46. See also Mark Bowden, "The Dark Art of Interrogation," *The Atlantic Monthly*, 292(3) (October 2003), 4.

is water-boarding or repeatedly simulated drowning.[84] Latin American torturers in countries that were subjects of investigation by the Inter-American Commission on Human Rights, when I was a member in the late 1970s and early 1980s, sometimes achieved equivalent effects by encasing a victim's head in a plastic sack which was then twisted shut.

Waterboarding in one form or another is an old technique, one used along with electric shock by military interrogators in Algeria and sometimes in Paris too during its war of independence. Here is the account of a 31-year-old Algerian interrogated in Paris in 1958:

I was taken off the bar [on which he had been hung and subjected to electric shock] and my guards started their football again [beating and kicking him], perhaps for a quarter of an hour. Then they led me, still naked and blindfolded, into a neighboring room... Then they laid me on a bench, flat on my stomach, head extending into the air, and tied my arms against my body with cords. Again the same question, which I refused to answer. By tilting the bench very slowly, they dipped my head into a basin filled with stinking liquid—dirty water and urine, probably.

I was aware of the gurgling liquid reaching my mouth, then of a dull rumbling in my ears and a tingling sensation in my nose.

'You asked for a drink—take all you want.' they said. The first time I did drink, trying to appease an insupportable thirst. I wanted to vomit immediately. 'He's puking, the bastard,' [one of them shouted]. And my head was pushed back into the basin... From time to time one of them would sit on my back and bear down on my thighs. I could hear the water I threw up fall back into the basin. Then the torture would continue.[85]

Here is the account of Irina Martinez, an Argentine student activist, who was arrested at her parents' house in Buenos Aires in 1977. She was immediately blindfolded. Her first torture session was in a basement full of soldiers, where she was stripped naked, tied, and beaten.

'They slapped my face, pinched my breasts. "You have to talk, this is your last opportunity, and this is your salvation." And then they put me on a table. And I thought, Well, if they are going to kill me, I hope they kill me pretty soon. They pushed my head underwater, so I could not breathe. They take you out, ask you things, they put you in, they take you out—so you cannot breathe all the time. "Who did you receive this from? Who do you know?" Who can control anything when you cannot breathe? They pull you out, you try to grab for air, so they put you back in so you swallow water, and it is winter and you are very cold and very scared and they do that for a long time. Even if you are a good swimmer you cannot stand it anymore.'[86]

[84] See, eg, Nat Hentoff, "The CIA's Kidnapping Ring," *The Village Voice*, 26 April 2005, 28. See also Brian Ross, "A History of an Interrogation Technique: Waterboarding," *ABC News Investigations*, 29 November 2005, available at <http://abcnews.go.com/WNT/Investigation/story?id'1356870>.

[85] See John Conroy, *Unspeakable Acts, Ordinary People: The Dynamics of Terror* (Berkeley: University of California Press, 2000), 170–1; as quoted in Danner, 35.

[86] See Stuart Lyle, *The Gangrene*, trans. Robert Silvers (New York: Lyle Stuart, Inc, 1960), 81–2; as quoted in Danner, 35–6.

Under the definition proposed by the Justice Department in its original memorandum on the subject, principally authored, it appears, by John Yoo, then a Deputy Assistant Attorney General on leave from the law school at the University of California, Berkeley,[87] Porter Goss is probably correct in suggesting that waterboarding falls below the threshold of torture, that it is merely cruel or inhuman, since in the average case it will not result in death. Moreover, I might note in passing, even if a court were to conclude it was torture, according to the memorandum the responsible agents could not be prosecuted, because it was not their intention actually to inflict suffering that would finally kill their subject, since that would have been counterproductive.[88] I believe it is fair to say that the Justice Department and the CIA Director's view that waterboarding is not torture does not command much support outside the precincts of the American Right and possibly of security agents in countries with uncertain democratic credentials or none at all. I can at least say with absolute confidence that during the years I was a member of the Inter-American Commission,[89] it would not have occurred to Commission members that this was anything but torture, a standard tactic in the repertory of Latin American state terror.

Nevertheless, in fairness to Professor Yoo and his colleagues, I must admit that their position is not *entirely* without legal foundation. They relied in part on a decision of the European Court of Justice in the Northern Ireland Case.[90] The case against the United Kingdom was first brought by the Irish Government to the European Human Rights Commission. The petitioner claimed that certain methods used by British security forces in order to penetrate and destroy the structure of the Irish Republic Army and at a minimum to prevent terrorist acts violated the European Human Rights Convention. This regional convention uses language almost identical to the International Convention on Torture. It too prohibits torture (which it does not define) and cruel, inhuman, and degrading treatment.

[87] See, eg, R Jeffrey Smith and Dan Eggen, "Justice Expands Torture Definition," *The Washington Post*, 31 December 2004, A1. *See also* Whitney, "The Devils Advocate," at 1. When asked for his personal opinion on the use of torture, Yoo replied: "Personally, I do not think that torture is necessary. But it may be the case that interrogation methods that go beyond questioning, but do not arise to the level of torture, may be necessary to get actionable intelligence from high-ranking al Qaeda leaders. I do not know whether that is true as a matter of fact; I do not have access to the information or data to make an informed decision. That is up to our elected leaders."

[88] Mayer, "A Deadly Interrogation," 46. Mayer reports that during testimony before Congress in March 2005 Porter Goss stated: "C.I.A. policies on interrogation have always followed legal guidance from the Department of Justice. If an individual violates the policy, then he or she will be held accountable."

[89] See generally, Inter-American Commission on Human Rights (IACHR), Organization of American States, <http://www.cidh.org/DefaultE.htm>. I was a member of the IACHR from 1976–83, and served as President from 1980–82.

[90] *Ireland v United Kingdom*, Case No. 5310/71, Judgment of the European Court of Human Rights, 18 January 1978.

The methods principally at issue in the case were:

(1) Wall standing. The prisoner stands spread-eagled against the wall, with fingers high above his head, and feet back so that he is standing on his toes such that all of his weight falls on his fingers.
(2) Hooding. A hood is placed over the prisoner's head and kept there except during interrogation.
(3) Subjection to noise. Pending interrogation, the prisoner is kept in a room with a loud and continuous hissing noise.
(4) Sleep deprivation.
(5) Deprivation of food and drink.

In addition, prisoners were sometimes beaten to the degree that a number of detainees suffered injuries later described by the European Court as "substantial" and in some cases the injuries were described as "massive." Indeed it is hard to imagine that prisoners would have subjected themselves to the progressive pain of wall standing without the credible threat of being beaten severely if they failed to perform.

The European Commission found these various measures to be part of a program of interrogation which taken in its entirety had to be regarded as torture.[91] But on appeal, the Court decided that though cruel and inhuman and degrading, neither the individual beatings nor the program as a whole attained the particular level of severity inherent in the notion of torture even though the program caused in its words "if not actual bodily injury, at least intense physical and mental suffering to the persons subjected thereto and also led to acute psychiatric disturbances during the interrogation."[92]

In relying on the Court's decision, the Justice Department might have taken into account that, for practical purposes, it made no difference whether the acts in question constituted torture or cruel, inhuman, and degrading treatment, since in either case they were prohibited under the Convention and the Court could assume with confidence that the British Government would obey its order to terminate them. Actually, in the face of internal and external denunciations, London had suspended them long before the case reached the Court. What the Court apparently thought it was doing was reinforcing a special stigma for "deliberate inhuman treatment causing very serious and cruel suffering," a purpose utterly different than the purpose of the Justice Department in invoking the decision.[93]

One may wonder whether the Court would have construed the Convention differently if it had been faced with the alternatives of finding torture and

---

[91] See 19 *Yearbook of the European Conventions on Human Rights* (1976), 516–20, para 794. See also Rodley, 91–3.

[92] *Ireland v United Kingdom*, European Court of Human Rights, Series A, No. 84, paras 167–8.

[93] See generally, Daniel Levin, *Memorandum for James B. Comey*, 30 December 2004, available at <http://www.humanrightsfirst.org/us_law/etn/pdf/levin-memo-123004.pdf>.

thereby ending the practices it found cruel or finding merely cruel, inhuman, and degrading behavior and thereby allowing them to continue. Whatever the Court might have done then had it envisioned the way in which the Government of the United States would employ its test of torture, we need not simply speculate about what it would today. We need not speculate, since in its 1999 decision in *Selmouni v France*, it has repudiated the previous threshold of "severity":

> ... having regard to the fact that the [Torture] Convention is a "living instrument which must be interpreted in the light of present-day conditions", the Court considers that certain acts which were classified in the past as "inhuman and degrading treatment" as opposed to "torture" could be classified differently in future. It takes the view that the increasingly high standard being required in the area of the protection of human rights and fundamental liberties correspondingly and inevitably requires greater firmness in assessing breaches of the fundamental values of democratic societies.[94]

Selmouni, the Court found, had been urinated on and beaten in various parts of his body over an extended period. He had not experienced organ failure or otherwise been deposited at death's door. The Court concluded that he had been "tortured." This decision, announced four years before Professor Yoo crafted his memorandum, seems not to have made its way into the Justice Department library. Perhaps information concerning it had been shipped by ass and sail rather than more contemporary modes of transportation. There are many reasons not to regard Professor Yoo's views of the Constitution as "conservative." Even he seems to think they are creative. But in one respect his evident self-perception as a conservative might be deemed literally accurate in that he clearly believes that old law is good law.

While for all we can know with confidence the Bush Administration may continue under its theory of Executive discretion in time of "war" to interrogate unregistered detainees by brutish means, what has been the posture of its natural opponents, persons of generally liberal disposition with a long history of support for human rights internationally and progressive interpretations of the Bill of Rights at home? The fair answer, I believe, is that a not trivial number are divided, divided from each other and divided inside themselves. Taken as a complex whole, this normative community has not been immune to the traumatic effects of 9/11. Like the prospect of being hung on the morrow, contemplation of a radiological much less an atomic bomb or a synthesized or genetically-altered super-bug, in the hands of terrorists committed suicidally to their cause, has concentrated the collective mind on that old standby of classes in ethical theory and, I should add, of classes for military officers in the law of war, namely the case of the prisoner and the ticking bomb.[95] The trauma of 9/11, in short, has not left this elite normative community untouched.

---

[94] *Selmouni v France* (1999).
[95] See, eg, John W Dean, "Shocking the Conscience of America: Bush and Cheney Call for the Right to Torture and are Decisively and Correctly Rebuffed by the House," *FindLaw.com*,

On the one hand, the leaders of the main human rights NGOs have consistently denounced torture, heavy or light.[96] Given their institutional positions, it is hard to see how they could do otherwise. After all, the underlying philosophy of human rights, indeed their very definition, is non-utilitarian. One may even say anti-utilitarian, for they protect the individual against injurious calculations of aggregate community well being. Let us assume it could be demonstrated that the collective happiness or well being of any particular community would be enhanced by killing all seriously disabled people or, as a character in Shakespeare proposes, all the lawyers. A strict utilitarian would have to say, "proceed." But from the perspective of human rights, at least with respect to the most profound interests, above all the interest in not being killed, mutilated, or subjected to intense pain, every individual is, as it were, a community of one. The human rights conventions and, as I have noted, the Geneva Conventions as well, give this view unambiguous legal form.

Opponents of torture and other cruel, inhuman and degrading treatment have not, however, taken a stand on law and ethical theory alone. In addition, they generally question the supposedly imperious necessity, even the bare efficacy of torture.[97] To that end they may cite reputable interrogators who testify that, with time, adroit interrogators can winkle out of the most intransigently militant detainees all that torture might ultimately extract.[98] Moreover, information secured by more subtle means has much greater reliability. In extremis, most people will scream out anything that might reduce the pain, even if temporarily. In fact, a favorite argument of torture's opponents is that it generates a mass of unreliable data.

No one these enlightened days admits to liking torture perhaps for its punitive or possibly its erotic attractions. Supporters of torture lite or heavy respond, more

---

17 December 2005, 3–4, available at <http://www.findlaw.com>. See also Dershowitz, *Why Terrorism Works*, 131–63.

[96] See generally, World Organization Against Torture (OMCT) (<http://www.omct.org>); Amnesty International (<http://web.amnesty.org/library/eng-313/index>); and Human Rights Watch (<http://www.hrw.org/doc/?t'torture>).

[97] *See especially* Jeannine Bell, "One Thousand Shades of Gray: The Effectiveness of Torture." *Indiana University School of Law-Bloomington Research Paper No. 37*, 15 August 2005, available at <http://ssrn.com/abstract=820467>. According to Bell, torture *can* produce useful information but is far less likely to do so than traditional forms of interrogation that are (largely) free of the enormous social, political, and legal complications and taint associated with torture: "The scant empirical evidence that can be uncovered regarding whether torture is good at eliciting information suggests that coercive mechanisms may not be especially effective interrogation tools." But compare Andrew C McCarthy, *Torture: Thinking the Unthinkable*, Benador Associates, Commentary, July–August 2004, 9, available at <http://www.benadorassociates.com/article/5900>. McCarthy suggests that because torture *can* produce useful information, it should be viewed as a viable option: "In fact, it could just as plausibly be asserted that torture is an ironclad guarantee of honesty as of misinformation... torture has been known to be a very effective method to get at the truth; that it is not foolproof is hardly a reason to prohibit its selective use."

[98] Bell, 13–17. See also Bowden, 57 and Joseph Lelyveld, "Interrogating Ourselves," *New York Times Magazine*, 12 June 2005, 43.

in sorrow than in anger, to the claims of professional human rights advocates by asking: Suppose there is not a great deal of time? Suppose you need intelligence now, not next week, or suppose in a particular case the softer methods simply do not work or suppose you need to process a whole lot of people in a relatively short time and you don't have on staff a regiment of Sigmund Freuds or even Carl Jungs, you just have a bunch of good ol' boys with thick necks, horny hands and heavy boots. Then what? The fall-back argument of the pro-torture crowd is, again, the ticking bomb case supplemented by the institutional reality that gifted people are always in short supply. To that case, they say, liberals have no answer.

Well, in fact there are answers, but not ones that will persuade everybody. One answer is that the ticking bomb case is really just a rhetorical device, a debater's fantasy. You could run torture operations for a century without encountering the smirking sociopath who credibly assures you that he's planted a small atomic device which will incinerate the population of lower Manhattan in three hours. That is not the real world.[99] The real world is Algiers, 1958. The resistance owns the Casbah by night. By day they are teens on street corners, shopkeepers, shoe-shine boys, vendors, students. But at night they own the Casbah. So one night you begin.

You cordon off a block and grab every male between the ages of 16 (or at least who look 16) and 40. You blindfold and shackle them and take them to some improvised detention center. You strip them and you let them sit naked on the stone floor. If they doze off, you kick them awake. After a while, maybe a long while, you bring them to the interrogation room. Maybe you begin softly, ask if they would like some water or a cigarette or to use the toilet. Maybe you don't. Maybe you start off as if you did not care what they have to say, as if you did not want answers to questions, you just want to experience the pleasure of hurting them. Silent colleagues strap them to the water-board or attach electrodes to their gums and ears and testicles and pour water on them. And you begin. And after a time, most will beg for questions to answer. And eventually they will get their wish. You will give them questions. And sooner or later they will give you answers, names and addresses; they will give them fulsomely, almost with pleasure. Finally, when you can't think of any more questions and they can't think of any more answers, you may just send them back to the bare room and the crawling vermin who share it with them or you may become soft, paternal, concerned, rueful, offer them some tea. Then you go and seize the people they named and search the houses and collect more names. And you discover that some lied, but others told the truth, because you find a pistol or a grenade or a pamphlet in the closet or under a floorboard. You continue, day after day, deliberately sorting through the cornucopia of screamed names, distinguishing the militants from

[99] See, eg, Andrew Sabl, "Torture as a Case Study: How to Corrupt Your Students," *The Chronicle of Higher Education*, 11 November 2005, B5. See also Dean, 3; paraphrasing David Luban, "Torture, American Style: This Debate Comes Down to Words vs. Deeds," *The Washington Post*, 27 November 2005, B1.

the sympathizers from the innocent until you have unpeeled the onion and the Casbah belongs to the parachutists and the Legion. Mission accomplished, sir. The battle of Algiers was won, but of course the French lost the war.[100]

Now let's move forward 46 years to another part of the Arab world. General Fay, in his report on what led to Abu Ghraib, writes that:

As the pace of operations picked up in late November–early December 2003, it became a common practice for maneuver elements to round up large quantities of Iraqi personnel [ie civilians], in the general vicinity of a specified target as a cordon and capture technique. Some operations were conducted at night... [101]

As Mark Danner has written, "In this way the Americans arrested thousands of Iraqis—or, as the Schlesinger Report puts it, they reverted to rounding up any and all suspicious-looking persons—all too often including women and children. The flood of incoming detainees contrasted sharply with the trickle of released individuals."[102] The release was a trickle, according to one US General, because combat commanders had the attitude: "We would not have detained them if we wanted them released."[103] The flood was a flood because, as General Fay points out, the combat soldiers, in their zeal to apprehend Iraqis who might conceivably be supporting those shadowy figures attacking American troops, neglected to filter out those who clearly did not belong in [prisons like Abu Ghraib]. The capturing soldiers, in Fay's words,

...failed to perform the proper procedures at the point-of-capture and beyond with respect to handling captured enemy prisoners-of-war and detainees (screening, tactical interrogation, capture cards, sworn statements...) Failure of capturing units to follow these procedures contributed to facility overcrowding... [104]

My main point is that once torture and cruel, inhuman, and degrading treatment become normalized, even if nominally restricted to the ticking bomb case, it will in fact be employed as an everyday means to the end of rolling up the whole carpet of the organization or organizations perceived to be potential planters of such a bomb and then rolling them up again and again as the kin and friends of the tortured and others who feel aggrieved by real or perceived

---

[100] See generally, General Paul Aussaresses, *The Battle of the Casbah* (New York: Enigma Books, 2006). See also Alistair Horne, *A Savage War of Peace: Algeria 1954–1962*. (London: Macmillan Ltd, 1977). But compare Slater, 203: "It may be rhetorically effective to say that it was torture that caused the French to ultimately lose in Algeria, but it is not accurate; they resorted to torture precisely because they feared defeat if they did not..."

[101] Jones-Fay Report, 37.

[102] Danner, 30; quoting the Schlesinger Report, 29.

[103] Ibid, 31; quoting the Fay-Jones Report, 39.

[104] Ibid, 32; quoting the Jones-Fay Report, 39. See also Human Rights Watch, "Leadership Failure," 3–4. Human Rights Watch conducted extensive interviews with US troops in Afghanistan and Iraq to determine how US forces were handling prisoners/detainees, and what directives/ orders they were given regarding this: "These soldiers accounts show how the administration's refusal to insist on adherence to a lawful, long-recognized, and well-defined standard of treatment contributed to the torture of prisoners."

oppression and humiliation resist. Your interrogators will not wait for the mastermind or the delivery agent to come into their nests. They are not sure who these people are or where they are. You have to start somewhere, they will say. Find the right thread and you can unravel the whole quilt. The trick is finding the right thread and, regrettably, mistakes will be made. To be sure, they are foreseeable, but so is the collateral damage of air and missile attacks. What's the moral difference? Are you a worse human being because you look your mistakes in the eye?

And perhaps, to toughen yourself or because people of a certain cast of mind will be drawn, by process of self-selection, into the game, you will begin to say: Maybe many of these people that did not actually seem to know anything, were not really innocent. After all, they were friends of the bad apples. Hell, that's how we got their names in the first place. Or they sympathized with the goals of the bad apples, even if they did not support or had yet to become involved with the means. Innocence is relative. Not everyone, but some may end up thinking just a little bit like the Argentine general in the days of the *desparacidos* who said: "First we will kill all the subversives. Then we will kill everyone who helped them. And then we will kill everyone who did not help us." Sure, that's a little extreme. Still, I think you can see that people who spend their working days inflicting pain and humiliation on other people and are not eager sociopaths or crazed fanatics, to begin with, will need to do something to thicken their mental skin. The utilitarian calculus sounds fine when you are sitting in your study in a thick leather chair and telling subordinates what results you want and making sure they understand you don't need to know about the means. But it is pretty weak medicine when human beings are screaming and vomiting blood in front of you. It certainly must help to convince yourself that they are at least a little bit guilty in most cases.

In short, beyond the extreme unlikelihood of the true ticking bomb case, a large part of the liberal answer is that torture like a taste for luxury goods once experienced has an irremediable tendency to spread beyond the small special places where governments may attempt to isolate it. Extreme necessity becomes routinized. And more and more people become implicated. To be implicated in an age or at least in a society where torture remains a dirty little secret is to become deeply wedded to keeping the secret, not just now, but forever.

The Israeli experience illustrates the difficulty of limiting the use of brutal means to ticking bomb cases. In the late 1960s, following the beating to death of two Palestinian detainees, the Israeli Government constituted a blue-ribbon commission (the eponymous Landau Commission), chaired by a Supreme Court Justice, to consider, among other things, the methods that the General Security Service, the state's internal security organization, could employ against suspected terrorists in detention. Following prolonged deliberation, the Commission concluded that "in cases where the saving of human lives necessarily requires certain information, the investigator is entitled to apply both psychological pressure and 'a moderate degree of physical pressure [not amounting to torture].' "[105] While the various apparently stringent conditions surrounding this license to hurt were set out in a secret part of its report, the general understanding was that the Commission intended to limit physical pressure to ticking bomb types of cases, that is cases where the threat of terrorist attack was strongly evidenced and imminent.

When defending physical coercion in a 1999 Supreme Court case concerning GSS interrogation methods, the Government implicitly confirmed this limitation.[106] It argued that GSS authority to employ physical coercion in certain circumstances is implied by the language of the criminal law defense of "necessity" prescribed in Israeli Penal Law. The relevant provision states that:

A person will not bear criminal liability for committing any act immediately necessary for the purpose of saving the life, liberty, body or property, of either himself or his fellow person, from substantial danger of serious harm, imminent from the particular state of things [circumstances], at the requisite timing, and absent alternative means for avoiding the harm.[107]

Despite this nominal policy, according to reliable reports, Israeli GSS personnel have long employed on a widespread and systematic basis practices that are unquestionably cruel and inhuman and sliding over into torture as understood by official inter-governmental institutions and by widely respected non-governmental organizations.[108]

---

[105] Report of the Landau Commission of Inquiry (1987); cited in Israel's report to UN Committee against Torture, 17 February 1997, CAT/C/33/Add.2/Rev.1.

[106] *Public Comm. Against Torture in Israel v The State of Israel*, 53(4) PD 817 (1999).

[107] Among other organizations, *B'tselem*, the most prominent Israeli human rights group monitoring activities both in Israel and Occupied Territories, has widely reported on torturous behavior of Israel's General Security Service: <http://www.btselem.org/english/Torture/Torture_by_GSS.asp>.

[108] See Human Rights Watch, *Israel's Record of Occupation: Violation of Civil and Political Rights*, 10(2E) (August 1998), available at <http://www.hrw.org/reports98/israel>; Human Rights Watch, *UN Should Condemn Israeli Torture and Hostage Taking*, 15 July 1998, available at <*http://hrw.org/english/docs/1998/07/15/isrlpa1214.htm*>; Amnesty International, *Israel and the Occupied Territories: Mass Detention in Cruel, Inhuman and Degrading Conditions*, MDE 15/074/2002, May 2002, available at <http://web.amnesty.org/library/index/engmde150742002>. The UN Committee Against Torture and the Special Rapporteur of the UN Human Rights Commission found that GSS practices identified by an official Israeli investigative body, the so-called Landau Commission, constituted torture (see Tom Lue, "Coercive Interrogations," app B of Philip B Heymann and Juliette N Kayyem, *Long-Term Legal Strategy Project for Preserving Security and Democratic Freedoms in the War on Terrorism*, Kennedy School of Government, available at <http://bcsia.ksg.harvard.edu/BCSIA_content/documents/LTLS_final_5_3_05.pdf>), 155, 161, a position, however, rejected by the Israeli Supreme Court in *Public Comm. Against Torture in Israel v The State of Israel*, 53(4) PD 817 (1999). For an eye witness account see Ari Shavit, "On Gaza Beach," *New York Review of Books*, 18 July 1991, available at <http://www.nybooks.com/articles/3202>. See, in addition, Chris McGreal, "Facility 1391: Israel's Secret Prison," *The Guardian*, 14 November 2003, available at <http://guardian.co.uk/israel/story/0,2763,1084796,00.html> and Israeli Information Center for Human Rights in the Occupied Territories, *Legislation Allowing the Use of Physical Force and Mental Coercion in interrogations by the General Security Service*, Position Paper (January 2000), 61–2, cited in Lue, above.

If substantial numbers of people, in high as well as low places, become members of a fraternity of the guilty, democratic governance can begin to erode. You need judges who will find they have no jurisdiction when complaints are brought by torturees who lived to tell the tale or who deliver summary judgments with one-line opinions, you need a compliant press, you need friends in Congress, and you will have them, because the members of the joint-intelligence committee probably knew and so they too are implicated. And you need a military institution and intelligence agencies staffed by persons who will rally round, if exposure is threatened, who will "understand," maybe even celebrate your ability to transcend your humanity in the name of humanity and Christian civilization. The fraternity needs to maintain a conspiracy of silence. And it needs to be large. Maybe it is sheer coincidence that French democracy barely survived Algeria. Maybe there is simply no comparison. I myself can think of a hundred differences. Still, there just might be a distant cautionary bit of history here. It is not hysterical to factor it into the liberal answer.

But perhaps the strongest strand in the liberal answer also connects to the French experience. As I said, the French lost the war. Mark Danner tells of meeting a young Iraqi from Falluja and peppering him with questions about the insurgency. Why were American troops being attacked? How many were carried out by foreigners? How many by local Islamists? And so on. Then Danner writes: "The young man—I'll call him Salih—listened, answered patiently in his limited but eloquent English, but soon became impatient with what he plainly saw as my American obsession with categories and particulars. Finally he interrupted my litany of questions, pushed his face close to mine, and spoke to me slowly and emphatically:

For Fallujans it is a shame to have foreigners break down their doors. It is a shame for them to have foreigners stop and search their women. It is a shame for the foreigners to put a bag over their heads, to make a man lie on the ground with your shoe on his neck. This is a great shame, you understand? This is a great shame for the whole tribe. It is the duty of that man, and of that tribe, to get revenge on this soldier—to kill that man. Their duty is to attack them, to wash the shame. The shame is a stain, a dirty thing; they have to wash it. No sleep—we cannot sleep until we have revenge. They have to kill soldiers.[109]

I suppose that, for that list of shames, torture is *a fortiori*.

A completely honest liberal should concede, I think, that torture can produce tactical benefits in some circumstances. The French did unravel the FLN networks in the Casbah. The Israelis at least claim that their methods, which include brute physical coercion, have averted some suicide bombings. A case was reported not long ago where police beat a suspect and eventually he told them where he had left the child he had kidnapped.[110] But if we are going to use the utilitarian calculus,

[109] Danner, 1.
[110] Dershowitz, *Why Terrorism Works*, 137–8. See also Phillip B Heymann and Juliette K Kayyem, *Protecting Liberty in an Age of Terror* (Cambridge, Mass.: MIT Press, 2005), 165; paraphrasing from Bruce Hoffman, "A Nasty Business," *The Atlantic Monthly*, January 2002, 49–52.

we need to think strategically and not only about terrorism, but also about all the other issues on which the national interest would be better served if a large proportion of the world's billion Muslims did not regard us as more of a threat to world peace than Osama bin Laden which appears now to be the case in a country like Indonesia, the world's largest Muslim country, where before the beginning of the Bush Administration's war, the United States was fairly popular.[111]

But even if we think strategically about terrorism alone, we might hesitate to normalize torture, even in the restrained way proposed by the good professor Dershowitz of Harvard who has for years represented clients not for money, he has assured us, but to defend the precious legacy of that central human right, due process of law.[112] Concerned about the ticking bomb case, concerned as we all ought to be about the prospect of the continuing, probably progressive, diffusion of the know-how to produce weapons of mass destruction, concerned as we must be that there are some people out there who are not deterrable, he believes that in the name of security against real threats, torture will occur and, perhaps he means to imply, should occur.[113] If we let it be subterranean, in dark places beyond the reach of the law, it could metastasize. Better to bring it within the law, keep it limited to means that do no permanent injury, at least to the body, and to persons about whom there can be little doubt of their knowledge and culpability. And so he proposes torture warrants to be issued by judges, rarely, perhaps reluctantly, but issued, because some day there may be a ticking bomb.[114] Can we say, in brief, that Professor Dershowitz takes his human rights with a dash of utilitarianism? Is it that the times are too dangerous for human right absolutism, in part because if absolutism leads or can plausibly be claimed to have led to another 9/11, perhaps

---

[111] See "What the World Thinks in 2002," *Pew Global Attitudes Project*, 4 December 2002, available at <http://pewglobal.org/reports/pdf/165.pdf>. Per the Pew Project, 61% of Indonesians viewed the United States favorably in 2002, down from 75% during 1999/2000, while 64% opposed the US-led "War on Terror." See pp 1–5 and 54–61 regarding opinions of the United States in the Middle East and the rest of the Muslim world.

[112] Alan Dershowitz, *Reversal of Fortune: Inside the Von Bülow Case* (New York: Random House, 1986). But compare, "Is there a Tortuous Road to Justice?" *The Los Angeles Times*, 8 November 2001. Dershowitz considers the possibility of whether using torture to avert bloodshed in a "ticking bomb" scenario should outweigh prevailing concepts of "due process."

[113] Dershowitz, *Why Terrorism Works*, 141–63. But compare Bell, 12–17. See also Sanford Levinson (ed), *Torture: A Collection* (New York: Oxford University Press, 2004), for an extensive collection of contrasting perspectives and arguments regarding both the legitimacy and efficacy of torture.

[114] "To the Editor," *New York Times Book Review*, 13 February 2005, 5. Dershowitz also seeks to ensure that the power/decision to torture rests at the highest level possible, to maintain a separation between the torturer and the approving authority: "My proposal would shift responsibility from the low-level interrogators to the president or another very high-ranking official who would have to sign the warrant." But compare Sanford Levinson, "The Debate on Torture," *Dissent Magazine*, Summer 2003, available at <http://www.dissentmagazine.org/article/?article=490>: "Making the judge complicit in torture would have certain consequences. One might be that certain judges would simply stand down, because of their adherence to the absolute proscription to the practice...whether or not the judge actually puts the hood over the head, he should have no doubt that he is collaborating in what even Argentinean torturers recognized as presumptively evil activity."

on a far grander scale, human rights will be one of the casualties? In part, at least, Professor Dershowitz and others who agree with him to one degree or another are proposing that in order to save popular support for human rights and their domestic constitutional equivalent, we may have to shrink them just a little.[115]

The never-say-never position in the debate over torture is not weightless.[116] It demands that we look inside ourselves and imagine what we ourselves might do if we were caught up in some analogue of the ticking bomb case. No one can say with certainty what he or she will do in moments of rage or fear. But from that uncertainty it does not follow that one must join Professor Dershowitz's camp. Laws cannot cope with the truly exceptional. They are generalizations. They prescribe the behavior which, in most instances, perhaps in almost all, will advance the general interest. Professor Dershowitz proposes that we legislate the exceptional case in order to keep it exceptional and in order to avert catastrophe when men and women to whom we have entrusted our security believe one is looming.[117] The alternative is to deal with torture as we do with euthanasia, to keep it beyond the law, to place upon the individuals contemplating this awful act the burden of persuading their judges that they should be excused, that the circumstances were so exceptional as to mitigate or even absolve. Let the burden be heavy on those who choose to act outside the value system that defines a liberal democratic state.

A state that tortures is not a liberal democratic state. Its officials may be elected through a process that is not manifestly fraudulent or coercive, and in that sense the state may be democratic, but it is not liberal. The progressive elimination of official torture is probably the most conspicuous marker on the Western road from government without consent of the governed to government by consent, the road from a world where the ordinary person was the object of power to the world of formally equal citizenship, the road from a world where the authorities defined identity to a world where individuals make and remake their identity. One sign of the visceral feeling within free societies that torture is bestial is its outlawry even

[115] *Why Terrorism Works*, 141–63. But compare Elaine Scarry, "Five Errors in the Reasoning of Alan Dershowitz" in Levinson, (ed), *Torture: A Collection*, 281–90.

[116] See especially Susie Linfield, "The Dance of Civilizations," *Dissent Magazine*, Winter 2005, available at <http://www.dissentmagazine.org/article/?article=269>: "To say that one is against torture, or that the Geneva Conventions must always be upheld, or that fundamental human rights are inviolable does not, unfortunately, end the discussion about ways and means in the war on terror." See also Slater, 210–12: "There are at least three possible scenarios... in which the issue of torture is certain to be, and must be, considered: the capture of terrorists at the field level who are about to engage in WMD attacks in cities, the capture of terrorists about to engage in non-WMD attacks on cities, and the capture of terrorist leaders who are planning or who know about the plans for future major terrorist attacks."

[117] *Why Terrorism Works*, 158–63. Compare McCarthy, 10–11. Similar in spirit to Dershowitz, McCarthy advocates the creation of one specialized "national security court" that would, among other duties, issue torture warrants: "Centralizing this sensitive matter in a single court would ensure that the standards developed for warrants win rigorous adherence rather than (as in Dershowitz's proposal) being subject to tinkering by hundreds of federal judges in scores of districts throughout the country."

in countries that retain the death penalty. The long-time official keeper of the American Conscience, the Supreme Court of the United States, has found cruel treatment of suspects and of prisoners to be unconstitutional, if it "shocks the conscience,"[118] but it has not prohibited the taking of their lives after conviction for grave crimes.[119]

But what of interrogation techniques that fall short of torture, yet may be effective in eliciting truths against the interrogated person's wish or will. If they are prisoners of war, then, as I have already noted, the Third Geneva Convention is prohibitory. If they are caught up in a conflict not of an international character, they are protected by Common Article 3 of the Conventions against not only torture, but also "cruel... humiliating and degrading treatment." The Torture Convention and Article 7 of the International Covenant on Civil and Political Rights protect everyone else against such treatment. And while the former might conceivably be construed, insofar as cruel, inhuman, and degrading treatment is concerned, to be subject to derogation in exceptional circumstances, the latter is explicitly made non-derogable. But arguably that still leaves some scope for methods effective at eliciting truths the suspect wishes passionately to conceal, methods like short periods of solitary confinement intermixed with lengthy interrogations, threats of particularly severe punishment in the event of conviction, threats to prosecute loved ones or to confiscate property on which they depend, and various forms of duplicity such as confining the suspect with a disguised officer or leading him to believe that a confederate has betrayed him.

Most of these techniques other than solitary confinement and prolonged interrogation do not vitiate the "voluntariness" of a confession under the due process clause of the US Constitution. Between them and that violent coercion that always causes intense pain and suffering (and is thus definable as "torture," even under the inventive definition of Professor Yoo and Attorney-General Gonzalez) lie techniques that the Report of the *Long-Term Legal Strategy Project*, sponsored by Harvard Law School and the Kennedy School of Government, labels "highly coercive interrogation (HCI)."[120]

The Project report offers an illustrative list of measures "that have been reportedly used or taught by US military personnel:

• putting on smelly hoods or goggles
• wall-standing for long periods of time

---

[118] *Rochin v California* 342 U.S. 165 (1953).

[119] See *Gregg v Georgia* 428 U.S. 153 (1976), which upheld the death penalty as not violative of Eighth Amendment prohibition of "cruel and unusual punishment." Compare *Rochin v California* 342 U.S. 165 (1953), in which the majority held that evidence extracted through use of brutal means is inadmissible in court.

[120] Philip B Heymann and Juliette N Kayyem, *Long-Term Legal Strategy Project for Preserving Security and Democratic Freedoms in the War on Terrorism* (Kennedy School of Government, Harvard University), available online at <http://bcsia.ksg.harvard.edu/BCSIA_content/documents/LTLS_final_5_3_05.pdf>.

- subjection to noise
- deprivation of sleep
- deprivation of food and drink
- deprivation of medical treatment (called 'borderline' by the Project report authors)
- exploiting sexual urges and/or religious prejudices
- preying on fears of the safety of relatives and family
- putting rats or cockroaches in cells
- keeping the prisoner naked and isolated
- threat of indefinite detention"[121]

To this list they might have added a number of other methods reliably reported to have been used. One is exposing naked prisoners to extreme cold (whether by pouring ice water on them or placing them in fiercely air conditioned rooms). A second is suffocation, principally by filling a detainee's nostrils with water, although long thick hoods, frequently employed by Israeli interrogators (according to the Israeli Supreme Court) and reportedly by American ones as well, can also create a suffocating sensation particularly for those with asthmatic symptoms. The third is cuffing or chaining a prisoner in a position calculated to cause gradually intensifying pain. Perhaps the authors felt these methods, although apparently authorized by the Secretary of Defense under the authority of the President, shade beyond HCI into torture pure and simple. The project authors might also have included the use of aggressive dogs in an effort to terrify prisoners, a measure also in the repertoire of American interrogators since sometime after 9/11.

The Many of these measures are similar or identical to those used by British interrogators against IRA suspects. They are also similar or identical to measures used by Israeli interrogators along with simple beating.[122] It would appear that when used in combination and/or for prolonged periods, today they would be found by the European Court of Human Rights to constitute torture.

The author of a special paper on "Coercive Interrogations" for the Harvard Project recognizes that "the combined or prolonged use of some HCI techniques may eventually cause severe pain or suffering amounting to torture."[123] He also expresses concern for the two-sided "slippery-slope" danger associated with HCI: Its tendency to spread far beyond the "ticking bomb" context to become a regular means of acquiring long-term strategic intelligence about groups deemed hostile; the tendency of its users to transition over to torture when HCI does not work or does not work fast enough for their purposes. Nevertheless, he

---

[121] Ibid, at app B, Tom Lue, "Coercive Interrogations," 166.

[122] See footnote 104 above. See also UN Commission on Human rights, Report of the Special Rapporteur on torture and cruel, inhuman or degrading treatment or punishment, UN Doc. E/CN.4/1994/31 Israel (1994).

[123] Lue, "Coercive Interrogations," 182, fn. 106.

endorses the Report's conclusion that HCI might properly be employed "under exceptional circumstances" and "adequate *procedural safeguards* to ensure that HCI techniques are applied strictly in the manner and circumstances in which they are authorized."[124]

The Report is plainly an effort by persons concerned about the future of civil liberties under the US Constitution and global human rights and about the reputation of the United States to prevent the metastasis of torture. In a time of popular anxiety, regularly aggravated by political entrepreneurs and ideologically extreme elements of the media, when government is in the hands of leaders with a Manichaean view of the world and contempt for international restraints on the exercise of national power, their concern is understandable. And so they have sought to construct a system of limits on executive discretion which affords just enough flexibility to relieve them of the charge that they have left the country with dangerously insufficient means to prevent a catastrophic attack.

In summary, they begin by seeming to reject torture and also "actions that the courts find [Have previously found? Might find in the future? Are closely analogous to such previously found actions?] 'shock the conscience.'" Then they require the President, on the recommendation of the Attorney General, to promulgate "guidelines stating which specific HCI techniques are authorized." The guidelines "shall address the duration and repetition of use of a particular technique and the effect of combining several different techniques together [sic]." Next they require the Attorney General to brief "both houses of Congress upon request, and no less frequently than every six months, as to which HCIs are presently being utilized by federal officials or those acting on their behalf." In addition, they limit the subjects of HCI techniques to persons with respect to whom "Authorized interrogators have probable cause to believe...are in possession of significant information, and there is no reasonable alternative to obtain that information, about either [a] specific plan that threatens US lives or [a] group or organization making such plans whose capacity could be significantly reduced by exploiting the information."[125] Probable cause must be determined by senior government officials on the basis of sworn affidavits and the factual basis for their determination must be communicated to congressional intelligence committees, the Attorney General, and the Inspectors General of the pertinent departments.

However, the authors also provide for an Emergency Exception allowing "an interrogation technique not specifically authorized in this way when it is used with the express written approval of the President on the basis of a finding of an urgent and extraordinary need, [the] finding must be submitted within a reasonable period to appropriate committees from both houses of Congress, must state the reason to believe that...the information sought to be obtained concerns a specific plan that threatens US lives...the information is in possession of the

---

[124] Ibid, 174.
[125] *Long Term Legal Strategy*, 33.

individual to be interrogated and...there are no other reasonable alternatives to save the lives in question."[126] Although as stated, the "emergency exception" can be construed to allow not only any combination or intensity of HCI but also torture itself in what the President alleges is a ticking bomb case, in their "Explanation" of the formal proposal the authors state clearly their intention that torture be banned under all circumstances.[127]

It is conventionally said that, at the end of the day, laws are no better than the people who enforce them. But that is too facile by half. At least in a democratic more-or-less liberal political system, law can create standard operating procedures, penalties, and taboos that will inhibit even men and women of malign intent, in part by encouraging resistance and exposure particularly by professionals with a stake in the regular and legitimate functioning of the public institutions in which they have made their careers and from which they draw their dignity and identity. It is not by chance that the main governmental opponents of torture and other illegal methods proposed by political appointees in the Department of Defense have been military lawyers backed by a considerable number of retired troop commanders.

The question for those who would have the United States display grace under pressure in our time is whether human rights can best be defended by conceding that the risk of catastrophic terrorism may require the formal legalization of methodical cruelty. Even the strict Utilitarian may doubt the correct answer, for we cannot predict with confidence the long-term impact on human rights of an absolute formal prohibition rather than highly qualified legalization of cruel means. In the end as we individually resolve that doubt, we can rely only on the frail reed of our intuition.

But if our concern is less with human rights than it is with security, then we have a good deal more than intuition on which to rest a judgment. We have experience. Terrorists are insurgents, insurgents prepared to transgress moral restraints. A first principle of counter-insurgency doctrine developed by democratic governments, particularly the British (who have been relatively successful in containing or ending low-intensity conflicts), is the primacy of the political. That is shorthand for a strategy combining a measure of force with a larger measure of non-violent measures (and acts of self-restraint) designed to minimize sympathy for the insurgents within that subset of the general population from which the insurgents spring. Those measures generally need to address both material and symbolic concerns of the relevant public, concerns the insurgents will always claim to champion against the authorities. Ideally the measures adopted will lead people to conclude that the insurgents are themselves threats to generally accepted norms of behavior, that they are literally "outlaws."

---

[126] Ibid, 34.
[127] Ibid, 40.

Insurgents employing terrorist means ought to be particularly vulnerable to this strategy, for those means by definition transgress commonly recognized limits on violence. But the opportunity to isolate the terrorist is lost where the authorities themselves employ transgressive means. The photos from Abu Ghraib—the terrified hooded prisoners, enraged dogs, laughing abusers— reached every corner of the Muslim world, the world to which Islamic radicals address their appeals. Those photos drove a hole through the wall of silence out of which in the succeeding months and years has poured evidence of worse trans- gressions against human rights and humanitarian law. By our means we have violated the first principle of successful counter-insurgency.

Inspired, apparently, by the resistance of many professionals, soldiers, and military lawyers to the brutal measures secretly authorized by the President and his closest advisors, by the cataclysmic decline of American prestige abroad, and, possibly, by the widespread view among experts on the Middle East and terrorism that cruel methods were helping deepen the pool of potential recruits for terrorist organizations, perhaps influenced as well by his personal experience of torture, in 2005 Senator John McCain introduced legislation designed to prohibit torture and, in effect, such cruel, inhuman, or degrading treatment as would shock the conscience of a majority of American Supreme Court Justices or had so shocked them in the past. Although bitterly opposed by the Administration, it gathered bi-partisan support to such an extent as to pass the Senate by a vote of 90–9 and with House of Representatives approval became law as the Detainee Treatment Act of 2005.[128] Did this action set the country on course to comply with its obligations under international law?

It would appear not. In his signing statement the President declared that:

[t]he Executive branch shall construe [the provisions] relating to detainees . . . in a manner consistent with the constitutional authority of the President to supervise the unitary executive branch and as Commander in Chief and consistent with the constitutional limitations on the judicial power, which will assist in achieving the shared objective of the Congress and the President . . . of protecting the American people from further terrorist attacks.

The "Torture Memorandum" emitted by the Department of Justice after 9/11, had invoked the President's authority as Commander-in-Chief (in a time of armed conflict) to justify the proposition that he could legally authorize tor- ture or other means irrespective of any legislative or treaty prohibition. Hence the pledge to interpret in light of his position as Commander-in-Chief seemed intended to restate the position taken previously by the Department of Justice and reaffirmed by his then Legal Counsel, later the Attorney-General. Moreover, the invocation of the President's power "to supervise the *unitary* executive branch"

---

[128] A tally of the votes and text of the amendment are available online through the Library of Congress database, <http://thomas.loc.gov/>.

implies adoption of a radically creative constitutional theory that has in recent years circulated among right-wing jurists intent on inflating executive power.

Most writers on the Constitution, whether liberal or conservative, have noted the intricate way in which it limits the risk of autocracy by overlapping the authority of the several branches, as well as by maintaining a federal system. Thus in the field of foreign affairs, although the President is Commander-in-Chief and, by strong implication, the organizer of the nation's diplomacy, the Constitution grants to Congress alone the authority to declare war, to appropriate funds for the support of the armed forces and to regulate their behavior through legislation defining the laws and customs of war to which they must adhere. Similarly, the President shares with the Senate the authority for binding the United States by treaty and the Senate must approve his choice of Ambassadors and high officials of the Defense and State Departments. While the Supreme Court and constitutional scholars have nevertheless envisioned a zone of responsibility where the Executive has unfettered discretion, for instance in the deployment of forces in war and peace and the conduct of battles, once war has begun, advocates of the "unitary executive branch" have urged an interpretation of the Constitution that vastly enlarges that zone. The torture memorandum was an instance in point. Thus by both references the President was obliquely challenging the authority of Congress to bar his authorization of torture and other cruel, inhuman, and degrading methods of interrogation.

But it was not the President alone who seemed to wink at the nominal preclusion of torture and other cruel measures. Congress itself seemed to collude with him by adding to the very legislation embodying the McCain Amendment another amendment that appears to eliminate habeas corpus as a means for detainees to challenge their treatment during detention. And just prior to the 2006 national elections, Congress added a prohibition on habeas corpus review to the Bill confirming the President's authority to establish Military Commissions to try such of the non-citizen "unlawful combatants" as the government decides it wishes to try.[129] In those trials, according to the legislation and implementing regulations, hearsay and evidence secured through cruel and inhuman means can be introduced if deemed reliable by the serving officers who will constitute the Commission. Moreover, the prosecution can withhold classified sources and also methods of interrogation from both the defendant and his counsel. It can also withhold exculpatory classified evidence, although it is required to provide a substitute regarded as "adequate."[130]

Detainees brought before the Military Commissions will be the lucky ones. The rest have no recourse other than a hearing before the Combat Review Status Tribunals. Most of the evidence about the operation of these tribunals has had to

---

[129] Military Commissions Act 2006; text available online at <http://thomas.loc.gov/cgi-bin/bdquery/z?d109:S.3930>.
[130] Ibid, § 949j(c)(2).

be extracted from the Government through the Freedom of Information Act or District Court orders in habeas corpus appeals.[131] Full records have been obtained for only 102 proceedings and some information has been obtained about another 292 out of the admitted total of 558 proceedings.

What is indisputable is that detainees are not allowed counsel; they are allowed personal representatives appointed by the military authorities, representatives who inform the detainee that "None of the information you provide me shall be held in confidence and I may be obligated to divulge it at the hearing."[132] Meetings are brief and occur shortly before the hearing. Requests by detainees for testimony of persons outside Guantánamo have been uniformly unsuccessful as it appears have requests for documents not available at the base. It is known that in three cases out of the 102 that are fully documented, the Tribunal found the detainee to be "not/no longer" an enemy combatant, whereupon the Defense Department ordered the convening of a new Tribunal. In two of those cases the new one found the detainee to be an enemy combatant and hence subject to indefinite detention. In the third case, the second Tribunal came to the same conclusion as the first, whereupon the Defense Department convened yet a third Tribunal and it finally found that the detainee was indeed an enemy combatant.[133] Such is the state of American due process in the war to make the Middle East safe for liberal democracy.

4. The Latin Americanization of the American "War" on Terrorism

I cannot hope to address in depth within a single chapter all of the problematical means that the Bush Administration has been employing in its declared "war" on terrorism. An entire volume would barely suffice. Being sensible of this constraint, I have obviously chosen to focus principally on torture and other cruel, inhuman (all too human), and degrading methods of interrogation. A number of factors dictated this choice. One is the clarity and virtually universal acceptance, in form, of the prohibitions on the use of these methods, above all torture. Another is their partial incorporation into US domestic law.

A third is the Bush Administration's preoccupation with them. Often seemingly obtuse about or indifferent to legal and moral constraints, being consecrated in the President's everyman's idiom to "kicking ass," when it comes to cruel methods of interrogation, the unease of the President and his closest

---

[131] Mark and Joshua Denbeaux, "No-Hearing Hearings: CSRT—The Modern Habeas Corpus," Seton Hall University School of Law, 17 October 2006, available online at <http://law.shu.edu/news/final_no_hearing_hearings_report.pdf>.

[132] Ibid, 15.

[133] Ibid, 37–9.

colleagues is palpable in their early solicitation of legal assurances that they could safely authorize very cruel means, in the clandestine character of their instructions down the chain of command, in their episodic insistence that they are treating detainees humanely, in their efforts to evade responsibility for particularly harsh measures by transferring detainees to regimes known to lack all inhibition, and in their insistence, when faced with a hew and cry about new evidence of gross abuse, that such abuse is the work of a few rogues who will be punished in accordance with law. A final factor in my choice of emphasis is the way in which revelations of brutal interrogation, perhaps more than any other single facet of US tactics in the counter-terrorist struggle, have engaged public notice around the world and lowered where they have not virtually emptied the reservoir of goodwill accumulated by the United States over the past two centuries.

Still, I feel something more must be said about the overall behavior of the Bush Administration, behavior that I find hard to reconcile with the values we are supposedly defending, behavior that, taken in the round, certainly appears to violate fundamental rights declared in the International Covenant on Civil and Political Rights and in Common Article 3 of the Geneva Conventions. I speak in the light of behavior by other governments I encountered not vicariously in the comfort of my study but in the grim world of practice when serving from 1976–83 as a member and, for a time, President of the Inter-American Commission on Human Rights of the Organization of American States.

During those years, authoritarian regimes from the Hemisphere's Central American throat to Tierra del Fuego terrorized critics of their political projects in the name of protecting public order and Western Christian Civilization against terrorists and revolutionary movements inspired by one or another variant of Marxist thought. Some of their presumed opponents they disappeared into clandestine torture centers from which few emerged. Others they simply murdered. Still others they rounded up and held indefinitely often in severe conditions or sentenced to long prison terms after trial by military tribunals. Guantánamos and Abu Ghraib's sprouted like poisonous mushrooms across the countries ruled by terror. The courts were suspended, supine, corrupted, intimidated, or simply ignored.

With a clarity then unprecedented for United Nations or Hemispheric institutions, the Commission, its seven members insulated from accusations of ideological collusion with left-wing insurgents by virtue of having been nominated and elected by the Governments of the OAS and coming for the most part from the most privileged sectors of their respective countries, illuminated the awful terrain of these torture states. Its reports bore witness to death and mutilation and trials that travestied due process. Its members accurately translated into the dignified language of officialdom the screams of the electric shocked and beaten and water-boarded, they translated, in other words, tales of torture and "highly coercive" or "professional" interrogation.

Although immune to labeling as a knowing accomplice of the insurgents, insurgents who themselves were not always scrupulous in their methods, the Commission was accused of failing to take into sufficient account the difficulties governments faced in protecting the citizenry from "the terrorists." To this accusation, the Commission responded as follows in its 1980 Report on the condition of human rights in Argentina:

In the life of any nation, threats to the public order or to the personal safety of its inhabitants, by persons or groups that use violence, can reach such proportions that it becomes necessary, temporarily, to suspend the exercise of certain human rights.... However, it is... clear that certain fundamental rights can never be suspended, as is the case, among others, of the right to life, the right to personal safety, or the right to due process. In other words, under no circumstances may governments employ summary execution, torture, inhumane conditions of detention, or the denial of certain minimum conditions of justice as the means to restore public order.[134]

The Commission went on to say that:

When the emergency situation is truly serious, certain restrictions may be imposed, for example, on the freedom of information... or... association. In more extreme cases, persons may be detained for short periods without it being necessary to bring specific charges against them. It is true that such measures can ultimately pose the risk that the rule of law will be lost, but that is not inevitable provided that governments act responsibly; if they register arrests and inform the families of the detainees of the detentions; if they issue strict orders prohibiting torture; if they carefully recruit and train security forces, weeding out sadists and psychopaths; *and lastly, if there is an independent Judiciary to swiftly correct any abuse of authority* (emphasis added).[135]

How does the Bush Administration's war against international terrorism stack up against the standards the Commission reaffirmed in its report concerning the Argentine Government's war against "terrorists"? The Administration's "declaration of war" in conjunction with a broadly worded mandate from Congress[136] can be read as equivalent to the declaration of a state of emergency referred to by the Commission. Though it has not attempted to suspend formally the writ of habeas corpus for the nation as a whole, it has encouraged legislation profoundly limiting the exercise of that right for detainees held in Guantánamo and has argued before the courts, ultimately without success, that they have no

---

[134] See *Inter-American Commission on Human Rights: Ten years of Activities 1971–1981* (Washington DC: OAS, 1982), 341. I am familiar with these words, not only because I have refreshed my recollection of the Report, but also because I wrote them in the draft document approved by the full Commission without a dissenting vote.

[135] Ibid., 342.

[136] On 18 September 2001, one week after the attacks, Congress passed Public Law 107–38 allocating $40 billion for the purpose of "(1) providing Federal, State, and local preparedness for mitigating and responding to the attacks; (2) providing support to counter, investigate, or prosecute domestic or international terrorism; (3) providing increased transportation security; (4) repairing public facilities and transportation systems damaged by the attacks; and (5) supporting national security..."

jurisdiction over claims of detainees held outside the country even in territory under the control of the US Government. In addition, the President has claimed that, given the state of war, he has authority to order the detention in the United States of citizens and aliens alike, if he or his designees believe such persons are engaged in terrorist conspiracies or have actually aided and abetted or committed acts of terrorism, and to hold them indefinitely without charge or trial. Whether or not he is using a "reasonable-grounds-for- suspicion" or some other test is unclear. On the theory that persons arrested for being parts of the terrorist conspiracy against the United States are, by definition, unlawful combatants unprotected by the Geneva Conventions, the President also claims the right to have such persons tried by military commissions created for this purpose rather than by civilian courts or courts martial under the Uniform Code of Military Justice.

Furthermore, the Administration has authorized or, at best, tolerated methods of interrogation that, at a minimum, satisfy widely accepted definitions of cruel, inhuman, and degrading treatment and, by seeking to limit the application of any Congressional limits on methods of interrogation to the Department of Defense, as distinguished from the intelligence agencies, has conveyed the message that the latter should be free to employ any means they deem useful. Moreover, a large body of evidence supports the conviction that the Bush Administration has seized suspected terrorists in various parts of the world and taken them for interrogation to secret places of detention abroad or turned them over to the intelligence services of countries that, according to its own official surveys of human rights violations, regularly interrogate by torture. In addition, consistent with the claim of right to attack terrorists wherever it may find them, it has carried out the assassination of at least one person it believes to have been an official of Al Qaeda.

The Bush Administration does not plead in extenuation of these actions extreme "necessity" under circumstances constituting an acute emergency such as the one reasonably apprehended by the Administration and many other Americans in the immediate aftermath of 9/11. On the contrary, the President and other high officials foresee a war that may extend for two generations. In practical effect, then, this is a condition of permanent emergency, precisely the situation that George Orwell in his classic novel *1984* envisions as an enabler of totalitarian control.[137] Moreover, under the theory of Presidential power voiced by the President, for instance in his "signing statement" accompanying the McCain Amendment, and urged by his Attorney General, at least in time of war, the President is empowered by the Constitution to override by his decision alone the existing laws of the land and any new ones that the Congress may pass over his veto. In addition, if respectable accounts of the President's vetting of

---

[137] Of course we are light years from that surreal world, but, in the event of further dramatic terrorist incidents in the United States, perhaps not quite so far removed from the serious risk of an authoritarian populism of the kind Benito Mussolini constructed in Italy during the early 1920s. Democracy, like other processes, has its tipping points.

candidates for Supreme Court vacancies are correct, a litmus test for prospective Justices is acceptance of the theory of the "unitary executive" which is the exotic constitutional ideology from which this President's claims spring.

Why do I mention the creeping emasculation of Judicial and Congressional restraints on Executive Power? Because in Latin America, the debility of Judicial and Congressional oversight and the corresponding hypertrophy of Executive Power have invariably coincided with gross violations of human rights like torture, cruel, inhuman, and degrading treatment, arrest without probable cause, arrest followed by disappearance, indefinite detention without charge, and trials (normally followed by conviction) in which defendants lack reasonable means to contest the accusations against them. That we truly live in dangerous times is a point I underscored early in this chapter. The capacity of non-governmental associations, even small ones, to wreak havoc is likely to increase over time as scientific knowledge and technological competence become progressively more diffused.

As one of the world's leading proliferators, the Pakistani nuclear scientist AQ Khan, has demonstrated,[138] a person may acquire technological sophistication without coincidentally coming into possession of humanistic values. Hence it would be Panglossian to pretend that the United States and other governments will not need to take measures for the protection of their citizens that would in the past have been properly regarded as intolerable intrusions on personal freedom. I fear that there will have to be permanently enhanced surveillance of movement and financial transactions, for example, and even of private communications. But this push of circumstance toward chronic insecurity makes it all the more important that we resist the emasculation of restraints on executive power particularly as it impacts on individuals caught up in fear-driven dragnets of persons who arouse suspicion often and inevitably by their ethnic or religious profile or their harsh criticism of government policy or their family connections or friendships with persons who become suspects. In intelligence and policing agencies, the whole incentive system will encourage aggressive use of power to arrest and interrogate. Failure to avert an attack will destroy careers. Mistaken arrest, surveillance without reasonable suspicion, abusive interrogation, and conviction achieved by unethical means usually will not.

A President satisfying the Hemingway test of grace under pressure would seek to reinforce the system's safeguards rather than taking the Latin American way of security that prevailed during my years on the Inter-American Commission. The Commission did not find, for instance, that trial of civilians by military tribunals was in itself a violation of due process. The case for such a finding is strong. Professional military institutions are by their nature relatively hermetic. Success in battle requires very high levels of mutual trust and confidence, intense bonding

---

[138] See Seymour Hersh, "The Deal: Why is Washington going easy on Pakistan's nuclear black marketers?" *New Yorker*, 8 March 2004.

of cohorts, and respect for authority. To find an accused not guilty is to reject the earlier findings of fellow officers who made the arrest, collected the evidence, and prosecuted the case. To reject evidence on grounds that it was obtained by torture is to indict fellow officers. But since most Latin American constitutions provided for or did not preclude trial of civilians by military tribunals under certain circumstances or with respect to a limited number of offences, it was very difficult for the Commission to find in Hemispheric practice a solid basis for construing the broad due process language of the American Convention to preclude all military trials.

So instead the Commission looked at military trials of persons not members of the military in order to determine their fundamental fairness on a case-by-case basis. One central concern was whether the defendants and their counsel could counter all of the evidence brought against them. Another was whether evidence obtained through torture and other abusive interrogation methods was admissible. And a third was the possibility of review by the regular civilian courts. Where these safeguards, particularly the first two were not available, most Commission members believed the process was fundamentally unfair. While President Bush's military tribunals have been moving targets, their features being frequently altered in the face of condemnation by lawyers and civil liberties organizations and, finally, the courts, the early reluctance to allow review of guilty verdicts by civilian courts and the insistence on being able to use secret evidence and witnesses revealed that indifference to considerations of fundamental fairness, indifference to the substantial risk of convicting the innocent, that I had previously encountered among the rulers of the terror states of Latin America in an earlier era. Those governments too had, in some cases including the Argentine one, faced serious threats to public security. Those governments too were graceless under pressure. But that was hardly surprising in their case, since they never imagined themselves as the champions of liberal democracy.

4

Terrorism, Communalism and Democracy: The Limits of Tolerance

We are very apt to think that we men and women understand one another; but most probably you know nothing even of the modes of thought of the man who lives next door to you.
(Anthony Trollope)

The main driver of terrorism in the post-Marxist age will be communal rather than class conflict. The fault lines of class may overlap and thereby aggravate communal ones. And in some cases, the reduction of the overlap—for instance by affirmative action to produce much greater equality of opportunity and outcome for the group producing armed challengers of the status quo—may reduce inter-communal animosity, particularly at the level of elites. But not in all. For many people, communal ties respond to a deep hunger for a kind of organic, almost familial identity (and often for a corresponding Satanic "other") that often trumps a merely material calculus. Before the First World War, many Socialists cheerfully predicted that the proletarians of the great powers would, in their transnational class solidarity, refuse to serve as the cannon fodder of bourgeois and aristocratic governments appealing to them in the name of *La Patria*.[1] Ten million deaths managed to dispel that optimism.

In commonplace scholarly and official discourse, the phrases communal conflict and ethno-nationalist conflict are often used interchangeably. Where religion is the fault line of group animosity, the term "religious nationalism" is sometimes employed. I prefer communal because it covers all cases, including ones, like the present struggle with the Al Qaeda network and its clones, that are not strictly speaking nationalist, but can still be usefully described as inter-communal, the conflicting communities in this case being a relatively small but probably expanding sub-set of Islam and, in the view of this sub-set, much or all of the West (including Israel) in league with various Muslim regimes that betray the interests of their peoples and of Islam in general.[2] Ethno- and

---

[1] See, eg, Niall Ferguson, *The Pity of War* (London: Basic Books, 1998), 174–211. Referencing copious primary sources, Ferguson finds that the large number of men who volunteered for service (well into 1916) were typically motivated by a diffuse "love of country."

[2] A vast array of scholarship (greatly varying in quality) on the conflicts and tensions between the West and the Islamic world has emerged over the past several decades. See, for instance,

religious-nationalism are two varieties of communalism. Often the two are indistinguishable, religion being in many places, like the Balkans, the principal source of "ethnic" identity. But not in all. The Kurds, for instance, are Sunni Muslims; they nevertheless constitute a self-conscious and sometimes persecuted minority even within countries of the Middle East like Iraq and Turkey where Sunnis have dominated the political terrain. Religion defines the murderous divisions of Ulster, but not of Spain: Basques are Catholic like the rest of the country's Christians.

Initially, as in the case of Al Qaeda, only one side in a potential conflict of communities may see the world in we/they terms. But by treating the otherwise disparate elements of its self-defined enemy as if they formed a single hostile community, those many elements can quickly morph into one for the purpose of confronting their assailant. By envisioning the "other," you may summon it. The Al Qaeda phenomenon is an effort by Islamic militants to create a vast transnational armed struggle by persuading otherwise heterogeneous Islamic communities to unite against Western states or at least the activities and influence of the West and particularly the United States and Israel (the latter being seen as an extension of the West) in the Middle East. To that end they benefit from and probably consciously seek to provoke a US-led response to their attacks that is conducted in such ways and on such a scale as to make Muslims generally feel targeted or, where not physically threatened, symbolically humiliated.[3]

Clashes inspired by a vision of global inter-faith conflict but often shaped by local conditions are one form of communal conflict. A second form, one which, as in the case of Kashmir, can overlap the first, is the classic struggle for autonomy, often for sovereign independence, waged in the name of self-determination by a community, or at least by militants claiming to represent it, that is numerically preponderant in some part of an existing state. Terrorist violence in furtherance of communal bids for territorial separation had been part of the modern European scene until very recently. Now, with the apparent decision of the IRA to abandon violence in pursuit of its political goals, other than the Basque insurgents the main terrorist threat in Europe (outside the Balkans, at least) seems to stem largely from the tensions immanent in the territorial co-location of secular liberal majorities and primarily Muslim immigrant minorities, themselves quite diverse

Edward Said, *Orientalism* (New York: Pantheon Books, 1978); but compare Ian Buruma and Avishai Margalit, *Occidentalism: The West in the Eyes of Its Enemies* (New York: Penguin Press, 2004). See also Bernard Lewis, *What Went Wrong? Western Impact and Middle Eastern Response* (Oxford: Oxford University Press, 2002). But compare Robert Fisk, *The Great War for Civilisation: The Conquest of the Middle East* (New York: Alfred A Knopf, 2005).

[3] See, eg, Sarah Lyall and Ian Fisher, "Many Muslims in Britain Tell of Feeling Torn Between Competing Identities," *The New York Times International Edition*, 13 August 2006, 6: One 23-year old British Muslim man interviewed by Lyall and Fisher angrily asserted that "the war on terrorism is the war on us." See also Alan Cowell, "British Muslims Criticize Blair and Policies; Police Broaden Search for Evidence," *The New York Times International Edition*, 13 August, 2006, 4.

in background,[4] carrying on traditional practices that in a variety of ways cut across the grain of liberal values. Even where it is not the immediate source of terrorist violence, the deep estrangement of an uncertain but clearly not trivial number of Muslims in Western Europe may be producing an emotional climate in which the *jihadi* virus can incubate and then kill, either locally or wherever its carriers may be drawn or directed, as Mohamed Atta, leader of the 9/11 hijackers, was directed from Hamburg to the United States.

On the risks and rigidities of communal profiling, I want to concede here at the outset that stating the terrorist problem in terms of communal conflict risks creating an insidiously misleading set of caricatures that will be taken, by some, as a mirror of reality. On the one hand is the caricature of the liberal democratic descendants of families resident in the West from time immemorial, heirs of the Renaissance and the Enlightenment. On the other is the caricature of the funda-mentalist Muslims of the first or second generation living rigidly in a pre-modern epistemological and normative universe. Yet within the ranks of the notional heirs of the Enlightenment are, among others, murderous skinheads who swarm to cripple persons of darker hues in various European cities and the drunken, foul-mouthed hooligans who haunt European and particularly British football and the sweet-tempered Volk who parade to the polls to vote for Le Pen and the polished gentlemen who collude with the Italian Mafia, to name but some. Meanwhile the ranks of European Muslims contain distinguished intellectuals like Tariq Ramadan of Switzerland,[5] Parisians in haute couture, and tens of thousands of families living quiet bourgeois and working-class lives informed by a range of views on education, democracy, and the organization of family life and moved by worldly aspirations hardly distinguishable from those of their Christian neighbors.

Still, detailed inquiries into the diurnal reality of Muslim minorities in Europe (including their treatment of women)[6] and the bombings and murders (like that of the filmmaker Theo Van Gogh in Amsterdam and the young Muslim woman in Berlin who broke away from her family in the hope of living an independent life) carried out in the name of Islamic family values,[7] and the furious denunciation

---

[4] *See* Fiona Adamson, "Islam in Europe: The Challenges of Institutionalization," *Council for European Studies at Columbia University*, 2006, available at <http://www.columbia.edu/cu/ces/pub/Adamson_sep05.html>. *See also* Frank J Buijs and Jan Rath, "Muslims in Europe: The State of the Research," *Essay Prepared for the Russell Sage Foundation*, October 2002, available at <http://dev.eurac.edu:8085/mugs2/do/blob.pdf?type=pdf&serial=1124274755830#search=%22euro-islam-a%20new%20understanding%20of%20islam%20within%20muslim%20diaspora%22>.

[5] Ramadan's website includes an extensive collection of his writings, thoughts and commentary; available at <http://www.tariqramadan.com/welcome.php3>. For an assessment of the man and his ideas, see Ian Buruma, *Tariq Ramadan Has an Identity Issue*, The New York Times Magazine, 4 February 2007, 36.

[6] See especially Ayaan Hirsi Ali, *The Caged Virgin: An Emancipation Proclamation for Women and Islam* (New York: Free Press, 2006). But compare Marlise Simons, "Muslim Women in Europe Claim Rights and Keep Faith," *The New York Times International Edition*, 29 December 2005, A3.

[7] See, eg, Peter Schneider, "The New Berlin Wall," *The New York Times Magazine*, 4 December 2005, 66–71. Schneider, a writer living in Berlin, chronicles his discovery of what "...Germans like me didn't care to know...an everyday life of oppression, isolation, imprisonment and brutal

by some Islamic religious teachers of majority culture, indicted for its sensuality and tolerance of practices and relationships proscribed by traditional Islamic principles,[8] testify collectively to deep estrangement between significant elements within the immigrant communities and the generality of West Europeans. Caricature, after all, exaggerates, often grossly, but generally it does not invent.

That said, it is nevertheless important to any balanced appreciation of the long-term risks to open, tolerant, and reason-based societies in Europe and North America to appreciate how the twinned caricatures tend to veil the liberal/ traditionalist fault line of culture that runs through the legacy populations of Europe much less the principally Caucasian multi-generational citizens of the United States. Terrorist violence on behalf of their idea of traditional values is not exactly alien to Europe's skinheads and America's militias, racists, homo-phobes, and radical anti-abortionists. Though few in numbers, they are the murderous edge of far larger groups that rage against the tolerance and cosmopolitan character of liberal society.[9]

The European and American cases differ in at least two important respects. The first is that in American the liberal/traditionalists fault line does not over-lap an ethnic one. The second is that, in America, traditionalists enjoy serious political power; hence they can advance their agenda through the political pro-cess. Because its liberal culture is hegemonic and the liberal/traditionalist fault line does overlap largely with ethnicity (and the rawest economic inequalities), Europe is the part of the West where the tension[10] between the majority culture and the traditionalist one is most threatening to peaceful (even if antagonistic) coexistence.

What are the generic features of the cultures I refer to as "illiberal" or "traditional"? They idealize and organize family life along patriarchal lines with women of any

---

corporal punishment for Muslim women and girls in Germany, a situation for which there is only one word: slavery." On the murder of Van Gogh, see Ian Buruma, "The Final Cut," *The New Yorker*, 80(41) (3 January 2005), 26–32.

[8] See footnote 5 above; and Ramadan's *To Be A European Muslim* (Leicester, UK: Islamic Foundation, 1999). See also Jytte Klausen, "Counterterrorism and the Integration of Islam in Europe," *Foreign Policy Research Institute, Watch on the West*, 7(1) (July 2006), available at <http://www.fpri.org>. Klausen notes that Muslims aren't the only voices of religious conservatism in con-temporary European (and American) society: "Abortion, gay rights, and bioethics are some of the issues where religious Muslims find common ground with other religious associations and lobbies."

[9] See, eg, "Summer 2006 Intelligence Report," *Southern Poverty Law Center*, Issue 122, Summer 2006, available at <http://www.splcenter.org/intel/intelreport/intrep.jsp>. See also Russell Shorto, "Contra-Contraception," *The New York Times Magazine*, 7 May 2006, 48, on the burgeoning movement in the United States to outlaw all forms of contraception. See also sources cited at footnote 8 in Chapter 1, particularly Dinesh D'Souza *The Enemy At Home: The Cultural Left and Its Responsibility for 9/11* (New York: Doubleday, 2006).

[10] See "Look Out, Europe, They Say," *The Economist*, 24 June 2006, 29–34: the article notes the growing belief in the United States that it is more successful at integrating Muslims because American culture is more comfortable with overt displays of religiosity than secular European culture; however, the article also notes that the majority of Muslims in America are considerably better-off economically than their peers in Europe. See also "Charlemagne: Talking of Immigrants," *The Economist*, 3 June 2006, 50.

age in a subordinate (traditionalists might say "protected") and constrained position insofar as legal rights, decisional power, and relations with the larger society are concerned. They assume that identity is inherited and permanent, not individually constructed. The moral life is defined by iron tradition; it is not a matter of personal choice. Virtue consists of adherence to received tradition and loyalty is owed first to the extended family and then to the community, the latter being constituted by co-adherents to the received tradition. Internal challenge to tenets of the tradition is punishable heresy. Voluntary departure is punishable apostasy. External criticism, satire, or insult is punishable blasphemy.

With those features, the illiberal minority must present public policy challenges to a liberal democratic state in a host of areas: sexual and reproductive freedom (eg contraception, abortion, sodomy, extra-marital intimacy); education (eg compulsory education, state regulation of religious school curricula, mixed-gender schools); marital choice (eg minimum age laws); gender equality (eg divorce, control of property, equal application of criminal law to spouses); treatment of children (eg again compulsory education and minimum age for marriage, protection of children from painful and harmful rituals like clitoridectomy, access to modern health); free speech and association for all citizens. I will return to these issues at a later point.

The encounter of liberal and illiberal communities occurs in an epoch where the integration of national economies and the revolution in communication and transportation, what might be called the material cosmopolitanization and consumerization of the world, coincide with the survival of parochial and traditionalist attachments. Hence there can be no accommodation by means of mutual willed isolation. The encounter compels consideration of the limits of liberal tolerance and the bases of social peace. It demands that we consider whether individual rights and alleged rights of groups are fully reconcilable, whether group rights are derivative of individual rights or a distinct category of human entitlements, and it further requires us to consider the rights of majorities as well as minorities. Finally it requires that we consider the compatibility of tolerance for illiberal ways of life with the long-term sustainability of liberal democracy. I look at these issues, as at all the others this book engages, through the optics of law and the moral values embedded in human rights norms (best expressed politically by American liberalism and European social democracy) which constitute a particular way of visualizing human dignity.

1. Civic Communities and Communities of Blood and of Faith

First I turn to the more familiar, relatively straightforward, self-determination struggles. Here the normative consensus among governments, a consensus witnessed by most scholars, seems clear. In sum, the effort at normative containment of the centrifugal principle of self-determination has been successful. It has not evolved into a general writ of secession available to any self-conscious group, predominantly occupying a determinate territory, wishing to secede from an existing state.[11] Other than in the matter of the Palestinian problem, which, for reasons I will explain in my next chapter, I see as the final knot in the unwinding of the Western colonial order, self-determination today is, at most, a special writ available as a last resort in cases where no other means of safeguarding the human rights of a group appear available.

I find it conceptually helpful to think of nationalism as one form of communalism, a form that shares many of the broader phenomenon's traits while having a few all its own. What exactly is this sub-species? Nationalism, one of its most sophisticated analysts, Ernest Gellner, has proposed, is a political movement designed to achieve symmetry between a nation or "people" (to use the UN's idiom) and its frontiers,[12] that is to make the people's space coterminous with the territory of a sovereign state or at least a political entity enjoying internal self-government.

What is it that bonds the individuals who constitute the movement? What, in other words, is a "nation?" "Two men are of the same nation," Gellner writes, "if and only if they share the same culture, where culture in turn means a system of ideas and signs and associations and ways of behaving and communicating."[13] Culture is, however, an insufficient condition, since it also is necessary that "they *recognize each other* as belonging to the same nation."[14] While also emphasizing the centrality of a shared *perception* of common nationality, another leading scholar, Yael Tamir, suggests that it is necessarily accompanied by the shared *belief* that members of the nation have certain features in common, the most important of them being ancestors, however remote, and a continuous genealogy.[15]

That claimed feature applies plausibly to the Basque but not at all, of course, to the great transnational communities of faith. The many-hued pilgrims who converge annually on Mecca cannot imagine themselves as offshoots of a common genealogical root, but they appear nevertheless to feel part of a community, however vast. What most writers agree on, the ones cited being typical, is that at its core, the nation is an inter-subjective phenomenon, what Benedict Anderson describes in his memorable phrase as "an imagined community."[16] The community may in fact share various objective features: language, religion, culture, distinguishing skin tone, long residence of a determinate territory, and so on. And these common features may help explain why the sense of collective identity arose. But while they may be a source, they should not be identified as integral to

[11] See generally, Tom J Farer, "The Ethics of Intervention in Self-Determination Struggles," *Human Rights Quarterly*, 25 (2003), 382–406.

[12] Ernest Gellner, *Nations and Nationalism* (Ithaca, New York: Cornell University Press, 1983), 1.

[13] Ibid, 7.

[14] Ibid, 7 (emphasis added).

[15] Yael Tamir, "The Enigma of Nationalism," *World Politics*, 47(3) (April 1995), 418–40.

[16] Benedict Anderson, *Imagined Communities: Reflections on the Origins and Spread of Nationalism* (London: Verso, 1991).

the phenomenon itself, because even where several of these features are present, it may not arise.

The essence of the phenomenon being subjective, it might seem dependent to some extent on free individual choice. However, as Margaret Canovan has perceptively noted,

> That choice is…experienced as a destiny transcending individuality; it turns political institutions into a kind of extended family inheritance, although the kinship ties in question are highly metaphorical; it is a contingent historical product that feels like part of the order of nature; it links individual and community, past and present; it gives to cold impersonal structures an aura of warm, intimate togetherness.[17]

This imagined national community, what I would call "the community of blood," can be contrasted with what some writers call the "constitutional nation,"[18] exemplified by the United States. The constitutional nation is, to be sure, a sovereign state, but, unlike many of its kind, it is not felt by its members to be a mere contingent cluster of institutions and legal norms, at most a temporarily useful contrivance, an impersonal thing that is better than anarchy but unimaginable as an object of devotion. The constitutional nation both in perception and fact is a community of choice. It has a beginning, often heroic, an identifiable historical beginning associated with a voluntary pact that is either the extant constitution or the core of principles on which the present one is based. The historical specificity of this nation's origins discourages notions about common genealogy. Members know that their ancestry predates the community, that their ancestors once were part of other political arrangements possibly in remote geographic space. Nevertheless the constitutional nation distinguishes itself from mere sovereign states by having acquired that "aura of warm, intimate togetherness"[19] shrewdly evoked by Canovan.

In the ideal case, though its members may differ in religion, race, domestic practices, and even language (consider Switzerland, for instance), they participate in a common political culture, call it "the constitutional culture," and it evokes that same passionate loyalty, that sense of belonging to a bounded, distinctive, and admirable association that characterizes the imagined nation, the community of destiny with its myth of common origin. In the real world, however, a sovereign state may be a constitutional nation for only a portion of its citizens. Others, like many Basques in Spain, may identify with a community of blood and feel in varying degrees alienated from the constitutional system. In other words, constitutional nations are not immune to self-determination challenges.

[17] Margaret Canovan, "The Skeleton in the Cupboard: Nationhood, Patriotism and Limited Loyalties," in Simon Caney *et al.* (eds) *National Rights, International Obligations* (Boulder, Colorado: Westview Press, 1996), 76.

[18] See, eg, John Charret, "What is Nationality and is There a Moral Right to Self-Determination?" *National Rights, International Obligations*, 53–68.

[19] Canovan, 36.

Imagined nations by their nature are more like billiard balls, all of a piece, unitary actors as long as the glue of extended family feeling continues to bind. Where the imagined nation is coterminous with a sovereign state, of course it controls the material means—the media, schools, patriotic rites, language of power, and opportunity—for the glue's perpetual renewal. Perhaps, even more important, its members automatically experience a quotidian sensation of separate and distinct existence from other unitary actors. So if we think of the imagined community as an organic thing and if we assume that the primal instinct of organic things is to survive, it seems natural in a world long organized into sovereign states that where community members predominantly occupy a substantial territory, particularly one which over the years has acquired for one reason or another distinct boundaries, it will experience an impulse toward sovereignty. For where it shares political space with other communities, it cannot monopolize the means of cultural reinforcement.

Since for the Muslims of Western Europe the sharing of space with other communities is unavoidable, traditionalists face a more daunting task in attempting to propagate beliefs and practices. Without spatial separation, community members may easily acquire cross-communal ties of friendship, family, love, and instrumental interest that progressively erode the primal communal identity. This risk is greatest within a liberal constitutional state, since in opening place and power to members of all its communities, that state creates conditions inimical to willed ghettoization.

2. Communalism and Liberalism

Suppose the world were divided into a neat checkerboard of imagined communities, each occupying continuously and exclusively a particular geographic space and that, whether by war or negotiation, each community had achieved independent national existence. Would this be a moral utopia? Would liberalism's respect for associational autonomy then be reconciled with all other liberal values? Or, to put the issue in a slightly different form, would communalism and liberalism be thus made compatible? Surely, even then, the answer is "no." It is "no" in this world where unparalleled ease of communication and movement and the global division of labor foster fraternity and identity across national lines and offer a smorgasbord of "histories" in place of a single myth. But it would have been "no" even before there was liberalism much less globalization.

When men traveled no faster than a ship could sail or an ass be made to trot, there was apostasy. And not just by the remarkable aberrant individual, because aberrancy is more than a matter of genius. It is encouraged by the contradictions between expectations and their fulfillment, by the failure of prophesy and the parsimony of justice, by the particularities of place, each with its layered history of successive myths. Aberrant individuals give passionate voice to doubt and disillusionment or to unsanctioned sources of hope. They challenge the tribal myths. They can be the offspring of merely endogenous contradictions, needs, and inspirations. In the middle ages, before there were nations, the Albigensian Christian heresy flourished less than a thousand land miles from Rome[20] and alongside areas unswerving in their conventional faith. The Albigensians constituted an internal challenge to the imagined community of Catholic Christianity which, in self-defense, extinguished them by fire and sword. As in the case of the Nazis and the Jews, mere ethnic cleansing seemed insufficient, assuming it even was an imaginable option.

If, as I suggest, communalism has an impulse toward cultural isolation (or, where possible, cultural monopoly) and if communalism has a corresponding susceptibility to the cultivation of intolerance by ambitious political adventurers, why would anyone who resonates to the liberal tradition in political philosophy find anything positive about it? One answer to that question is that communalism's vices are the other side of its considerable virtues.[21] It sustains a sense of fraternity among a host of strangers. In the framework of a sovereign state, it is an emotional adhesive that fosters domestic peace and, by clothing governmental institutions in an aura normally associated with the warm intimacy of kinship ties, it enables these strangers to do more justice to each other and to cooperate more in the production of public goods than would be plausible without this sense of deep connection.

Without some feeling of fraternity, what will as effectively evoke generosity among the "haves" and soften resentment among the "have nots"? Communal feeling fills the gap left when Divine Sanction for inequality and compassion loses its authority. In a secular, consumerist age, the imagined community may seem the most effective basis for consensual government. To the extent it facilitates government by consent and sympathetically connects the privileged and the needy, communalism serves liberal values, according to this line of argument. Civic nationalism, where it takes root, is a happier alternative to the same end. But up to now it has only occasionally found nourishing soil.

Within the human rights value system (which, as I have previously indicated, I associate closely with modern liberalism and its social democratic cousin), the sympathetic connection of the privileged and the needy must be reckoned a virtue belonging to communalism in general, not just the genealogical form, one that

---

[20] See generally, Joseph R Strayer, *The Albigensian Crusades* (New York: Dial Press, 1971). See also Michael Costen, *The Cathars and the Albigensian Crusade* (Manchester, UK: Manchester University Press, 1997).

[21] See, eg, Hasan Hanafi, "Alternative Conceptions of Civil Society: A Reflective Islamic Approach," in Simone Chambers and Will Kymlicka (eds), *Alternative Conceptions of Civil Society* (Princeton: Princeton University Press, 2002), 171–89: "Individual human beings cannot live alone...in Islam, civil society protects the rights of its members by anchoring these rights in a conception of universally binding duties or obligations that resemble Western conceptions of natural law." See also Richard Madsen, "Confucian Conceptions of Civil Society," *Alternative Conceptions of Civil Society*, 190–204.

resonates with particular strength where all communities within the territorial state contain a wealthy elite whose generosity can increase the life chances of each community's poor. Viewed from a human rights perspective, increasing life chances is not communalism's only virtue. In addition, even if members of a community visualize membership as their fate, communalism is in fact an exercise of the individual human right of association for any licit purpose, certainly including cultural preservation.

Some liberal writers propose a third virtue, one they wrest through a kind of intellectual judo move from liberalism's emphasis on personal autonomy.[22] Their argument runs along the following lines. In order to be self-directed, individuals need a stable framework of meaning that filters and channels the tsunami of sensations roaring toward them after they enter the world. Their cultural legacy provides that framework. It organizes and filters sensation. It lends a sense of identity, a distinct place in the world, a menu of constraints and actions. The legacy both poses and provides answers to life's elementary questions. Who am I? What should I do? What impulses must I restrain? Which actions should I celebrate and which should I condemn? To what can I aspire? What should I avoid? What are the consequences of doing A rather then B or C? By providing individuals with cues for action, culture generates confidence. In a totally alien world, we could not make rational choices because the consequences of any action would be unknowable. A deep, institutionalized culture is thus claimed to act like a flashlight handed to an individual who would otherwise be frozen with uncomprehending fear in a dark and precarious place.

A deep institutionalized culture, even an isolated one, is not, however, a closed, frictionless system. Cultures are riddled with cues for action that lead to disappointment. Their explanations sometimes fail to explain, their prophesies fail to predict. And the societies they organize also disappoint individual hopes, in part because many valued goods—power, wealth, celebrity, reciprocated sexual desire—are scarce. Disappointment and surprise force thought and self-consciousness and introspection. Thought need not lead to apostasy. It does lead to the subjective experience of choice, the human faculty liberalism celebrates and protects. Thus even illiberal cultures have a profoundly liberal consequence. Conversely, the argument concludes, the destruction of minority culture even in the name of human rights and liberal values has the illiberal consequence of reducing the experienced capacity to choose. And that consequence ensues whether destruction results from state-coerced assimilation or state prohibition of practices important in the minority culture but incompatible with the majority's values, or through mere failure of the state to protect minority culture from the gradual but progressive erosion that results where access to power, privilege, and

[22] See, eg, Will Kymlicka, *Politics in the Vernacular* (Oxford: Oxford University Press, 2001), 250–3, quoting and paraphrasing Yael Tamir, *Liberal Nationalism* (Princeton: Princeton University Press, 1993). See also Charles Taylor, "The Politics of Recognition," in Amy Gutmann (ed), *Multiculturalism and the Politics of Recognition* (Princeton: Princeton University Press, 1992).

respect is implicitly conditioned on changes in cultural style, often in language and sometimes in religion, in order to mirror the majority.

That we cannot make reasoned choices if we cannot make sense of the world and of our place in it seems indisputable. As the Puritan theologian, Jonathan Edwards once hypothesized, a donkey standing exactly mid-way between two equally sized, equally succulent bales of hay will not starve to death, but the decision to wander over to one rather than the other and begin nibbling is not a reasoned choice (Edwards saw it as evidence of Predestination by the will of God).[23] And the proposition that what enables us to make sense of the world initially, and thus to make reasoned choices, are cues provided by society is intuitively persuasive. But does the individual need a single set of cues in order to organize the world effectively? And, in any event, are single sets now available?

To be sure, the inhabitants of long-isolated societies, organized on the basis of a rationally elaborated system that comprehensively explains and integrates the social and natural worlds[24] appear to experience a catastrophic loss of confidence in their values and understanding of the world when representatives of technologically more advanced societies intrude.[25] For these inhabitants the multiplication of cues seems to constrict the capacity for reasoned choice, to reduce or even destroy their sense of agency. But such societies were exceptional even two centuries ago.

Today, as Jeremy Waldron notes,[26] when millions of people flow across oceans and borders, when radio and television and film are omnipresent, almost everyone is born in effect into a buffet of cultural cues. For better or worse, individuals draw on this buffet to construct an identity, an understanding of themselves in relationship to others and to the institutions and norms that surround them, construct a way of being in the world that works for them, although it may not in all cases work very well for society. But simply because the personality an individual assembles, consciously and unconsciously, from cultural fragments may in some cases be sociopathic, he or she is still an agent, a maker of reasoned albeit by many standards badly reasoned choices. This being, as I see it, the real

---

[23] *Freedom of the Will*, Paul Ramsey (ed) (New Haven: Yale University Press, 1957), 128–9. See also "John Buridan," *Stanford Encyclopedia of Philosophy*, updated 10 July 2006, available at <http://plato.stanford.edu/entries/buridan/>. This parable is commonly known as "Buridan's Ass" in reference to fourteenth-century Parisian philosopher John Buridan, although it is not found in any of Buridan's writings and earlier versions of story are known to exist, including one by Aristotle.

[24] See especially Claude Lévi-Strauss, *The Savage Mind* (Chicago: University of Chicago Press, 1966).

[25] Such scenarios are not limited to small, neolithic-like tribal groups living in exotic, physically isolated locales; arguably, any unique and insular culture can suffer severe cultural trauma from such encounters. See, eg, Jonathan D Spence, *The Search for Modern China* (New York: WW Norton and Co, 1990), 139–91, on the devastating impact of Western intrusion into China during the nineteenth century.

[26] See Jeremy Waldron, "Minority Cultures and the Cosmopolitan Alternative," *University of Michigan Law Review Journal*, 25(3), 751–93. But compare Kymlicka, *Multicultural Citizenship* (Oxford: Oxford University Press, 1995), 101–5.

cultural condition of our time, the liberal case for not merely tolerating but actively supporting illiberal cultures does not rest securely on the ground that culture provides the cues prerequisite for the exercise of reasoned choice and thus for individual autonomy.

Still there may be something to the argument. Inevitably persons living in the West who are born into a family that is patriarchal, essentialist in its view of gender, devout, sexually constrained, deeply absorbed in questions of honor, and strongly inclined to favor family and communal over civic interests are aware at an early point of multiple and sometimes conflicting cues. In theory they could construct a personality by synthesizing cues from their traditionalist culture and from the surrounding secular liberal one. But what the simmering anger among second generation immigrants recorded by researchers suggests[27] is not a creative synthesis of cultural elements, but rather an estrangement far more intense than that of their parents, an estrangement intensified if not generated by a feeling that the majority disrespects their family culture and hence them.[28]

If this is true, if there is a tendency toward polarization which is likely to worsen to the degree the minority culture appears to its members as being under siege, then minority families would seem more likely to resist the majority culture, to withdraw into psychological (as well as geographic) ghettos, and in the process narrow their range of conceivable choice. Polarization intensifies identification with one's birth community and thereby reduces autonomous decision-making for the individual. It follows that respect for non-liberal, even strongly illiberal cultures may, paradoxically, promote one of liberalism's core values, arguably its defining ones.

3. Reconciling Liberal Government and Minority Claims: General Principles and Human Rights Norms

What, however, does respect entail in terms of public policy? Must liberals refrain from using state power to restrain any practices of illiberal communities? Must they agree to deploy state power to enforce minority community practices against dissenting or deviant community members? Must they do more and

---

[27] See, eg, Catherine Fay de Lestrac, "The Malaise of Second-Generation Muslim Immigrants," *iafrica.com*, 28 July 2005, available at <http://iafrica.com/news/features/466650.htm>. See also Stéphane Beaud and Michel Pialoux, "The Children of Hatred," *Le Monde diplomatique*, English language edition, July, 2001.

[28] See, eg, David A Bell, "The Shorn Identity," *The New Republic*, 28 November and 5 December 2005, 20–9, commenting on the language used to describe ethnic minorities in France: "The very use of the word 'immigrant' for these second- and third-generation French youths is an insulting reminder of just how little attention official France has given them. Nicolas Sarkozy is more of an immigrant than many of them." See also Abdellah Taïa, "The France I dreamed of, the France I Lived in," *International Herald Tribune*, 14 April 2006, 9; and "Multicultural Hysterics," *The Economist*, 22 April 2006, 52–3.

restrain private members of their own community from acts that the illiberal minority are likely to regard as disrespectful? Does avoiding polarization also require liberals to support positive governmental action on behalf of the minority's cultural preservation projects including elimination to the extent possible of societal incentives for greater assimilation such as a preference for fluency in the majority's language? Before turning to the details of public policy, I want to consider background moral principles and human rights norms.

A central problem for contemporary liberal moralists is how to reconcile communalism, possessing in all of its forms inherently parochial interests, and twenty-first century liberalism with its universal ones implicit in the conviction that all human beings, regardless of their circumstances, possess a great constellation of rights. The dilemma is dangerously edged precisely because the instrumental virtues of communalism appear to be a function of its exclusionary self-conception. It seems futile to ask the devoted not to favor their own. So where one community shares space with others, the logic of fraternal feeling as well as group survival tilts toward communal bias in the recognition of individual merit and also toward inter-communal struggles for power. In the right circumstances, a balance of communal power or a widely shared cost-benefit analysis in favor of stability where the status quo is relatively comfortable, particularly for elites of all communities, dictates incremental accommodation of differences and a sharing of public goods that benefits the minority in a manner disproportionate to its numbers (but not, perhaps, to its capacity for disruption). But is this not the purchase of peace, an instrumental value, at the expense of core substantive values?

The liberal's philosophical response to the dilemma stemming from the two moral faces of communalism contains two analytically distinct albeit related strategies. One is to take communalism as an organism anti-liberal at its core, not without virtues, to be sure, and useful in its way, but a perpetual threat to humanistic values, demanding anxious vigilance and close restraint by human rights norms. To the extent a particular instance of communalism accepts those constraints, it deserves acceptance. The other intellectual strategy is to insinuate liberal values into the communal core and to insist that the only good communalism, and hence the only one that merits a liberal's respect and support, is a liberal one.

How can "liberal communalism" avoid being an oxymoron? Liberalism emphasizes the essential moral identity of all peoples. Communalism in all its forms and instances celebrates their differences. Boundaries, whether geographic or legal, social and psychological are, for liberals, contingent and instrumental. For fervent communalists they are destined and essential. At the same time, liberalism is no enemy of groups. It values all free association. It respects difference and prohibits coerced assimilation. Rights are universal, but one of those rights is to act collectively. Communalism is liberal when it respects the rights of all other communities to flourish. Being liberal does not prevent it from being communal in the sense of acting to promote the interests of its members in competition with other groups. But it remains liberal only if in the course of that competition it respects the rights necessarily shared by all human beings if life is to be anything other than a war of all against all. To put it in Rawlesian terms,[29] liberal communalists acknowledge as universal those forms of respect they would propose behind a veil of ignorance which prevented them from knowing to which group they would belong.[30] The liberal-communalist distinction between goods that must be shared and those available for competitive appropriation works up to a point with respect both to the relations between sovereign states and those among communities within a state. In inter-state relations liberalism commands mutual respect for political independence and territorial integrity. These are the basic shared goods. It does not enjoin anything like an equal sharing of the benefits and burdens of participation in the global system of political economy. Within states, it arguably requires consultation with all communities in matters requiring collective action and it clearly prohibits ethnic cleansing and forced assimilation. The extent to which it correspondingly commands public assistance to every community's cultural self-defense projects is rather less clear.

Liberal communalism envisions competition between communities and, without self-evisceration, can tolerate up to a point the unequal outcomes implicit in competition. Success in political competition equals control over state institutions. Consistent with the restraints of liberal communalism, to what extent can a victorious community insinuate its distinctive cultural traits, language for instance, into the public realm? Does the "liberal" dimension of liberal communalism require that there be as many languages of public business as there are communities within the envelope of the sovereign state? What does liberal communalism imply for favoritism in the distribution of public goods and the state's obligations, if any, to combat private discrimination in favor of ethnic kin? The more forms and degrees of communal preference liberal communalism is construed to preclude, the less it appears as a coherent form of communalism.

A. The Human Rights of Illiberal Minorities

Does human rights law steer the outcome of that mediation or does it at least provide some guidance? One way of seeing the issues posed by the rapidly growing non-Western communities within European states is in terms of minority entitlements that form a sub-category of human rights law. Some liberal analysts contend that its provisions offer minorities all of the protections and opportunities compatible with liberal values. If minority communities wanted no more than equal treatment for their members within the framework of the established

---

[29] See generally, John Rawls, *A Theory of Justice* (Oxford: Oxford University Press, 1972).
[30] Ibid, 11–12.

majority's ongoing nation-building project, along with the opportunity to associate for purposes of reproducing their traditional culture to the degree that it does not conflict with the majority's core values and public policies, the provisions of the International Covenant on Civil and Political Rights[31] would appear to provide most, perhaps all of the necessary guarantees. Article 18, for instance, confirms the individual right to "thought, conscience and religion." "This right shall include freedom to have or to adopt a religion or belief of his choice, and freedom, either individually or in community with others and in public or private, to manifest his religion or belief in worship, observance, practice and teaching." The article further provides that the states parties to the Covenant "undertake to have respect for the liberty of parents ... to ensure the religious and moral education of their children in conformity with their own convictions." However, the rights declared in Article 18 are subject "To such limitations ... as are necessary to protect public safety, order, health, or morals or the fundamental rights and freedoms of others." I am confident that if the French law forbidding ostentatiously religious clothing and accessories in the public schools and universities[32] were challenged under Article 18, it would be defended precisely on grounds that it is necessary to protect public order by maintaining all public space as a secular realm, and that the principle of secularization or laisization is in turn an instrument the state uses to protect fundamental rights and freedoms.

Article 19 of the Covenant adds to the safeguards for what multi-culturalists would call a minimalist version of communal rights. It guarantees the right to hold opinions without interference and also the right to freedom of expression which shall include freedom to seek, receive, and impart information and ideas of all kinds, regardless of frontiers, either orally, in writing or in print, in the form of art, or through any other media of choice. But, as in the case of Article 18, freedom of expression may be restricted by law where necessary for public order, health or morals and also, in this case, for national security. The Dutch Government would doubtless invoke that exception in defense of a law requiring all Muslim teachers to be trained in Dutch seminaries or one allowing the state to forbid guest appearances by foreign Imams deemed to have encouraged violent *jihad*. I anticipate that restrictions on the expression of militant Islamist views might also be grounded on Article 20's requirement that "Any advocacy of national, racial or religious hatred that constitutes incitement to discrimination, hostility or violence shall be prohibited by law." Also relevant to the protection of

---

[31] International Covenant on Civil and Political Rights, UNGA Res. 2200A (XXI), GAOR, 21st Session, Supp. No. 16, 52 (1966).

[32] See especially Jane Kramer, "Taking the Veil," *The New Yorker*, 22 November 2004, 59. See also Dawn Lyon and Debora Spini, "Unveiling the Headscarf Debate," *Feminist Legal Studies*, 12(3) (January 2004), 333–45: Within their discussion of the broader legal, political and social/cultural implications of the headscarf ban Lyon and Spani astutely observe that, "in all these debates a gender perspective is often absent or marginalized ... where gender is raised, it most often takes the form of a distinction and opposition between 'the Western/European woman' and 'the other Oriental/migrant women'."

minority rights are Article 21's declaration of the right to assemble peacefully and Article 22's declaration of the right to freedom of association, both being subject to the usual qualifications.

The ambiguity or, shall we say, uneasiness, that pervades these articles appears again in Article 23 which declares the family to be "the natural and fundamental group unit of society and entitled to protection by society and the State." So far, so good from the view of traditionalists. However, it turns out that the family being preserved is not necessarily their idea of a proper family, since the Article also provides that "States Parties . . . shall take appropriate steps to ensure equality of rights and responsibilities of spouses as to marriage, during marriage and at its dissolution." Moreover, "No marriage shall be entered into without the free and full consent of the intending spouses." So much for arranged marriages, particularly of the very young.

The final article on individual rights, Article 26, can fairly be seen as the quintessential statement of the liberal integrationist project. It declares all persons "equal before the law and entitled to the equal protection of the law. And it requires state parties to prohibit discrimination and guarantee to all persons equal and effective protection against discrimination on any ground such as race, colour, sex, language . . . or religion." Only Article 27 addresses the minorities issue directly, although arguably in a way that merely summarizes the guarantees already expressed. It provides that:

In those states in which ethnic, religious or linguistic minorities exist, persons belonging to such minorities shall not be denied rights, in community with the other members of their group, to enjoy their own culture, to profess and practice their own religion, or to use their own language.

The Covenant on Economic, Social and Cultural Rights[33] adds nothing to the picture, since it simply declares rights that should be available to all citizens without discrimination.

The Covenants reflect the thoughts and concerns of their time which was the middle years of the last century. At the time they were opened for ratification in 1967, the minorities problem was doubtless seen as one of pervasive discrimination in political, social, and economic life. Within the United States, for instance, formal desegregation of schools was just under way in an atmosphere of often furious resistance from the white majority.[34] The last lynching of an African-American was less than a decade old. African-Americans were still routinely snubbed in hotels, restaurants and other institutions open to the public. In society and the private economy Jews also suffered from embedded discrimination although

[33] International Covenant on Economic, Social and Cultural Rights, GA Res. 2200A (XXI), 21 UN GAOR Supp. (No. 16), 52, UN Doc A/6316 (1966).
[34] See generally, Taylor Branch, *At Canaan's Edge: America in the King Years, 1965–1968* (New York: Simon & Schuster, 2006). See also Mark Kurlansky, *1968: The Year that Rocked the World* (New York: Random House, 2005).

doors once closed to them, particularly in the professions and corporate America, were by then opening in a rapidly growing number of once exclusive domains. Of course in such an environment the demand for change was expressed in terms of equal opportunity for all. Similarly, in many countries of Latin America, still unassimilated indigenous peoples could only dream of equal opportunity to compete for social opportunities and public goods.

Gradually over the last three decades of the century, there began a determined assault on the perception of the minorities problem as one simply of vicious discrimination blocking the exercise of rights and the seizure of opportunities open to the majority. The assault came from many sides. In the world of ideas, post-modernism's[35] attack on the unconscious premises of the status quo (with its partially veiled hierarchies of power) and its coincident citation of the hidden cultural foundations of political hegemony and post-modernism's related devaluation of all canons of propriety and achievement as mere social constructions based on and designed to perpetuate unequal relations of power, inspired among other things a critique of models of integration into the prevailing order of things and a valorization of non-liberal modes of thinking and creating. In the world of brute fact, the difficulty of overcoming centuries of discrimination led to disillusionment in certain minority communities about mere equal opportunity. It is unclear whether much greater equality of opportunity, perceived as such by minorities, would gradually achieve their strong identification with the legacy civic culture.

B. The Evolution of Minority Rights in the Post-modern Era

Minorities were enabled by the tendency of all ideational systems, in this case liberalism's, to perfect themselves, that is to realize their paradigms completely in the material world. For liberalism in countries where it is dominant that has meant less will to coerce, however subtly, in all realms and more will toward penitential responses to groups like Native Americans or colonial peoples brushed aside or repressed by the liberal West in its ebullient epoch of expansion.

Liberalism's constitutional respect for self-determination, whether of individuals or individuals united in groups, heightened its moral sensitivity to minority claims whether for autonomy, even independence, or for a constellation of rights and privileges within existing liberal political orders. Inside Europe, the end of its intra-mural animosities, the de-glorification of war and the opening of borders dulled the state's and the majority's rationale for central control and coercive nation-building and gave more operational space and practical opportunities to the expression of communal particularities and residual grievances and

---

[35] See, eg, Iris Marion Young, "Together in Difference: Transforming the Logic of Group Political Conflict," in Judith Squires (ed), *Principled Positions: Postmodernism and the Rediscovery of Value* (London: Lawrence and Wishart, 1993). See also Kymlicka, *Politics in the Vernacular*, 44–8.

aspirations. Being a Flemish or Catalan or Scottish nationalist began to seem neither very threatening, on the one hand, nor risible on the other. The end of the Cold War and the dissolution of the Soviet Union along with the increasing integration of the European economies sharply enhanced the environment for communal self-assertion.

But of course in the case of Europe, by far the most important change came, as it often has in world history, from migration and demographics, their weight amplified in this instance by the revolutions in the cost and speed of communications and transportation networks and acute unevenness in the global incidence of economic growth. By the last decade of the twentieth century, European nations had uniformly lost their homogeneity. Every one of them had acquired critical masses of non-European minorities and problems of assimilation undreamed of in 1948 when, along with the United States and Canada, West European governments had served as principal authors of the Universal Declaration of Human Rights. On the North American Continent, while both Canada and the United States were experiencing their own immigration surges, it was primarily in the former that the integrationist model was most seriously challenged. And the challenge came not from the new immigrant but rather from the old national minorities of Native Americans and French-speaking inhabitants of Quebec.

Both communities (the former really a coalition of communities) took equal rights and opportunities in liberal-social democratic Canada as a given, but nowhere near enough. Both sought, in addition, to preserve what each saw as a distinctive culture, in the Native American case a whole way of life. And neither thought that its ambition to survive and reproduce itself indefinitely as a living culture could be achieved without a very extensive degree of legal autonomy, if not outright independence in the territories where it predominated. Both communities held this ground in part because of their shared conviction that reproduction in perpetuity required the aid of measures that at least on the surface clashed with the values of a liberal state. It is no wonder, then, that some of the most thoughtful writing on the rights of minorities as living cultures rather than clusters of individuals should have come in recent years out of Canada.[36]

With old-fashioned militant nationalism rending the bloody Balkans and threatening order in other parts of the former Soviet bloc, with growing internal tensions between majorities and new minorities in EU countries and with a hodge-podge of minority issues in the Western Hemisphere, particularly, as noted, in Canada, but also in the many Central and South American countries where indigenous people were gaining voice, it is no wonder that the final years of the twentieth century and the first ones of the twenty-first have witnessed a proliferation of international and regional conventions and other legal or law-related actions addressing the minority rights issue as a problem of collectives not simply individuals. A representative sample would include the 1992 UN

---

[36] See especially the work of Will Kymlicka and Charles Taylor variously cited in this chapter.

Declaration on the Rights of Persons belonging to National or Ethnic, Religious and Linguistic Minorities[37] and its 1994 Draft Declaration on the Rights of Indigenous Peoples,[38] the Council of Europe's 1995 Framework Convention for the Protection of National Minorities,[39] and the minorities provisions of the Document summarizing the consensus of the 1990 Copenhagen meeting of the Conference on the Human Dimension of the Commission on Security and Cooperation in Europe.[40]

Nowhere is the change in perception more frankly stated than in the Preamble to the International Labor Organization's 1989 Convention on Indigenous and Tribal Peoples:

Considering that the developments which have taken place in international law since 1957, as well as developments in the situation of indigenous and tribal peoples in all regions of the world, have made it appropriate to adopt new international standards on the subject with a view to removing the assimilationist orientation of the earlier standards.[41]

Where is the law moving? And for those who believe that nothing should be allowed to compromise the first generation of human rights, how far should we go? That in answering the second question we are moving across contested ground is illustrated by a recent decision of the Dutch Government. The Netherlands, for decades seen as one of the most liberal, asylum- and immigrant-friendly countries in Europe, issued a Declaration in 2005 purporting to make the Council of Europe's Framework Convention for the Protection of National Minorities applicable only to the country's traditional Frisian minority. In a critical comment on the Dutch Declaration, the British-based Minority Rights Group noted that the Declaration implicitly excludes Moroccans, Turks, and other of the principal de facto minorities in the country from being able to make claims against the government on the basis of the Convention.[42]

---

[37]   GA Res. 48/138, 48 UN GAOR Supp. (No. 49), 258, UN Doc A4/48/49 (1993), available at <http://www.minorityrights.org/Declaration.asp>. See also UNESCO Universal Declaration on Cultural Diversity, UNESCO Doc. FS82/WF.32 (1982), available at <http://www.unhchr. ch/html/menu3/b/d_minori.htm>. The introduction notes: "Considering that the process of globalization, facilitated by the rapid development of new information and communication technologies, though representing a challenge for cultural diversity, creates the conditions for renewed dialogue among cultures and civilizations."

[38]   UN DOC E/CN.4/SUB.2/1994/2/Add.1(1994), available at <http://www.unhchr.ch/ huridocda/huridoca.nsf/(Symbol)/E.CN.4.SUB.2.RES.1994.45.En?OpenDocument>.

[39]   Strasbourg, 1.II.1995. European Treaty Series (ETS) No. 157, available at <http://conventions. coe.int/Treaty/Commun/QueVoulezVous.asp?NT=157&CL=ENG>.

[40]   Document of the Copenhagen Meeting of the Conference on the Human Dimension, 29 June 1990, available at <http://www.csce.gov/index.cfm?FuseAction=AboutCommission. SecurityDimensionOfHelsinkiProcess&CFID=18849146&CFTOKEN=53>.

[41]   C.169, 27 June 1989, available at <http://www.ilo.org/ilolex/cgi-lex/convde.pl?C169>.

[42]   "Dutch Declaration Excludes Minorities from Minority Rights Convention." *Minority Rights Group News Bulletin*, 3 October 2005 (previously available online but not currently achieved). But compare "The New Dutch Model," *The Economist*, 2 April 2005, 24.

Scholars and political activists fueled the legal project with moral theories, historical constructions, and programmatic claims, all under the label of "Multiculturalism."[43] It was and remains a large umbrella under which a fairly wide range of normative ideas and corresponding political programs can shelter. For all their differences, I think it fair to say that multiculturalists have at least two things in common. One is their hostility to any policy of state-driven assimilation of cultural minorities into the cultural majority. The other is their fierce rejection of the claim that before multiculturalism, the liberal state had a laissez faire policy toward culture, laissez faire in this context meaning that the state neither helps nor hinders the reproduction of cultures, and that a laissez faire policy (cultural survival of the fittest, as it were) is the only one consistent with the liberal state's formative values.[44] Historically, multiculturalists argue persuasively, the liberal state, epitomized by France, has sought to construct a corresponding nation out of the various cultural communities in place at the time of its inception. Viewed from one angle, Liberty, Equality, and Fraternity were bright ideals. But in order to construct the fraternity of shared national citizenship, it was necessary to flatten more parochial identities, identities constituted by local cultures like those of Brittany and Languedoc.[45] Fraternity being seen as the foundation of Liberty and Equality, parochialisms had to go. And go they gradually did, helped along by the army of school teachers, animated by the secular-democratic nation-building project, that the nineteenth-century French state marched into every village and town to construct the minds of the young.[46]

In France the project was peculiarly evident, in part because at the time of the Revolution the country had so many strong regional cultures,[47] in part because by the nineteenth century, France already had a relatively strong centralized state which the Revolutionary authorities and then Napoleon made much stronger and more intrusive. But the project was also evident in the United States where central government was relatively weak throughout the nineteenth century, where there was no tradition of centralized authority, and education was a distinctly local enterprise. Nevertheless, the Anglo-Scottish culture of the

[43] See, eg, Kymlicka, *Multicultural Citizenship*, 10–19 and 198: "...various senses of culture are reflected in the different meanings attached to the term 'multiculturalism' in different countries." For an introduction to Canada's official policy on multiculturalism, see "What is Multiculturalism?" *Canadian Heritage*, last modified January 2004, available at <http://www.canadianheritage.gc.ca/progs/multi/what-multi_e.cfm>. But compare "Impact: Multiculturalism; the New Racism," *Ayn Rand Institute*, November 2002, available at <http://www.aynrand.org/site/DocServer/newsletter_multiculturalism.pdf?docID=162>.

[44] See, eg, Will Kymlicka and Wayne Norman, "Citizenship in Culturally Diverse Societies: Issues, Contexts, Concepts," *Citizenship in Diverse Societies*, Kymlicka and Norman (eds), (Oxford: Oxford University Press, 2000), 3–5.

[45] See generally, David A Bell, *The Cult of the Nation in France: Inventing Nationalism, 1680–1800* (Cambridge, Mass.: Harvard University Press, 2001). See also Bell, "Recent Works on Early Modern French National Identity," *The Journal of Modern History*, 68(1), 1996, 84–114.

[46] Bell, "The Shorn Identity," 28 (see note 28 above).

[47] See footnote 45 above.

Founders[48] operated hegemonically through a variety of political, social, and economic institutions and assimilation became the stated goal of established elites[49] once the bulk of immigrants began to arrive from places other than England, Scotland, Wales, and Northern Ireland.

What the American experience demonstrates is the disingenuousness of claims that as long as the government does not as a matter of policy press assimilation on minorities, a laissez faire policy toward cultures can be deemed neutral on the issue of which cultures survive. Once a particular culture has becomes dominant in public and private institutions, once fluency in its language and its style are important if not decisive criteria for political, economic, and social success, then new arrivals from different cultural zones will feel tremendous pressures to assimilate. The state can choose to ease those pressures, for instance by requiring civil servants and judicial process to be multilingual, by relaxing or diversifying style codes, and by guaranteeing representation of new communities in political decision-making and thus creating channels for upward mobility of unassimilated leaders within the migrant community. But if the state does nothing more and nothing differently than it did when the society was mono-cultural, it is by the nature of things reinforcing the legacy culture. In short, there is no laissez faire option.

On this point the multiculturalists all agree and their position seems unassailable. Beyond it, however, multicultural unity breaks down. For all the variety of their differences over public policy, I think they can usefully even if somewhat artificially be divided into two groups. One group sees multiculturalism as a program for renegotiating the terms of integration into what is conceded to be the majority culture.[50] The object of that renegotiation is to achieve access to opportunity for members of the minority without wholesale sacrifice of their cultural values and hence the individual and collective sense of self-worth and self-respect. The other group proposes instead of integration on more favorable terms something like a confederation of cultures constantly re-negotiating the terms of their coexistence.[51] In the final section of this chapter I will consider the premises of each position and its policy implications. At this point, I turn to the concrete claims of traditionalist minorities as seen through a liberal optic.

---

[48] See Peter Kivisto, *Multiculturalism in a Global Society* (Oxford: Blackwell Publishers Ltd, 2002), 43–52. See also Samuel P Huntington, *Who Are We: The Challenges to America's National Identity* (New York: Simon & Schuster, 2004). But compare Alan Wolfe, "Native Son," *Foreign Affairs*, 83(3), May–June 2004, 120–5.

[49] Ibid. See also Kymlicka, *Multicultural Citizenship*, 178–80.

[50] See, eg, Tyler, "Strangers and Compatriots," 20–2, analyzing and considering Kymlicka's *Multiculturalism: A Liberal Perspective*, and *Liberalism, Community and Culture*; and Joseph Raz's *The Morality of Freedom*. Tyler observes that "liberal multiculturalists support, both materially and symbolically, the efforts of non-dominant cultural groups to maintain the central features of their particular way of life…this particular combination of respect for personal autonomy and cultural engagement leads both Kymlicka and Raz to reject a static and homogenised conception of culture."

[51] See especially Chandran Kukathas, "Cultural Toleration," *Ethnicity and Group Rights*, Ian Shapiro and Will Kymlicka (eds), (New York: New York University Press, 1997), 69–111.

C. Minority Claims and Liberal Values

What are the main practices of non-liberal, faith-based communities that have aroused a sense of the intolerable among individuals and peoples for whom the idea of tolerance is integral to their conception of a just society? As I sketched earlier, for the most part they relate to the treatment of women, children, dissenters, apostates, and external critics and satirists. With respect to women, along with violent abuse and cruel punishment of unconventional behavior, principally so-called honor killings particularly of girls who have violated sexual taboos or otherwise defied conventional morals, they include restrictions on the opportunities of females to have an education, to choose their spouses, and to enjoy equality within the family and within the community's prestige-bestowing and decision-making practices. With respect to children, the most neuralgic matters involve practices that are both painful and physically harmful, such as clitoridectomy, or which deny them modern medical attention or which are seen as failing to prepare them to participate effectively, if at all, in the economy and government of the larger society. Physical threats to dissenters or apostates or their exclusion from the community and threats to persons outside the community deemed to insult its beliefs are a third source of liberal anxiety. Beyond these concrete concerns there is a more general anxiety over the perceived erosion of that society-wide agreement on first principles of morality that are believed to hold societies together and thus to facilitate the compromises and adjustments and sense of a single overarching national community that many believe essential for the long-term survival of liberal democratic government.

Not all claims of minority communities conflict with liberal values. In fact they run the gamut from those that indisputably do to those that arguably advance the liberal project. Jacob Levy's seven categories of minority claims is the most useful analysis that I have found.[52] In his scheme, one claim is for *exemptions* from laws of general applicability which incidentally penalize or burden a minority's cultural practices without thereby advancing an important majority interest. Among his illustrations are the impact of motorcycle helmet laws on turban-wearing Sikhs and of hunting restrictions on certain Native American tribes for whom hunting is essential to preservation of the traditional way of life. A second is *"assistance to do those things the majority can do unassisted"* like voting or testifying in the majority language." The claim for assistance may extend to the funding of cultural activities for poor minority communities and affirmative action to enable community members to overcome obstacles to business and professional opportunities arising, for instance, from their newness, the time they

---

[52] Jacob Levy, "Classifying Cultural Rights," *Ethnicity and Group Rights*, 22–6. See also Kymlicka and Norman, 25–30. *Compare* Robert Ted Gurr, *Minorities at Risk: A Global View of Ethnopolitical Conflict* (Washington, DC: United States Institute of Peace Press, 1993), 294–312. Levy, at 49, notes that "Gurr sorts cultural rights-claims into demands for exit, autonomy, access, and control, with various further subdivisions."

need to acquire fully the majority language, their poverty, or previous formal or de facto discrimination. A third set of claims is for *laws restricting the liberties of non-members* of the community in order to protect its culture, for instance laws limiting hunting and fishing by outsiders in the traditional domain of Native American groups or setting long residence periods as a condition of participating in local elections, and central government laws allowing a sub-unit numerically dominated by a minority (ie French-speakers in the Canadian Province of Quebec) to restrict use of languages other than that of the minority community in order to sustain indefinitely the language's regionally dominant position.

A fourth category consists of *rules and practices internal to the community designed to express, enforce, and reproduce its values* and enforced by itself through informal sanctions including ostracism, excommunication, and other forms of coercion including deprivation of interests in communal property. A fifth is demand for *recognition of its rules and practices and enforcement thereof by the national legal system*. A sixth is guaranteed or at least specially facilitated *representation in legislative, administrative and other government bodies*. Finally there are claims for *symbolic acknowledgment or respect* through the naming of public places, declaration of holidays, public art exhibits and the content of history books. The claims in this typology that now agitate West European states fall, obviously, in categories three through five.

For the last several decades, claims in categories one, two, and seven have not encountered much resistance in Western Europe because in principle they seek only equal treatment and can be defended as low-cost means for instantiating liberal values in societies no longer homogeneous. Most if not all of the state obligations declared in the Council of Europe Framework Convention[53] and the UN Declaration on Minority Rights[54] fall within these three categories. Still, at least the second category, claims to assistance for, among other things, maintaining the traditional cultures of sub-national communities, can be considered problematical to the degree they impede the established majority's interest in maintaining a national identity that for the purposes of civic peace, civil liberties, and social justice is more compelling than any communal one.

In a liberal democratic state, that is a state where first generation human rights are realized far beyond the global norm, maintaining the preeminence of a national identity is plausibly connected to protecting human rights. Particularly with high immigration levels, maintenance probably requires state policies consciously designed to foster rapid integration of new arrivals into the national project. Whether we should call that project one of cultural construction and maintenance probably depends on our conception of how thick and affective the civic culture needs to be, how deeply it needs to penetrate the consciousness of all citizens and find a prominent position in their symbolic worlds, and

[53] See footnote 39 above.
[54] See footnote 37 above.

how extensively it conflicts with and needs to displace the cultural legacies of newcomers. The more the national project is seen as a full-blown culture, the more integration becomes indistinguishable from policies of assimilation that the conventions and declarations of recent times and their politically correct advocates, our contemporary *bien pensants*, have condemned.

In practice, the tension between the cultural self-preservation claims of sub-national communities and the claims of the national project may express itself with special sharpness in the area of primary and secondary education. To advance its ongoing nation-building project, the state may rationally insist on the dissemination of a version of history which reflects favorably on the nation's past and exalts its prominent actors, persons without any natural symbolic connection to migrants, persons, indeed, who may have been implicated in the conquest or spoliation of the very communities from which migrants spring. Schools may, however, be only one venue for the sometimes more profound clash over language use. A classic feature of nation-building, after all, has been the consolidation and dissemination of a national language. Nation-building can collide head-on with minority cultures when, as in the case of Hispanics in the United States, or Arabic and Turkish speakers in Western Europe, language is a central feature of minority identity.

The moral status of guaranteed representation is still more problematic. To the extent it privileges leaders of minority communities, it could be seen as unfair to their counterparts in the majority community who must compete for relatively fewer positions. It also could be seen to privilege ordinary members of the minority community, since at least in form, they are guaranteed a larger measure of influence on public affairs than their numbers warrant. On the surface, in other words, it enjoins inequality in the application of the right to participate in government. However, particularly in countries where members of the majority community transcend differences of class and ideology and vote as a hostile bloc against the interests of minority communities or where they and, consequently their representatives, are insensitive to the interests of minorities, representation may be necessary to safeguard their participatory rights. Certainly this was true in parts of the United States for African-American citizens until the last decades of the twentieth century.[55]

Not all of the claims that fall within the third, fourth, and fifth categories grate harshly across the liberal sensibility. Limiting the freedom of non-Native Americans to slaughter animals, by denying them the exercise of that right in tribal areas, may fairly be seen as an acceptable accommodation of conflicting liberty

---

[55] The key legislation establishing and protecting the voting rights of African-American citizens is the Voting Rights Act of 1965; see *Introduction to Federal Voting Rights Laws*, United States Department of Justice, Civil Rights Division, Voting Section, available at <http://www.usdoj.gov/crt/voting/intro/intro.htm>. But compare "Faith, Race and Barack Obama," *The Economist*, 6 July 2006, 30, on how racial gerrymandering may be diminishing the voice of African-Americans in the electoral process.

interests where game is relatively scarce and hunting is essential for maintaining the core traditions of tribal society. Similarly, such formal privileging of a minority's language in business and public life as now occurs in Quebec is arguably not distinguishable in any morally consequential sense from the de facto privileging of the majority language in all countries. But categories three through five do include all of the practices and claims that grate. Does it then follow that governments seeking to defend the liberal values embedded in human rights norms should prohibit those practices and deny the claims? What, in other words, are the appropriate limits of liberal tolerance?

4. Liberal Values and Minority Claims: Toward Practical Accommodation

How one answers the above question depends in part on one's conception of Liberalism's core value. In my first lecture I defined it as individual autonomy, the equal right to liberty to which John Rawls, in his magisterial work, assigns priority among the virtues of a just political order.[56] But it is also possible to argue in favor of "tolerance" as the central virtue and few have done so more effectively than Chandran Kukathas.[57] He urges liberals to begin their inquiry into the limits of respect for other cultures by thinking of cultures as coming together in a position of initial equality of right to reproduction. Most persons writing about the clash of liberal and traditionalist cultures in the West, he says, begin by privileging the liberal culture of the Western status quo, the culture reflected in the political arrangements and constitutions of Western States. That is they begin, really as I have, by asking to what degree they should tolerate cultural practices they find alien. Professor Kukathas contrastingly asks us "to consider the possible virtues of a regime in which there is no 'common standpoint of morality.'"[58]

In a response to Kukathas' proposal, Michael Walzer argues that no long-settled political order other than an imperial one has ever had this characteristic. Why? Because stable relatively free political orders arise from a consensus among their members about a just organization of society. That consensus embodied in a regime may not have come easily. On the contrary, it is almost invariably constructed or we might say negotiated over time among groups of residents with different views and interests, constructed through great effort and possibly violent conflict and profound sacrifice. Hence once it is achieved, once a moral settlement is reached, those present at its birth are committed to its defense. As Walzer writes eloquently:

[E]very settlement is or is on its way to becoming a way of life. Important things are at stake here . . . they represent the gradual shaping of a common life—at least, a common

---

[56] Rawls, *A Theory of Justice*, 214–15.
[57] See footnote 51 above.
[58] Ibid, 83.

political life. Their participants come to value the rules and practices that they slowly settle on; they want the settlement to endure; they want to pass on their ways of doing things [ways that become customary and are seen as valued traditions] to their children and grandchildren. So they celebrate the key moments of the settlement process. The result of all this is that every domestic society develops "a common moral standpoint"...[59]

Walzer concludes with the assertion that "[r]eligious difference and cultural pluralism are entirely compatible with this kind of commonality; indeed, they are likely to make for social conflict and civil war without it."[60]

The lyrical character of Walzer's response to Kukathas is seductive. But is it entirely persuasive? As one might expect of a political theorist, he seems to regard ideas ("a common moral standpoint") as the principal glue of social order. Of course social order has three other dimensions: the organization of violence (military and paramilitary institutions and practices); the structure and functioning of the economy; and the organization and strength of the state.[61] Arguably, a society where the state bureaucracy selects and promotes largely on the basis of talent, where the organs of violence are centralized, also meritocratic, and amenable to direction by elected officials, and where the economy permits easy entry for aspiring entrepreneurs and readily absorbs new cohorts will be very stable, however diverse the moral standpoints of the electorate. But, Walzer might fairly ask, will all these other dimensions obtain without a common moral standpoint? For instance, does not the subjection of the military and police to civilian control and the operation of meritocracy in the state and the economy imply and depend on a widely shared set of values that are prior to ideas about the merit of certain political arrangements? These questions of causality—of which are the dependent and which are the principal independent variables— have long been the grist of the political theorist's and scientist's mills and promise to remain so.

The complexity and unique histories of societies and the brief historical incidence of very open ones make it hard in arguments about causation to move convincingly beyond close study and comparison of national instances. From the standpoint of the natural sciences, the sample is very small. But it is all we have.

Ignoring for purposes of argument the old dictum that "for example is not proof," consider the United States. The social order appears stable. Despite the vicious character of contemporary political rhetoric, the wanton talk of "culture wars" by militants of the Right and the evident decline of private sociability across party lines in Washington, the country does not appear to be trembling on the

---

[59] Michael Walzer, "Response to Kukathas," *Ethnicity and Group Rights*, 108.

[60] Ibid.

[61] See generally, Michael Mann, *The Sources of Social Power, Vol. II: The Rise of Classes and Nations-States, 1760–1940* (Cambridge: Cambridge University Press, 1993). See also Scott McLemee, "Delving into Democracy's Shadows," *The Chronicle of Higher Education*, 51(4), A10, commenting on Mann's four-dimensional model of power, the so-called "IEMP Grid" (Ideological, Economic, Military, and Political).

brink of civil war or widespread terrorism. But can its electorate be said to enjoy a "common moral standpoint"? Where is the point of commonality between those who believe: that abortion is largely a matter of free choice for women and those who label it murder; that physically intimate same-sex relationships are sinful and should be subject to prohibitions enforced by the criminal law (ie sodomy laws now held unconstitutional)[62] and those who believe sexual relationships between consenting adults are entirely a matter of personal preference; that the United States is endowed by Divine Providence with the duty to make the world in its image by all necessary means[63] and those who believe it is subject to the limits on the use of force generally accepted by other states; that disparities of wealth and power, no matter how pronounced, are not morally suspect and those who believe they are; that the state should protect all members of the population from chronic destitution and those who believe that poverty, however, extreme, is the result of personal failings and hence should be deemed self-imposed (other than in the case of those suffering from extreme physical or mental disabilities); that the death penalty is a barbaric relic and those who deem it condign punishment? Can any society deeply divided over such profound issues be deemed to have a "common moral standpoint"?

To this question there are at least two possible responses. One is that it depends on what Walzer means by a "common moral viewpoint." It is a viewpoint, he stresses, that not only can coincide with religious and other cultural differences, but actually makes peaceful coexistence and shared positive governance possible despite those differences. What he clearly has in mind *at a minimum* is a common viewpoint on the justness or fairness of political institutions, as distinguished from the outcomes they produce. If, for instance, a large majority of Americans agree that recourse to private violence on behalf of moral values is wrong, agree that values can be enforced only through constitutional means and that the basic restraints on political authority—an independent court system, the impartial enforcement of law, separation of powers at the national level and a zone of protected authority for state governments—should not be altered, then arguably Americans have a common moral standpoint of a type sufficient for the survival of a liberal democratic society.

But I believe that Walzer's common morality implicates more than political arrangements. If it did not, then his sense of contestation with Kukathas is groundless in that the latter, when speaking of culture, clearly has in mind not political arrangements but the beliefs and practices concerning the human fundamentals

---

[62] See *Lawrence et al. v Texas*, No. 02–0102, available at <http://www.supremecourtus.gov/opinions/02pdf/02-102.pdf>. But compare Randy E. Barnett, "Justice Kennedy's Libertarian Revolution: *Lawrence v. Texas*," *Cato Supreme Court Review, 2002–2003*, James L Swanson (ed), September, 2003, available at <http://www.cato.org/pubs/scr/2003/revolution.pdf>.

[63] See, eg, Walter Russell Meade, *Special Providence: American Foreign Policy and How it Changed the World* (New York: Alfred A Knopf, 2001). But compare Walter McDougal, *Promised Land, Crusader State: The American Encounter with the World Since 1776* (Boston: Houghton Mifflin, 1997).

of birth, childhood, eroticism, marriage, gender, family, and death that give shape and meaning to and drive action in quotidian life. Moreover, the idiom of institutions and norms is a dry one. Compare the rhetorically pedestrian specifications of the US Constitution with the sonorities of the American Declaration of Independence. The latter speaks to the heart, proffers a majestic vision of the human condition, that of being endowed with *inalienable* rights to life, to liberty, to happiness. It is the picture of a Lucullan Feast for the entire race, while the constitutional document is the feast's prosaic recipe: "remove the intestines; add two tablespoons of salt, one garlic clove, five crushed peppercorns, a rasher of bacon and three slices of masticated bread, then roast for an hour." Perhaps I am wrong. Perhaps a nation's historical achievements or at least the heroic representation of them in official and popular histories and the generations of the dead alleged to have died to preserve its institutions, and in addition the sacrilized lives of their original architects all conspire to hallow those institutions, to lend them the color and drama with which successive generations can identify.

Still my intuition is that some grand conception of human dignity is the taproot that gives life to Walzer's common moral standpoint. In the case of the United States, for instance, one could argue that the moderate center of the electorate and the strength of political values and meritocracy in public institutions and even the laissez faire economic system all stem ultimately from a very widely shared valorization of the individual as agent of his or her fate whether in isolation or in relationship to God. And arguably it is this standpoint that connects NASCAR Man to readers of *The New York Review of Books* and thereby helps to contain their furious differences. On this thesis, an originally Anglo-Scottish Protestant value inseminated and continues to make morally effective the institutions and practices that are the outcome of that long process of contestation and compromise that Walzer invokes,[64] an outcome now instinctively identified with the economic buoyancy and relative order of contemporary American life.

A second response to the question I posed above is that the profound divisions enumerated above are less than meet the eye when it is riveted on television shout-fests. For what public opinion surveys consistently reveal is a broad middle ground on all of these issues, a ground where differences are very much questions of degree. For instance, large majorities oppose, on the one hand, the re-criminalization of abortion and, on the other, abortion on demand without qualifications respecting such matters as the age of the foetus, juvenile notification of parents, and state funding.[65] With respect to same-sex relationships, large majorities oppose discrimination in the workplace and have come in recent years to favor equality of material rights for same-sex couples even while opposing,

---

[64] See footnote 58 above.

[65] See, eg "Abortion and Rights of Terror Suspects Top Court Issues," *The Pew Research Center for the People and the Press*, 3 August 2005, available at <http://people-press.org/reports/display.php3?ReportID=253>. See also Gardiner Harris, "F.D.A. Approves Broader Access to Next-Day Pill," *The New York Times*, 25 August 2006, A1.

albeit in declining numbers, the formal recognition of a marital relationship.[66] If, as survey data suggests, the bulk of Americans are not divided by a cultural-values chasm, then one does not have to hypothesize that political values trump cultural ones in America in order to explain its political stability.

As I noted above, however, even if there were a deep cultural-values split down the middle of American society, one might still be able to explain its stability in terms of other features of American life, particularly the diversity of political cultures among its 50 states and the mobility of its population, its relatively competent national bureaucracy, political parties, dispersion and checking of political power through separation in some respects and overlap in others, the early establishment of military subordination to democratic political leadership, and laissez faire economic institutions together with the opportunities for individual advancement those institutions foster. One could nevertheless argue, to be sure circularly, that neither the national bureaucracy nor the vertical and horizontal restraints on arbitrary power nor the economy would function as they do without the stability owed both to the mere differences of degree on cultural issues that mark the electorate's broad center and to the ethic of individualism instinct in much of American society.

If political institutions in the liberal democracies do not stand on their own feet, as it were, but rather draw their authority from a conception of human dignity strongly at odds with the cultural practices of immigrant communities, then Kukathas' plan for inter-communal harmony undermines the authority and hence the capacity of liberal democratic institutions. He would deny them the right to defend the deep values that sustain them. In his scheme, as I understand it, the liberal state cannot, for instance, preclude the forced marriage of pre-pubescent children to old men or the denial of economic, social and political opportunities to women or the mutilation of their genitals. In his scheme socially egalitarian and grossly inegalitarian societies shall exist side by side. And presumably, under his scheme the state must license, perhaps even subsidize, a minority educational system designed to perpetuate belief in the divine necessity of gender-based subordination and inevitably to promote contempt and loathing for the social practices of the majority and to discourage the fraternization of children across communal boundaries.

It is not easy to see this scheme achieving its instrumental objective of long-term comity between majority and minority communities living, perforce, cheek by jowl. Majority and minority will constantly chafe each other. Particularly in Europe, militant defenders of minority traditions are bound to resent as subversive the omnipresent expressions of the majority's sunny hedonism and to find insulting even heretical any comment on their practices by artists and human

---

[66] See, eg, "Less Opposition to Gay Marriage, Adoption and Military Service," *The Pew Research Center for the People and the Press*, 22 March 2006, available at <http://people-press.org/reports/display.php3?ReportID=273>. See also Pam Belluck and Katie Zezima, "Proposal to Ban Same-Sex Marriage Renews Old Battles," *The New York Times*, 11 July 2006, A12.

rights advocates within the majority community. Hence as the minority increases in its numbers and political power, it will inevitably seek to limit through state action the perceived insults and the incidental seduction of its young. And the majority, frightened by what it will see as the threatened erosion of its way of life, is likely to respond with growing intolerance. It is therefore at least arguable that multicultural schemes for the ongoing reproduction of illiberal cultures are more likely to promote communal conflict than peaceful coexistence.

5. Then . . . What is to be Done?

Defenders of undiluted multi-culturalism, among whom I would number Kukathas, plainly believe that social peace is most at risk where the secular majority tries to coerce immigrant communities into jettisoning deeply rooted practices. Their claim, it seems to me, is that both for the instrumental end of minimizing communal tensions and as a matter of liberal principle, it would be better if the moral settlement, to which Walzer refers, were seen by the liberal majority to be in constant motion and that new arrivals should have as much right as the descendants of the settlement makers to negotiate the constantly shifting terms of coexistence. For Liberalism as a moral way of life, they argue, is informed by respect for multiple views of what is honorable and what is true. It abjures certainty about the good life; it is committed only to maintaining the conditions in which individuals, alone or in association, can decide on how to shape their lives.

Does it follow that every practice traditional to some group be tolerated? Won't Kukathas' approach turn society into something like a mosaic of tyrannies or at best a sea of human rights marked by large islands of tyranny? He believes, I think, that in liberal societies, the islands, whatever their initial size, will diminish sharply over time, because the dominant culture and consequently the state-supported institutions for the transmission of culture are infused with liberal values. So, for instance, he would allow communities to establish their own schools in which non-liberal practices might initially be re-enforced. But the advantages of using the public schools, he seems to believe, will as a practical matter result in many children from traditional communities attending them. Still, as a scrupulous scholar, he concedes that in his scheme of tolerance some children may be brought up illiterate, marriage may be coerced, conventional medical care may be denied children and persons may be subject even to cruel punishments.[67] The one rule he would, however, enforce on all communities is a right of exit for their members.[68] Of course, exit is an option least likely to be exercised by the most vulnerable members of a community, a fact which he himself concedes.

---

[67] Kukathas, "Cultural Toleration," 87.
[68] Ibid.

Will Kymlicka, a leading North American analyst of multi-cultural societies,[69] finds merit in Kukathas' approach only where it is applied to old highly institutionalized, territorially concentrated cultural groups, like the French-speaking community in Quebec or Native American communities in various parts of North America, originally embedded against their will in what are today liberal democratic societies. These communities he perceives as captive nations. They may themselves be liberal and democratic in culture as are the Quebecois and seek nothing more than the opportunity to perpetuate their language and a few associated cultural nuances. But where, as in the case of certain Native American communities, some traditional practices are illiberal,[70] within broad limits Kymlicka favors non-intervention. In short, these captive nations should enjoy internal self-government.

With respect to minorities resulting from immigration, including refugees and asylum seekers, he proposes tolerance of cultural differences only up to the point where minority cultural practices violate human rights,[71] presumably including the detailed rights of women and children set out in the relevant specialized human rights conventions. Given the inequality of gender rights within many Islamic communities and also many non-Islamic African ones, this formula is a mandate for extensive state intervention to the end of altering traditional practices. However, it is in no way hostile to affirmative efforts by the state to facilitate civic and economic integration through such measures as special language programs, the provision of translators and interpreters in public offices and the judicial system, affirmative action to facilitate immigrant access to higher education and the public service, and special support for primary and secondary schools in areas of high immigrant population densities.

On what basis does Kymlicka justify distinguishing the "captive nation" minorities from immigrant ones? If I understand him correctly, he is moved in part by a sense of historical justice, a sense of justice integral to liberal values. Captive nations did not choose to subject themselves to the cultural preferences of the majorities among whom they are embedded.[72] Immigrants, conversely, chose to leave the place where their culture is the warp and woof of life and

---

[69]   See, eg, *Politics in the Vernacular* (2001); *Finding Our Way* (1998); *Ethnicity and Group Rights* (1997); *Multicultural Citizenship* (1995); and *Liberalism, Community and Culture* (1989).

[70]   See, eg, Kymlicka, *Multicultural Citizenship*, 44 and 205, citing two rulings by the Canadian Supreme Court that focused on the rights of aboriginal groups to engage in illiberal activities against their own members: *Sparrow v Regina* [1990] 3 CNLR SCC; and *Thomas v Norris* [1992] 3 CNLR BCSC.

[71]   Ibid, 152–76.

[72]   See Kymlicka, "Ethnicity in the USA," *The Ethnicity Reader: Nationalism, Multiculturalism and Migration*, Montserrat Guibernau and John Rex (eds), (Malden, MA: Blackwell Publishers Inc, 1997), 241–2. Commenting on Michael Walzer's *The Politics of Ethnicity* and Nathan Glazer's *Ethnic Dilemmas: 1964–1982*, Kymlicka notes that "having emphasized the difference between immigrants and national minorities, one might have expected Walzer and Glazer to endorse the self-government demands of American Indians, Puerto Ricans, native Hawaiians, etc. These groups, after all, really are conquered and colonized peoples, like the national minorities in Europe."

enter the physical space where another people has developed its own distinctive cultural ways and enjoys a long-and-widely-recognized right, inherent in the idea of national sovereignty, to protect that culture by precluding or conditioning access to its territory.

This argument is not without its problems. True, one could reasonably describe immigration in terms of choosing to leave the place where one's culture is rooted and to enter an alien culture zone with only the rights guaranteed by international conventions and granted by the national law of the receiving country. But if entry was not explicitly conditioned on the surrender of all cultural traditions abominated in the receiving country or on agreement to integrate fully into the receiving country's predominant culture, would it be unreasonable to describe the admission of immigrants in terms of a decision by the indigenous inhabitants to accept the benefits incident to the immigrants' arrival even at risk to the relative homogeneity of their culture?

Should it make a difference whether immigrants came first as guest workers expected to return ultimately to their countries of origin? In that case, receiving governments would have been less likely to be concerned about integrating the new labor force into the nation-building enterprise. So they would have seen no need for conditions. But once they allowed guest workers to morph into permanent residents, the issue was plainly in front of them. So one could argue that if there were no conditions at that point, the immigrants are entitled to a presumption that they were at liberty to continue being their cultural selves except where cultural practices arguably threaten not the values of the majority but its constitutional rights and material well being or general social peace and good order. In response, however, one could argue along Walzerian lines that a threat to majority values deprives the society of its hard-earned common moral standpoint and thus imperils the long-term sustainability of liberal democracy.

The extreme conditions that drive some immigrants constitute another conceptual difficulty attending the effort to use *choice*, the exercise versus the inability to exercise agency, as the basis for distinguishing the rights of captive nations from those of relatively recent immigrants. In some Western European countries, refugees and asylum seekers are a substantial part of the immigrant population. Their very status makes the attribution of choice to them rather tenuous: "You chose to emigrate from your cultural homeland rather than die." (Ironically, it may have been their distinctive culture in a multi-cultural country of origin that made them targets of persecution. In such cases it can reasonably be said that they have fled to the receiving country in order to preserve their culture.) In Anglo-American common law, the imminent threat of death mitigates or exculpates otherwise illegal acts precisely on the grounds that the defendant's actions were not voluntary.[73]

---

[73] The roots of this concept are centuries-old; for contemporary examples, see generally, *People v Unger* 66 Ill. 2d 333 (1977); *State v Mannering* 150 Wn.2d 277 (2003); and *People v Anderson*, 28 Cal. 4th 767 (2002).

Despite the distinction international refugee law draws between threats with a malignant human provenance and those stemming from "natural conditions" like drought, locusts, and plagues, the attribution of choice to migrants fleeing lethal natural conditions seems hardly less tenuous than its attribution to those fleeing genocide.[74] Many migrants, however, have fled not imminent death but simply poverty of one degree or another while others no doubt have simply sought to live a more affluent life. In other words there is undoubtedly a continuum of felt necessity, of constraint on choice. Moreover, all human choice is in some measure constrained. If we disparage the presence of choice wherever immigrants are poor or "have a reasonable fear of persecution," then we must disparage it wherever one of two options available to a person is very unpleasant. That would dramatically shrink the notion of free will on which the whole liberal enterprise rests. In sum, despite the problems I have tried to sketch, I don't think that Kymlicka's reliance on choice is meretricious.

In any event, choice is not the only basis for his proposal to treat captive nations differently than immigrant communities. He also argues, again assuming I interpret him correctly, that for immigrants as distinguished from the members of captured nations, cultural change is in general less traumatic.[75] He rests this hypothesis, it seems to me, on the belief that the act of leaving one's native cultural milieu and heading for what is known to be a very different one, this process of self-uprooting, prepares migrants for cultural change. For through the process of migration they have already experienced the trauma of separation and have had to visualize and psychologically to accept the prospect of living outside the deeply institutionalized culture that has hitherto surrounded them.[76] Moreover, even though they will probably integrate first into immigrant communities already established in the host country, so that at the outset of their new lives they are not engulfed by the alien culture of the receiving nation, their insulation is partial and progressively attenuates. For in order to work and be educated and obtain social benefits, they cannot avoid pervasive contact with their new cultural environment. Kymlicka postulates a psychologically important difference between living in an environment where your native culture is institutionalized, which he sees as the condition of captive nations, and one where it is not or at least not anywhere near to the extent it is institutionalized in the migrant's

---

[74] See Tom J Farer, "How the International System Copes with Involuntary Migration: Norms, Institutions and State Practice," *Threatened Peoples, Threatened Borders: World Migration and US Policy*, Michael S Titlebaum and Myron Weiner (eds) (New York: WW Norton & Co, 1995).

[75] See footnote 72 above: "I think that Glazer and Walzer are right to emphasize the difference between immigrants and national minorities, and to focus on the fact that (in most cases) the decision to emigrate was voluntary."

[76] Ibid. But compare Kukathas, "Cultural Toleration," 96–7, arguing that the voluntary consent of the migrating, first generation "... [does not] establish the obligations of descendants who did not voluntarily enter into any agreement or arrangements. Children are clearly *involuntary* immigrants [emphasis in original]."

birth country.[77] Kymlicka's conclusion, then, is that on his assumptions, the prohibition of traditional practices that violate human rights like the unequal treatment of women is less traumatic for the generality of migrants than it would be for the citizens of sovereign countries or captive nations if they were subjected to intervention by an external authority.

The legitimate claims of captive nations are, I suppose, conceivably relevant to the broader issue of how to treat minorities in the Western World because one of the conventional criteria of social justice is the essentially identical treatment of essentially identical cases.[78] So concrete policies that differentiate between groups on grounds that will appear arbitrary, particularly to the subjects of those policies, are more likely to be resented and may therefore aggravate already dangerous social tensions. In this instance, however, the operational need for persuasive distinctions is probably not very great, since the captive nation phenomenon is not pervasive in most West European countries. It seems to me unlikely that Moroccans in The Netherlands, for instance, will assess their treatment by the Dutch Government in the light of the Spanish Government's treatment of the Basques, particularly because the latter, like the Quebecois or the Hungarian minorities in various Central and Eastern European countries, are not seeking to sustain a traditionalist culture.

Kymlicka's normative distinctions are, however, relevant to the problem posed by illiberal minorities quite independently of the claims or even the concept of captive nations. He is proposing that the West uphold core values it shares with people all over the world who believe in the universality of human rights or at least aspire to secure the life chances human rights norms affirm. In part on the basis of his analysis, I agree in principle with his position. Western governments should defend those rights within their respective territories because the values informing them are not parochial, because those rights are essential to the moral identity of Western peoples who have, like all peoples, a collective right to defend and reproduce their identity, subject to the limits imposed by international law, because they constitute that common moral viewpoint which, on the basis of the historical experience of successful and unsuccessful democratic experiments, seems to me necessary for the maintenance of liberal democratic government, and because I believe their even- but not ham-handed enforcement is a necessary but by no means sufficient element of a long-term strategy for the peaceful integration of persons from traditionalist cultures into secular democratic societies.

There are diverse ways in which this element might be translated into the details of public policy. The ultimate objective of policy is to achieve incorporation of a

[77] Kymlicka, *Multicultural Citizenship*, 76–80. But compare Rawls, *Political Liberalism* (New York: Columbia University Press, 1993), 222.

[78] See, eg, Rawls, *A Theory of Justice*, and *Political Liberalism*. But compare especially Amartya Sen, *Development as Freedom* (New York: Alfred A Knopf, 1999), on his concept of "Substantial Freedom."

universal human rights perspective into the moral universe of immigrant families and also, of course, illiberal constituencies within the native majority. This cannot occur to the extent immigrants see themselves as objects of the majority's hostility and contempt. If the government is ungenerous in responding to the sorts of claims, enumerated earlier,[79] that do *not* cut across the grain of liberal values, then perceptions of hostility are virtually certain to result. Conversely, if governments act affirmatively to limit the adoption or application of laws that incidentally burden certain minorities without being necessary means for advancing important public interests, to facilitate the upward mobility of immigrant populations and their use of and participation in the administration of public services, if they build channels that permit regular consultation with immigrant communities at the local level on matters calculated to affect them, if they find ways of incorporating the emerging young leaders of immigrant communities into political office and other institutions of social power, and if they act to protect immigrant communities from physical and moral assault, members of those communities are likely to relax their instinctive defensive crouch and thus to become more accessible to cultural forces emanating from the wider society.

To varying degrees Western governments are in fact attempting to balance tolerance of immigrant community traditions and symbolic expressions of respect with affirmative efforts at *integration* of immigrants into the civic culture and the associated opportunity structures of their respective societies.[80] But reports of isolation and alienation, more (and more disturbingly) among second and third generation youth than new adult arrivals,[81] and events, most strikingly the French riots of Fall 2005, argue for the proposition that these attempts are inadequate. One structural factor inhibiting them, obviously, is the torpid growth[82] and associated high unemployment, particularly among the young,[83] that now mark European society. Resulting anxiety and pessimism among middle-class youth, evidenced in France by their winter 2006 demonstrations against half-hearted efforts by the country's government to liberalize labor markets,[84] impedes expansion of the service sector which in the United States absorbs large numbers of migrant family members. That pessimism (and the alienation it generates) is also

---

[79] See footnote 52 above.

[80] See, eg, "Big Dominique and His Struggle Against the Islamists," *The Economist*, 18 December 2004, at 73–4. See also "The Kiss of Death," *The Economist*, 12 August 2004, 50–1. But compare Parekh Report, *The Future of Multi-Ethnic Britain* (London: Profile Books, 2001).

[81] See, eg, Bell, "The Shorn Identity." See also "Tales from Eurabia," *The Economist*, 24 June 2005, 11.

[82] See, eg, "Gloom in France: The Unbearable Lightness of Being Overtaken," *The Economist*, 2 February 2006, at 45–6. See also Stéphanie Giry, "France and Its Muslims," *Foreign Affairs*, 85(5), September–October 2006, 87–104.

[83] See, eg, "France's Troubles: A Tale of Two Frances," *The Economist*, 30 March 2006, 22–4. See also "In Rare Praise of Domenic de Villepin," *The Economist*, 16 March 2006, 13–14: "France has acute problems getting its young people into work. The unemployment rate for 15–24-year-olds is almost 22% [as of January, 2006], one of the highest in Europe."

[84] Ibid.

likely to hamper any conspicuous affirmative action program designed to increase progressively the proportion of second- and third-generation migrants in public and private sector managerial positions and in the police and security services, and also in politics.

Over time, the large-scale liberalization of labor markets, an incidental increase in the pace of economic growth, and robust affirmative action programs might, in combination, increase the integration of migrant populations. Then again, these indirect means of increasing psychological integration, the form of integration that, in the end, really matters, might leave a large sector of that population isolated from the civic culture. In any event, these indirect means take time to work their effects. Meanwhile there are legions of alienated youth susceptible to the appeals of *jihadi* entrepreneurs. What seems to follow is that European societies need immediately to imagine and win public support for large-scale integration initiatives which will not appear punitive and invidious to immigrant populations. Their basic purpose would be to reduce social isolation dramatically by networking immigrant youth with young men and women from the middle and upper classes.

In some measure the United States attempted this in the early years of the American civil rights revolution of the 1960s and 1970s through school integration and full-bore integration of the armed services and through affirmative action. These measures undoubtedly accelerated the growth of the black middle class,[85] but they left behind millions of African-Americans in a swamp of poverty and alienation. While this very mixed result is sobering, European countries have characteristics which make the prospects for integration initiatives more favorable than one might conclude from the American experience. Among those characteristics are stronger state structures, much more centralized authority (education, particularly the execution of education policies, is largely a local responsibility in the United States), a much more concentrated and less mobile population, a more social-democratic political culture and one more accepting of top-down social initiatives, and, probably a greater sense of urgent self-interest: a growing unintegrated Muslim population poses the kind of threat, in the long term even an existential one, that African-Americans never posed to the American majority.

One possible instrument of national integration would be compulsory national service in late adolescence carefully designed to mix young men and women of all classes and backgrounds in small groups, led by well-trained mentors, that would

---

[85] See, eg, Derek T Dingle, "Then and Now," *Black Enterprise*, 36(1), August 2005, 134–9. For an interesting discussion on the complexities of "fitting" African-Americans into the lexicon of minority groups, see Walzer and Norman, "Citizenship in Culturally Diverse Societies," at 23–4: "African-Americans do not fit the voluntary immigrant pattern, not only because they were brought to America involuntarily as slaves, but also because they were prevented (rather than encouraged) from integrating into the institutions of the majority culture."

live and work together either on domestic projects of an ecological or welfare character or on similar projects abroad. A national system of sporting clubs integrated by class and ethnicity could be used to reach pre- or early adolescents. Still, schools will probably remain the principal agency for achieving integration and, at the same time, facilitating upward mobility. In self-defense of the liberal civic culture, it may be prudent to make public education compulsory, although this might require constitutional change in some European countries, as it clearly would in the United States.[86] But before taking the liberty-inhibiting and possibly provocative step of precluding private education (except as a supplement to the public schools), countries could attempt to incentivize use of the public system by developing integrated magnet schools of superior quality that would plainly open access to higher-status occupations.

The foreign policies of European states are bound to affect the success of integration projects as means to foster a civic culture shared by majority and minority, all to the end of reducing the immediate risk of terrorism and the corrosion over time of liberal democracy. Muslims are not going to identify with the national project if the nation in which they live is seen to have a foreign policy contemptuous of Muslim interests and indifferent to Muslim lives. There is evidence that rage over the terrible fate of fellow Muslims in places like Iraq, Gaza, Lebanon, and the West Bank and humiliation over the apparent impotence of Islamic states in the face of Western power burn within Western Islamic communities.[87] Even if integration projects increase trans-communal networks and open opportunities for social mobility, they will not eliminate the transnational religious identity of Muslims any more than the integration of Jews in American society has attenuated their sense of identity with Jews generally and with Israel in particular.

Therefore, both for purposes of lubricating the integration process and accomplishing its main purpose, the concerns of their Muslim populations will need to figure more prominently in the foreign policies of European states than they have done to date. For instance, over the past four decades, neither the principal European states nor the European Union as an institution have employed their economic power in a serious effort to block cruel treatment of Palestinian detainees by the

---

[86] The US Supreme Court ruled that the "right" to an education was not among the fundamental rights protected by the US Constitution. See *Rodriguez v San Antonio Independent School District*, 411 US 1, (1973) available at <http://caselaw.lp.findlaw.com/scripts/getcase. pl?court=US&vol=411&invol=1>. See also Kymlicka and Norman, "Citizenship in Culturally Diverse Societies," 37–9, on the merits of the state-school system as a focal-point for citizenship training. For a discussion of recent debates over religious schooling in Canada, see Eamon Callan, "Discrimination and Religious Schooling," *Citizenship in Diverse Societies*, 45–67.

[87] See footnote 2 above. But see also, eg, Lubna Hussain, "Justice Is Dead, If You're Born an Arab," *Arab News*, 4 August 2006, available at <http://www.arabnews.com/?page=7&section =0&article=77354&d=4&m=8&y=2006>; and "Angry Islamic States Tell US to Get Out of Iraq," *Agence France Presse*, 13 October 2001, available at <http://www.commondreams.org/ headlines03/1013–03.htm>.

Israeli occupying authorities[88] or Israeli expansion into the occupied territories or the conscious squeezing of the Palestinian presence in East Jerusalem.[89] For all their occasional rhetorical demurrers, they have trailed flaccidly behind the de facto US policy over much of this period of indirectly underwriting the expansion of settlements in the occupied territory and the attempted bantustanization of Gaza and the West Bank.

In sharply focusing a deep integration project, European countries will be playing catch-up. It is regrettable that a determined policy of integrating migrants did not begin as soon as the first waves of Third World migrants and, in particular, migrants from Islamic countries, began streaming into the continent to help support Europe's economic recovery from the devastation of the Second World War. Ideally, an integration project should begin before migrants arrive and should serve not only to prepare those who seem able and willing to embrace the civic culture which they will enter, but also to screen out those who seen unlikely candidates for integration. The need for this sort of preemptive effort has not abated. If the pulling effect of dynamic economies has abated, the push of poverty remains, as does the pull of the European welfare state, even in its somewhat diminishing form.

Both the existential national interest in preserving, indeed enhancing, the culture of liberal democracy and the justness of informing prospective immigrants about the cultural adjustments they will have to make argue for the investment of money and administrative energy in such a preemptive project and for its comprehensive application, its application, that is, to all prospective immigrants, whether they would come as spouses and close family members of previous immigrants or as refugees and asylum seekers. It would be unwise permanently to exempt the latter from preemptive screening, for if more demanding criteria are imposed only at one categorical point of entry, more people will be drawn to the other and will tailor their narratives accordingly. Moreover, given the incidence of failed states, brutal regimes, and grim social conditions even in countries where regimes are merely normal, the number of persons from countries with deep traditional cultures, many of them Islamic, who could arguably qualify for refugee and asylum status, will continue to swell Europe's minority population.[90] A decision to add "capacity for integration" to the criteria for

[88] See, eg, "Palestinian Detainees in Israel: Inhuman Conditions of Detention," *International Federation for Human Rights (FIDH)*, Number 365/2, July 2003, available at <http://www.fidh.org/IMG/pdf/ps365a.pdf#search=%22israeli%20treatment%20of%20palestinian%20detainees%20european%20union%22>. See also "Israel and the Occupied Territories," *Amnesty International: Report 2005*, available at <http://web.amnesty.org/report2005/isr-summary-eng>.

[89] See, eg, Nabeel Kassis, "International Torpor Can Only Prolong Conflict," *Palestine-Israel Journal of Politics, Economics and Culture*, 11(2) (2004), 12–17: "The EU is Israel's biggest trading partner. If the EU was serious in its position on illegal Israeli settlements in occupied territory, one would have thought that it would have used this most potent weapon to apply pressure on Israel . . . *But nothing has happened* [emphasis in original]."

[90] See, eg, Jeffrey Stinson, "Europe in Quandary as Immigrants Flood In," *USA Today*, 7 June 2006, available at <http://www.usatoday.com/news/world/2006–06-07-eu-immigration_x.htm>.

allowing refugees to enter and asylum seekers to remain will, of course, require the amendment of international legal instruments[91] and of arguably crystallized international practice.[92]

I am not proposing wholesale abandonment of the long-established distinction in favor of those who are threatened by vicious people (and may therefore qualify for refugee or asylum status) rather than cruel conditions, although the latter too have in the end human provenance. The distinction makes a great deal of moral sense when most potential beneficiaries are a relative handful of persons seeking protection in liberal democracies from the focused malice of illiberal regimes. It also makes sense as a response to a humanitarian crisis of potentially genocidal dimensions. But when, as in recent decades, refugee and asylum criteria are inflated to the shifting limits of the politically possible to succor the victims of chronic albeit awful political and even social and cultural conditions,[93] the distinction begins both to lose its moral coherence and to short-circuit democratic deliberation about immigration policy.

But if the distinction is reduced by a harsh tightening of criteria for refugee and asylum status *without any concomitant effort to address the conditions that drive many migrants from their native lands*, the net result would be still greater human misery. Today there exists neither the collective will among the leading actors in world politics (even among the leading actors in the West) nor the institutional framework for mobilizing and deploying the economic, administrative, and military resources needed to address those conditions in more than an occasional and incidental way. Therefore, there remains a strong humanitarian case for maintaining the privileged status of credible applicants for refugee and asylum status with the qualification suggested above, namely requiring an explicit commitment from them, as well as from "economic" immigrants, to embrace the core values of the liberal societies where they seek safety.

Integration is not a panacea for the plague of catastrophic terrorism. In our brittle world, a handful of unintegratable sociopaths, inspired by any one of the several ideologies of hate with which every society is laced, can cause inestimable damage. Still, the inability to eliminate risk is hardly an argument against limiting it. For this historical moment in the West, the greatest risks are

See also "Views on Immigration Differ in Eight Countries," *Angus Reid Global Scan: Polls and Research*, 8 June 2006, available at <http://www.angus-reid.com/polls/index.cfm/fuseaction/viewItem/itemID/12152>.

[91] See, eg, "HLS Library: Immigration and Asylum Law," *Harvard Law School*, last updated 29 June 2005, available at <http://www.law.harvard.edu/library/services/research/guides/international/web_resources/asylum.php>. See also "Towards a Common European Union Integration Policy," *European Commission*, July 2006, available at <http://ec.europa.eu/justice_home/fsj/immigration/wai/fsj_immigration_intro_en.htm>.

[92] See, eg, "International Migration and Multicultural Policies," *UNESCO: Social Transformation Themes*, updated 1 August 2006, available at <http://www.unesco.org/migration>.

[93] In the United States, for instance, political asylum has been successfully claimed for at least one young African woman threatened by her family with ritual cutting of her clitoris.

likely to arise from estranged immigrant communities, principally Muslim ones. Reducing estrangement in the various ways suggested reduces the pool of recruits for terrorist grouplets. Coincidentally, integration of minority communities will reduce if it does not altogether drain the lake in which terrorist entrepreneurs could otherwise swim indistinguishably while they recruit and conspire, and it will add to the social capital available for identifying these grotesque fish before they strike.

5

The Iconic Conflict between Israelis and Palestinians: The Normative Parameters of a Settlement

I sit on a man's back, choking him and making him carry me, and yet assure myself and others that I am very sorry for him and wish to lighten his load by all possible means—except by getting off his back. (Leo Tolstoi)

Visiting contemporary Syria, the writer Andrew Lee Butters finds that "[t]here are plenty of imams ... who preach brotherhood and peace." But, he adds, "there's also an angry religious sentiment growing in the country, fueled by what Syrians see as Western atrocities in the Middle East: the US occupation of Iraq, the Israeli occupation of Palestine and the Syrian Golan, and the recent Israeli bombardment of Lebanon."[1] Nasir Nathalia, a 15-year-old student at a state-supported Islamic academy in Leicester, England, tells a reporter that the sight of Muslims under attack in Palestine areas or Iraq "makes us want to help ...". To be sure, the forms of help he lists are "giving or charity" and he himself may well stop there. But when a classmate, Yusuf Parekh, is asked whether violence is justified, he responds affirmatively albeit only when it is "a last resort."[2]

For almost six decades Israel's conflict with Arabic-speaking peoples around and inside its domain has been squeezing a slow poison into international relations and now, as a result of the massive and continuing migration of people away from poverty toward centers of opulence and opportunity, it poisons the relations of communities within many Western states. As the conflict envenoms communal relations, it inevitably enlarges both the pool of potential recruits to terrorist groups and the larger number of sympathizers. The latter, if they do nothing else, psychologically enable violent militants and thin the flow of information about terrorist organizations and operations to the police and intelligence agencies.

The conflict's iconic character, the way it feeds perceptions among Muslims that they are under siege from the West led by the United States, the latter seen as the

---

[1] Andrew Lee Butters, "Clerical Era," *The New Republic*, 2 October 2006, 16.
[2] Alan Cowell, "Islamic Schools Test Ideal of Integration in Britain," *The New York Times*, 15 October 2006, 12.

principal enabler of Israeli policies, is one reason for making the Israeli-Palestinian conflict the only chapter with a narrow territorial focus in a book otherwise devoted to broad issues illustrated by multiple instances. A second reason is the way it collects in one thrashing bundle virtually all of the issues and arguments I have explored to this point, in particular the legitimate occasions for resort to force, the legitimacy and morality of various applications of force, the role of international law, the often felt tension between the categorical character of human rights norms and the visceral demand for security from political violence, and the complex mediation between liberal and communal values. In explaining the reasons for focusing on this conflict, I aim to preempt the all-too-common charge that, irrespective of the accompanying discussion, such a focus implies a concealed bias against Israel or Zionism as a nationalist movement, a bias hinting at a covert anti-Semitism even when, as in this case, the author is himself Jewish.

Typical of this sensibility is an institution, based apparently in Jerusalem, that purports to monitor anti-Israeli bias among human rights organizations.[3] In its angry indictments, it adduces as evidence of their bias the *number* as well as the substance of their reports or references to Israel in comparison to reports on or references to other countries, the apparent premise being that the investigative and reporting resources of an organization like Human Rights Watch should be spread evenly across the globe. In the event, then, that more is said about Israel than, let us say Guinea-Bissau or North Korea, bias is deemed incontestable. Since reports are only a means to the end of actually enhancing the protection of human rights, the mindless character of this claim, even if it were accurate (which it is not)[4] should be evident. Reports can advance human rights to the extent their exposure of violations embarrasses the elites of target countries or mobilizes internal opposition to such violations or activates external pressure on the delinquent government. If elites are insusceptible to embarrassment, largely insulated from external pressure, and ruthlessly in control of their population, reports will have little or no effect. Investigative resources being all too finite, clearly they should be concentrated in areas where the prospect for using them effectively is relatively great. By analogy, my focus on this particular conflict is dictated, as I suggested above, by its peculiarly illustrative and symbolic importance.

---

[3] See the website of NGO Monitor at <http://ngo-monitor.org>, whose mission statement discusses "the obscuring or simply the removal of context alongside highly misleading reporting, often through incomplete images, [that] have made widespread gross distortions of the humanitarian dimension of the Arab-Israeli conflict."

[4] See Aryeh Neier, "The Attack on Human Rights Watch," *New York Review of Books*, 2 November 2006, 41 at 42: "In all [Human Rights Watch] issued more than 350 reports [on human rights violations in particular countries] in 2003, 2004, and 2005 on the 70 or so countries that it monitors. Of these, just five deal with Israel and the Palestinian occupied territories, while another 60 reports deal with various Arab countries and Iran. The largest number of reports concerned abuses in Iraq, Sudan, and Egypt, but reports were also published on Iran, Saudi Arabia, Syria, Algeria, Tunisia, Morocco, and Jordan."

The debate over the question of whether Israeli policy contributes to the terrorist phenomenon, being neurotic in its ferocity, is marked as such debates always are by attribution of fantastical claims. The one most relevant to this chapter is that those who assign a measure of responsibility to Israeli policy are alleging that a settlement of the Israeli conflict principally with the Palestinian people would transform the Middle East into The Peaceable Kingdom where lion and lamb lie down and gently nuzzle each other. This rhetorical attribution, for instance, seemed implicit in much of the on-the-whole rather frenzied reaction to the paper of two eminent academicians, John Mearsheimer of the University of Chicago and Steve Walt of Harvard, about the influence of the Israeli lobby on American foreign policy.[5] Perhaps there exist some crackpot writings, unknown to most of us, that evidence the presence somewhere of such an hallucination. Be that as it may, I at least propose only the following: First that Israel's subjugation of the Palestinian people living in the Gaza strip and the West Bank *contributes* to a widespread perception among people of the Islamic faith that Islam is under brutal assault not simply by Israel, but also by the United States and to some degree by the "West" in general; Arabs most intensely, but Muslims in general experience, as it were, pain and humiliation by proxy which in turn enlarges the pool of recruits and sympathizers for jihad against the West. My second hypothesis is that the means by which Israel seeks to maintain its freedom of action also contributes to Islamic rage, but, in addition, they help to undermine the distinction, so vital to the struggle against terrorism, between legitimate and illegitimate methods for employing force even in a just struggle.

These propositions, particularly the first one, seem to me so self-evident, and so frequently confirmed both by polling data and persuasive anecdotal evidence, as to be banal. And yet within the community of policy advocates who write about the conflict and whose writings justify with marked consistency the general thrust, sometimes every twist and turn, of Israeli policy, there is a perceptible effort to discount the impact of Israeli policy on Muslim attitudes toward the West.[6] One small but, to me, revealing example among many others: In writing about Osama bin Laden's bill of particulars against the West, certain publicists parsed his words with Talmudic rigor to prove that the Palestinian issue had little if any importance for him.[7]

As I noted in my opening chapter, Western implication in the convulsive traumas of life in the Arabic and wider Islamic world takes a variety of forms. The Israeli-Palestinian relationship is only one, albeit an important one. Not only

[5] John Mearsheimer and Stephen Walt, "The Israel Lobby," *London Review of Books*, 28(6) (23 March 2006). See also Stephen Walt, John Mearsheimer, Zbigniew Brzezinski, Aaron Friedberg, Dennis Ross, and Shlomo Ben-Ami, "Does the Israeli Lobby Have Too Much Power?", *Foreign Policy*, July/August 2006, 56.

[6] See, eg, Abraham Foxman, "We are one but not the same," *Jerusalem Post*, 31 August 2006, 14. See also Josef Joff, "A World without Israel," *Foreign Policy* 146 (January–February 2005), 36.

[7] See Brendan O'Neill, "The Man Who Believes in Nothing," *New Statesman*, 26 February 2006.

is it important in itself, but in addition, it probably influences other facets of the Western particularly the American impact on life in the Middle East and West Asia, including the decision to invade Iraq. After all, a number of the most determined advocates of invasion within the senior reaches of the Bush administration were persons who, while out of government, had identified themselves with and encouraged Israeli opponents of a negotiated settlement with the Palestinians[8] and who appeared to see a relationship between regime change in Iraq and the ability of Israel to impose a settlement to the Palestinian conflict on whatever terms it alone finds agreeable.[9] I am not hinting at anything conspiratorial. The views to which I refer have been expressed openly. And certainly people may actually believe that American and Israeli interests, as defined by the right wing of Israel's political elite, are perfectly coincident. One can hold unpersuasive ideas in good faith.

The Israeli government may also have influenced the American government's relationship to the Arab and wider Islamic world by providing a model for visualizing and defining terrorism and for fighting it.[10] Among countries seen by friends and enemies as a part of the West, Israel either pioneered or has rationalized and sought to legitimize such practices as assassination (both within territories it controls and abroad) of suspected terrorists and terrorist facilitators, the use of torture and other cruel forms of interrogation, arrest and indefinite detention without trial, trial by special tribunals, collective punishment, use of deadly force where order could be restored by milder means, and the employment of aerial and artillery assault under conditions where heavy collateral damage to innocent civilians is foreseeable.[11] More generally, it has championed the view that groups and governments employing terrorist means either have non-negotiable ends or should at least be treated as if they had them, the view that negotiation or even the examination of the substantive claims such groups make merely feeds the terrorist appetite.[12] So the response to terrorist methods should be force alone rather than force coincident with a declared readiness to pursue reasonable compromises of material differences over defined interest, the approach ultimately adopted, for instance, by the British government in its dealings with groups using terrorist methods in Northern Ireland. In the later stages of that conflict, essays in repression coincided with the beginning of negotiation.

---

[8] See James Mann, *Rise of the Vulcans: The History of Bush's War Cabinet* (New York: Viking Press, 2004), in which a connection is drawn between Richard Perle, Paul Wolfowitz, Douglas Feith, and other Administration officials and their affiliation with an organization that was close to Benjamin Netanyahu and argued fiercely against creation of a Palestinian State.

[9] See Daniel Schorr, "Has War Inspired Global Conciliation?" *Christian Science Monitor*, 18 April 2003.

[10] See Matthew Brzezinski, "Fortress America," *The New York Times Magazine*, 23 February 2003, 38.

[11] On Israeli methods before the escalation of violence after Camp David, see Tom J Farer, "Israel's Unlawful Occupation," *Foreign Policy*, 82 (Spring 1991), 37–58 and sources cited there.

[12] See Yossi Klein Halevi, "Unsettled," *New Republic*, 29 December 2003, 14–15.

During most stages of the Israeli-Palestinian conflict, with a brief pause after the Oslo agreement of 1993 and again during the Prime Ministership of Ehud Barak, successive Israeli governments have encouraged the view that conflicts in the Middle East have an existential character, that the struggle with Islamic militants is about abstractions like ways of life, which by their nature are non-negotiable, rather than concrete and possibly accommodatable grievances, the same view often echoed by neo-conservative writers[13] and by President George W Bush in his Axis-of-Evil imagery which has inhibited bi-lateral negotiations with the North Koreans and the Iranians and has probably encouraged their pursuit of a nuclear deterrent.[14]

At least some of the Israeli leaders and the writers who have purveyed this conception of the conflict have doubtless been sincere in their belief that governments and popular organizations in the Middle East and, for that matter, the "Arab street" have as their long-term goal the eradication of Israel to which end negotiations and compromise agreements of whatever kind are merely means. This view long preceded the 1948 war of independence. It has roots in the pre-state Zionist movement. One of its most formidable figures, Vladimir (Ze'ev) Jabotinsky, ideological forbear of Likud, which has been the Israeli right's main political expression, put it as follows: "The Arab is culturally backward, but his instinctive patriotism is just as pure and noble as our own; it cannot be bought, it can only be cured by...*force majeure*."[15] It coincides with a cultural stereotype, namely that all the Arabs understand is force,[16] that all other forms of influence such as appeal to common material interests or shared values or universal norms is futile in dealing with them.

Certainly one can find evidence of an unalterable eradication mentality in the sea of rhetoric fed over the decades by Arab governments and leaders of political organizations like Fatah and Hamas,[17] just as one can find evidence of a willingness to accept Israel as a fait accompli if it will satisfy certain not patently unreasonable conditions.[18] As simply one example of the former position, one could cite the provision to that effect in the original charter of the Palestine Liberation Movement.[19] Conversely, one can also find in the writings of Zionist

[13] See, for instance, "Defending and Advancing Freedom," *Commentary*, 120(4), 21–68 and James Bamford, *A Pretext for War* (New York: Doubleday, 2004), 261–2.

[14] The proposition that Arab peoples and states seek the destruction of Israel and that Islamist movements are incorrigible aggressors against the West is implicit in the repeated claim of the Israeli authorities and their American advocates that their efforts to achieve peace have invariably been rebuffed. As personified, allegedly, in the behavior of Yasser Arafat, the Arabs have never missed a chance to miss a chance for peace which is indisputable testimony to their intransigence. For a detailed historical account of the chances Israel chose to miss, see Avi Shlaim, *The Iron Wall* (New York: WW Norton & Co, 2001).

[15] Quoted in Benny Morris, *Righteous Victims* (New York: Knopf, 1999), 108.

[16] See Stuart Schoffman, "On the Couch," *Jerusalem Report*, 3 November 2003, 43.

[17] See Robert Wistrich, "The Old-New Anti-Semitism," *National Interest*, Summer 2003.

[18] See "Mainstreaming Terrorists; Democracy in the Middle East," *The Economist*, 25 June 2005.

[19] Article 23 of the Palestinian National Charter, the official charter of the Palestine Liberation Organization, explicitly declares: "The demand of security and peace, as well as the demand of right

leaders and, after the establishment of Israeli, of high officials of the Israeli state a desire to extend its boundaries south into Lebanon as far as the Litani River, east to the edge of Saudi Arabia (ie conquering today's Kingdom of Jordan) and north to the Suez Canal.[20] Mirroring the selective reading of their militant Jewish counterparts, Arab writers have cited those utterances in order to characterize Israel as an irreducibly aggressive state. In other words, two can play at the game of demonization.

Whatever their dreams, when faced with the impossibility of realizing them or realizing them at a price they are willing to pay, many people decide to settle for less, not necessarily because they conclude that their dreams were meretricious or perverse, but often simply because they or at least their followers grow tired of the struggle, as may have been the case of the IRA. Or they may recognize that circumstances have changed, so that what once seemed realizable no longer does. Or they may hope that over some vast reach of time, their dream might occur through processes of social and political evolution. Or where the dream is more like a nightmare, that is where people think they are fighting for their very identity, they may discover in the process of negotiation that far less has been at stake, that their opponents had mirror image fears rather than ravening ambitions.

Because deeply rooted communal conflicts have sometimes been settled or their scale of violence dramatically reduced, observers like myself are agnostic in any given case about the possibility of mitigation, even, perhaps, of settlement in the long term. To us, neither terrorist methods, however loathsome, nor examples of extreme rhetoric prove, a priori, that force alone is the only means for protecting our legitimate interests and that a readiness to consider the claims of the communities from whose ranks the violent militants have come, even as we engage the militants forcefully, demonstrates weakness of will and constitutional naivety. Hence we necessarily see the rise to dominance within the Israeli elite of the view that the only road to peace is through battering the Arabs into submission, into the acknowledgment and misery and humiliation of utter defeat and abject dependence on Israeli good will, as dangerous to Israel's interests. And to the extent it has reinforced what Walter Russell Mead has called the "Jacksonian" impulse in America's foreign policy culture,[21] the impulse simply to exterminate the nation or group that is seen to challenge the United States, it is inconsistent with the American interest as well.

and justice, require all states to consider Zionism an illegitimate movement, to outlaw its existence, and to ban its operations, in order that friendly relations among peoples may be preserved, and the loyalty of citizens to their respective homelands safeguarded."

[20] See Benny Morris, *Righteous Victims: A History of the Zionist-Arab Conflict 1881–1999* (New York: Knopf, 1999), 108, 261, 653. See also Joel Beinin, "When Doves Cry," *Nation*, 17 April 2006, 31–9.

[21] Walter Russell Mead, "God's Country?" *Foreign Affairs*, 85(5) (September/October 2006). See also Walter Russell Mead, *Special Providence: American Foreign Policy and How it Changed the World* (New York: Routledge, 2002), 218–64.

The premise from which this chapter stems is that the Arab world generally and the Palestinian people in their entirety are open to a negotiated sustainable settlement with Israel, a settlement that concedes the permanence of Israel as a Jewish state located in the Middle East, and that such a settlement is a necessary (albeit not sufficient) condition for achieving a *modus vivendi* between the Islamic peoples and the dominant groups of the West, above all the United States. A sustainable settlement of any bitter and broadly resonant conflict must be seen not only by the immediate parties to it but also by their friends and sympathizers, really by the generality of the international community of consequential actors, as just. It will not be so seen if the vastly stronger party to the conflict extracts it like fingernails from the weak one. Hence, unlike the case where two more-or-less evenly matched adversaries negotiate, where the parties to a negotiation are hugely unequal in bargaining leverage, the mere fact that a signed text emerges from such a negotiating process does not attest to the agreement's "justness." Rather it is seen to have all the value a legitimate court would impute to a confession obtained by torture.

Since Israel is a rich, well-integrated state with powerful conventional and nuclear-armed forces utterly superior to those of its neighbors, while the Palestinians are a fractured community with a rag-bag of ill-armed, mutually antagonistic militias and a nominal, insolvent government lacking sovereignty much less true operational control over a single hectare of land, it is hard to envision more unequal parties to a negotiation. How is it possible, then, to negotiate an agreement that will be seen as a just, ie a "legitimate" outcome?

As I noted above, where parties are roughly equal in negotiating leverage, legitimacy is generally a function of the process. The parties are deemed to be the best and rightful judges of whether, on balance, an agreement to end a conflict is more in their respective interests than a decision to let it continue. But where because of the inequality of the parties, the process itself cannot confer legitimacy, then it must arise from the agreement's substance, that is from the coincidence of its terms with external criteria of justness or fairness. Where do we find those criteria? The most obvious place is in the norms of international law. For those norms are the historical moment's synthesis of ideas of justness and shared national interests that, unlike the Bible or the Koran or any other text commanding the loyalty of only one community, transcends the fault lines of culture and faith.

Believing, as I do, that a settlement of the Israeli-Palestinian conflict is in the US national no less than the human interest, my purpose in this chapter is to sketch the profile of a settlement consistent with prevailing norms of international law. In doing so, I work in previously cultivated but presently rather neglected ground. Rivers of blood in the Middle East have for the moment washed away most of the landmarks of hope. Discourse even among those eager for a sustainable settlement seems concerned with minor tactical moves to contain violence. And yet, I would argue, it is precisely the predominant emphasis, particularly at the level of official discourse, on minor tactical moves, on settlement processes ("road maps") rather than outcomes, that has consistently failed to produce an irresistible momentum toward peace. Whether hypocritical or sincere, insistence on "confidence-building" steps, invariably on steps the divided, battered, occupied and brutalized Palestinians must take to earn Israeli confidence, have led only to more violence and diminished popular belief in the possibility of peace.

The "step-by-step" approach having manifestly failed, the only rational option for those who actually seek an end of the conflict is to identify the terms of a just settlement and then to demonstrate the will to employ sanctions and incentives in order to achieve that end in the face of predictable intransigence from "spoilers"[22] on both sides. Only on the basis of such terms is there a hope of isolating the fanatic rejectionists in the Palestinian and the wider Arab camp and in the Israeli polity, just as the rejectionists in Ireland were isolated and defeated once Britain, the party vastly superior in force, conceded Irish sovereignty (except in the northern provinces) in the early 1920s.

The main function intellectuals can play in the realm of public policy is to influence the policy agenda. They do so in part by demonstrating the applicability of norms, legal or moral, that enjoy official sanction, in part by demolishing mendacious narratives that obscure the equities of an issue and the prospect for its resolution. Twisted narratives serve the opponents of a sustainable peace, whether in the media or the halls of government, by enabling them to depict peace advocates as bigots or fools and one of the parties as hopelessly obdurate and hence irremediably evil.

1. The Legal Parameters of a Just Settlement

Certain norms embodied in two almost universally ratified international agreements set the main legal parameters for the settlement of the long and sanguinary conflict between the Israelis and Palestinians. One agreement is the International Covenant on Civil and Political Rights (hereinafter the "Covenant").[23] The other is the Fourth Geneva Convention of 1949[24] dealing with the treatment of civilians in "occupied territory." Israel is a state-party to both treaties, without any substantial reservations. In addition, Israel is a state-party to a number of other human rights treaties that have significant bearing on the topic under discussion here, in particular the International Covenant on Economic, Social and Cultural Rights.[25]

---

[22] See generally, Edward Newman and Oliver Richmond (eds), *Challenges to Peacebuilding: Managing Spoilers during Conflict Resolution* (Tokyo: United Nations University Press, 2006).

[23] GA Res. 2200A (XXI), 21 UN GAOR Supp. (No. 16), 52, UN Doc. A/6316 (1966), 999 UNTS 171, entered into force 23 March 1976.

[24] Adopted on 12 August 1949 by the Diplomatic Conference for the Establishment of International Conventions for the Protection of Victims of War, held in Geneva from 21 April to 12 August 1949, 75 UNTS 287, entered into force 21 October 1950.

[25] GA Res. 2200A (XXI), 21 UN GAOR Supp. (No. 16), 49, UN Doc. A/6316 (1966), 993 UNTS 3, entered into force 3 January 1976. Israel became a state-party to the ICESCR in 1991. In

I conclude that these key human rights treaties support the Palestinian claim of a legal right to be accorded sovereign authority in the territory occupied by Israeli in the course of the 1967 war, including East Jerusalem subject, however, to such conditions as, in the judgment of the Security Council acting pursuant to Chapter VII of the Charter, are necessary to assure international peace and security. Those conditions could, of course, include internationalization of all or a part of the city of Jerusalem.

A. Self-Determination of Peoples

The principal driver of my conclusion is the right of "peoples" to self-determination. First claimed more than two centuries ago most famously by the American revolutionaries, and the guiding principle thereafter for a plethora of national integration and national liberation struggles, it is declared in Article 1 of the UN Charter and reiterated, albeit again without definition, in the first article of both Covenants.[26] Through the practice of states acting both within and outside the organs of the UN, there has formed a broad consensus about the substance of that right which can fairly be summarized as follows. First there is the issue of who constitutes a "people." In general, peoples have been seen as falling into one of two categories: Either they are the sum of the inhabitants of any overseas territory occupied by Western states during the imperial era and organized for the benefit of the occupier into a separately administered unit or they are minorities within recognized states who, whether on the basis of common color, religion, ancestry, language, culture or any other real or imagined characteristic, share a sense of common identity that distinguishes them in ways felt to be important from other persons living in the particular state. (So-called "Indigenous People" are a specially-protected minority sub-set.) The former (we will call them "colonial peoples") are entitled to form a new sovereign state out of the colonial administrative unit. The latter ("minorities" or "indigenous people") must generally content themselves with equal treatment and the opportunity to sustain their distinctive identity within the sovereign state where they live.

1998, at its 19th session, the Committee on Economic, Social and Cultural Rights, which oversees the implementation of the treaty's provisions, issued a Concluding Observation that expressed its grave concern with ongoing violations of the rights of Palestinians in Israeli occupied territory, noting especially the discriminatory aspect of violations of Palestinian rights to housing, work, health, education, and an adequate standard of living (CESR e/C.12.1/Add.27).

[26] As early as 1920, an advisory committee to the Council of the League of Nations opined that self-determination was generally considered a legal right. See John Quigley, *Palestine and Israel: A Challenge to Justice* (Durham, NC: Duke University Press, 1990), 15. But its content was uncertain, particularly in light of the incongruence between such a right and colonial practice in the period between the two World Wars. The 1961 Declaration on the Granting of Independence to Colonial Countries and Peoples (GA Res. 1514 (XV), 15 UN GAOR Supp. (No. 16), 66, UN Doc. A/4684 (1961)) reduced that uncertainty by calling unequivocally for the rapid transfer of authority to the inhabitants of non-self-governing territories and rejecting the view that such peoples might require long periods of tutelage before they could be granted independence.

Within the idiom of UN practice, colonial entities acquired the generic name of "non-self-governing territories." Palestine, a former Ottoman territory acquired by the United Kingdom as a Mandate at the close of the First World War but reduced in size by the British decision to spin off part of it as the sovereign state of Jordan, fell by common understanding under that label.[27] Most such territories contained a miscellany of ethnic groups some of which felt more of a common identity with persons in other territories than with each other. Nevertheless, as decolonization evolved in the first decades of the post-War era, not surprisingly a consensus favoring preservation of the territorial integrity of the Colonial-era administrative entities formed among two clusters of governments often in conflict on other matters. Western governments joined it because they were avid for stability in a world challenged by a Soviet state apparently bent on the indefinite expansion of its zone of control. The governing elites of territories newly independent or on the verge of such independence bonded with the West on this issue because they were eager to legitimate their rule throughout all the metes and bounds of their respective colonial legacies. Consensus among the new rulers on the imperative character and yet restrained dimensions of national self-determination achieved formal expression in General Assembly Resolution 1514[28] which declared the obligation of governments to facilitate a rapid transfer of authority to the inhabitants of the territories but without prejudice to the integrity of existing national states, ie peoples who were deemed to have already determined themselves in the hastening process of decolonization.

By the time of the Resolution's adoption, however, there were two important precedents for dividing non-self-governing territories where the desire for separation from each other was plainly felt by groups within the territory, rather than fomented by the colonial authorities and/or where, in the judgment of the political organs of the UN, attempting to preserve them as unitary states threatened long-term disruption to peace and security. The two major precedents for such a division were India and Palestine, the former division unilaterally executed by the colonial power, the latter ordered or at least recommended[29] by the United Nations and, after more than six decades, still pending. In the case of Palestine, the political organ responsible for the fate of the Mandates inherited from the League of Nations, that is the General Assembly,[30] found the territory to be occupied by two peoples whom it identified as Jews and Arabs. Of course this was an oversimplification, though arguably one that was not inappropriate

---

[27] See generally, Quigley, above, chs 1–3.

[28] Declaration on the Granting of Independence to Colonial Countries and Peoples, above.

[29] In UN General Assembly Resolution 181 (the "Partition Resolution"), A/RES/181(II) (A+B), 29 November 1947. Quigley (above 5, at 45) supports the position that 181 was more a recommendation than a determination of legal entitlement. He cites also the fact that in March 1948, the United States recommended to the other members of the Security Council that the 181 recommendation be abandoned, and urged it seek alternative solutions besides partition.

[30] To be sure, the authority of the General Assembly in this regard, is not entirely uncontested. See Quigley, above, at 47–53.

under the circumstances. It ignored other self-identities such as Sephardic and Ashkenazi Jew, Christian, Muslim, or Druze, not to mention tribal identities or an indigenous rural person's self-identification with a particular place and an urban intelligentsia's identification with an hypothesized Arab nation spreading from Baghdad to Cairo or even Marrakesh.[31] On the other hand, it accounted for the already intense although incomplete polarization of Palestine's inhabitants along the fault line of Jewish and non-Jewish identity and conceded the difficulty of translating the more complex mosaic into a political idiom.

Whatever the tangled reality of group identity, the fact is that, in 1947, the community of nations determined that there were two peoples in Palestine, that each had a right to self-determination and that the exercise of that right could not be managed, without intolerable risks to the peace of the region and the security of the inhabitants, other than by division of the territory. Neither the establishment of the State of Israel nor its admission to the United Nations nor Israel's occupation of all of the Mandate's territory as a result of its victory in the 1967 Middle East War has altered that original judgment by the generality of member states of the international community. Rather the contrary.

As the great Palestinian writer Edward Said has noted, a Palestinian national identity transcending both more local and more cosmopolitan identities did not fully crystallize and achieve a well-defined political form until after the Arab defeat in 1967, although an inter-subjective identity that can fairly be characterized as Palestinian nationalism preceded it by many decades.[32] The full political crystallization of Palestinian nationalism included a commitment to resisting the occupation of the territories taken in the '67 war and securing "justice" for the persons who had fled or been expelled[33] from the territories assigned to the Jewish inhabitants of Palestine under the 1947 Resolution of the General Assembly and from the West Bank and Gaza after Israel's military triumph in 1967.[34] Israel's expansion as a result of the '67 war together with the maturation of Palestinian nationalism produced in the wider world a much deeper appreciation for the Palestinians as a distinctive "people" (as opposed to a mere agglomeration of refugees, as former Prime Minister Golda Meir had once described them)[35] living in and, as a result of exile, around the former Palestinian Mandate territory,

---

[31] Pan-Arabism was an ideology especially of the early Ba'thists and articulated by its leading theorist, Michel 'Aflaq. See Albert Hourani, *A History of the Arab Peoples* (Cambridge, Mass.: Harvard University Press, 1991), 404–5.

[32] Edward Said, *The Question of Palestine* (New York: Vintage Books, 1979), esp. 157–69.

[33] See, generally, Benny Morris, *The Birth of the Palestinian Refugee Problem, 1947–1949* (New York: Cambridge University Press, 1987).

[34] Said, above. For a comprehensive treatment of the development of post-1967 Palestinian nationalism, see generally Glenn E Robinson, *Building a Palestinian State: The Incomplete Revolution* (Bloomington, IN: Indiana University Press, 1997).

[35] In an interview with the *Sunday Times* in June 1969, Meir was quoted as stating, "there is no such thing as Palestinians...[I]t was not as though there was a Palestinian people in Palestine considering itself as a Palestinian people and we came and threw them out and took their country away from them. They...did not exist" (June 15), 12.

a people with an unrealized right to self-determination. One concrete and at the same time formal legal expression of this phenomenon was recognition by UN organs of the Palestine Liberation Organization as a "national liberation movement" comparable to the ones fighting for independence under majority rule in the various African colonies of Portugal and also at that time in Southern Rhodesia.[36]

To be recognized as a national liberation organization was to be conceded the status of the government of a latent sovereign state. In the case of the PLO, that posture was formalized in part through its admission to Observer status within the United Nations.[37] What made the Palestinian case unique, however, was the initial lack of consensus among governments about the boundaries of this latent state. In 1948 most Arab governments had condemned as illegal the division of Mandate Palestine into two states.[38] According to them it was a violation of the Arab population's right to majority rule in a unitary state.[39] The principal—perhaps only—dissenter among them, albeit more by its actions than its words, was Jordan. Roughly coincident with Israel's declaration of independence, Jordan's ruler, King Abdullah, had negotiated an understanding with Israel's political leaders pursuant to which he would occupy the territories allocated by General Assembly Resolution to the Mandate's Arab population.[40] In essence, then, he and his Israeli counterparts implicitly recognized a right to self-determination for the Mandate's Jewish population but not for its Arab inhabitants. Apparently, it was for this act, treasonous from the broader Arab community's perspective, that he was assassinated in 1951. Under the subsequent rule of his grandson Hussein, Jordanian policy evolved from nominal trustee of Palestinian interests to formal cession of responsibility for the Palestinians' fate to the Palestinian Liberation Organization in 1974.[41]

Believing the division of Palestine to be an act beyond the authority of the United Nations because it violated, in their judgment, the indissoluble right to self-determination of the indigenous majority, ie persons of some sort of Arab ethnicity,[42] the Arab governments refused initially to recognize a sovereign Israeli

---

[36] Quigley, above, 48–50. See also Yonah Alexander, "The Nature of the PLO: Some International Implications," in Michael Curtis (ed) *The Middle East Reader* (New Brunswick, NJ: Transaction Publishers, 1986), 275.

[37] UN General Assembly resolutions 3236 and 3237, 22 November 1974.

[38] Ibid, 62–5.   [39] Ibid.

[40] See Avi Shlaim, *Collusion Across the Jordan: King Abdullah, the Zionist Movement, and the Partition of Palestine* (New York: Oxford University Press, 1988), 62.

[41] The "Rabat Resolution" of the Arab League in 1974 designated the PLO as the "sole legitimate representative" of the Palestinian people. Seventh Arab League Summit Conference, Resolution on Palestine, Rabat, Morocco, 28 October 1974, full text online at <http://mondediplo.com/focus/mideast/a2287> (accessed 5 August 2004). King Hussein severed all legal and administrative ties with the occupied West Bank on 31 July 1988. Joel Brinkley, "Hussein Reduces Ties to West Bank and Palestinians," *The New York Times* 30 July 1988, A1.

[42] In the late years of the Palestinian Mandate, Zionist leaders had rejected Arab and British proposals to establish an elected government precisely because their followers constituted a minority. So elections, they reasonably believed, would result in a unitary state with an Arab electoral majority.

state within any borders. Gradually, however, in the face of American pressure and Israeli power, a majority of Arab states came to concede Israeli sovereignty albeit with varying degrees of explicitness.[43] But until the 1990s, Israel continued to insist either that there was no Palestinian people with a right to self-determination or that the right could be exercised only within the territory of Jordan, the large, dusty slice of the original British mandate that the British had decided after the First World War to convert into a kingdom for the benefit of their ally in that conflict, the Hashemite Dynasty of the Arabian Peninsula.[44] Although the British decision to create a new state East of the Jordan seems to have been made primarily for reasons of perceived self-interest, possibly reinforced by some residual sense of guilt at the betrayal of Hashemite expectations it had encouraged during the war,[45] it was arguably compatible with the terms of the Mandate. In a bow to the liberal rhetoric with which the Anglo-French alliance had clothed itself, particularly in the later reaches of the war when it was desperate for American entry, mandatory rule over the German colonies (as distinguished from colonial rule in general) was supposed to be conducted for the benefit of the indigenous population. Allowing independence to a part of that population, albeit under an imposed King aided and advised by British handlers, would appear compatible with that vague injunction, when the legitimate alternative[46] was indefinite rule by the government of Britain.

2. The Problematics of Borders

In the twentieth century, borders made abruptly by main force proved unpredictable things. Some, like the ones that now define North and South Korea or separate India and Bangladesh, so quickly acquired general acceptance that, not long after their violent creation, they seemed as indisputably fixed as those that had been settled for centuries. Others, like the one resulting from the coercive extension of Indonesian sovereignty to include the former Portuguese colony of East Timor, remained contested even when it appeared unlikely that they would ever be effectively challenged. Through an intricate moral, legal, and strategic

[43] Egypt was the first of the Arab states to sign a peace treaty with Israel and recognize its sovereignty, in March 1979. The Jordanian-Israeli Treaty was signed in October 1994. Negotiations for treaties with Syria and Lebanon were underway under the Madrid framework, but the Syrian process has been stalled since 1998. Israel and Lebanon concluded a ceasefire agreement in 1996, and Israel ended its 18-year presence in Lebanon in May 2000.

[44] See David Fromkin, *A Peace to End all Peace: Creating the Modern Middle East, 1914–1922* (New York: H Holt & Co, 1989).

[45] Ibid.

[46] "Legitimate for two reasons: (a) Because at that time there was no legal right to self-determination nor for that matter anything like a consensus among democratic states in favor even of a moral basis for such a claim; (b) Because the Mandates were declared by the League of Nations, an organization established by treaty among all the leading states of the time other than the United States which did not object to the Mandate system."

metric, the international community of states and other consequential actors decide which should be accepted as fixed and which should remain in play.

Palestine offers examples of both responses. The de facto borders Israel established in its war of independence, concluded in 1949, gradually achieved broad tolerance if not formal recognition, even though they left Israel with almost 30 per cent more of Mandate Palestine as it existed in 1947 than the General Assembly had recommended[47] or, depending on one's construction of the Resolution's meaning and the Assembly's power, had granted to the Jewish inhabitants of Palestine in Resolution 181. By contrast, Israel has not been able to induce widespread acceptance of the de facto extension of those 1949 borders achieved through its victory in the 1967 war.

Is that simply because it has not tried? Well, not exactly or at least not entirely. Of the territories acquired in 1967, Israel, by declaring an undivided Jerusalem to be an integral part of its territory and treating it as such has implicitly claimed sovereignty over the Jerusalem piece plus a chunk of the so-called West Bank it dragged within the Municipal boundaries.[48] With respect to the rest of the shrunken West Bank and of Gaza, it has modestly declared itself to be in effect the legitimate custodian of territories belonging to no one (*terra nullius*) pending some final determination of their disposition.[49] However, in statements made over the past three-and-a-half decades and in positions adopted by Israel following the inauguration of a peace process in the early 1990s, the country's government has consistently declared an intention to maintain sovereign control over some pieces of the West Bank at least for security if not for other purposes. Its insistence, made effective through US power, on eliminating the word "the" (referring to "territories") from the English language version of Security Council Resolution 242, marking the end of the 1967 conflict and calling for Israeli withdrawal from "territories" occupied in the course of the war, heralded this position.[50]

The key point here is that the State of Israel has failed, both with respect to the West Bank in general and Jerusalem in particular, to reproduce its post-1949 success in legitimizing the de facto extension of its governing power. The best evidence of that failure in the case of Jerusalem is the refusal of virtually all countries, even the United States, to move their embassies to the city despite the fact that the Israelis have made it their official Capital and the site of their

---

[47] Benny Morris, *Righteous Victims* (New York: Knopf, 1999), 653.

[48] Obviously all of 1947 Palestine was on the West Bank of the Jordan River. After the June 1967 war, Israel expanded the municipal boundaries of East Jerusalem from the 6.5 square kilometers that existed under Jordanian rule, to 64 square kilometers. See Cheryl Rubenburg, *The Palestinians: In Search of a Just Peace* (Boulder: Lynne Rienner, 2003), 197.

[49] This is based on what Quigley (above, at 91) calls the "sovereignty-vacuum" theory, first advanced by the Israelis upon the departure of the British in 1948. In this *terra nullius* that was mandate Palestine, Israel created itself through "auto-emancipation." For a contrary view, see Ian Brownlie in his semi-authoritative *Principles of International Law* (Oxford, UK: Clarendon Press, 1966), 596: "[an inhabited territory] cannot be regarded as *terra nullius* susceptible to appropriation by individual states in case of abandonment by the existing sovereign."

[50] See Quigley, above, at 170.

governmental institutions.[51] Israel's failure to achieve recognition of Jerusalem as its capital is consistent with and to a degree confirms my conclusion that the right of the Palestinian people to self-determination applies, *inter alia*, to some part of the Holy City.

This conclusion does not, however, rest exclusively or even primarily on the refusal of governments to move their embassies to Israel's seat of government. Its principal base is the observation that Jerusalem is so entwined with Palestinian self-identity, so culturally and socially central to that identity and to the possibility of expressing that identity in the form of a sovereign state, that ripping it out of any plan for the realization of the Palestinian right to self-determination is to mutilate the right. This might not be so if the entire city were to be internationalized, as the UN originally proposed. Palestinian national identity has matured, after all, through a dialectical relationship with Zionism[52] and then with Zionism's creation, a Jewish state centered emotionally and symbolically on Jerusalem. Having achieved full self-consciousness through this dialectical process, the Palestinian national movement cannot visualize a completed self-determination process that does not grant it too a place in Jerusalem as long as Israel has one.

That fact, or at least that hopefully persuasive hypothesis about the psychological conditions of Palestinian nationalism, has two kinds of normative implications. Behind the norm of self-determination lies a powerful moral concern, namely the creation of conditions that enable people to give coherent shape to their sense of collective identity and thereby to enhance their search for meaning and value in their individual lives. The core condition is association with other human beings in a felt community of shared ideas of meaning and self respect and of the morality of action.[53] A gathering of people in a place to which they have been randomly or arbitrarily assigned, cannot accomplish that. Community is the sediment of shared and similarly understood experiences. It is an inter-subjective phenomenon centering normally around a shared place and always around a shared identity. After all, a place—Palestine—and above all the city of Jerusalem, was at least an aspect of Jewish identity during the millennia of exile.[54] Even if, as some argue, the so-called "psychological longing" of Diaspora Jews for Jerusalem is a foundational myth brought to life by late Nineteenth Century Zionism, by the time Palestinian self-identify began to take shape, Jerusalem had become a focal point of identity for Israeli and most Diaspora Jews.

---

[51] Both the UN Security Council (in Resolution 478, 20 August 1980) and the General Assembly (in Resolution 35/169, 15 December 1980) found the 1980 Knesset "basic law" declaring Jerusalem the capital of Israel to be in violation of international law, and thereby nullified.

[52] Said, above.

[53] See eg, Benedict Anderson, *Imagined Communities: Reflections on the Origin and Spread of Nationalism* (London: Verso, 1983) and Ernest Gellner, *Nations and Nationalism* (Ithaca, NY: Cornell University Press, 1983).

[54] How important an aspect is a matter of some dispute with some arguing that it did not achieve centrality until the Zionist movement succeeded in establishing the state of Israel. See Quigley, above, at 66–81.

Recognition of the importance of place to human beings is manifest in the contemporary addition of ethnic cleansing to the list of crimes against humanity.[55] The crime of exclusion is independent of the murderous means generally used to execute it. Thus to honor the right to self-determination in a given case, one needs to respect the importance of place for a people. The latter can be seen as a corollary of the former. It follows that where a colonized people's collective identity has a geographic locus which is not already an integral and generally recognized part of another sovereign state or a place internationalized by a universal treaty or by the United Nations (itself established by a universal treaty), that locus must be subject to the particular people's self-determination right. Where, however, the place is also the legitimate focal point of another people's self-determination right, it must be shared in one way or another.

A second normative implication springs from the prospect of endless threats to international peace and security, particularly in this age of porous borders and catastrophic terrorism, when a people's self-identity is mutilated. Legal norms do not simply implement public policies; in a real sense they are linguistic forms wrapped around the body of those policies. According to the words of the Charter, reinforced by its allocation of a carefully delimited decisional authority to the Security Council, the central public policy of the community of states is the maintenance of international peace and security, by implication a policy deemed consistent with, if not essential for, the other declared policies of promoting self-determination, protecting human rights and preserving the territorial integrity and political independence of the various sovereign states.[56] Mutilating a people's self-identity is not merely a moral wrong or a violation of human rights norms. It is also the creation of an infection in the political order that will continually ooze violence. Hence it manages to be a blunder no less than a crime.

3. The Question of Forfeiture

But can it not be argued that whatever a people's initial rights, they can be forfeited, particularly by illicitly threatening the exercise of parallel rights by other claimants? And so in the case of Palestine in general and Jerusalem in particular, it has indeed been argued, at least implicitly, that since the UN's division of the Palestine Mandate in 1947, the Arab population, by its rejectionist position, has successively forfeited first the territorial accretions won by Israel during its war of independence, then rights in the remaining territory, if not at the time of the 1967 war (when arguably Jordan was the steward of Palestinian interests), then in

---

[55] Rome Statute of the International Criminal Court, UN Doc. A/CONF.183/9 (1998), entered into force 1 July 2002, art 7.

[56] See Tom J Farer, "Panama: Beyond the Charter Frame," *American Journal of International Law*, 84 (1990), 503 at 507.

2000–01 when the Palestinian National Authority in the person of Yasser Arafat rejected Israel's proposals for a peaceful settlement without making a counter-offer and then failed to prevent the second *intifada* or uprising against Israel rule, or to terminate it once it had begun.[57]

I agree that the general principles contained in the various national legal systems, which constitute a subsidiary source of public international law,[58] probably include a relevant doctrine of forfeiture in one form or another. But the view of practically all states, manifested repeatedly since 1947 in resolutions of the General Assembly and the Security Council and in other ways, is that the doctrine does not apply to this case. Even the Government of the United States, a Government that normally dissents from widely shared views about the legality of Israeli actions vis-à-vis the Palestinians, and has frequently vetoed Security Council Resolutions condemning Israeli actions in the occupied territories,[59] recognizes that the Palestinians have the right to form a sovereign state,[60] a position apparently reaffirmed on more than one occasion by President George W Bush. Since international law is constituted by a broad consensus of states about the identity and interpretation of authoritative norms, the widely shared view that Palestinians have not forfeited their rights is decisive on the legal issue.

The roots of that view are not obscure. One surely is the special character that the right to self-determination for colonized peoples has come to assume even as the occasions for its application have shrunk. Arguably it is a principle of *jus cogens*,[61] that is a core value of the sovereign state system. As such, it creates a presumption against any claim that it has been lost whether by waiver, forfeiture, or other means. It is also a human right, the only one iterated in both of the International Covenants.[62] To declare it forfeit, therefore, is to imply that other human rights, like the ones to life and due process, are susceptible to forfeiture. To draw again on analogies in national legal systems, arguing for forfeiture of the right to escape from colonial or alien rule is much like arguing before a domestic court that persons accused or even convicted of a crime can waive their constitutional right not to be tortured, for instance, as a condition of receiving

---

[57] On the idea of forfeiture as stemming from events in 1948 and 1967, see Frank LM van de Craen, "The Territorial Title of the State of Israel to 'Palestine': An Appraisal in International Law," 14 *Revue belge de droit international* (1978–79), 500 at 508; and Shabtai Rosenne, "Directions for a Middle East Settlement—Some Underlying Legal Problems," *Law and Contemporary Problems*, 33 (1968), 44 at 51.

[58] Statute of the International Court of Justice (26 June 1945), 59 Stat. 1055, T.S. No. 993, 3 Bevans 1179, art 38, section 1(d).

[59] The United States has vetoed over 40 UN Security Council resolutions since 1972. See <http://www.jewishvirtuallibrary.org/jsource/UN/usvetoes.html> (accessed 6 November 2006).

[60] See the Statement by the President of the United States, 14 April 2004, at <http://www.whitehouse.gov/news/releases/2004/04/20040414-2.html> (accessed 6 November 2006).

[61] Article 53 of The Vienna Convention on the Law of Treaties (1155 UNTS at 331, entry into force 27 January 1980) defines *jus cogens* as "a norm accepted and recognized by the international community of States as a whole as a norm from which no derogation is permitted and which can be modified only by a subsequent norm of general international law having the same character."

[62] ICCPR and ICESCR, art 1(1) in each.

a non-capital sentence, [63] or should be deemed to have forfeited it for having committed a crime so heinous that under law of some states, it could justify the imposition of the death penalty.

Forfeiture, after all, is a remedy, a drastic remedy in a case like this. Depriving people of a human right, like the right to life, in the case of an individual, and the right to a free and independent communal life, in the case of a collection of people, would seem appropriate not as punishment but only as a last resort for protecting the human rights of others. Given the disparity of power today between the Israeli state and the Palestinian people, it is hard to see any basis for the application of so exceptional a remedy, even if one assumes three things: first, that the Palestinian failure prior to the late 1980s to acknowledge the legitimate existence of the Israeli state constitutes in itself an international delinquency; secondly, that Yasser Arafat's failure at the Camp David meeting, organized in the year 2000 by US President Bill Clinton, to accept proposals formulated by the Government of Israel for a settlement evidences a secretly sustained or a renewed rejection of the right of the Jewish inhabitants of Mandate Palestine to self-determination, a right they exercised in 1947 to form the state of Israel; thirdly, that Yasser Arafat ordered the second *intifada* and could have halted it at will.

All three assumptions are, in fact, contestable. With respect to the first, as noted above, Palestinian refusal to recognize Israel corresponded to Israel's long-enduring insistence that the Arab inhabitants of the Palestinian Mandate territory had no right to self-determination within that territory as it existed at the time the Mandate terminated. The second has been a source of lively contention between, among others, two of the principal Middle East experts in the Clinton Administration who participated in the year 2000 Camp David negotiations, Dennis Ross[64] and Robert Malley.[65] I do not believe that any fair-minded person can review the facts and circumstances illuminated by their respective accounts without concluding that the failure is reasonably subject to diverse interpretations; in other words, that failure to reach agreement does not compel the conclusion that the Palestinian Authority is still unwilling to acknowledge Israel as the result of a legitimate act of self-determination carried out by the Jewish inhabitants of Mandate Palestine.[66]

[63] Such an act would certainly be deemed as an "unconstitutional condition." See, eg, "The Supreme Court 1959 Term," 74 *Harvard Law Journal* 95 (1960–61), 153.

[64] Dennis Ross, *The Missing Peace: The Inside Story of the Fight for Middle East Peace* (New York: Farrar, Straus & Giroux, 2004).

[65] See Malley's review of Ross in Robert Malley, "Israel and the Arafat Question" *New York Review of Books*, 7 October 2004. See also Hussein Agha and Robert Malley, "Camp David and After: An Exchange" (A Reply to Ehud Barak), *New York Review of Books*, 13 June 2003.

[66] Moreover, quite apart from the position of Yasser Arafat, public opinion polls conducted among the Arabs of the West Bank and Gaza at the time of Camp David showed very substantial majorities in favor of a solution that would produce an Arab and a predominantly Jewish state. While for most international legal and diplomatic purposes, a people participates in the international order through its official representatives, with respect to human rights issues, the individuals constituting a "people" have independent standing.

Any post-Camp David forfeiture argument rests on the claim, often reiterated by the Israeli Government and its supporters both at home and abroad, that prior to the second *intifada*, the Israeli Government offered the Palestinians the opportunity to form a viable sovereign state, that is the opportunity to exercise their right of self-determination if it could be done without unreasonable risk to the equally legitimate self-determination rights of Israelis, ie to the state of Israel. And this offer did not bar the possibility of some official Palestinian presence within the municipal boundaries of Jerusalem. On the contrary, in the form it finally assumed when representatives of the two parties met in Taba at the end of the Millennium, such a presence was explicitly envisioned.[67] And while rejection of the Israel proposals made earlier that year at Camp David might not constitute a forfeiture, the launching of the second *intifada*, rather than a counter-offer or at least a call for additional negotiations, could reasonably be deemed a forfeiture of rights because it was an act of low-intensity but still lethal aggression against the Israeli State, because it evidenced a continued unwillingness to accept a two-state solution and because it threatened the peace and security of the entire region and thereby violated the UN Charter.

I am unable to conclude that the facts bear the weight of these linked claims. The Israeli Government in the person of its prime minister did not initially offer the Palestinians any sovereign rights in historical Jerusalem, a failure which struck at the heart of Palestinian identity. By the end of the Camp David negotiations there were hints of movement on that point, but not a concrete offer.[68] Such an offer was made at Taba, but by negotiators who were not authorized to make binding commitments and represented a government plainly on the edge of replacement by political figures hostile to key elements of the Camp David proposals much less the further concessions made by the Israelis at Taba.[69] The inauguration of a Sharon Government meant the withdrawal of any proposals consistent with the exercise of a right to self-determination, for that government was publicly committed to maintaining settlements in the occupied territories and exclusive Israeli sovereignty over all of historical Jerusalem and its post-1967 territorial additions.[70]

[67] Section 2.2 of the Agreement suggests joint Israeli/Palestinian administration of a number of city services. Section 2.3 states that both sides would agree to Jerusalem serving as the capital of both Israel (Yerushalaim) and Palestine (Al-Quds). See the non-paper prepared by EU Special Representative to the Middle East Process, Ambassador Moratinos, available online at <www.mideastweb.org/moratinos.htm> (accessed 6 November 2006).

[68] In the words of one observer, "Barak's performance in office was so strange that it does not seems an exaggeration to term it schizoid... [H]e continuously subverted his own peace plan and the rational analysis on which it was based." Jerome Slater, "What Went Wrong? The Collapse of the Israeli-Palestinian Peace Process," 116 *Political Science Quarterly* 171 (2001), 179. But compare Dennis Ross, *The Missing Peace: The Inside Story of the Fight for Middle East Peace* (New York: Farrar, Straus & Giroux, 2004).

[69] Gidi Grinstein and Dennis Ross, "Camp David: An Exchange," *New York Review of Books*, 9 August 2001.

[70] In June 2003, the Associated Press reported Sharon as telling his cabinet that Israel should continue quietly constructing settlements in the West Bank and Gaza, despite the construction freeze required by the US-backed road map to Mideast peace. Sharon was quoted as saying the

I do not claim to know the real goals of Yasser Arafat and his closest colleagues at the time of the Oslo Accords, Accords that permitted them to assume a limited form of authority in fragments of the West Bank, or the Camp David meeting. Certainly it is possible that they clung to the vision of a unitary state in the territory of the former Palestinian Mandate which through the power of demography would eventually be governed by an Arab majority.[71] And it is even possible, given the human capacity for fantasizing, that this was an operational goal, not a merely whimsical dream, self-understood to be such. What one can say with certainty, however, is that neither the failure to counter-offer at Camp David (a meeting for which Arafat was ill-prepared at least in the sense of not yet having taken the political risks of preparing his own constituents for concessions, as he told Clinton in explaining his initial extreme reluctance to attend)[72] nor to accept formally as a final deal the compromises sketched at Taba by Israeli representatives who, as noted, did not have the power to commit the Israeli state, are conclusive evidence of a rejection of a two-state solution. Certainly, at least according to credible accounts, the representatives of Arafat attending the meeting believed that they were very close to an agreement that could be sold to the Palestinian people.[73]

Arafat's failure to prepare his various constituencies, including the 1½ million Palestinians surviving in refugee camps outside Palestine, often invoked as evidence of his treacherous evasion of the spirit of the Oslo Accords, surely does no more than parallel the Israeli Government's evasion by continuing to foster expansion of Jewish settlements in the very territories that would have to be turned over to the envisioned Palestinian State if it were to be anything more than a mockery of statehood. "In September 1993," one distinguished Israeli scholar has noted,

there were 33,000 family housing units in the settlements. By July 2000, 19,000 were added (3,000 of them under Barak). At the end of 1993 there were, according to Israeli statistics, some 116,000 settlers in the West Bank and Gaza. In view of the yearly population growth of 8 percent (natural increase and newcomers combined), we can assume that there were about 200,000 settlers at the beginning of the second Intifada in late September 2000...[74]

continuation of settlement construction was "my personal commitment." Mark Lavie, "Sharon: Settlements can expand, despite road map" (23 June).

[71] In the abstract an ideal no more objectionable from a moral perspective than the pre-state Zionist ideal of a Jewish-dominated state in all of the Palestinian Mandate (plus, for at least some Zionist luminaries, contemporary Jordan, Egypt's Sinai Peninsula, and contemporary Lebanon south of the Litani River).

[72] See Benny Morris, "Camp David and After: An Exchange" (An Interview with Ehud Barak), *New York Review of Books*, 13 June 2003; and the response to it, Hussein Agha and Robert Malley, "Camp David and After: An Exchange" (A Reply to Ehud Barak), *New York Review of Books*, 13 June 2003.

[73] For an analysis of Arafat's positions throughout these negotiations, see Robert Wright, "Was Arafat the Problem?" *Slate* (18 April 2002), online at <http://slate.com/?id=2064500>, 6 November 2006.

[74] Avishai Margalit, "Settling Scores," *New York Review of Books*, 20 September 2001, 1–2.

Arafat's failure may also have reflected his political weakness. By signing the Oslo Accords, Arafat had recognized the legitimacy of Israel, a principal bargaining chip of the Palestinians, and thereby conceded the loss of nearly 30 per cent of the territory that the original 1948 UN partition plan had assigned to the proposed Palestinian state, leaving him with two slices of land, the "West Bank" and Gaza, separated by Israeli territory and constituting little more than 22 per cent of the British Mandate of Palestine at the time of its termination. Moreover, it did not even guarantee that 22 per cent, since it did not require the removal of the settlements. Nor did it explicitly preclude their expansion. Nor did it offer anything explicit for the million plus Palestinians still living in refugee camps. And finally, it provided no assurances of an eventual capital in some part of the City of Jerusalem.[75] Hence for signing the Accords, he had been excoriated in the Arab press as a traitor.

The continued expansion of the settlements thereafter seemed only to confirm Israel's determination to withhold even a part of that 22 per cent and to allow, at most, a mock, bi-furcated state that would enjoy no more real autonomy than had South Africa's Bantustans. Hence, Arafat might reasonably have calculated that, until he had in hand an unequivocal agreement, guaranteed by the Security Council, conceding the establishment of a sovereign Palestinian state with borders approximating those of 1967 and with a capital in East Jerusalem, an agreement assuring generous compensation for Palestinian property confiscated in 1948 and 1967, he might suffer a total implosion of his authority if he advocated before he could plainly deliver a settlement which, from the Arab point of view, made huge concessions. A larger man might have risked that. I merely propose that given the political risks and the reasonable doubt that any such settlement could be negotiated with the Israelis, Arafat's failure to "prepare" the Palestinians does not require the conclusion that he and his colleagues had no intention of settling for a two-state solution if it were obtainable.

In addition, there is a respectable legal argument for the proposition that renewal of violent resistance to continued Israeli occupation, even assuming the resistance was organized or was at least amenable to suppression by the Palestinian Authority, which is by no means clear, was not an act of aggression but rather an exercise in national liberation[76]—albeit one carried out in part by atrocious and clearly illegal means, namely attacks on non-combatants.[77] If it were aggression, then the forfeiture argument would have more traction. The atrocious acts themselves are grounds for criminal punishment of persons implicated in their

---

[75] See Chris Hedges, "The New Palestinian Revolt," *Foreign Affairs*, January/February 2001, 124, 134.

[76] Eide, below.

[77] While I recognize that in past debates at the General Assembly, some governments have insisted that no violent act committed to advance a war of national liberation could be labeled terrorist, I believe that in recent years a broad spectrum of international opinion has repudiated that position and that it is no longer widely held, at least in official circles.

commission, but, because of forfeiture's implications for the long-term human rights prospect in the occupied territories, not for a loss of national rights.

Violent resistance after 37 years of occupation was not illegitimate.[78] On the contrary, one can reasonably argue that it was justified by international law. This would not have been the case had the uprising occurred shortly after the 1967 war. For in exercising their right to self-defense under Article 51 of the UN Charter, the Israelis were entitled to an active defense which included not merely driving back hostile or threatening forces, but pushing them back from its de facto borders.[79] So the initial Israeli occupation of East Jerusalem, and also of Gaza and the West Bank, was seen by many commentators at the time as licit. And in the official Israeli view it remains licit to this day because no other state has even an equal much less a greater claim to the territories.

For the reasons already sketched in the discussion of self-determination rights, the Israeli claim is meretricious. Occupation of Gaza, the West Bank, and East Jerusalem by the Arab states following Israel's declaration of statehood was not a violation of Israel's rights,[80] because under the UN partition, Israel had no rights to those territories.[81] Nor, during the years between the end of the war of independence in 1949 and 1967, did Israel—much less any other country—argue that the presence of those states in the territories constituted some delinquency vis-à-vis Israel. To be sure, few if any states formally recognized their occupation as licit. And after Israel drove them from the territories in 1967, it denied that it could be said to have "occupied" the territories because their prior occupants had not been present in them legitimately.

One could argue, I suppose, that if an initial occupation of any territory is illegitimate, then the exercise of effective authority over the illegally occupied place can never ripen over time into an extension of sovereign rights. That is one possible explanation for the position of Israel *vis-à-vis* Jordan and Egypt after the 1967 war, and for the refusal of other countries before 1967 to concede the

[78] *Pace* Hillary Clinton, who when running for the US Senate in New York had denounced as "offensive and outrageous" the statement of a New York community leader that international law supported the right to resist an occupation. Quoted in Brian Urquhart, "Living in an Impasse," *New York Review of Books*, 21 September 2006, 52 at 53.

[79] Itzhak Rabin, Matitiahu Peled, Ezer Weizman, and Menachem Begin later admitted that they had not anticipated an imminent attack by Egypt when Israel struck it on 5 June. Thus the preemptive strike against Egypt needs to be distinguished from the case of Jordan, which Israel attacked after it had struck Israel "in response to Israel's attack on Egypt in exercise of collective self-defense permitted under Article 51 of the UN Charter." See Quigley, above, at 162–5.

[80] But it probably was a violation of the UN Charter as a "breach of the peace." However, the Arab states argued that they entered at the request of the de facto Palestinian authorities to assist in protecting Palestinian villages in territory allocated to the envisioned Palestinian state by Resolution 181. From the vantage point of 2004, it is difficult to unravel the sequence of Jewish-Arab violence within the Mandate following the British withdrawal.

[81] It is important to note that in its declaration of statehood transmitted to the United Nations—as well as in the declaration itself—Israeli authorities cited Resolution 181 (and presumably the borders it suggested) as a basis for their claim of statehood. See Quigley, above, at 64.

legitimacy of the Jordanian and Egyptian occupations.[82] But by far the more powerful explanation of the attitude of states other than Israel is that those claims could not become licit because they violated the rights of the territories' inhabitants to self-determination. In other words, Gaza, the West Bank and Jerusalem were not *terra nullius*: they were Palestinian terra; they were part of the latent Palestinian state implied by the recognition of the Palestinians as a "People." For if they were not, then there was no place for that right to be exercised. A right incapable of being exercised is a logical absurdity. In this connection surely it is suggestive that excepting the standard instances of long-time colonial rule, the clearest if not the only other case of a failure, despite decades of effective control, to legitimate a claim to sovereignty over territory acquired through armed force—as were Jerusalem, Gaza, and the West Bank—was another colonial legacy. I refer of course to East Timor.

What follows from the argument to this point is that when Israel sent its troops into Gaza, the West Bank, and East Jerusalem in 1967 in exercise of its right to self-defense, its legal position was essentially the same as the one that would accrue to the United States in a hypothetical case where it occupies Mexico to preempt an attack by Chinese forces that had previously invaded Mexico, destroyed its political institutions and ruled it as a province of China for 18 years. In that hypothetical case, the United States' initial entry into Mexico would be licit, but the United States would be obligated to turn de facto authority over to representative Mexican officials and withdraw its forces as soon as it could establish conditions consistent with the security of its southwestern frontier. If, for instance, some Mexicans had collaborated with the Chinese, had, indeed, formed commando units to assist in the attack on the United States and those units were not only intact but were led by officers aspiring to reverse the result of the Mexican-American War, that is to reacquire for Mexico the southwestern part of the United States plus California, the United States would arguably be entitled to remain in Mexico until it had eliminated the units or succeeded in helping more pliable Mexicans to reestablish a government willing to coexist peacefully with the United States and able to deal with the revisionist commandos.

In this hypothetical case, the United States could do nothing to diminish Mexican sovereignty, even temporarily, that was not essential to the exercise of its rights under Article 51 of the Charter. In effect, the United States would have under international law a conditional license to deploy troops on foreign territory

[82] The Jordanian parliament formally incorporated the West Bank in 1950—but said it did so "without prejudicing the final settlement of Palestine's just case within the sphere of national aspirations, inter-Arab cooperation and international justice." The incorporation was only recognized by Great Britain and Pakistan. Egypt administered Gaza as "an inseparable part of the land of Palestine." Quigley, above, at 153. The Jordanian parliament formally incorporated the West Bank in 1950—but said it did so "without prejudicing the final settlement of Palestine's just case within the sphere of national aspirations, inter-Arab cooperation and international justice." The incorporation was only recognized by Great Britain and Pakistan. Egypt administered Gaza as "an inseparable part of the land of Palestine." Quigley, above 5, at 153.

without authorization from the territorial sovereign. The license's conditions would necessitate, among other things, a maximum effort to preserve Mexican natural resources, including land and water, and to reestablish or reanimate indigenous political institutions so that the Mexicans themselves could thereafter prevent their territory from being used by indigenous paramilitary groups or foreign powers to threaten the United States. These conditions are a corollary of national sovereignty, the central organizing concept and value of the entire international order. Once it was the privilege of mostly Western states. But in the nineteenth century, it began to morph into a universal right belonging, as we have noted, to peoples, a morphological process completed in the twentieth century.

There is one further point that needs to be made concerning the legitimacy in a legal but even more strongly in a moral sense of armed resistance to occupation. The spirit of the UN Charter and the letter of just war doctrine, as it has evolved over the centuries in the West, is that recourse to force in conflicts between peoples and states should be a last resort. Can the Palestinians make a reasonably persuasive case that their widespread armed resistance since the year 2000 satisfies that condition? Shortly after the beginning of the 1967 occupation, Palestinian notables appealed to the Israeli authorities for the grant of autonomy in the territories. This was rejected. Indeed, the authorities prohibited all political activity. After a period of quiescence, Palestinians attempted passive resistance of a Ghandian sort, a policy of non-cooperation with the occupation, such as the withholding of taxes. The attempt was crushed by Israel by means of curfews, mass detention, termination of essential services, and beatings. There followed 20 years of submission, summarized by the Israeli writer, Amos Elon, as a "low maintenance...military occupation that for more than two decades has held 1.5 million Palestinians as pawns, or bargaining chips, as a source of cheap menial labor, while denying them the most basic human rights."[83]

Finally, in 1988 Palestinians revolted, "led by a few thousand teenagers and even younger boys and girls, armed with nothing but stones and slingshots and occasional Molotov bottles—a children's crusade."[84] This could be described as a form of resistance lying between non-cooperation (Ghandian passive resistance, already tried and failed) and armed rebellion. Still, it was an escalation of resistance in response to which the Israelis escalated their repression. Writing at an early point in that first *intifada*, Amos Alon described the Israeli response as follows:

More than ninety Palestinians have died so far.... Most were shot; twenty-one are said to have died by asphyxiation by tear gas (including three babies less than seven months old, a boy of twelve, and one man a hundred years old). Seven are said to have died as a result of beatings (including one fourteen-year-old boy and a man aged sixty).... Hundreds have

[83] Amos Elon, "From the Uprising," *New York Review of Books*, 14 April 1988, 1.
[84] Ibid, 2.

been wounded and beaten up by truncheon-wielding troops who follow orders that are at best confused and at worst downright brutal....The hospitals in Gaza and elsewhere are filled with youngsters suffering from broken arms or legs, or both....Thousands of Palestinians have been arrested, hundreds of thousands more have been intimidated and placed under prolonged house arrest in the recurrent curfews imposed upon villages, refugee camps, and entire cities....Curfews often mean disconnected telephones and cuts in the supply of electricity....Men are hauled out of their houses in the middle of the night and made to stand in the village square until morning, and there are many similar acts of collective punishment....Yet in three months of uprising the rioters have not fired a single shot.[85]

That was 1988. The rising and the brutal repression was still going on three years later on the eve of the First Gulf War. In testimony submitted to the US House of Representatives Foreign Affairs Committee in May 1990, Amnesty International USA conclude on the basis of its inquiries that "thousands of Palestinians have been beaten while in the hands of Israeli forces or tortured or ill-treated in detention centers....Wounded Palestinians have been dragged out of hospitals against the advice of doctors and beaten before being taken to detention centers."[86] By that time, as I wrote in 1991,

more than 700 Palestinians have been killed and many thousands wounded by troops firing live ammunition or plastic bullets at lethally close range. Of those killed as of May 1990, close to 150 were aged 16 or younger; Amnesty International USA reports that about 35 were less than 12 years old. The Israeli government does not claim that most or even many of the persons killed in confrontations with security forces have carried or used firearms or grenades. Indeed, according to Israeli Defense Force (IDF) figures, only about 5 percent of violent activity by Palestinians involves the use of clearly lethal weapons, defined as guns, knives, and gasoline bombs; 85 per cent is stone throwing, 60 per cent is carried out by children 12 years old or younger. The great majority of shootings by the IDF are associated with either alleged incidents of stone throwing and other riotous behavior, or attempted flight to avoid capture.[87]

In light of this history first of passive resistance, then of resistance largely by non-lethal means designed to make the territories ungovernable (as was the purpose of passive resistance), and in light as well of the ongoing confiscation of private and collective Arab lands and their use to create and expand and link Israeli settlements and the total control exercised over economic activity and movement in and out of the territories, and the seizure of water resources and the grossly disproportionate allocation of those resources to the settlers or to Israel itself, the Palestinians could certainly make a reasonable case for the proposition that they had exhausted options other than recourse to arms before launching the second *intifada*.

[85] Ibid, 43.
[86] Quoted in ibid, 44.
[87] Tom J Farer, "Israel's Unlawful Occupation" *Foreign Policy* 82, Spring 1991.

4. Israel and the Occupied Territories in Light of Human Rights Law and the Law of War

Returning to my hypothetical case of a US occupation of Mexico as a conse-quence of war with China and a resulting conditional license for the United States to remain pending the establishment of secure conditions, a position I analogize to that of Israel at the close of the 1967 War: The license's conditions in my hypothetical case or the real Israeli one do not stem only from the broad organizational and moral principles of national sovereignty/self-determination. In addition, they are required by the very concrete provisions of the almost universally ratified Fourth Geneva Convention on the rights of civilians in occupied territory. The key provision is Article 49 which prohibits the Occupying Power from expel-ling any of the people in the territory, except on a temporary basis and for exi-gent reasons of security, and from transferring of parts of its own population into the territory. Also relevant is Article 53 which prohibits "any destruction... of real or personal property... except where such destruction is rendered absolutely necessary by military operations." Article 53 includes the confiscation of property belonging to or held for the use of the citizens of the Occupied Territories.

Since the beginning of the occupation in 1967, both openly and by relatively subtle means, Israel has grossly and persistently violated these prohibitions in Jerusalem as well as the other occupied territories. Violations of the applicable prohibition were not long delayed. Immediately after driving the Jordanians from East Jerusalem, Israel demolished buildings around the Western Wall primarily in order to provide a large space for Jewish worshippers at this site of great religious significance in the Jewish faith, certainly not for reasons of military necessity, since none existed then or thereafter. That was only the first of various confiscations of property in Jerusalem and the other territories most of which were designed to affect the demographic balance in the city.

Successive layers of policy decisions enacted by Israeli governments since 1967 constitute violations of the Fourth Geneva Convention, the International Covenant on Civil and Political Rights, and a number of other treaties to which Israel is a party—most notably the International Covenant on Economic, Social and Cultural Rights.[88] These violations are a result of Israel's failure to fulfill obligations of both conduct *and* result contained within the treaties.[89] They have inevitably led to a dramatic shift in the demographics of East Jerusalem,

[88] I note here that the Jerusalem example provides support for the claim that the two covenants and the rights contained within them are indivisible and interdependent. For example, the "standard of living" right enumerated in art 11 of the ICESCR (which includes a right to housing) is inextricably tied to the ICCPR's art 12 which enumerates the human right to choose one's own place of residence.

[89] An obligation of *conduct* represents a duty to act in the realization of a right, including promoting the conditions necessary for rights to be realized. An obligation of *result* is a goal that must be achieved, such as the obligation to ensure the right to housing or education. See the

creating "facts on the ground" intended to make any future division of Jerusalem impossible, and to strengthen Israel's grip on the West Bank with its network of settlements—hence a move clearly designed to thwart the development of a Palestinian state. I emphasize Jerusalem because in that area Israeli transgressions are particularly transparent.

To create the demographic facts on the ground, the Israeli government has actively pursued a set of policies "designed to isolate Jerusalem from the West Bank hinterland or to impede institutional development."[90] The two-sided Israeli policies of Judaization/Israeliazation (promoting and encouraging settlement activity) and de-Arabization (actively encouraging the departure of legal Palestinian residents from the city) of East Jerusalem are inextricably linked. According to one observer, the overall objective of these meta-policies is "to transform Jerusalem into an overwhelmingly Jewish metropolis—demographically, culturally, socially and politically."[91]

Policies designed to alter the demographic make-up of East Jerusalem were implemented immediately after the 1967 war, beginning with the expansion of the "newly unified" city's municipal boundaries eastward.[92] After dissolving the local Palestinian city council, offers of citizenship to the existing Palestinian residents of East Jerusalem were extended. But the requirements to obtain citizenship were so strict (including especially the demand that Palestinians be fluent in Hebrew and renounce any other claims of citizenship—presumably Jordanian) that many opted instead to become "permanent residents." And that offer was extended only to those Palestinians who were actually residing in the newly defined borders of Jerusalem. Many who had fled the fighting during the Six-Day War lost all legal claims of residency and their property, declared "absentee," was confiscated by the Israeli government in blatant disregard of Articles 49 and 53 of the Fourth Geneva Convention.

In addition to reducing the Palestinian population though this legal maneuver, the Israeli government has taken incremental steps since 1967 to make life in East Jerusalem difficult, and especially to make the prospects of living elsewhere in the West Bank or Gaza more attractive. Increasingly stringent residency requirements have been the most obvious method of promoting de-Arabization of the city. Whereas Palestinian residents initially enjoyed freedom of movement in and out of East Jerusalem (especially for those looking for work), in 1995 a new "center of life" policy (completely unannounced) was implemented, whereby Palestinian residents had to certify that they lived and worked within the boundaries of the city—certifications that required extensive tax documentation that

---

"Maastricht Guidelines on Violations of Economic, Social and Cultural Rights", *Human Rights Quarterly*, 20 (1998), 122, note 21, para 7.

[90] Michael Dumper, *The Old City of Jerusalem in the Middle East Conflict* (Boulder, CO: Lynne Rienner, 2002), 27.

[91] Cheryl Rubenburg, *The Palestinians: In Search of a Just Peace* (2003), 194.

[92] Benny Morris, *Righteous Victims* (New York: Knopf, 1999), 331.

was often difficult or impossible to obtain. As a result of this maneuver, between 1995 and 1999, more than 3,000 Jerusalemite Palestinians lost their right to reside in the city.[93]

Severely restrictive zoning and housing construction laws (which do not apply to Jewish residents) are additional policy tools designed to encourage Palestinians to leave the city. Between 1967 and 1999, only 12,490 new housing units in East Jerusalem were built for Palestinians, compared to 122,376 units for Jews.[94] Palestinians are allowed to build in a mere 7 per cent of the entire expanse of East Jerusalem—and restrictions on that building are stringent (eg no building in open areas or vacant lots) and restrictive (eg no buildings of more than two storeys). The authorities deal swiftly with illegal building activities by Palestinians—including those who have added to existing structures in order to ease crowding. In 1999, for example, 10,000 housing units were declared illegal and slated for demolition.[95]

For those Palestinians who have managed to maintain their residency, Israeli administration of East Jerusalem has led to a dramatic deterioration in their quality of life. For instance, Palestinians pay 31 per cent of the taxes and receive only 2 to 12 per cent of the services offered to residents. In per-capita terms, in 1998 the city spent six times more per Jewish resident than per Palestinian one.[96] As a result, in 1998 there were 414 public schools for Jewish children, and 35 for Palestinian children. Jewish residents enjoy the services of 26 libraries, while Palestinian residents have access to two. One hundred per cent of Jewish neighborhoods get regular garbage collection, whereas 60 per cent of Palestinian neighborhoods have sporadic or no garbage collection at all.[97]

Increasingly restrictive residency policies and stringent zoning and housing rules, coupled with gross discrimination in the provision of public services and lack of attention paid by the public authorities to the quality of life for Arabs in East Jerusalem, conspired for years to make the prospect of finding housing elsewhere in the West Bank or Gaza highly attractive. Of course, once legal residents leave, they lose their residency. The impact of 40 years of Israeli de-Arabization policy can be summed up thus: 86 per cent of East Jerusalem has been effectively removed from Palestinian control through expropriation and confiscation of land and property; 42 per cent of the land has been appropriated for Jewish settlements; 44 per cent has been declared "green" (eg not for development), although past practice suggests that ostensibly "environmental" set-asides are the first step before settlements are actually built.[98]

---

[93] Rubenburg, above, at 206–7.   [94] Ibid, 209.   [95] Ibid, 210.

[96] Ibid, 200. It is important to note that since the Israeli government considers Jerusalem to be a "united" city, it does not disaggregate data between East and West. In 1998, Jews made up 68.4% of the Jerusalemite population, and Palestinians comprised 31.6%. But in 1998 nearly all of the 200,000 Palestinians lived in East Jerusalem—alongside 170,000 Israeli "settlers."

[97] Ibid.

[98] Ibid. 210.

Since any attempt to reconcile its policies with the terms of Article 49 would be risible, successive Israeli Governments have defended their actions in the Occupied Territories by claiming that the Fourth Geneva Convention is inapplicable to them. The Convention, they have argued, applies only where State A occupies territory that enjoys general recognition as an integral part of State B another party to the Convention. Since neither Jordan nor Egypt (in the case of Gaza) had the legal right to occupy those territories in the first place, much less to remain in occupation thereafter, and since Israel acquired them through pre-emption of imminent Arab aggression, that is not true of the territories occupied as a result of the 1967 war. Ergo, the treaty is inapplicable. This position has gathered very little support within either the diplomatic or the international legal community. And it has been rejected by the neutral steward of the Geneva Conventions, the International Committee of the Red Cross.[99]

To be sure, as the Government of Israel notes, certain procedures of the Fourth Convention only become operative when land occupied in the course of an armed conflict is indisputably part of another Belligerent's national territory. But it is hard to find in that fact a persuasive rationale for denying the applicability of the convention's substantive guarantees. They were designed, after all, to provide international protection for a people in circumstances where the fortunes of war have stripped from them the legal and institutional framework of quotidian existence hitherto provided by the Belligerent forced from the territory. Suddenly they are under the authority of a state that has expended blood in order to occupy the territory and which normally has no historic ties to its inhabitants. The condition is aggravated where the occupier is engaged in self-defense, because then the territory may well have been the launching pad for the aggression to which it is responding. At best, therefore, it will regard the inhabitants with suspicion; at worst it will feel vengeful.

A convention of treaty interpretation is to interpret those in the realm of human rights so as to maximize their humanitarian impact.[100] Ambiguities should be resolved in favor of protection. In the case under consideration, the reason for the rule could hardly be more relevant.

It is no doubt anomalous for an international agreement designed for the extreme conditions of war to continue as a principal legal framework for a territory four decades after the fighting ceased. But that anomaly, rather than casting doubt on the continuing applicability of the Fourth Convention, underscores the anomalous nature of Israel's position in relation to the territories and

---

[99] See, eg, Official Statement of the International Committee of the Red Cross, Conference of High Contracting Parties to the Fourth Geneva Convention, 5 December 2001, esp. para 2, available online at <http://www.icrc.org/Web/eng/siteeng0.nsf/htmlall/57JRGW?OpenDocument> (accessed 6 November 2006). See also Tom J Farer, "Israel's Unlawful Occupation," 37 *Foreign Policy* 82 (Spring 1991), 40–1.

[100] See, eg, the Advisory Opinion of the International Court of Justice on Reservations to the Convention on the Prevention and Punishment of the Crime of Genocide (28 May 1951), available online at <http://www.icrc.org/web/eng/siteeng0.nsf/html/5FLDPJ> (accessed 6 November 2006).

the extraordinary conditions under which its inhabitants labor to survive as individuals, as families, and as a People. It coincidentally underscores the importance of assessing Israel's behavior in terms of the Covenant on Civil and Political Rights, designed as it is to cover all the conditions of existence, as well as the Geneva Conventions, designed as they are to protect the population under the acutely threatening but normally transitory conditions of war.

A focus on Articles 25 and 26 of the Covenant helps one to appreciate the legal gravity and the human reality of those conditions. Article 25 states that:

Every citizen shall have the right and the opportunity...

(a) to take part in the conduct of public affairs, directly or through freely chosen representatives;
(b) To vote and to be elected at genuine periodic elections...;
(c) To have access, on general terms of equality, to public service in his [sic] country.

Article 26 in its entirety reads as follows:

All persons are equal before the law and are entitled without any discrimination to the equal protection of the law. In this respect, the law shall prohibit any discrimination and guarantee to all persons equal and effective protection against discrimination on any ground such as race, colour,... national or social origin,... religion...

What is the reality of life in Jerusalem and the other occupied territories? Jews and Arabs live in close proximity. The former participate vigorously in shaping the laws and the administration of the Israeli state. The latter participate not at all. The former are subject to all of the due process protections afforded by Israeli law. The latter are subject to arrest, detention, interrogation by means found by the UN Special Rapporteur on Torture to constitute torture,[101] all under a system run by the military and the security services, and can be detained indefinitely without charge or trial. Which is to say that they live and have lived since 1967, decades before the first *intifada,* under the rigorous conditions that one might expect in an occupied territory at the height of a murderous inter-state conflict. Denial of the right to participate in government and to equal treatment of the law is compatible with the Covenant only in time of war.[102] At that time, the Fourth Geneva Convention offers some floor for the population of the occupied territory to prevent their sinking into an abyss of rightlessness. While it continues to provide a floor after the war is concluded, it can hardly be deemed to be the entire legal structure governing the treatment of a People. That is why the Covenant comes into full play once the crisis of war has passed.

---

[101] UN Commission on Human Rights, *Report of the Special Rapporteur on torture and cruel, inhuman or degrading treatment or punishment,* UN Doc. E/CN.4/1994/31 (1994) (Nigel Rodley, Special Rapporteur).

[102] ICCPR, art 4 allows states parties to derogate from certain provisions of the treaty "in times of public emergency."

During the many debates at the United Nations on Wars of National Liberation, often conducted in conjunction with discussions of terrorism, most non-Western states took the position that populations under colonial rule or alien domination had the right to rebel and many argued third parties had the right to provide material assistance.[103] Suiting deed to word, many states did assist insurgents attempting to overthrow colonial regimes or, in the case of Southern Rhodesia and South Africa, regimes with colonial roots and governments that discriminated grossly on ethnic grounds. Even some Western states, Sweden for example, gave some non-lethal aid. And by ultimately supporting sanctions against Southern Rhodesia and later South Africa, even Western states like the United States and the United Kingdom most hostile to third party support of insurgencies under any circumstance seemed to endorse the impropriety of third parties assisting the colonial regime in suppressing national liberation movements. This history implies broad support for a right to revolt against colonial and alien domination.

I raise this history not to reargue the question of the responsibilities of third parties in colonial conflicts. My purpose here has been quite modest, namely to explain why, given the conditions imposed on the population of the occupied territories, I do not believe that the launching of the first or even the second *intifada* provides grounds for declaring forfeit the Palestinian right to self-determination. The first one did not begin until after 20 years of an occupation marked by illegal acts seriously prejudicing the day-to-day lives of the inhabitants of the territories and the second occurred in the face of a continuing expansion of illegal settlements in the occupied territories despite the reasonable expectation of at least a standstill of settler expansion in the wake of the 1993 Oslo Accords.

5. A Legal Right in Search of a Remedy

The right of the Palestinians to a state and to the restoration of land and property in East Jerusalem being clear, what are the obligations of the state of Israel with respect to its enforcement? Assuming as I do that the original occupation of the territories in 1967 was licit (albeit a close case)—an exercise of Israel's right to self-defense under the Charter *vis-à-vis* Jordan and Egypt—cannot Israel argue, by analogy, that even if the Palestinian people have a right to form a sovereign state, as long as the representatives of that people are unwilling or unable to suppress threats against Israeli territory, a condition for the realization of self-determination rights is missing? By retaining control over the territories or the right to intervene in them at its discretion, Israel might argue, it is still exercising its rights under Article 51 of the Charter against the latent Palestinian state, as previously it did against the actual states of Egypt and Jordan.

---

[103] See generally, Asbjorn Eide, "International Law, Dominance, and the Use of Force," *Journal of Peace Research*, 11(1) (1974).

One not unreasonable legal response is to turn the forfeiture argument on its head, that is to argue Israeli forfeiture of rights to remain in the territories, pending an agreement and conditions providing it with reasonable security guarantees. Forfeiture would arise from the violations of the Covenant and the Convention described above. It follows from this line of argument that if, after occupying the territories in 1967, Israel had not introduced elements of its own population into the territories, had encouraged local self-governance and had declared its readiness to hold a referendum on the future status of the territories, including East Jerusalem, once representatives of the inhabitants had provided reasonable assurances of respect for Israel's territorial integrity, then Israel could have legitimately remained an Occupying Power until those conditions were sat-isfied whether through the emergence of a local leadership with which it could negotiate a two-state solution or negotiations with Yasser Arafat if he were chosen by the territories' inhabitants to represent them. In order to assure Jewish access to the Holy sites in Jerusalem, it could, in addition, have insisted on some sort of internationalization of the city along lines charted by the original UN resolution of 1947.

Remedies are a distinct part of any legal system providing it with needed flexibility in bringing general rules and principles to bear on particular cases. However appealing the forfeiture argument, demanding in its name immediate implementation of Palestinian rights to a separate state without any plausible plan for securing a settled constitutional order in the occupied territories and organ-izing its relations with Israel is to ignore the implications of a sudden change of status for the welfare of all the people of Israel and the occupied territories and the interest of the broad international society of states in the establishment of sustainable peace and regional security. What is needed first at this point, then, is recognition that Palestinians retain a right to self-determination and that settlements beyond the 1967 boundaries are presumptively illegal, although final boundaries are subject to minor adjustment through negotiation in order to maximize the prospects for peaceful coexistence of the two states and to protect the religious interests of all interested parties, a major concern of the United Nations since it first confronted the question of Palestine. Next would be action by the Security Council to compel a beginning to the dismantling of settlements and the corresponding replacement of Israeli with third-country forces in the occupied territories to assure secure conditions for the population and for Israel. Israel would of course remain free to erect security barriers at its 1967 frontiers. In Jerusalem itself, all changes in the status quo need to be halted pending nego-tiations informed by the proposition that one of the probable conditions of a sustainable settlement is placing stewardship at least of the holy sites, if not all of the old city, in the hands of the Security Council which would then sub-delegate its administrative (but not its ultimate supervisory) authority to representatives of the various major factions of the three monotheisms that have historically sought to control them.

6. Conclusion: The South African Analogy

In the past 60 years, the years in which universal human rights took root in the soil of international law and grew into the principal idiom of moral discourse, only two countries have been sites of the following phenomenon. One group of people enjoying all the freedoms and the opulent comforts that characterize life in West European and North American states exists cheek-by-jowl with and controls the life chances of another group of people among whom none enjoy the most basic freedoms and most endure conditions of Third World poverty. Members of one group participate in a vibrant political process and set the parameters of government policies, above all its treatment of the other group's members. The latter's members can elect officials theoretically entitled to govern them, but in fact those elected officials cannot prevent their constituents either from being detained indefinitely without judicial review or assassinated, cannot assure them due process in the event they are accused, and cannot secure them the opportunity to move freely within the national territory. And finally, in neither case can members of the subordinate group as a practical matter migrate to membership in the dominant group, because each dominant group has defined its identity in a way that permanently excludes members of the minority. Minority persons can acquire or possess what qualities they will: wealth, superior education, excellence of intellect, musical virtuosity, it makes no difference. They remain "the other."

In both cases it would be fair to say that the subordinate group lives in a collection of concentration camps with their only means of exit being exodus from the land of their birth. These concentration camps are not duplicates of Auschwitz: their inhabitants are not slated for extermination, although individual members are from time to time exterminated if they are suspected of plotting against the dominant social group. In one case the possibility of mass expatriation to a neighboring state is mooted in the majority's political discourse,[104] but it is not yet a settled aim. Among the different historical analogies perhaps the closest is the reservation system used by the United States to isolate the surviving members of Native American tribes at low cost in what could fairly be described as spatially extensive, largely open-air prisons in which the inmates enjoy a certain degree of quotidian self-administration. Looking to more contemporary instances, a plausible analogy is the Serbian Province of Kosovo where, as readers will recall, the demographic imbalance between Russian Orthodox Serbian-speaking inhabitants, on the one hand, and the Muslim, Albanian-speaking majority on the other made domination increasingly costly as the majority pressed its resistance

---

[104] See "Shutting Itself in, Hoping for the Best," *The Economist*, 25 March 2006 for a discussion of Avigdor Lieberman, a leader of the right-wing Yisrael Beiteinu ("Israel is Our Home") party who has been vocal about his advocacy for expulsion of Arab-Israelis, so as to maintain a strong Jewish majority.

to the point where the Serbian government initiated a mass expulsion of the latter that was halted by NATO's bombing campaign.[105]

In both of the principal cases I am describing, the dominators imagine themselves as part of Western civilization, as the forward edge of that civilization in a nasty part of the world, and invoke the West's support in terms of their common values. And in both cases the dominators justify the arrangements I have described as compelled by an extreme and permanent necessity, namely the existential threat they face in the form of the subordinate group. In one country the camps or reservations, as you will, were called Bantustans. In the other, they are generally referred to by outsiders as the "occupied territories."[106]

The comparison has been all too clear for Israelis and Diaspora Jews who have not yielded to the chauvinistic self-absorption endemic to national movements. Here is the witness of one such person, Israel's Attorney-General from 1993–96, Michael Ben-Yair:

[After the 1967 war,] we enthusiastically chose to become a colonial society, ignoring international treaties, expropriating land, transferring settlers from Israel to the Occupied Territories, engaging in theft and finding justification for all these activities. Passionately desiring to keep Occupied Territories, we developed two judicial systems: one—progressive, liberal—in Israel; and the other—cruel, injurious—in the Occupied Territories. In effect, we established an apartheid regime in the Occupied Territories immediately following their capture.[107]

Since it is not very pretty, this comparison of South Africa's *apartheid* system, as it was before the great transition, and Israel's governance of the occupied territories is resisted with some considerable ferocity, witness the reaction in most Western countries to the 1975 UN General Assembly's effort to connect the two cases by equating Zionism with Racism.[108] The equation was seen as much like the blood libels that had for a millennium been used to justify the massacre of Jewish minorities particularly in various parts of Europe. And of course the emphasis on race, that is on differences in skin pigmentation and, perhaps, physiognomy, was absurd. Israel's Jewish citizens are a full-spectrum of pigmentation including very dark-skinned refugees from Ethiopia. Moreover, as even the UN delegates voting for that stupid and pernicious resolution must have known, about 18 per cent of Israel's citizens living within the pre-1967 boundaries are Arabs in the sense that they are descendants of the predominantly Arabic-speaking population of

---

[105] To be fair, some argue that the bombing triggered mass expulsion. Others contend that expulsion was planned and in its early stages and the bombing merely accelerated implementation of a plan to alter the area's demographics. Until historians have access to the Serbian archives, we will not know with certainty. What is certain is that the dialectic of repression and resistance was spiraling upward to the point where, in light of the butchery in Bosnia, one had to anticipate an early replay of the Bosnian massacres in Kosovo.

[106] For a comparison see "A Safety Measure or a Land Grab," *Economist*, 11 October 2003, 25–8.

[107] Brian Urquhart, "Living in an Impasse," *New York Review of Books*, 21 September 2006, 53.

[108] United Nations General Assembly Resolution 3379, adopted 10 November 1975.

Palestine long-settled there in numbers vastly greater than the residual Jewish population before the organized migration of Jews to the area under the banner of Zionism beginning in the very late nineteenth century.[109]

But is exclusion and subordination on the basis of a form of communal identity other than race less objectionable in principle? Arguably yes, in that members of a community distinguished on merely religious or linguistic grounds, two of the most common forms of communal or "ethnic" identity, can in theory choose to exchange these legacy properties of their identity for those of the majority and thereby integrate into its privileged status. Pigmentation (and physiognomy where it too differs) are rather more difficult to alter. Thus subordination on the basis of race is seen to lie entirely outside the realm of individual choice.

That may partially explain the particular emphasis on racial discrimination in human rights discourse and its iterative indictment in UN Conventions and Declarations,[110] and the associated identification of *apartheid* as a grave international crime.[111] Of course it is also explicable in terms of the West's peculiarly abominable treatment and perception of "black" Africans.[112] But although religion, unlike race, is in theory a matter of choice, for people of faith it is woven so integrally into the core of their being that ripping it out and replacing it with another is an act of self-mutilation inconceivable for many and psychologically disabling for those who might feel compelled to do so by the extremity of their conditions. The importance of religion for many people's ability to construct a meaningful and coherent existence explains why religious freedom also has been singled out for special protection in human rights law.[113]

As I noted earlier, however, communal identity, whether or not religion is one of its properties in a given case, is itself strongly protected, most notably in the inclusion of ethnic cleansing among common enumerations of "Crimes Against Humanity."[114] And like race, that identity may not be alterable (we cannot very well change our ancestors); and like religion, even where it can be altered by a

---

[109] Benny Morris, *Righteous Victims* (1999), 17–20.

[110] See the documents produced at the World Conference Against Racism, Durban, South Africa, 2001, available at <http://www.unhchr.ch/html/racism>.

[111] Apartheid was officially criminalized by the General Assembly with the passage of the Resolution 3068 (1973), also known as International Convention on the Suppression and Punishment of the Crime of Apartheid. This concept was further elaborated upon with the 2002 passage of the Rome Statute, establishing the International Criminal Court. In the Statute, apartheid is given the weighted distinction on the specific list of crimes against humanity (Part 2, art 5).

[112] For a magisterial overview of European-organized slavery and of racism in European thought see David Brion Davis, *The Problem of Slavery in Western Culture* (Ithaca, NY: Cornell University Press, 1966) and Martin Bulmer and John Solomos (eds), *Racism* (Oxford, UK: Oxford University Press, 1999) respectively.

[113] Besides art 18 of Universal Declaration of Human Rights, the United Nations revisited this issue with the 1981 adoption of General Assembly Resolution 36/55, Declaration on the Elimination of all Forms of Intolerance and of Discrimination Based on Religion or Belief.

[114] Ethnic cleansing was defined as a crime against humanity in the foundational documents of the International Criminal Tribunal for the former Yugoslavia (1993) and the Rome Statute inaugurating the International Criminal Court (2002).

public act of choice, its coerced abandonment can be psychologically crippling. The long and the short of it, then, is that there is no important moral difference between a system of *apartheid* based on race and one based on religion or an historical communal identity.

But, one might plausibly object, this is not the Israeli case, since those members of the Palestinian ethnic group living in Israel have been granted formal legal equality as citizens of the Israeli state, while in the South African case, all blacks were denied citizenship and arbitrarily expatriated to the shrunken and impoverished bit of territory set aside for people with their respective tribal origins. The case would be analogous, the argument goes, only if Palestinians who remained in Israel after the War of Independence were driven from their homes thereafter and concentrated in swollen refugee camps on the Occupied Territories. This argument is not entirely without force (although, as Benny Morris and other Israeli historians have now demonstrated, a part of the pre-Independence Arab population of Israel was driven out in 1948[115]), but is it ultimately persuasive in its attempt to draw a crucial moral difference insofar as the population of the Occupied Territories rather than the totality of Palestinians are concerned?

Suppose the *Afrikaaner*-dominated government of South Africa had calculated that it would be useful to allow a modest number of blacks to live in white areas and be granted citizenship. In doing so, the government might have concluded, it could demonstrate to the world that its *apartheid* policy rested on security not racial grounds. Assume further that the number chosen was about 18 per cent of the white population. At that percentage, there was no danger in the foreseeable future of a black majority in the electorate. And to avoid any danger of the minority seriously influencing public policy, the South African political parties in my hypothetical case agreed informally that none would form a government dependent on parties or politicians representing the black community. Moreover, government leaders agreed among themselves that if demographics ever threatened to make that minority into a formidable force, the government could periodically scrape off a part of the minority population and send it to the Bantustans perhaps through a notional exchange of territory which would be facilitated by informally fostering residential segregation. Meanwhile the Bantustans would hold in close and miserable confinement—albeit under the immediate authority of fellow blacks allowed by the South African Government to govern each Bantustan so long as they maintained order—the 40 million or so blacks seen to constitute an existential threat to white South Africans. In this way, political leaders declared, we can avoid pariah status while assuring that South Africa remains both democratic and Afrikaaner.

If the South African Government had pursued that strategy, would it have avoided the moral obloquy and isolation that haunted it? I think not. For at the end of the day there would have remained the objective reality of two societies,

---

[115] See Morris (1999), 253 and Avi Shlaim, *The Iron Wall* (2001), 31.

one dominant and one subordinate, one with a plumply comfortable citizenry enjoying the liberties of a Western democracy, the other (cheek-by-jowl) filled with impoverished people subject to detention, torture, and assassination if suspected of conspiring against either their local Quisling governments or the government of South Africa.

To avoid pariah status, the South African Government would have had either to hive off a very considerable part of its territory and there allowed non-whites to establish a truly independent state, a state enjoying the prerogatives and the dignity of genuine sovereignty, or to take the course which it ultimately took, which was to concede full citizenship to all of the indigenous peoples living in the all of the territory it controlled directly or by proxy. Perhaps a third possibility, a blend of the two, would have been confederation of the two territories, along the lines of the European Union, with the aim, as it has been in the European Union, to accelerate the economic development of the poorer territory through economic assistance and the largely unimpeded flow of goods and services and capital; but in this hypothetical case, unlike the European Union, the movement of people would be restrained.[116]

All of these options involved risks, as does any effort to resolve a bitter, long-running communal conflict. Ironically, it is the community with the greater existential risk that chose to end the conflict by jettisoning its *apartheid*. Why that choice? I know of no grounds for believing that its leaders were inspired by a more elevated conception of human rights. The far more plausible hypothesis is that they weighed the costs and benefits of unending conflict and found more potential cost than benefit. Intensifying international sanctions, isolation, and moral revulsion against them in the very Western countries with which they identified probably influenced that calculation.[117] So did the difficulty of maintaining a high standard of living without allowing a large number of black African workers to live in close proximity and to work within the large areas set aside for white occupation. And over time, the long borders and hostile neighbors whom they could batter but not wholly control might have made it increasingly difficult to prevent guerrilla infiltration, although up to the moment *Afrikaans* leaders opted for comprehensive democracy and thus minority status, they were little troubled by insurgency.

Ah, one could say, the difference is they had Nelson Mandela, perhaps the most morally enlightened and far-sighted leader of the twentieth century with whom to negotiate, while the Palestinians had only Yasser Arafat. True, but Mandela was far from a young man. And the South African state had stolen from him much of his adult life. Who could be sure that he did not nurse a terrible sense of grievance or that he could control his liberation movement once it achieved political power

---

[116] See F Stephen Larrabee, "Danger and Opportunity in Eastern Europe," *Foreign Affairs*, 85(6) (Nov/Dec 2006).

[117] For a definitive account of the various causes of the end of apartheid see Adrian Guelke, *Rethinking the Rise and Fall of Apartheid* (New York: Palgrave Macmillan, 2005).

or that the elite of the African National Congress, however sophisticated and wise and ready to cooperate in running a multi-ethnic state, would not lose place quickly to a new generation of leaders quite prepared to play the racial card on behalf of the tens of millions of black South Africans who, for decades after the political transition, would remain miserably poor in the midst of great wealth.[118]

Israel's security problems seem tame by comparison. At the time of the abandonment of *apartheid* in South Africa, the demographic lineup was roughly 4 million whites and more than 35 million persons classified as black. By contrast, the population of Gaza and the West Bank combined is about 3.5 million.[119] An additional 1.4 million Arabs live in Israel as citizens (who may or may not in the end prefer identifying with the wealthy, stable and democratic state of Israel than with a sovereign Palestinian entity).[120] The Palestinian refugee population in surrounding Arab states numbers around 4.4 million according to credible sources.[121] The Jewish population of Israel today is approximately 5.4 million.[122] One key element of any sustainable peace would be generous compensation for all refugee families and opportunities for some to achieve citizenship in countries where they now reside or elsewhere. The compensation payments would make them far more attractive as potential citizens. But even assuming that all preferred moving to a Palestinian state established beyond the pre-1967 borders of Israel, the population disparity between Jews and Arabs in the two states combined would be well short of 2 to 1. In the South African case it was more like 7 to 1. Israel is not dependent any more on the Palestinians for cheap labor. It can therefore opt for physical separation, except in Jerusalem. Moreover, given the resources of Western countries hungry for peace in the area, not to mention the wealth of Israel itself, the standard of living for Palestinians in the Occupied Territories or who moved there from the external refugee camps could be raised quickly and dramatically, as soon as orderly and reasonably efficient government was in place, a condition that has proven impossible to achieve without the removal of the illegal and hated settlements and the establishment of a Palestinian capital in Jerusalem and generous recognition of the rights of refugees to compensation for the loss of their land and property and

---

[118] The story of Nelson Mandela's life, imprisonment and involvement in the struggle against apartheid is told beautifully in his autobiography, Nelson Mandela, *Long Walk to Freedom* (Boston, MA: Back Bay Books, 1995).

[119] Palestinian Central Bureau of Statistics, Palestinian National Authority, available at <http://www.pcbs.gov.ps>.

[120] Central Bureau of Statistics, State of Israel, "Statistical Abstract of Israel 2006," available at <http://www1.cbs.gov.il/reader/shnatonenew_site.htm>.

[121] United Nations Relief and Works Agency for Palestine Refugees in the Near East, "Who is a Palestinian Refugee?" available at <http://www.un.org/unrwa/refugees/whois.html>.

[122] Central Bureau of Statistics, State of Israel, "Statistical Abstract of Israel 2006," available at <http://www1.cbs.gov.il/reader/shnatonenew_site.htm>.

a general amnesty for Palestinians in Israeli prisons[123] and a UN-authorized force able through its presence to protect the Palestinians from Israeli missiles and bombs and to protect their air space and territorial sea and assure their free movement throughout the territories and the freedom to leave and enter their country. Only then could there emerge Palestinian leaders willing and equipped to marshal the popular support needed to build a stable and prosperous state, a state able, at least when supported by the UN-authorized forces who could flood the small area we are discussing, to meet its responsibility to prevent its territory from being a haven for transnational terrorists.

Israel, moreover, has a security trump the *Afrikaaner* elite did not, namely an implicit guarantee from the United States which, under the conditions I hypothesize, would doubtless be formalized if Israel made it a condition of peace. Indeed were it to exhibit generosity in concessions to the Palestinians, it could probably secure from the United States and the Europeans an invitation to join NATO. In addition, certainly if it accepted international forces on both sides of its border with Lebanon, it could shift to them the principal front-line responsibility to guarantee protection on that front. That might, however, be unnecessary, if a Palestinian settlement were part of a larger Middle Eastern one.

During the summer of 2006 when Israeli planes were reducing Lebanon's infrastructure and Shia urban neighborhoods to rubble while the United States delayed calls for a cease-fire, US Secretary of State Condoleezza Rice looked cheerily beyond the bouncing rubble to see the birth of a new Middle East.[124] As far as one could tell, it was the same new Middle East heralded by the Administration as it hurled itself into Iraq, one in which the United States could at little cost arbitrate the destiny of the region's peoples while Israel decided unilaterally on what fragments of Mandate Palestine it would allow the intentionally cowed[125] and exhausted residue of Palestinians to endure under such form of self-rule as it deemed consistent with its national interests. In September 2007, the one thing that now appears exhausted is that vision. The framework of a more stable

---

[123] The amnesty, a frequent feature of the end games for internal conflicts, could be extended as well to Israelis who have conducted brutal interrogations (see footnote 103 of ch 3 above) and, more generally, persons at high and low levels of officialdom who have committed or colluded in violations of the Geneva Conventions and other international criminal law norms.

[124] See "Friends See Things Differently," *The Economist*, 7 October 2006.

[125] The distinguished director of Middle East Programs at the Council on Foreign Relations, Henry Siegman, writes: [The Sharon Government (this was in 2003)] maintain[s] that its only option is to wage an unrelenting war against the Palestinians that, in the words of the Israeli Defense Force's chief of staff, Lieutenant General Moshe Ya'alon, will 'sear deep into the consciousness of Palestinians that they are a defeated people' before any peace process can begin." "Sharon's Phony War," *New York Review of Books*, 18 December 2003, 16. Subsequently, however, the same General Ya'alon took a very different view of the matter. Sharon's policies, he declared far from defeating terror, "'increase hatred for Israel and strengthen the terrorist organizations,'" Siegman, ibid. "General Ya'alon's sudden conversion was followed by an even more extraordinary event. On November 14 [2003], former heads of the Shin Bet [the Israeli secret intelligence organization] joined in a dramatic warning to the Israeli public that their government's policies are leading the country to a 'catastrophe,'" ibid.

order apparently will require negotiation. It cannot be imposed. And all players, including the Iranians and the Syrians, the religious and the secular, will need to be at the negotiating table(s) and will need to be shown positive benefits, not simply mailed fists.

It is hard to see how either the larger negotiation over the broad frame of Middle Eastern security or the smaller but integrally related one over the rights of the Palestinians to a dignified existence can be convened much less exit in durable arrangements without some preliminary recasting of the narratives that psychologically fix the actors in their present positions. Just as narratives evolve dialectically from the conflict of peoples,[126] they can be unwound dialectically. Adjusting the narratives requires confession and rhetorical acts of contrition. Confession does not enlighten the victims; they, after all, know what has been done to them. Rather it enlightens the people in whose name those sins were committed and third parties who, although not engaged in the past, can now contribute to a more benign future.

Take the US–Iranian relationship, for instance. The Bush Administration's contribution to its bitterness was to label the country a part of the "Axis of Evil," while President Amadinejhad's corresponding contribution has been to doubt the Holocaust and anticipate with apparent pleasure the incineration of Israel.[127] Suppose the United States, as the many-times stronger partner to this envenomed dialectic, were to propose a new narrative structure, one with some potential for convergence. It would have to start at the confessional. President Bush could use his bully pulpit to recall with regret the successful 1953 putsch organized by our Central Intelligence Agency to overthrow the elected government of Mohamed Mossadegh and thus abort the momentum toward that consolidated democratic regime which the President has said is his goal for every Middle Eastern country.[128] And he could additionally regret the support the United States gave to Saddam Hussein's aggression against Iran in 1980 which included use of poison gas against the decimated youth of Iran. The President of Iran is one of those young men who survived and whose world view must have been inflamed in the charnel house of that awful conflict. In these actions, we violated our national ideals, President Bush could justly say, adding that the occupation of the American Embassy in 1979 and the cruel treatment of its inhabitants may well have been triggered by the fear of militant young Iranians that the Embassy which had engineered the restoration of autocracy in 1953 might be conspiring to restore the Shah (or some member of his family) again.

---

[126] I noted earlier how the Palestinians sense of themselves as a "people" with rights of national self-determination developed dialectically out of their confrontation with a Jewish nationalism, Zionism, that transcended the many cultural and historical and religious differences among Diaspora Jews.

[127] See "A Government that Thrives on Defiance," *The Economist*, 6 May 2006.

[128] See Stephen Kinzer, *Overthrow* (New York: Henry Holt, 2006), 117–28.

It is not inevitable, but certainly it is plausible that such an honest revision of the American narrative declared to be a first step toward mutual understanding and reconciliation would induce a reciprocal softening of rhetoric on the Iranian side. The two national narratives would begin to shift from their established orbits even if President Ahmedinejad remained obdurate. For narratives are the stuff of popular thought, of a people's view of the world. Popular world views translate into political frames constraining the discretion of leaders.

The need for a narrative that corresponds more closely to historical truth is nowhere more apparent than in the relationship of the United States to the conflict between Israelis and Palestinians. I noted earlier that because of the vast inequality of power between the principals, no sustainable settlement is possible without the effort of third parties, primarily the United States in part because of Europe's default, to balance the scales, which in the nature of things means pressing Israel to make territorial concessions successive governments have striven to avoid. Among the central elements in the American narrative that grossly distort history, distortions exposed by *Israeli* historians of varying political allegiances, are the following.

First, from the inception of the Zionist movement, its leaders held out the hand of friendship to the Arab inhabitants of Palestine only to have it repeatedly bitten. Well, not exactly. Some were initially surprised at the extent of Arab settlement.[129] Despite popular poetic fantasies, Palestine was not "a land without a people for a people without a land" and this was perfectly apparent to most of the movement's luminaries.[130] They sought not a sanctuary, but a state in which they were dominant. And that meant, they recognized, political subordination of the indigenous Arab inhabitants.[131]

What most distinguished the so-called "Revisionist" Zionists, led by Vladimir (Ze'ev) Jabotinsky, from the main stream led in the pre-state years by Ben-Gurion was the former's candor on this point. As a hawkish but fastidious Israeli historian has written,

… Jabotinsky had no problem in recognizing that Zionism had a legitimate rival in the Palestinian-Arab nationalist movement. Hence the Jews would have to settle and spread throughout Palestine, and eventually dominate the country, by force. A collision was inevitable.[132]

---

[129] Morris (1999), 61.
[130] Ian Lustick, *Arabs in the Jewish State* (Austin, TX: University of Texas Press, 1980), 36.
[131] Morris (1999), 91.
[132] Ibid, 108; In his own words, Jabotinsky is quite revealing on this point: "Zionist colonisation must either stop, or else proceed regardless of the native population. Which means that it can proceed and develop only under the protection of a power that is independent of the native population—behind an iron wall, which the native population cannot breach. That is our Arab policy; not what it should be, but what it actually is, whether we admit it or not" Vladimir (Ze'ev) Jabotinsky, "The Iron Wall," *Jewish Herald (South Africa)* 26 November 1937; also available at <http://www.mideastweb.org/ironwall.htm> (accessed 11 November 2006).

Consistent with this goal, as the years of the Palestinian Mandate were drawing to a close, Jewish leaders opposed Mandate-wide elections until, as they optimistically saw it, continuing Jewish migration would give them a majority.[133] Moreover, to assure that the homeland would be a Jewish-dominated state, as early as the beginning of the twentieth century, Zionist leaders contemplated the necessity of large-scale transfer of the Arab population from Palestine into neighboring countries and consciously avoided public statements of that purpose for fear it would harden Arab resistance to the growing Zionist presence in Palestine and also provoke European and American antagonism to the Zionist project.[134]

A second critical falsehood in the popular narrative is that the Palestinian refugee problem arose in 1948 because Palestinians were instructed by their leaders to move out of the way of the invading Arab armies of Syria, Egypt, and Jordan which were expected to throw the Jews into the sea after which the Palestinians would return to a Jew-free land. The leading Israeli historian of the period, Benny Morris, has demonstrated that this is nothing more than a tissue of lies. To begin with, there was no well-developed Palestinian leadership. On the contrary, partially because of the parochial and fragmented character of Palestinian society, including deep fissures between a wealthy land-owning and urban elite and a great mass of villagers and urban poor, and partially because of the British decimation of Palestinian leaders during the Arab revolt of 1936–39, and partially because of splits between leading Palestinian families, a national leadership able to organize and direct the Palestinian people was precisely what they lacked.[135] Moreover, even if there had been a Palestinian leadership, unless its members were very badly informed, they had no grounds for optimism about the success of the Arab armies or even about their goals. For in fact those armies were small (before the end of 1948, Jewish forces outnumbered them), poorly equipped, ill-trained and untested. Nor were their prospects for improving their armaments favorable, since the UN arms embargo declared after fighting broke out proved effective in blocking shipments of arms to the Arab states (at that point the Soviet Union as well as the United States supported Israel), but was easily eluded by the nascent Israeli authority.[136]

Palestinians fled in part for the same reason that people flee zones of conflict in most wars: fear. Even if troops of both sides are well disciplined, under effective command, and not inclined to target the civilian population, to be at the scene of armed conflict is to court death. But that was not the only source of their fear. Rather, Morris demonstrates that both the military arm of the Zionist

[133] Morris (1999), 81.
[134] Ibid, 254.
[135] "The structural weaknesses that characterized Palestinian society on the eve of the war make it especially susceptible to collapse and flight. It was poorly organized, with little social or political cohesion. There were deep divisions between rural and urban populations, between Muslims and Christians, and between various elite clans, and there was a complete absence of representative leaders and effective national institutions" ibid, 253.
[136] Benny Morris, *Righteous Victims* (New York: Knopf, 1999), 171, 184.

Revisionists, the followers of Jabotinsky led by Menachem Begin, a future Prime Minister, and the Israeli Defense Forces committed a number of atrocities, the most infamous being the massacre of civilians, including women and children at the village of Deir Yassin.

Deir Yassin is remembered not as a military occupation, but rather for the atrocities committed by the IZL and LHI troops during and immediately after the drawn-out battle: Whole families were riddled with bullets and grenade fragments and buried when houses were blown up on top of them; men, women, and children were mowed down as they emerged from their houses; individuals were taken aside and shot. At the end of the battle, groups of old men, women, and children were trucked through West Jerusalem's streets in a kind of a "victory parade" and then dumped in (Arab) East Jerusalem.[137]

In addition, after May of 1948, in the face of the penetration of Arab armies into Palestine, the Israeli Prime Minister, David Ben Gurion, authorized the Israeli Defense Forces to expel the Arab inhabitants of certain parts of Palestine under their control. As Morris notes, although ethnic cleansing was not part of Israel military planning at the beginning of the conflict, the move to forceful transfer was made against the backdrop of a long-standing sentiment in favor of mass transfer of Arabs out of Palestine, a sentiment dating back to the very early days of the Zionist movement.[138]

A third deviation of the narrative from the facts concerns the use of terrorist methods. In the narrative, the Jewish population and the Israeli state have always fought with honor, according to the norms of civilized people, while the Arabs are brutal, callous, indifferent to the suffering of others, even of their own. Typical of this narrative strand is the claim, made among others by former Prime Minister Benjamin Netanyahu, that suicide bombers are brainwashed by Mullahs or bred by their morally crazed parents to kill Jews,[139] rather than being young people brutalized by the humiliations and hopelessness and quotidian pain stemming from a four-decade occupation and from the experience of friends, parents, and brothers having previously been killed, grievously wounded or detained and tortured by occupation forces. What Morris depicts in telling detail is a dialectic of terrorism between Israelis and Arabs:

Until mid-1937 the Jews had almost completely adhered to the policy of restraint. But the upsurge of Arab terrorism in October 1937 triggered a wave of Irgun bombings against Arab crowds and buses.... Now for the first time, massive bombs were placed in crowded Arab centers, and dozens of people were indiscriminately murdered and maimed—for the first time more or less matching the numbers of Jews murdered in the Arab pogroms

[137] Morris (1999), 208.
[138] As quoted in Morris (1999), 21, Theodore Herzl wrote in 1895, "We must expropriate gently...We shall try to spirit the penniless population across the border by procuring employment for it in the transit countries, while denying it any employment in our own country...Both the process of expropriation and the removal of the poor must be carried out discreetly and circumspectly."
[139] See, eg, Efraim Karsh, "Arafat Lives," *Commentary*, 119(1) (January 2005).

and rioting of 1929 and 1936. This "innovation" soon found Arab imitators and became something of a "tradition"; during the coming decades Palestine's (and, later, Israel's) marketplaces, bus stations, movie theatres, and other public buildings became routine targets, lending a particular brutal flavor to the conflict.[140]

He goes on to give examples. Among them: "On July 6, 1938, an Irgun operative dressed as an Arab placed two large milk cans filled with TNT and shrapnel in the Arab market in downtown Haifa. The subsequent explosion killed twenty-one and wounded fifty-two."[141]

Terrorist tit-for-tat has continued the length of the conflict. During the first Arab-Israeli War, Morris writes, In

Tel Aviv, Jaffa, Haifa and Jerusalem, in December and early January 1948, hundreds of Arab civilians [were] killed or wounded by IZL [Irgun] terrorism.... Another such operation set in motion one of the bloodiest, most vicious cycles of terror and retaliation of the period: On December 30, an IZL squad threw a number of bombs into a crowd at a bus stop outside the Haifa oil refinery, killing six people and wounding dozens more. In a spontaneous response, the Arab workers in the refinery turned on their Jewish coworkers with hammers, chisels, stones, and clubs, massacring 39 of them and wounding another fifty ... [In Retaliation, the Israeli Defense forces ordered a raid on a cluster of villages around Haifa where many refinery workers lived. Their] order was to "kill a maximal number of adult males, destroy furniture, etc." but to avoid killing women and children. The raiders moved from house to house, pulling men out and executing them. Sometimes they simply threw grenades into houses and sprayed them with automatic fire. The villagers suffered more than 60 dead, some of them women and children.[142]

This cycle of awful, transgressive brutality has continued through all the years of the conflict. Yet because of the power of the narrative, when Israeli forces strike, often from the air, and hit targets resulting in terrible civilian casualties, the inevitable claim that it was an unfortunate but reasonable error seems reflexively assumed to be true, as if it were outrageous to imagine that the Israeli Defense Force might target civilians in order to terrorize them into non-cooperation with militant movements whether it be Fatah, Hamas, or Hezbollah or might simply be recklessly indifferent to the impact of its operations on civilian lives.[143]

---

[140] Morris (1999), 147. Hannah Arendt had this to say about Jewish terrorism: "They think it is all right to murder anyone who can be murdered—an innocent English Tommy or a harmless Arab in the market of Haifa." In Jeremy Waldron, "What Would Hannah Say," *New York Review of Books*, 15 March 2007, 8 at 8 and 10.

[141] Ibid.

[142] Ibid, 198.

[143] In putting down the first *intifada*, the evidence supports the conclusion that, unlike South Korean and Japanese police suppressing violent demonstrations, the Israelis acted with reckless disregard for human life, as I discussed previously in "Israel's Unlawful Occupation," *Foreign Policy* (Spring 1991), 44. For further details as to the extent of the violence see, "Israel-Occupied West Bank and Gaza Strip" in *Human Rights Watch World Report 1993*, <http://www.hrw.org/reports/1993/WR93> (accessed 7 November 2006).

And yet, preferring like any other government to present an amiable face to the world, the Government of Israel or senior civilian or military officials thereof have been known to lie about violations of the Laws of War and the norms of humanity. Morris illuminates two particularly repulsive cases. One was the infamous massacre carried out in 1982 in the Palestinian refugee camps of Sabra and Shatilla in Beirut by Christian militia permitted to enter the camp by General Ariel Sharon whose troops ringed the area.[144] Testifying after the slaughter, Prime Minister-to-be Sharon declared that he had no idea that the militia would slaughter the inhabitants. Morris demonstrates that this had to be a lie. To be sure, Sharon was later found by an Israeli investigating commission to deserve the brunt of the "main blame."[145] But he was never prosecuted and went on to become Israel's Prime Minister.

Morris also recalls the retaliatory mission in 1953 launched against the village of Qibya on the frontier with Jordan. An Israeli Defense Force Unit, also in this case commanded by Sharon, with orders to undertake "destruction and maximum killing," moved methodically through the village, firing blindly through windows and doorways and blowing up houses.[146] The dead were put at 60.[147] In the face of foreign outrage and Washington's suspension of economic assistance, Prime Minister Ben Gurion "went on the air with a wholly fictitious account of what had happened," claiming that the killing had been carried out by Israeli settlers on the frontier outraged by attacks on them.[148] " 'The Government of Israel rejects with all vigor the absurd and fantastic allegation that 600 men of the IDF took part in the action.... We have carried out a searching investigation and it is clear beyond doubt that not a single army unit was absent from its base on the night of the attack on Qibya.' "[149]

A final strand in the narrative is that Israel has relentlessly sought peace snatching at every opportunity but only in the cases of Jordan and Egypt finding, belatedly, takers for its offers and being rewarded for its generosity in the case of Egypt, generosity in returning the Sinai, with coldness and distance rather than the promised reconciliation. Both Morris and Avi Shlaim have demolished that claim in general and in detail. They have shown, for instance, that in the immediate aftermath of the first Arab-Israeli War, King Abdullah of Jordan was eager to conclude a peace agreement, but felt he could not do so unless Israel would allow a substantial return of refugees and yield some of the territory it had taken beyond that allocated by the United Nations.[150] Israel's refusal may

[144] Morris (1999), 543–6.
[145] Ibid, 548.
[146] Ibid, 278.
[147] Ibid.
[148] Ibid, 279.
[149] Ibid. With respect to Israeli raids on Arab settlements in the 1950s, Hannah Arendt wrote: "The shortest statement to be made would be: Thou shalt not kill, not even Arab women and children." Quoted by Jeremy Waldron, see footnote 140 above.
[150] See Shlaim, *The Iron Wall* (2001), 64.

have made good strategic sense and was consistent with Ben Gurion's aspiration to incorporate all of Palestine ultimately into the Jewish State. But it can hardly be said that Abdullah's proposition was not made in good faith and was not reasonable from the Arab perspective or even from the perspective of the United Nations members who had voted to divide Palestine.

The coldness of the peace with Egypt was foreshadowed by the refusal of Prime Minister Begin to consider any change in the status of the Palestinians in the Occupied Territories. While in the end Egyptian President Sadat seemed disinterested in their fate, his acting Foreign Minister Boutros Boutros Ghali pressed Begin on this point repeatedly but unsuccessfully.[151] Boutros Ghali seemed to foresee that true reconciliation with the Arab world required reconciliation with the Palestinians.

An important sub-set of the narrative is that after the 1967 war, Israel offered land for peace and met a wall of resistance. The narrative does not stop to note that the land offered was to Jordan and Egypt, not to the Palestinians whom at that point and for a long time thereafter Israel did not acknowledge as a "People." Nor does the narrative call attention to the fact that the offer never included East Jerusalem or the West Bank in its entirety. Settlement activity began immediately after the war.

As for the most recent period in the conflict, the Israeli government dismissed out of hand consideration of a minutely detailed draft for a final settlement negotiated by teams of Israelis and Palestinians meeting in Switzerland and led, respectively, by the Israeli political leader Yossi Beilin and his prominent Palestinian counterpart Sari Nusseibeh, an agreement that would have left in Israeli hands the largest settlement blocs which are adjacent to Jerusalem.[152] In a similar vein the government dismissed as not worthy of discussion a Saudi Arabian proposal for a comprehensive Middle East peace settlement if Israeli would withdraw to the 1967 boundaries which, I repeat, would leave the Palestinians with a state constituting about 22 per cent of the territory of Mandate Palestine as it was in 1948.[153]

Early in his abortive term as President of Harvard University, Lawrence Summers condemned as "anti-Semitic in their effect, if not their intent" actions and statements that unfairly "single out Israel."[154] Among the acts he deemed to fall in that general category was a petition he had rejected calling for disinvestment by Harvard from companies doing certain kinds of business with Israel. The last disinvestment campaign of this kind had been directed against

[151] See ibid, 48 and Amos Elon, "At Pharoah's Court," *New York Review of Books*, 44(11) (26 June 1997).

[152] To view the text of the Geneva Accord, visit: <http://www.mideastweb.org/geneva1.htm>.

[153] "What is in the Saudi Peace Initiative?" Available online at: <http://news.bbc.co.uk/1/hi/world/middle_east/1844214.stm> (accessed 12 March 2007).

[154] David H Gellis, "Summers Says Anti-Semitism Lurks Locally," *The Harvard Crimson Online Edition*, 19 September 2002 (accessed 6 November 2006).

South Africa. I believe that what I have written satisfies the test, a test I find perfectly reasonable, of not "unfairly" singling out Israel. But in light of the rabid ferocity displayed by numbers of otherwise thoughtful and reasonable people to critical writing about Israeli policy, even when accompanied by criticism of the Palestinians and/or Arab government policy,[155] I fear that I too will be indicted for being, in Professor Summer's words "anti-Semitic in effect if not in intent," even though, like Summers (in his words), "I am Jewish, identified but hardly devout."[156] I expect that critics will take particular exception to my comparison of Israel in the Occupied Territories with South Africa, a comparison, I tried to demonstrate, that I am hardly the first to notice.[157] They may, among other things, seize upon my reference to a confederation of Israel with a Palestinian state as a veiled endorsement of the bi-national state solution proposed from time to time over the years, perhaps most prominently in recent years by Tony Judt.[158] Believing that the settlement movement and its supporters within Israel's 1967 borders have achieved a veto status in Israeli politics, thus burying any prospect of a credible two-state solution, he concluded that, although the idea of a bi-national state "is an unpromising mix of realism and utopia,... the alternatives are far, far worse."[159] For his pains, he was accused among other things of advocating "genocidal liberalism,"[160] of "pandering to genocide,"[161] and of being "party to preparations for a final solution."[162] The ever-thoughtful Alan Dershowitz merely drew an analogy between Judt and Hitler's "one-state solution for all of Europe."[163]

Unlike Judt, whose scholarly work taken as a whole seems to me as fine an example of contemporary Enlightenment erudition and moral illumination as one can find, I think that the two-state solution is still conceivable or is, at least, more likely to be implemented than the bi-national one. Moreover, my hope is that in the event of a sustainable settlement of the conflict (which means one satisfying the conditions I listed earlier),[164] what Amos Elon has accurately described as the "crass discrimination against Israeli Arabs by means of punitive

[155] See, eg, the examples enumerated in Aryeh Neier's article, cited at footnote 4 above.

[156] See footnote 147 above.

[157] I could also have cited, among others, Tony Judt, "Israel: An Alternative," *New York Review of Books*, 23 October 2003: "Palestinian Arabs, corralled into shrinking Bantustans, subsist on EU handouts," and Amos Elon, "An Alternative Future: An Exchange," *New York Review of Books*, 4 December 2003: "The tragedy is that neither Sharon nor Arafat is likely to emulate the statesmanship of de Klerk and Mandela" (accessed both 6 November 2006). See also Jimmy Carter, *Palestine Peace Not Apartheid* (New York: Simon & Schuster, 2006).

[158] See, eg, Tony Judt, "A State Out of its Time," *The Weekend Australian*, 6 December 2003.

[159] Tony Judt, "Israel: An Alternative," *New York Review of Books*, 23 October 2003.

[160] David Frum, "David Frum's Diary," *National Review Online*, 14 October 2003, <http://frum.nationalreview.com> (accessed 6 November 2006).

[161] Andrea Levin, "Tony Judt's Pandering to Genocide," *Jerusalem Post*, 27 October 2003.

[162] Ibid.

[163] Alan M Dershowitz, "Rules of Engagement: a PR primer; the Consensus Cases," *Jerusalem Post*, 5 December 2003.

[164] See text at 37–38 above.

legislation as well as judicial, budgetary, and administrative measures"[165] will gradually diminish.

What distinguishes a confederation from a federation, of course, is the sovereignty of its parts, hence the right of each unit to arrange and rearrange its domestic affairs and foreign policies in all ways consistent with its obligations under international law, to provide for its security, and to enjoy the indisputable right to political independence and territorial integrity. What characterizes a confederation is an unusual abundance of commercial and social links and of institutionalized cooperation between its units, together with a formal commitment to consultation on all matters of common interest. But because they are sovereign, the two units can thin or thicken the ties they initially accept if one or the other fails to satisfy the commitments each made when entering the confederation. And when push comes to shove, either can end the formal relationship by an act of will, even if, in doing so, it violates the treaty by means of which the confederation was established.

Perhaps the most important aspect of the confederation is symbolic. It is the formalized recognition of an unavoidable interdependence. Still, it also has important material consequences. For it establishes the channels as well as the legal commitment to consult and cooperate and thereby enhances the opportunities for the two parties to maximize the benefits of an unavoidable interdependence while working to minimize its burdens. Confederation implies quiet, unpublicized, quotidian conversations among officials at various levels of authority and with operational responsibilities as various as law enforcement, public health, and environmental protection.

Still it is the symbolism that seems to me paramount. Any settlement will need to be pressed onto the parties or appear to be so pressed, so that they can justify their concessions to their constituents. And it will need to be collectively recognized and guaranteed by leading Islamic states, by the United States and Europe, and, ideally, by all consequential states, in part through the medium of a Security Council Resolution under Chapter Seven. I believe that no form of guarantee would be stronger than the incorporation of the two states into NATO and/or into a special relationship with the EU[166] which provides them with most of the benefits of formal membership. Being able to incorporate them as a single

---

[165] Amos Elon, "An Alternative Future: An Exchange," *New York Review of Books*, 4 December 2003. For details on the treatment of Arabs in Israel, see among other works Sabri Jiryis, *The Arabs in Israel*, translated from the Arabic by Inea Bushnaq (New York: Monthly Review Press, 1976), Ian Lustick, *Arabs in the Jewish State* (1980), and David Kretzmer, *The Legal Status of the Arabs in Israel* (Boulder: Westview 1990), esp. 49–134.

[166] Which, of course, Israel now possesses on its own. For a discussion of this relationship see Roberto Aliboni, "The Geopolitical Implications of the European Neighborhood Policy," *European Foreign Affairs Review*, 10(1) (Spring 2005), in which Albioni states: "For, although it is true that in principle the Arab countries and Israel will have the same status and opportunities within the ENP [European Neighborhood Policy], there can be no doubt that while Arab countries are not ready to grasp ENP opportunities, Israel is...Thus it will single out the EU-Israel relationship in Arab eyes and consolidate in their minds a negative geopolitical vision in which Israel is confirmed

entity, albeit one composed by two sovereign states, underscores the end of the epoch of brutal conflict and expresses a determination of the immediate parties and the guarantors to foster amity and joint development of the human and material resources of Israel and Palestine and to reduce as quickly as possible the significance of the border between them so that at some point the descendant of a Jewish family that was forced out of Hebron many decades ago can buy a home there and the descendants of a Palestinian family that had to flee Jaffa can buy a condominium on that crowded shore overlooking the Mediterranean Sea.

To be sure, from the standpoint of the present moment, such happy visions are nothing short of hallucinatory. And they will remain so, I am proposing, until the Israeli and American publics, recognize in their very guts that Israel in the Occupied Territories is where South Africa was before the epiphany of its elite, above all of its remarkable President, FW de Klerk, who invited Nelson Mandela, in the late years of his almost ruined life, out of his Robbins Island dungeon. The iconic status granted to Ariel Sharon, enabler (arguably the orchestrator) of the butchery of Sabra and Shatilla and Quibya, just as he was completing a wall and road system and expanding the settlements that would complete the Bantustanization of Gaza and the West Bank,[167] testifies to the ferocity with which otherwise moderate, morally lucid people evade the South African analogy.

This is perfectly understandable on at least six grounds. One is the memory of the Holocaust and of the moral failure of Western countries to facilitate the flight of Jews from Europe when there still was time and to declare publicly at the first news of the slaughter of Jews that at the end of the War, everyone who colluded in that slaughter would be hunted down, tried, and hung, a declaration which by 1943, that is the time an eventual Allied victory appeared certain, might have slowed the engine of destruction. At an unspeakable price, Jews accumulated an extraordinary quantity of IOUs in the moral bank of the peoples of the West. Secondly, and partially related to the first point, since the end of the Second World War, every medium of cultural production in the United States has elaborated a Manichean narrative of the creation and defense of the Israeli state in which a Zionism virtuous beyond human capability wrestles with a villainous Arab world. A third, in turn related to the second but with an independent root, is the resonance the Jewish return to Zion and Israel's conflicts with the Arab world has for a strong body of Protestant thought in the United States (Armageddon, the Second Coming, and so on).

---

as an intruding appendix of the Western world and Arab-European and Arab-Western relations are inherently governed by a fault-line."

[167] Three years ago, the former deputy mayor of Jerusalem, Meron Benvenisti, wrote that the Sharon plan "to disengage from Gaza and build a security wall along—and beyond—the eastern frontier of the West Bank was tantamount to making Israel 'a binational state based on apartheid.' It meant, he said, 'the imprisonment of some 3 million Palestinians in bantustans.'" See Joseph Lelyveld, "Jimmy Carter and Apartheid," *New York Review of Books*, 29 March 2007.

The fourth, an enduring psychological legacy, is the history of Israel's Cold War cooperation with the United States juxtaposed against the security ties for part of that era between Israel's chief antagonists at the time, Syria and Egypt, and the Soviet Union. The fifth is the ready access of Western journalists to the Israeli heartland where, in the setting of a prosperous developed state and with flawless English, brilliantly articulate spokespersons for the government assure them that every building destroyed in Arab territory was either the haven of terrorists or an incidental and terribly unfortunate casualty of a carefully focused military operation. Foreign journalists can arrive quickly at the scene of an attack on Israeli civilians in Jerusalem, or Tel Aviv, or Haifa, and record the carnage and the grief of people who look exactly like people one could see in the streets of any Western city. Naturally both journalists and their readers and viewers experience a profound sense of identity with the bereaved and the larger society, even more so after 9/11. Conversely, media access to the Occupied Territories is substantially regulated by the Israeli authorities. The media often arrives late even at scenes of terrible carnage and will miss the merely diurnal killing and maiming of a person here and there by Israeli troops or, in some cases, by settlers. And its representatives come nowhere near the inside of Israeli interrogation centers. Unlike Abu Ghraib, there are no photos illuminating those dark spaces where systematic torture and cruel and inhuman treatment have long been practiced with impunity.[168] And in the Occupied Territories there is no host of skillfully trained explainers or bi-lingual witnesses accustomed to massaging the Western media. And the grieving, furious people in their makeshift uniforms or shabby and alien garb do not evoke the same sense of "there but for the grace of God go I." If the increasingly professional Arab media had unencumbered access to the Occupied Territories, then we would see much more than we do of the extraordinary suffering of the Palestinian people, although far less in the United States, where the media increasingly shields its viewers from cognitive dissonance, than in Israel itself, Europe and particularly the Islamic world where, in any event, the presumptions are different and the dissonance correspondingly less.

Even-handed portrayal of the diurnal suffering of Palestinians would produce peculiarly intense cognitive dissonance for persons who have visited Israel and witnessed a society where artistic, intellectual, and entrepreneurial virtuosity are on unself-conscious display, where the very issues I have attempted to illuminate, the issues ignored or at best muted in the American media and political discourse, are engaged in a fierce open debate that testifies to the existence in Israel of a vital democratic society. "How can you propose a close identity," the returning visitor will ask rhetorically, "between a society so open, so free, that it allows an historian

---

[168] Although preserved with relative secrecy, "Facility 1391" is among the most notorious locales of torture. Termed the "Israeli Guantanamo," the prison is described as not even allowing its detainees the privilege of knowing their whereabouts. See Aviv Lavie, "Inside Israel's Secret Prison," available online through *Ha'aretz.com*; see also sources in footnote 106 in ch 3.

to expose the ethnic cleansing and massacre that may have accompanied the violent birth of the state and South Africa in the era of Apartheid?"

Having never visited South Africa, my hypothetical but very real interlocutor will not realize that had he visited South Africa before the end of *apartheid*, he might well have returned saying much the same thing, saying "how can you condemn as a gross violator of human rights a society in which a fierce and talented critic, like the novelist Nadine Gordimer, can publish what amount to assaults on its most profound premises, a society with fine universities, an efficient state, exquisite wines, brilliant professionals? How can we dream of sanctioning the country of the gentleman golfing champion, Gary Player, or the heart-transplant pioneer Dr Christian Barnard a society, after all, that must defend its very existence from the Communist-terrorists of the African National Congress and the hordes of enemies on its doorstep?" Few ordinary travelers to South Africa, after all, visited the Bantustans as well as the wine country, any more than the average visitor to Israel spends time in Gaza as well as in Jerusalem's luminous streets.

The sixth and final ground is possibly the most difficult one to cross. Down at the very core of their being, at the roots of their identity, most people in my experience, from the knuckle-dragging British soccer hooligan to the most soft-spoken and erudite scholar, is a pool of communal (if we were speaking of Africa, many people would call it "tribal") loyalty that a lifetime of learning can leave untouched. For some it is a naked "My community right or wrong." For others it is: "If you were not an unconscious bigot or if you understood the situation properly, you would see that my community is not wrong." For every rule your community, when need be, is the exception.

This primal communal loyalty narrows vision, mutes sound, closes the heart. How many decent people have I heard saying something to the effect: Of course I grieve for every maimed Palestinian child just as I do for every Israeli one.... But: The fault is Arafat's or their parents breed them to sacrifice themselves or their injury was an unfortunate incident of war or... How sharp the irony that one motive for the anti-Semitism of the European Right-Wing nationalists in the century preceding the Holocaust was their conviction that the Jews could never be good nationalists because by their nature they were rootless cosmopolitans; hence they truly could grieve with equal intensity for a death on either side of a frontier.

Of a hundred instances one could cite, none depressed me more than a piece written during the escalation of regional violence in July 2006. For more than three decades Michael Walzer has been a valuable contributor to the discourse on the moral limits of violence in the service of politics. Armed always with an unabridged Thesaurus, considerable erudition, and a lightly veiled taste for polemics, and armed as well with the affect of a sensitive man agonized by the perceived need in the world as it is to use violence for just ends, he has undoubtedly helped to illuminate the application of just war theory in our time. Disagree with him as I sometimes have, I have nevertheless seen him as a person actually attempting to clarify the facts of particular cases, to grasp the perspectives of the antagonists, and to identify and apply consistently rules for negotiating the moral maze constituted by recourse to war. Then, in that bloody July, I read the following paragraph:

I was recently asked to sign a condemnation of the Israeli operation in Gaza—a statement claiming that the rocket attacks and the military raid that led to the capture of Gilad Shalit are simply the inevitable consequences of the Israeli occupation: There "never will be peace or security until the occupation ends." In the past, I am sure, some Palestinian attacks were motivated by the experience of occupation. But that isn't true today. Hamas is attacking *after* the Israelis departed Gaza and *after* the formation of a government that is (or was until the attacks) committed to a large withdrawal from the West Bank.[169]

Let us suppose that after acquiring power through electoral means in the 1940s, the white Afrikaans government of South Africa had decided that rather than transferring the black population to notionally autonomous reserves organized on the basis of traditional tribal identities (ie the Bantustans), it would create four reserves in different parts of the territory into which it would concentrate blacks regardless of their tribal identity. Letting thought be father to the act, they created the reserves, one of which lay in a stretch of already impoverished land along the sun-drenched Indian Ocean coast and called it Gozo. Into it they herded something like a third of South Africa's black population and for three decades held them there in close confinement under conditions of squalid and hopeless poverty. In addition, as a statement of intention to maintain the status quo in perpetuity, the government planted in the midst of this heaving slum a group of armed Afrikaner settlers, protected by army units, who, with the aid of various subsidies, built an enclave of prosperous farms in which civilians lived a comfortable middle-class existence that provided to the inhabitants of the wretched slum around them a reminder of their misery. For blacks, ingress and egress from Gozo was tightly controlled. Although many Gozo families had relatives and friends living in the other reserves, no visit was possible without a permit from the military and anyone receiving it had then to travel along carefully designated routes, through many check points notable for their long delays and not infrequent humiliations, until they reached another of these reserves.

In part because poverty levels and crowding were even worse in Gozo than the other reserves, resistance to the occupation was particularly fierce. Largely unemployed, with only the most limited opportunities for education and miserably poor prospects for using an education to improve their conditions, and faced with the twinned images of a free life—the prosperous settler colonies and the shimmering sea (carefully patrolled by the South African Navy), Gozo's youth, suffocating in rage and hopelessness, acted as the main arm of the resistance. They attacked the occupying army and the settlements with suicidal courage.

---

[169] Michael Walzer, "War Fair," *The New Republic*, 31 July 2006, 15, 16.

Some were killed and maimed. Many others were picked up in search and grab missions and taken off to camps where they were brutally interrogated.

Although the main life support for the black inhabitants of the Gozo reserve came from foreign aid donors, nevertheless, because of the resistance, the costs of occupation rose over time. Furthermore, the South African soldiers rotated through occupation duties included many reservists who hated its risks, squalor, and tedium. Even the professionals found it intensely disagreeable and tried to serve elsewhere. Furthermore, unlike the other reserves, Gozo had no resources that were of any value to the South African regime. It did not, for instance, lie on top of large aquifers used by the white population as did the other reserves. So at last the Afrikaaner government decided that the costs of occupation outweighed its benefits.

The President and his advisors decided that their ends could be achieved at lower cost simply by, as it were, letting the inmates run their prison while they controlled it at minimum cost from the outside. Moreover, by withdrawing to the periphery and pulling out the small group of settlers, the President noted, they could appease international opinion by saying that this was a first step toward dividing the entire country between the black and white population and letting the latter enjoy all the benefits of self government. "What we will do," he told his colleagues, "is declare Gozo and the other reserves to constitute a single state within the South African confederation. If we can't find toadies to sign a treat, we will simply draft a declaration of separation in which we recognize them as a state while retaining the right to control their airspace and obviously we control their borders, since none of them will share a frontier with any country except us. And in the case of Gozo, we will, of course, have to retain control of their access to the sea. Then, if they get unruly, if, for instance, they try to infiltrate white territory, we will simply claim aggression and go in and smash them up or hit them from the air." And so the withdrawal was quickly carried out. Life in Gozo remained essentially unchanged: squalid and miserable and hopeless.

I have to believe that, if the South African Government had in fact employed such a stratagem, and if, after the withdrawal, the residents of Gozo continued within their exiguous means to attack South African targets, a fastidious moral philosopher like Michael Walzer would have dismissed with contempt any claim by the South African Government that in light of its withdrawal, and its previous plan to unite the reserves into a state, the continuing attacks could no longer be attributed to the conditions of occupation.

For moral philosophers no less than knuckle-draggers, the deep primal identity with some community of first loyalty rather often translates into the dictum: "My community: May it be right; but if it be wrong, give me the means to make it appear right." And that is why, at the end of this effort to communicate to an audience that will include many who wish above all to avoid cognitive dissonance, I am reminded depressingly of the old Welsh proverb: "He who knocks at the door of the deaf, knocks forever."

6

Toward a Liberal Grand Strategy

When a man has to be on the alert to keep Ireland quiet, or to prevent peculation in the dockyards, or to raise the revenue while he lowers the taxes, he feels himself to be saved from the necessity of investigating principles. (Plantagenet Palliser, the Liberal Party leader, in Anthony Trollope's *The Prime Minister*)

1. Ideas and Actions

Anyone who has served inside the US government, as I have on two brief occasions, and has thought with any depth at all about the experience, will recognize both the aptness and the partiality of Trollope's dictum channeled through the protagonist of his political novels. Besieged by the nation's endless alarms and commotions and the related fear of political death, high officials do indeed have little time to consult their "principles" as they try, however sluggishly, to respond while holding their place on the greasy pole of power. To that extent Trollope is right. But although there often is no conscious consultation, and although many officials when taking action picture themselves as no more or less than pragmatists armed with experience and common sense, "principles" in the sense of core values and rooted ideas about cause and effect, as well as partisan interests, invariably influence their choices in part by censoring their repertoire of possible responses. The great economist John Maynard Keynes noted this phenomenon in his *General Theory of Employment, Interest and Money* when he wrote:

Practical men, who believe themselves to be quite exempt from any intellectual influences, are usually the slaves of some defunct economist. Madmen in authority, who hear voices in the air, are distilling their frenzy from some academic scribbler of a few years back.[1]

The men and women who constitute the electorate in democratic countries also have little time for reflection on first principles as they register their assessment of official action in surveys of public opinion and, episodically, at the polls, and yet

---

[1] John Maynard Keynes, *General Theory of Employment, Interest and Money* (New York: Harcourt, Brace & World, Inc, 1964), 383.

they too are influenced by principles. Hence the function of policy intellectuals: through the confluence of chance, effort, and choice we occupy positions in society that give us the time and the incentive to assist both officials and the electorate in clarifying the principles implicit in public policy choices. And those privileged positions obligate us, I believe, to employ all the methods of rational inquiry to the end of anticipating and illuminating the moral and material consequences of presently mooted policy choices and also those the conventional wisdom has yet to concede.

I see policy analysis as an ongoing conversation not only with officials and citizens and fellow analysts, but also with oneself. For however firmly settled our core values, our appreciation of means for realizing them must be provisional. We cannot like natural scientists test our hypotheses in controlled experiments. History is our laboratory. We test our hypotheses about cause and effect by extrapolating from precedents perceived as essentially like the case before us. But not only is every historical "precedent" unique (once it is examined in any detail), in addition, the precedent is not an object awaiting discovery; it is, rather, a collage constructed by each of us out of objects that arrest our attention as we observe the passing stream of history. All we can see with any certainty is that one thing that has caught our eye precedes another; whether the latter pulled the former into place behind it is at best a reasoned hypothesis. For the historical stream's turbulence and the stunning variety and number of things in close proximity sped along on its heaving shoulders, together with the natural desire to confirm one's intuitive preferences, obscure our observations. No wonder that even in the best of cases, the forces set in motion by those with the final say (the "deciders" to use President Bush's idiom), whether moved by the supposedly reasoned conclusions of analysts or those voices in the air of which Keynes wrote, have unanticipated consequences.

So we have many good reasons for humility, for thinking of our work as one of successive approximation, and for recognizing that our values influence not only our ends but also our judgments about means. Take war for instance. Most liberals are not pacifists; in fact their values may place them in the forefront of appeals for violent intervention to halt butchery in other countries. But because liberalism expresses and stems from faith in the moral equality of people across the boundaries of nation, class, ancestry, gender, pigmentation, and other accidental conditions of human existence, and because the one thing war is guaranteed to do is kill and maim, to liberals war can never be a good in itself, it is always a lesser evil[2] demanding, therefore, the imperative justification of self-defense or the need to prevent crimes against humanity. To intellectuals of the Right, exemplified by the nineteenth-century German historian Heinrich von Treitschke, war, by contrast, has profound intrinsic virtue.

---

[2] Compare Michael Ignatieff, *The Lesser Evil* (Princeton: Princeton University Press, 2004).

We have learned to perceive the moral majesty of war through the very processes which to the superficial observer seem brutal and inhuman. The greatness of war is just what at first sight seems to be its horror—that for the sake of their country men will overcome the natural feeling of humanity, that they will slaughter their fellow-men who have done them no injury…Man will not only sacrifice his life, but the natural and justified instincts of his soul; his very self he must offer up for the sake of patriotism; here we have the sublimity of war. When we pursue this thought further we see how war…weaves a bond of love between man and man, linking them together to face death, and causing all class distinctions to disappear. He who knows history knows also that to banish war from the world would be to mutilate human nature.[3]

Von Treitschke urged his German audience "to once more join hands with Clausewitz in calling war the forceful continuation of politics."[4] Hence like militants of the contemporary American Right he would have despised the UN Charter restraints on the use of force, seeing them as do John Bolton, Charles Krauthammer, and other right-wing militants as intolerable restraints on the employment of military power and on the pursuit of national greatness.

   To be sure, in their rhetoric conservatives of the "neo" sub-species equate that pursuit with the long-term advance of liberal values and in that respect differ from unembarrassed rightists like von Treitschke. But their liberal rhetoric is hard to reconcile with their hostility to most of the domestic liberal agenda, their acquired hostility to government, their imperial triumphalism, and their alliance with Christian sects on the Right [5] that are proudly illiberal. And it crashes on the rocks of practice, for instance its ardent support of terrorist regimes and movements in Latin America during the 1980s and its championing of uninhibited executive power post 9/11 whatever the consequences for civil liberties and human rights. If criticism of cruel interrogation and due process violations after 9/11 came from the Right at all, it came mostly from Burkeian traditionalists like the columnist George Will,[6] not from neo-conservative publicists like the denizens of the *Wall Street Journal*'s editorial page.

   There is here, moreover, not really a question of sincerity but rather of moral instincts profoundly in conflict. The valuation of means is not simply a function of their contested efficiency in promoting ends. Idealistic Marxists imagined a blessed time after the transitional dictatorship of the proletariat when, as a result of the Proletarian revolution and the resulting overthrow of the tyranny of capitalist production, the human condition would be marked by unprecedented freedom of choice. The cause of conflict having been removed, people could live in peace. And with goods and services made abundant through technological

---

³ Heinrich von Treitschke, *Politics*, Hans Kohn (ed) (NY: Harcourt, Brace & World, 1963), 245.
⁴ Ibid, 244.
⁵ See, eg, Joshua Muravchik, "God Squad," *Commentary*, 122(4) (November 2006), 78–80; and Wilfred M McLay, "Is Conservatism Finished?" *Commentary*,123(1) (January 2007), 13–19.
⁶ See, eg, "No Flinching From the Facts," *The Washington Post*, 11 May 2004, A19; but compare "Hot Topic: A 'Tortured' Debate," *The Wall Street Journal*, 12 November 2005, A6.

progress and distributed to each according to their need, people could work in the morning, fish in the afternoon, and write in the evening. Arguably a liberal paradise. But the means, a cruel class war followed by dictatorship of unclear temporal limits, were unacceptable to liberals, devotees of a political philosophy centered on human freedom not at some indefinite point in the future but in the here and now. Just as in the liberal value system there are limits to what present majorities can demand for the general good, there are even greater limits to the demands that can be made on basic individual rights for the arguable benefit of generations yet to be conceived, even if one believes that the demanded sacrifice is more likely than not to achieve the hypothesized millennium. In their readiness to loose the dogs of war and the national security state to the end of building a more perfect liberal world, in their means, that is, neo-conservatism bears the same incompatible relationship to liberalism as did Marxism.

For instance, it follows from the evident difference in normative instincts between liberals and rightists of various stripes that in assessing whether a conventional reading of Charter restraints on the use of force is compatible with confronting terrorism effectively and advancing other American interests, liberals and rightists start with different presumptions in any given case and therefore tend to arrive at different conclusions (see Chapter 2). Moral instincts dominate assessment because only in retrospect is it at all clear whether recourse to force outside the Charter norms served the national interest. And even then, consensus is unlikely. In the case of Iraq, for instance, while so-called "liberal hawks" like Peter Beinart of *The New Republic*, beat the drum for war, in retrospect they admit errors of judgment.[7] Meanwhile neo-conservatives will concede no more than a failure to prosecute the war effectively.[8] The same differences in normative instinct will also color assessments of the efficacy of cruel treatment (see Chapter 3).

But while all strong belief systems—liberalism, Marxism, fascism, nationalism, Christianity, Islam, etc—color prediction and post hoc assessment, liberalism by virtue of its origins and nature is the most open to reasoned and fact-based argument about the probable consequences of means, it is the most provisional in its judgments. Why should that be? Remember that central to the liberal belief system is the conviction that there is no one great truth or some cluster of irrefutable truths available to all human beings through right reason or divine inspiration. Rather life consists of individuals, both alone and in groups, struggling to understand the world and then constructing meaning out of the mute elements of life. Liberalism is at its heart simply a conscious choice to protect their efforts. It is a scheme for the coexistence of peoples who live on the basis of irreconcilable ideas about the meaning of existence, the nature of the good life, and the laws of right conduct. Thus it seems to me that skepticism about truth-claims in general

<hr />

[7] "To the Brink," *The New Republic*, 235(22/23) (27 November 2006), 6.
[8] Reuel Marc Gerecht, "Running from Iraq," *The Weekly Standard*, 12(6) (23 October 2006); and Frederick W Kagan, "No Third Way in Iraq," *The Weekly Standard*, 12(9) (13 November 2006).

is built into the character and ethos of Liberalism. It is embedded as well in its genealogy. As Richard Tarnas neatly puts it:

The new psychological constitution of the modern character had been developing since the high Middle Ages, had conspicuously emerged in the Renaissance, was sharply clarified and empowered by the Scientific Revolution, then extended and solidified in the course of the Enlightenment. By the nineteenth century, in the wake of the democratic and industrial revolutions, it had achieved mature form. The direction and quality of that character reflected a gradual but finally radical shift of psychological allegiance... *from the transcendent to the empirical, from myth and belief to reason and fact, from universals to particulars*... [9] (emphasis added).[10]

Liberalism itself emerges in the nineteenth century as the institutionalized political expression of that centuries-long development.

Years ago a minister-to-be in sundry British Conservative governments, anxious to enlighten me about the true nature of British politics and the peculiar virtues of his Party, relished describing it as "the stupid party." He meant that in contrast with the Labor party, then still committed to old socialist dogmas about state ownership and class conflict, it had no ideology, no rigid conceptual limits on its ability to choose whatever policies best served the general interest of the British people. Of course, although he read books, he was hardly a self-critical intellectual. That on many domestic matters there might be no "general interest" but rather conflicting parochial interests concerned with the division of opportunity and wealth and, in the foreign policy realm, conflicting ideas about the role a diminished United Kingdom ought to play in the world never seemed to occur to him. But he was right in seeing the post-Second World War Conservative Party as less bound than Labor by rigid ideas about reality or identification (psychological or electoral) with any single-issue constituency and therefore freer to improvise and experiment in its policies, free even to conscript parts of the Labor Party program for its own electoral uses. That seems to me the condition of liberalism today in relation to the American Right whether in its neo-conservative, nativist, corporate, or Christianist sub-sets which collectively control the Republican Party.[11]

---

[9] Richard Tarnas, *The Passion of the Western Mind* (New York: Ballantine Books, 1991), 319.

[10] As a matter of definition, no liberal could say, as a high official of the Bush Administration said to the writer Ron Suskind: "The aide said that guys like me were 'in what we call the reality-based community,' which he defined as people who 'believe that solutions emerge from your judicious study of discernible reality.' I nodded and murmured something about enlightenment principles and empiricism. He cut me off. 'That's not the way the world really works anymore,' he continued. 'We're an empire now, and when we act, we create our own reality,'" "Without a Doubt," *New York Times Magazine*, 17 October 2004, 44.

[11] I refer to liberalism rather than the Democratic Party, because unlike the Republican one, which I see as having become an almost pure aggregator and reconciler (to the fullest extent possible) of right-wing programmatic ideas and values, it cobbles together political activists, social movements, and electoral groups with values and interests only some of which could be accurately described as liberal. In that sense it is somewhat like the British Conservative Party on the eve of Thatcher and more like the current Labor Party as transformed during the era of Tony Blair.

2. Toward a Liberal Grand Strategy of Containment

A. Pluralists and Reductionists

However provisional, however open to revision in the face of new facts and more persuasive interrogations of precedent, what grand strategy for confronting contemporary terrorism should liberals propose? Strategy must begin with a description of the problem that gives us a useful sense of its dimensions and its sources, that locates it in our historically based understanding of the world. In other words, in outlining a grand strategy we need to begin by attempting to answer the following threshold questions: Who are the terrorists? What do they want? How sizeable a threat do they pose and how dependent is that threat on conditions we can influence?

The present occupant of the White House has identified them in a variety of ways, some more expansive than others but every one of them large. At its broadest, his conception seems to cover all non-governmental groups that employ violence against the United States or friendly governments, whatever their means and goals, and any government that assists them. Thus it covers those who attack US targets, whether at home or abroad, whether civilian or military. His feats of rhetoric in their breadth equate groups with wildly different origins and goals, groups as varied as the exotic Japanese nihilists of Aun Shinrikio, who appeared to have as their goal the destruction of society to the end of purifying it,[12] and the Tamil Tigers, a conventional ethnic nationalist group killing and destroying to the end of secession from Sri Lanka. At other times the focus narrows from the generically satanic to "radical Islamists" or "Islamo-fascists."

In Chapter 1 of this book, I explored the definitional debate, to the extent it seemed still useful, and it would be tediously redundant to rehearse it again here, except in one respect which is perhaps not so much a matter of definition as it is of visualization. Persons participating through their writings in the debate about terrorism policy tend to divide into two groups because of their sharply contrasting answers to the following two linked questions. One is whether terrorism or at least something called "global terrorism" is a movement sufficiently organized and concentrated that it can be comprehensively engaged and "defeated," as one defeats an enemy state in a traditional war, or is rather a multitude of geographically scattered plots, conspiracies, and insurgencies, each with its own grievances and organizational peculiarities, its particular relationship to the social group from which it springs, its distinctive identity. The other is whether global terrorism is a response to or at least is susceptible to the influence of US policies or simply to the way we are, in President's Bush's words, "the brightest beacon for freedom and opportunity in the world."

---

[12] See Robert Jay Lifton, *Destroying the World to Save It* (New York: Henry Holt and Co, 2000).

For me the most persuasive analyst of contemporary terrorism is Louise Richardson, a Harvard scholar and the author of *What Terrorists Want*.[13] Her work is grounded in close study of every variety of insurgent movement employing terrorist tactics. In addition to having the scholar's familiarity with the general literature on the subject, she has interviewed insurgents, read accounts of interviews and interrogations, and read or listened to the statements of insurgents about their motives, means, and ends. Her analysis, in other words, is the product of empirical scholarship informed by historical perspective and integrated by the exercise of reason.

With respect to the first question I listed above, she clearly arrives on the side of those who see a multiplicity of groups, motives and ends, as must anyone who examines the global incidence of terrorism. Some, like the IRA and the Tamil Tigers, have a localized focus, but if provoked by perceived foreign intervention in their parochial conflicts, they can strike across borders. The Tigers, for instance, assassinated the Indian Prime Minister, Rajiv Gandhi, when they decided that he was interfering with the flow of assistance to them from south India. Others, like Al Qaeda, have a transnational self-identity and a corresponding transnational set of grievances. Still others, like the Algerian organization that set off bombs in Paris during the 1990s, seemed to span the two, in the sense that its Islamist members presumably felt some connection to the wider struggle of Islamist parties against more-or-less secular Arab governments or foreign governments deemed inimical to Islamic interests, but were nevertheless responding to a localized grievance, namely the French Government's perceived cooperation with its Algerian counterpart's efforts to destroy them.[14]

Terrorism, Richardson argues on the basis of her studies, needs to be understood and countered in detail, not in the round. Its causes in each case are "a lethal cocktail that combines a disaffected individual, an enabling community, and a legitimizing ideology." Long-term political motives "differ across groups." Terrorists on the whole do, however, share three immediate motives: "they want to exact revenge, to acquire glory, and to force their adversary into a reaction" that swells their renown, confirms their efficacy, and enhances their ability to recruit and to increase support from the society with which they identify.[15]

Neither Richardson nor other empiricists are arguing that diverse groups of insurgents may not also share in varying degrees a legitimating ideology and an associated narrative, the latter being a tale that invariably includes acts of injustice to which the insurgency with its terrorist methods is deemed by its participants to be a just response. And the injustice in the narrative need not be local; its victims can be anywhere as long as they are persons with whom the latent or actual insurgent identifies. The central point, however, is that while personal networks

---

[13] Louise Richardson, *What Terrorists Want* (New York: Random House, 2006).
[14] See, eg, "Wanted: An Algerian Policy," *The Economist*, 20 March 1997, 47.
[15] Richardson, *What Terrorists Want*, xxii.

in dozens of different geographic and social settings may share the ideology and the narrative, each has its own grievances, frustrations and aspirations embedded in a particular time and place.

There is a Cold War analogy to the present conflict between the Reductionist and what we might call the Pluralist perception of terrorism. The writings of Karl Marx and his epigones presumably provided ideological inspiration to self-described communists in, for example, Vietnam, China, Yugoslavia, and South Africa But each set of communists had its distinctive parochial grievances, challenges, and goals stemming from its unique social, political, and historical conditions and experiences. The Marxist narrative did not create those grievances; rather it provided a coherent explanation of their causes and a legitimization of transgressive responses, a guide to remedial action, and the empowering sensation of being part of a larger historical movement.

The defining impulse of American rightists and also so-called Cold-War Liberals, the impulse that killed 50,000 Americans in Vietnam and several million Vietnamese, was to treat communist movements and governments as a single, integrated enemy that needed to be confronted everywhere with hard power. Fortunately the impulse did not always shape national policy. It yielded quickly to realization that Marshall Tito's communist government in Yugoslavia could be drawn into a de facto anti-soviet alliance. It yielded very slowly to the opportunity for playing triangular diplomacy with China and the Soviet Union. It also helped delay strong sanctions against the regime of apartheid in South Africa. And it triumphed in the case of Vietnam where, during the colonial era, the communist party became the main expression of national resistance to foreign domination.

The call for differentiation is not limited to the academy. It comes also from a new generation of counter-insurgency experts in or consulting with the State and Defense Departments at an operational level so far untouched by the they-all-hate-us-because-we-are-good-and-they-are-evil-fascists mentality that characterizes the highest reaches of the American Government during the Bush Administration and its intellectual kin among media talkers and scribblers. In a recent sympathetic summary of the views that characterize this small cohort of experts, the journalist George Packer writes: "Even if we think that a jihadi in Yemen has ideas similar to those of an Islamist in Java, we have to approach them in discrete ways, both to prevent them from becoming a unified movement and *because their particular political yearnings are different*"[16] [emphasis added].

David Kilcullen, a former officer in the Australian Army who served as a counter-terrorist advisor in the Department of State before going to Iraq as an advisor to General David Petraeus, commander of US forces in that country, has plotted out a "ladder of extremism" that shows the progress of a jihadist. At the bottom is the vast population of mainstream Muslims who are potential allies against radical Islamism as well as potential targets of subversion,

---

[16] George Packer, "Knowing the Enemy," *The New Yorker*, 18 December 2006, 60 at 68.

and whose grievances can be addressed by political reform. The next tier up is a smaller number of "alienated Muslims," who have given up on reform. Some of these join radical groups, like the young Muslims in North London who spend afternoons at the local community center watching jihadist videos. They require "ideological conversion". A smaller number of these individuals, already steeped in the atmosphere of radical mosques and extremist discussions, end up joining local and regional insurgent cells, usually as the result of a biographical trigger— they will lose a friend in Iraq, or see something that shocks them on television. With these insurgents, the full range of counter-insurgency tools has to be used, including violence and persuasion. Finally there are the very small number of fighters who are recruited to the top tier of Al Qaeda and its affiliated terrorist groups and they are beyond persuasion or conversion. "They're so committed you've got to destroy them," Kilcullen said. *"But you've got to do it in such a way that you don't create new terrorists"*[17] (emphasis added).

A colleague of Kilcullen's, the anthropologist and Defense Department consultant Montgomery McFate, explicitly dismisses the one-size-fits-all rhetoric of all right-wing publicists along with a cluster of writers who, drawing on the Cold War analogy, imagine themselves as the avatars of that epoch's so-called liberal hawks. "Terms like 'totalitarianism' and 'Islamofascism' " she tells Packer, "which stir the American historical memory, mislead policymakers into greatly increasing the number of our enemies and coming up with wrongheaded strategies against them."[18]

Perhaps the person who best exemplifies the homogenizing cast of mind McFate deplores is an essayist called Paul Berman, a self-described liberal. In his book *Terror and Liberalism*,[19] first published in 2003, he declares us to be at war with nothing but Islamo-fascism, an Islamic derivative of European Fascism and Marxism as well,[20] both of which, for all their superficial differences, he sees as expressions of the inherently aggressive totalitarian impulse and the culture of death and both of which, like all totalitarian movements, "rise up against the liberal values of the West." While admiring the values, he writes with contempt of many of those (ie liberals) who hold them, since, according to him, large numbers have ceaselessly misread or funked the totalitarian challenge, scrambling to rationalize its crimes, and indulge its pretended motives (where they sound at all in the liberal idiom).

What makes the author interesting is neither his risible smugness nor swollen conceit nor cloying cuteness of self-reference, but rather his ability to exemplify characteristics of the homogenizing or we might call it the reductionist mind. One is its ability to soar into the realm of ideas unhindered by attachment to an empirical base. To understand the contemporary challenge you need to read

[17] Ibid.
[18] Ibid, 68.
[19] Paul Berman, *Terror and Liberalism* (New York: WW Norton and Co, 2003).
[20] Ibid, in particular, 52–60.

some Sayyid Qutb, intellectual leader of Egypt's Muslim Brotherhood. Then, with a dose of Albert Camus, supplemented by Baudelaire, you can grasp the essence of Islamism and see the connection to the European culture of death. Dip lightly into the secondary literature, rely on a moderately well-informed knowledge of history and recent events, scan the leftist-reductionist works of Noam Chomsky—a marginal figure among liberal policy intellectuals—and then set him up as typifying liberals who have a more complex view of reality than Berman[21] and...Eureka! You understand all that needs to be understood about the Islamo-fascist threat.

Well, almost all. For although Berman has shunned the hard slog of analysts like Richardson and McFate and Kilcullen, like them (and unlike people on the Right who want simply to "exterminate the brutes"[22]), he believes we need "to offer political solutions to people around the world who might otherwise become our enemies."[23] Exactly. But how can you offer those solutions, how can you even begin to imagine them, if you have convinced yourself that everyone who joins a terrorist organization or sympathizes with it, indeed great swathes of societies like the Iranian and the Palestinian are immured in a culture of death and, moreover, how can you begin to imagine solutions if you despise anyone who takes seriously the particular political claims of insurgent groups and reserve your fiercest mockery for those, like Richardson, who have concluded, on the basis of their detailed inquiries, that "terrorists are human beings who think like we do[24] [and] have goals they are trying to achieve, and in a different set of circumstances they, and perhaps we, would lead very different lives"?[25]

It appears from his writing that for Berman, people like Richardson, although they provide empirical stiffening for his plaintive claim that we need to find "political solutions," bear a heavy burden of responsibility for 9/11 and other atrocities. Near the end of his Philippic, he asks bitterly:

What have we needed for these terrorists to prosper? [He is speaking not just of bin Laden, but apparently of every violent Muslim organization, religious or secular, and of political

---

[21] Berman ignores, for instance, the strategically and methodologically sophisticated work of an iconic left-liberal intellectual, Richard Falk, who did not oppose the use of force in Afghanistan to eliminate the terrorist haven. For Falk's nuanced views on responding to terrorism see *The Great Terror War* (Brooklyn: Olive Branch Press, 2003).

[22] They see the world like the dying and maddened Mr Kurtz, the once idealistic Belgian adventurer in the Congo, in Joseph Conrad's *Heart of Darkness* (Oxford: Oxford University Press, 2003), 50.

[23] Berman, 208.

[24] Richardson, xvii. In her book Richardson describes a secret conference she organized, bringing together academics and senior figures from a number of violent ethnic-nationalist groups (she frankly says "terrorist" groups). Among other things, mixed groups of terrorists and academics war gamed in an effort to figure out what factors drive a group to escalate to a different level of violence. "I participated in a group that was a Chechen cell based in Moscow. The scenario called for us to be placed under increasing pressure by the authorities, as we were trying to establish what kinds of pressures would force a decision to escalate...[o]n the...important question of when one should escalate, the insurgents were not more prone to escalation than the academics. (Indeed, the insurgents were quite taken aback by the belligerence of the academics in the mixed groups.)"

[25] Ibid.

elites in Iran, Syria, Iraq before the invasion and elsewhere] ... We have needed handsome doses of wishful thinking—the kind of simpleminded faith is a rational world that, in its inability to comprehend reality, sparked the totalitarian movements in the first place.[26]

Scholars of the rise of Bolshevism and fascism may be surprised to learn that as a spark for totalitarian movements, liberal "faith in a rational world" trumps such factors as Czarist absolutism, urbanization, the Industrial Revolution, the First World War, historical anti-Semitism, right-wing views on race and democracy, European class structures, the poverty of economic theory, the Great Depression, the Weimar inflation, to name but a few. Fortunately for his progress in life, as a free-floating scholar of ideas Mr Berman enjoys immunity from the rigors of peer review.

The Manichaean vision of reductionists like Berman parallels the vision of President Bush who in turn mirrors Osama bin Laden. The President declares that this is a war about freedom and "[e]ither you stand for freedom or you stand with tyranny." Bin Laden declares "we fight because we are free men who don't sleep under oppression."[27] Bin Laden invokes Allah as the supporter of his efforts. President Bush invokes his version of God on behalf of the United States. As Richardson notes: the invocation of God "'absolutizes'" the conflict and demonizes a monolithic enemy.[28] Such a vision is inimical to the search for, much less the finding of the "political solutions" schizophrenically summoned by Berman, in part because it produces myopic appreciation of particular cases.

In writing of the Palestinian-Israeli case, for instance, Berman finds no possible explanation of the Palestinian resort to suicidal terrorism other than mass pathology, the triumph of the culture of death with children driven by their parents to fatal self-sacrifice. He is blind to the "biographical trigger" identified by Kilcullen that impels the merely aggrieved into violent networks and Richardson's similar observation that "revenge" for some act of violence personally or vicariously experienced is an immediate terrorist motive. The Palestinian experience is filled with triggers; so is the Israeli.

Chris Hedges, the journalist who has actually covered the conflict, sees *both* Israelis and Palestinians embracing death because of the dialectic of their tit-for-tat killing and their respective visions of themselves as "victims." He describes one instance he personally witnessed in Gaza that begins with a loudspeaker on the Israeli side of the fence separating the refugee camp of Khan Younis from a Jewish settlement, now abandoned, daring Palestinians in invective-filled language to come and fight.

...boys [mostly no more than ten or eleven years old] darted up the sloping dunes to the electric fence ... they lobbed rocks towards a jeep, mounted with a loudspeaker and protected by bulletproof armor plates and metal grating, that sat parked on the top of the hill. The

---

[26] Berman, 206–7.
[27] Richardson, 9, quoting bin Laden's "Message to America," 30 October 2004.
[28] Ibid, 196.

soldier inside the jeep ridiculed and derided them.... There was the boom of a percussion grenade. The boys...scattered, running clumsily through the heavy sand.... The soldiers shot with silencers. The bullets from M-16 rifles, unseen by me, tumbled end-over-end through their slight bodies. I would see the destruction, the way their stomachs were ripped out, the gaping holes in their limbs and torsos, later in the hospital.[29]

Similarly, in discussing the failure of diplomacy, Berman relies only on Dennis Ross's account of the failed Camp David negotiations, ignoring the account of Robert Malley another participant, and the other disconfirming views I cited in Chapter 5, and ignoring as well the historical context of the conflict which shaped Palestinian assessment of the compromise they were being offered.

Once having embraced the homogeneous account, the reductionists, as I suggested above, are disposed to fashion a confirming historical narrative by ripping or hallucinating factoids out of a complicating context. Here again Berman is typical except perhaps in the sheer tsunamic volume of his distillations. To illustrate the power and ubiquity of bin Laden's "army" as well as to insist that we are at "war" and have been for years against a single enemy, he invokes "the attack on the US Marines in Mogadishu in 1993."[30] Is he poorly informed or does he simply assume that few readers will recall that the marines were attacked when they launched an assault on a group of sub-clan leaders in the midst of an ongoing civil war between sub-clans into which the United Nations and the United States had blundered after the mission to feed starving Somalis had been completed, a civil war having everything to do with power and nothing to do with the religious views of the various sub-clans?

To illustrate the congenital naivete of liberals in the face of a totalitarian threat, he cites the failure of some (he implies many) liberals to recognize the Nazi threat in the 1930s, while ignoring the powerful, Right-Wing appeasers like England's Cliveden set[31] brought to life by Kazuo Ishiguro in his brilliant novel *The Remains of the Day*.[32]

In seeking to show the ubiquity and ruthlessness of Islamism in the Arab World, he reduces the sanguinary Islamist insurgency in Algeria to a massacre "of the impious" by Islamist parties after the "secular" government prevented them from seizing power by electoral means.[33] To have noted, as he does not, that the "secular" government, whose annulment of an electoral victory for religious parties catalyzed the insurgency, was a massively corrupt, self-sustaining military junta that had spent years dissipating the country's oil and gas wealth even as its population metastasized and that it was accused by human rights

---

[29] Chris Hedges, "A Gaza Diary," *Harpers Magazine*, October 2001, 59 at 64, reprinted in Chris Hedges, *War Is a Force That Gives Us Meaning* (New York: Public Affairs, 2002), 93–4.

[30] Berman, 13. I am familiar with the case, having been in Mogadishu serving as legal consultant to the head of the UN intervention force in the months preceding the attack.

[31] Berman, xv.

[32] Kazuo Ishiguro, *Remains of the Day* (New York: Vintage Books, 1990).

[33] Berman, 110.

organizations of delinquencies as grave as those of the insurgents would no doubt have complicated the story, making it a less-than-seamless fit for his narrative.

To strengthen his claim to personal prophetic insight into the Islamist-totalitarian danger, the author as a lantern in the engulfing darkness of naivete about the threat, Berman slams the "commanders and strategists" who failed to anticipate before the invasion of Iraq "an enemy who [would be] driven by fanatical zeal."[34] He seems to have forgotten that the "commanders" (presumably he is referring to senior military officers) had called initially for a minimum of several hundred thousand troops in order actually to occupy the country, an estimate dismissed by the Secretary of Defense who also dismissed the Chairman of the Joint Chiefs for his unseemly candor.[35] And he also fails to note that a former commander, Secretary of State Colin Powell, had his staff prepare elaborate occupation plans which were dismissed by the Secretary of Defense with the acquiescence of his fellow reductionists in the White House.[36] As for the "fanatical zeal" of those who have resisted the occupation, might the zeal have anything to do with the fact that the improvisations of the ideologically vetted civilians dispatched by the Bush Administration to Iraq included dissolving the Iraqi army without pay and banning the hundreds of thousand of Bathist Party members from public employment?[37] Perhaps, but conceding such conventional motives for resistance, not to mention garden-variety nationalism, would hardly fit a narrative constructed to demonstrate that America is fighting a vast horde of maddened militants intoxicated and united by a culture of death.

In addition to carrying out a general advance of his Islamo-fascist cum culture-of-death explanation of the terrorist threat to the West, Berman more specifically wants to persuade liberals that the invasion of Iraq was both morally justified and strategically prudent. To conscript the war for those joint purposes, he employs two polemical tactics. One is to argue that Saddam, moved not by a prosaically cruel judgment of military efficiency but by a desire to exhibit through superhuman cruelty his superior love of the Arab nation, that is to promote the Baathist version of Islamo-Fascism, "organized his side of the Iran-Iraq war on the cruelest of bases…gas attacks…[and] *minefields, too*"[38] (emphasis added). Even a writer who so evidently knows so little about war might be presumed to know that minefields have been commonplace for a long time in many wars including those fought by democracies like the United States and that the United States insists on their continuing utility and their consistency with the law of war which prohibits the use of peculiarly cruel weapons (if their efficiency is problematical). Surely this silly ploy is unnecessary for demonstrating that Saddam was a sociopathic Stalinist tyrant.

---

[34] Berman, xv.

[35] David Rieff, "Blueprint for a Mess," *New York Times Magazine*, 2 November 2003.

[36] Walter Isaacson, "Colin Powell's Redeeming Failures," *The New York Times*, 9 May 2003.

[37] Eric Schmidt, "Top Baathist Officials to be Barred from Government", *The New York Times*, 9 May 2003.

[38] Berman, 108.

Berman's second polemical game is to sound the theme common to advocates of the 2003 invasion that Saddam, presumably like other culture-of-death totalitarians, had proven himself not susceptible to the logic of deterrence. Berman makes the point by combining in one paragraph reference to the massacre of Kurdish civilians, an atrocious crime against humanity, and the 1991 invasion of Kuwait. A writer uncommitted to retailing the vision of a single vast Islamo-Fascist threat understandable only in cultural terms might have added a second dimension to Berman's account, namely the role of the United States. The Reagan Administration did not simply ignore Iraq's aggression against Iran; it facilitated it, if not initially then subsequently when it began to appear that the Iranians might win.[39] Moreover, following Saddam's initial assault on the Kurds, including a gas attack on Kurdish villagers which occurred before the war was over, Rumsfeld flew to Iraq on behalf of the Reagan administration to reassure Saddam that the US policy of quiet support would not be altered.[40]

The very mild admonitions communicated to Saddam in 1991 by the Administration of Bush the father in response to Saddam's pre-invasion threats against Kuwait[41] were consistent in tone with the previous decade's policy of treating Saddam as a valued regional balancer of Iranian power, an implicit ally. Hence it is quite likely that he was genuinely surprised when, after the invasion, he was confronted with a US demand to retreat or be thrown out. In short, an historian open to a variety of explanatory narratives would not find in the history of Saddam's behavior from 1980–91 conclusive proof that he was immune to the logic of deterrence.[42]

It is not only liberalism's genealogy and ethos that make it less susceptible to the reductionist account of the terrorist threat. In addition there is the feature that induces Berman's mocking charge that liberals enable totalitarianism through their "simple-minded belief in a rational world."[43] Liberalism's respect for the individual does rest on the presumption that all human beings have a capacity for agency, a capacity, that is, to formulate goals, both immediate and long term, and

---

[39] See, eg, "Shaking Hands with Saddam Hussein: the US Tilts Towards Iraq, 1980–1984," *National Security Archive Briefing Book No. 82*, Joyce Battle (ed), 25 February 2003, The National Security Archive, George Washington University, available at <http://www.gwu.edu/~nsarchiv/NSAEBB/NSAEBB82/>.

[40] Ibid; see also Christopher Marquis, "The Struggle for Iraq: Documents—Rumsfeld Made Iraq Overture in '84 Despite Chemical Raids," *The New York Times*, 23 December 2003, 10.

[41] See Steven A Yetiv, *Explaining Foreign Policy: US Decision-Making and the Persian Gulf War* (Baltimore: The Johns Hopkins University Press, 2004), 20–6.

[42] See, eg, Stephen M Walt and John J Mearsheimer, "Keeping Saddam Hussein in a Box," *The New York Times*, 2 February 2003, 15. There was a powerful case in 1991, one having nothing to do with deterrence, for destroying Saddam's grip on Iraq by decimating his elite troops and providing air cover for the post-war rebellions in the north and south of Iraq. It was a moral case based on liberal values and it was dismissed by the conservative realists who ran the Administration of Bush the father, just as they had previously ignored liberal values in supporting Saddam prior to 1991.

[43] Berman, 207.

to choose means that, given the limits of their knowledge and understanding, are plausibly related to realizing those goals.

To put it another way, liberals presuppose that human beings have reasons for their actions. Liberalism also presupposes that, in addition to agency, individuals share certain primal non-material needs like respect and belonging and that they have a shared capacity to feel and be moved by injustice, although they may conceive of injustice in quite different ways.[44] In order to understand their actions, we need to understand their reasons.

Understanding need not correspond with sympathy. Indeed if the reasons are hostile to the exercise of agency by other people, liberals are bound to resist. But reasons there are and liberal are moved by their convictions to seek to understand them.

Understanding requires empathy, an effort to imagine yourself into the life experience of another person, possibly one with very different goals and ideas about how to realize them, but one who presumably shares with you a need at least for respect. Most people also presumably seek justice. (Those who do not, who reject the elements of justice—reciprocity and the equal treatment of people in identical circumstances—in favor of self-aggrandizement are by definition socio-paths with whom there is no basis for co-existence other than a balance of power favorable to you.)

In the process of attempting empathy, particularly where you are empathizing with a person in another community, you are likely to experience a more complex historical view of your own behavior and that of the community with which you identify. Suppose, for instance, you were trying to understand the behavior of the Hezbollah leaders, in particular their attitude toward the United States and Israel too. Obviously this is not an exercise you have any need to attempt once you have persuaded yourself that they are simply the embodiment of the totalitarian culture of death. But if instead you regard that as only one possible explanation and therefore proceed with the thought experiment of imagining yourself into their shoes, you would, I think, end up seeing a more complex picture than the one that seems embedded in the mind of a writer like Berman.

For him Hezbollah is merely an emanation of Iranian Islamism.[45] He seems to attribute its attacks on the United States in 1983 and its battling with Israeli forces then and thereafter as nothing more than the noxious result of Iranian cultural modeling, as if the militants of Hezbollah were inert clay. A writer not gripped by a passion to simplify would sketch a more complicated narrative. He or she would mention, for instance, the 1982 Israeli invasion of Lebanon with all its attendant hardships for the country's large Shia community, many of whom lived in the southern part of the country through which the Israeli army had rolled on the

---

[44] Thus, while they may both believe that justice requires treating like cases alike, they may have very different ideas of what makes two cases "alike."

[45] Berman, 109.

way to Beirut and which Israel continued to occupy after its withdrawal from the capital.[46] Hezbollah grew in numbers, belligerence and fighting capacity in the course of that harsh military occupation with its inevitable spiral of vengeful action and retaliation. Given the occupation, the culture-of-death hypothesis surely is not necessary to explain the behavior of Hezbollah *vis-à-vis* the Israelis. Its termination after years of pitiless conflict between the occupying forces and the Shia insurgents has left on both sides a residue of deep bitterness and suspicion. And given the intimate military, financial, intelligence, and political links between Israel and the United States, it is not incredible to suppose that whatever its religious views, the resistance movement that evolved among the Shia during the occupation would have seen the United States as complicit in its agonies.

Had President Ronald Reagan followed the precedent of 1956, when President Dwight Eisenhower used American economic and political pressure to abort the Anglo-French invasion of Egypt, and forced the Israelis to abort their drive to Beirut and to withdraw from Lebanon, there would have been no marines in Beirut and therefore no suicide attack on the Marine barracks there, no prolonged Israeli occupation.

Change that train of events and Hezbollah would probably not be the formidable organization it has become. And even if it had become an important player—at some point the Shia were bound to demand a place in the Lebanese power structure more in proportion to their large slice of the country's population, without the Israeli invasion and occupation and all that followed from it, Hezbollah's relations with the United States, even possibly with Israel, might be far less antagonistic. I know of no evidence that the Arab Shia of Lebanon, any more than the Arab Shia of Iraq, are puppets of the Persian Shia in Tehran. As the Bourbon-Hapsburg wars of the seventeenth and eighteenth centuries suggest, a mere common religious identity, like the common ideological one with which it is closely analogous, does not guarantee even peace[47] much less willed subordination.

The short of the matter, then, is that the reductionist's blinkered reading of the past makes it virtually impossible for the United States "to offer political solutions to people around the world who might otherwise become our enemies," for how can we contemplate offering solutions until we can begin to see how those people visualize their problems which may include ourselves?

B. Hearts and Minds

Once we reject the reductionist account of our terrorism problem, which as I have argued, it is natural for liberals and empiricists generally to do, once we see the

---

[46] See generally, Jonathan C Randal, *Going All the Way: Christian Warlords, Israeli Adventurers, and the War in Lebanon* (New York: Random House, 1983); and Robert Fisk, *Pity the Nation: The Abduction of Lebanon* (New York: Atheneum, 1990).

[47] After all, during the Cold War the Chinese clashed militarily with both the Soviet Union and Vietnam.

constituents of the problem as globally scattered intimate social networks whose members are standing on various steps of Kilcullen's "ladder of extremism," all linked by a legitimizing ideology and a constantly refreshed narrative and embedded in communities that are susceptible to the narrative but whose disaffection and hence potential complicity with violence will depend on the interplay between local grievances and the narrative (which is driven by real events), once we understand the problem in these terms, we can begin to see the organizing elements of a grand strategy.

The first of those elements is to cease thinking and speaking of the terrorist challenge in terms of a "war." Calling it "war" associates terrorists with the titanic clash of peoples, history-changing battles, and storied feats of arms by half-mythic figures like the great Muslim general Saladin who defeated the Crusaders and reconquered Jerusalem. Thus it plays into the hands of the terrorists by allowing them to achieve a key objective, which is glory and renown. It empowers them psychologically and, by enhancing their stature, it is bound to facilitate their efforts to recruit new members. Moreover, calling it "war" fosters a political environment in the United States supportive of increased investment in military instruments when a central principle of counter-insurgent doctrine, and insurgency is the closest analogy to the present threat, is the primacy of political and economic measures and information operations designed to isolate the violent.[48] Calling it "war" activates what the historian Walter Russell Mead calls the "Jacksonian" side of the American foreign policy culture,[49] the side marked by wrath and blind hatred, an impulse to exterminate, a ferocious xenophobia, all-in-all a set of emotions not exactly conducive to the search Berman sensibly urges for political solutions to grievances that, if aggravated, can give the relatively few terrorists a whole sea of sympathizers in which to hide: empathy, after all, is one of war's first casualties. And calling it "war", and if war it is one that promises to be perpetual, will surely mean that at home we will have fewer freedoms to defend.

Rejecting the rhetoric of war, cold or hot, does not entail declaring that we do not have a serious challenge to our security. Even small groups now have the capacity to make catastrophes and both their numbers and their capacities could grow. Liberal strategists need to act on the assumption that a sound majority of the American people are not infantile, that they can grasp and accept the proposition that we face a substantial danger which is too dispersed and resilient to be exterminated, but which can be limited in its capacity to affect our lives if we address it resolutely and creatively, in close and respectful cooperation with other states and peoples, at considerable expense, and with a mix of means unlike the mix required to wage inter-state wars. The expense will not necessarily require more revenue; it will certainly require a substantial reallocation of existing

---

[48] See Richardson, 215–24; and Packer, 62–3.
[49] See generally, Walter Russell Mead, *Special Providence: American Foreign Policy and How it Changed the World* (New York: Alfred A Knopf, 2004).

defense expenditures in ways responsive to the real features of the terrorist threat which is unlike the threat arising from conflict with a powerful state. Such a conventional adversary is not now even on the horizon; yet we are investing more in our regular armed forces than the combined military expenditures of the next 13 strongest nations.[50]

The cost will not be financial only. There will be costs in privacy. The government will need to engage in more intrusive surveillance than has ever before been possible or deemed acceptable. And there may be other strains on civil liberties including, in some cases, the security vetting of lawyers defending persons charged with plotting or participating in terrorism whether at home or abroad. As a result, not all defendants will have lawyers entirely of their own choice.

Under a right-wing government we have already gone much further than measures of that character. In its successful effort to eliminate habeas corpus review of detentions of persons declared to be "enemy combatants"[51] and in its fierce opposition to Congressional restraints on interrogation methods,[52] the Bush Administration has evidenced its indifference to core constitutional values relating to security of the person from the power of the state: the right to a judicial process that gives all individuals a fair chance to defend themselves within a reasonable time against charges of criminal activity and the right not be brutally interrogated. In its overall performance it has confirmed two propositions of paramount importance. One is that when the executive branch is in the hands of the right wing of American politics, that branch will not be guided by the principles (a) that intrusions on constitutional and human rights should be only those plainly required by the severity of the danger, and (b) that certain absolute limits on unfairness and inhumanity must be respected. The other proposition is that if, in the face of a prolonged threat of catastrophic terror attacks, the United States is going to maintain its traction on the slippery slope of expanded executive power, it needs a congress and federal courts willing and able to force adherence to those principles through rigorous oversight.

In the course of the Cold War, American commentators and officials often described it as a struggle for "hearts and minds." But whether under Democratic or Republican Administrations, the US Government generally acted as if the "War" were a conventional conflict between powerful states, acted, that is, as if the nation's safety lay principally in its ability to deploy large military assets capable of defending territory, industrial capacity and material and human resources in Europe, Japan, and the Middle East from violent appropriation by the Soviet Union and its satellites. It was to that end that we invested by far

---

[50] Charles V Peña, "More Defense Spending, Less Security." *Antiwar.com,* 16 February 2006, available at <http://www.antiwar.com/pena/?articleid=8546>.

[51] See "Military Commissions Act of 2006—Turning Bad Policy into Bad Law," *Amnesty International,* 29 September 2006; available at <http://web.amnesty.org/library/pdf/AMR51154 2006ENGLISH/$File/AMR5115406.pdf>.

[52] Ibid; see also "A 'Tortured' Debate," above, footnote 6.

the largest part of the public revenues earmarked for national security purposes and decided how large the earmark should be. Although the rhetoric of "hearts and minds" sounded more loudly when the United States was engaged in the conflict's side-shows, the hot and, with the exception of Vietnam, generally little insurgent wars in what we then called "The Third World," there too the emphasis was on military means, on engaging and destroying Marxists, far more than on limiting their appeal or converting them. In general we followed the wisdom of that nameless General who remarked that "once you have them [the insurgents] by the balls, hearts and minds will follow."

To be sure, the psychological dimension of strategy was never ignored altogether. Very early in the conflict, when American officials feared the formation of communist-dominated governments in Western Europe, the CIA in particular sought to influence public opinion by quietly encouraging non-communist but left-leaning European intellectuals to repudiate revolutionary doctrines, to condemn the betrayal of socialism by the Soviet Union, and to endorse democratic reform within a capitalist economic framework. To that end covert sources funded organizations and publications, conferences and workshops often involving writers and teachers who in America would have been regarded as dangerous leftists, indistinguishable from hard-core communists,[53] which is one reason this project needed CIA rather than State Department funding: concealing it from the American right and its Neanderthal constituencies was possibly more critical than shielding it from general awareness in Europe. And later in the conflict, when, following Fidel Castro's consolidation of power in Cuba, signs of revolutionary ferment and little nodules of insurgency began to appear in Latin America, the Kennedy Administration, newly in power, initiated a broad effort, the "Alliance for Progress,"[54] to foster and facilitate a positive response by generally conservative governments to popular grievances and to associate the United States with reform. But the difficult and costly effort to overcome the rooted structures of injustice in Latin societies quickly got crowded out by a visceral identification of leftist movements as the generic enemy of the United States and a consequent refusal to risk the fall of anti-reform Neanderthals by activating the reform-oriented conditions rhetorically attached to our support for them. Moreover, it proved relatively easy simply to crush leftist political and insurgent movements rather than to risk the tricky task of working with them to leverage systemic reform. In any event, transforming rooted systems of injustice would have required the very large financial resources and senior decision-makers' attention that within a few years of the founding of the Alliance for Progress were being sucked into the quick-sands of Vietnam.

[53] See Frances Stonor Saunders, *Who Paid the Piper: The CIA and the Cultural Cold War* (London: Granta Books, 1999).
[54] See generally, *The Alliance for Progress: A Retrospective*, L Ronald Scheman (ed) (New York: Praeger, 1988).

Presidential-level interest in the hearts-and-minds dimension of national strategy resurfaced shortly after the Vietnamese disaster in part because of the alienation of hearts and minds within the United States itself. For the first time an American President explicitly internationalized American constitutional liberalism by equating it with the body of internationally recognized human rights and declaring their promotion a major concern of American foreign policy. And while Jimmy Carter's rhetoric far outran his actions, he deviated with sufficient frequency from the convention of unquestioning endorsement and material support for right-wing governments, regardless of their human rights records, to convince the media, the American people, and the American Right, as well as some targeted regimes, of his seriousness.[55]

In Chapter 2 I sketched the appropriation and transformation effected largely by neo-conservatives in the Reagan Administration of Carter's effort to give some heft to the ideological dimension of American strategy in what proved to be the final years of the Cold War. Initially, as I noted, neo-conservatives kept the international human rights wrapping for their ideological warfare project. Following the dissolution of the Soviet Union, however, they quickly, perhaps unconsciously, discarded the wrapping as they shifted the target of the project. Whereas before the primary target had been citizens of other countries, it now became citizens of the United States; the project's goal correspondingly changed from victory in the Cold War, now won, to victory in the battle to impose their imperial vision onto American foreign policy. The ultimate goal remained the same, they claimed, namely transforming the global security environment and universalizing American values by multiplying laissez-faire capitalist democracies.[56] To those ends it was necessary to harness the now incomparable military power of the United States and to release it from the restraints of international law and power-sharing international institutions, principally the United Nations. Thus the international human rights promotion project had to morph into the oxymoronic-sounding doctrine of American Universalism.[57]

Measured by its share of government revenues and its influence on US foreign policy, the effort to influence hearts and minds never played more than a bit part in the historical drama of the Cold War. In the context of the new terrorist threat to US national security, the most prospectively effective grand strategy requires the

[55] See Lars Schoultz, *Human Rights and United States Policy Towards Latin America* (Princeton: Princeton University Press, 1981); and "US Policy to Human Rights in Latin America: A Comparative Analysis Between Two Administrations," in Ved P Nanda, James R Scarritt, and George W Shephard (eds), *Global Human Rights, Public Policies, Comparative Measures and NGO Strategies* (Boulder: Westview Press, 1981).
[56] See generally, Tom J Farer, "The Interplay of Domestic Politics, Human Rights, and US Foreign Policy," *Wars on Terrorism and Iraq*, Thomas G Weiss, Margaret E Crahan and John Goering (eds) (New York: Routledge, 2004).
[57] See Robert Kagan, *Dangerous Nation* (New York: Knopf, 2006); but compare Walter Russell Mead, *Power, Terror, Peace and War: America's Grand Strategy in a World at Risk* (New York: Knopf, 2004).

former bit player to assume a leading role. It can only play that role, however, if the substance as well as the idiom of the strategy is liberal. Of course it is substance, the quotidian acts and omissions of the many arms of a powerful and complicated government, that matters most. But the inevitably freighted language in which a president sets the general thrust and character of national policy influences that quotidian output, as it also influences the ways in which the acts and omissions of the United States and of its democratic allies are understood and assessed.

The neo-conservative language and policy of American universalism adopted by Bush the younger, the declared intent and at least the notional attempt to advance freedom on the end of American bayonets, with such allies as are willing to conform to American tactical and strategic judgments, was hardly calculated to have much appeal beyond the borders of the United States. This is one element of reality that Paul Berman grasps.

Laws, formal treaties, the customs of civilized nations, the legitimacy of international institutions—these were the dross of the past, and Bush was plunging into the future. And, as he plunged, he had no idea, nobody in his administration seemed to have any idea, that international law [and]…human rights had willy-nilly become the language of liberal democracy around the world.[58]

To have a chance at effecting that "ideological conversion" of alienated Muslims that the counter-terror strategist David Kilcullen envisions, at "creating resistance" to the message of violent Islamist leaders, the idiom of our grand strategy must be the only idiom we have that connects our constitutional values with the values of people all over the globe, the idiom of international human rights and international law, the idiom of liberalism.

That should be the normative frame of our grand strategy. The electorate and the chattering classes, having experienced through the medium of the Iraqi debacle the consequences of imperial overreach, should in general be amenable to changing the frame. The way in which leaders then fill that frame will determine whether we, in alliance with governments that share our values or at least our interest in containing the risk of catastrophic terrorism, address the political grievances that if ignored will widen the pool of recruits for terrorist projects and incline local communities to complicity. The acts and omissions which constitute the substance of policy will also determine the incidence of those "biological triggers" that propel the alienated from latent to active terrorists.

Of course policies consistent with the liberal values embedded in human rights norms will not address all grievances, in part because not everyone now shares those values. Particularly in Chapter 4, I tried to suggest the normative limits of a liberal majority's efforts to accommodate the beliefs and sensibilities of non-liberal minorities within Western countries. Those limits are also relevant to the transnational scene. Hence, being true to our principles is not a panacea. It hardly

---

[58] Berman, 193.

follows, however, that because we cannot address all grievances we should address none. In any event, it is the nature of liberals, political heirs of Enlightenment thought, to believe in the gradual spread of liberal values wherever people are given the practical opportunity to have dreams and to realize them. Thus the project of liberalism is to create grounds for hope that those conditions can be achieved and for belief that the nations and the communities within nations that already enjoy those conditions actually wish to admit others to the same world of opportunity. In that spirit I have urged new and undoubtedly difficult social integration projects for Islamic immigrants in Europe and endorsed more selective criteria for prospective immigrants and much more effort to prepare them to live comfortably in societies saturated with a liberal ethos.

The United States has its own full measure of problems with alienated youth, but not particularly with the children of immigrants from the Muslim world, and alienation here has led largely to ordinary crime—contained through heavy policing and relatively massive incarceration—not political violence. But as the European phase of Mohammed Atta's incubation suggests, Europe's problems can migrate to America, just as America's problems can make their way to Europe by one route or another: it certainly appears that the victims of the Madrid and London bombings would be alive today if President Bush had not induced British and Spanish participation in the occupation of Iraq.

The security of the North Atlantic countries is so closely linked, in part because they are seen by other peoples as working in harness, that just as the United States has an interest in how European states cope with Islamic minorities, the Europeans have an equal or greater interest in how the United States relates to the Islamic world. That is one of the reasons the normally compliant Tony Blair has pushed the Bush Administration to press for a sustainable solution to the iconic Israeli-Palestinian conflict instead of giving a wink and a nod to Israel's colonizing enterprise in the Occupied Territories.[59] What I have tried to do in Chapter 5 of this book is to explain why the Occupation, ie the ever-advancing colonization of West Bank territory and the violence that has inevitably attended it, inflames Muslims from Karachi to London and violates liberal principles. And I have tried also to suggest how the North Atlantic States working with Islamic regimes, themselves threatened by the furies the conflict has unleashed, should address it within the framework of international human rights and humanitarian law.

Like any world view, Liberalism as the normative framework of a grand strategy has broad operational implications. One, implied by Paul Berman in the quotation above, is a strong preference for acting in concert with other states, that is for multilateralism over unilateralism which would then become the means of last resort. Ad hoc coalitions of the willing, the "willing" being those states that will doggedly follow wherever the United States Government chooses

---

[59] See, eg, Alan Cowell, "Blair Urges Strategy Change in Mideast, Spotlighting Iran," *The New York Times*, 14 November 2006, A10.

to lead, is functionally indistinguishable from unilateralism in that the United States determines tactics, strategies, and goals (and decides when those have been achieved) just as it would if it acted alone. What events have shown is that the insistence on dictating the terms of cooperation prevents the United States from securing the cooperation of important states.

Multilateralism is a commitment to *institutionalized* cooperation on the basis of a readiness to negotiate the terms of cooperation which in fact means a readiness to compromise on matters of tactics and strategies and instrumental (intermediate) goals. Institutions signify and facilitate systematic consultation and joint action over time. Any given action in any given case will probably benefit some states more than others. Those others need assurance that there will be compensation down the road where action will disproportionately benefit them. Because institutions are a commitment to cooperation over time, they are storehouses of IOUs. In addition, when established to address concrete problems, they facilitate cooperative action in two ways: by encouraging the evolution of convergent views about the nature of the problems and broad strategies for addressing them; and by developing operational plans for tackling particular instances of those problems, so tactics and strategies and the allocation of responsibilities do not have to be improvised case-by-case. Furthermore, by making consultation obligatory, they provide members with a feedback mechanism that will inhibit poorly considered, impulsive responses to shocking events by isolated deciders in individual states who, among other things, fail to calculate into their decisional equations the probable responses of other important states.[60]

Multilateralism is not an anodyne synonym for the United Nations. After the Second World War, inspired by liberal values, the United States acted as the principal architect of multilateral institutions—the United Nations, the World Bank, the Organization of American States, NATO, the General Agreement on Tariffs and Trade (GATT), to name some—institutions that structured a global order in which the United States has thrived. Addressing the festering grievances that feed recruits into terrorist networks and provide them with a social base and restraining the spread of weapons of mass destruction and, indeed, addressing all of the main twenty-first century threats to national and human security will in the longer term require close and systematic cooperation between the United States and other consequential countries including China, Japan, India, Brazil, Mexico, Indonesia, South Africa, as well as our traditional NATO allies.[61]

---

[60] Compare Freeman Dyson, "The Bitter End," *The New York Review of Books*, 28 April 2005, 4, at 5: "The third lesson of World War II is the value of international alliances…Leaders of international alliances…must make compromises and accept delays in order to achieve consensus. They cannot make brilliant and disastrous decisions as Hitler did. They cannot lead their people to destruction. To fight a war within the constraints of an international alliance is a good protection against fatal mistakes and follies."

[61] I have previously tried to make the case for and sketched the features of a new organization of consequential states in "Toward an Effective International Legal Order: From Coexistence to Concert?" *Cambridge Review of International Affairs*, 17(2) (July 2004), 219–38.

As presently constituted the Security Council has neither the requisite membership nor broad mandate nor skilled secretariat for operational planning. Reconstituting it may not be possible within the constitutional and political constraints immanent in the United Nations. So it may be necessary to build a new parallel institution or to develop new regional security organizations with overlapping membership and other linkages to each other and to NATO, organizations with a conception of security threats that includes all of the fortifiers and accelerators of terrorist networks. At this point the only things one can say with complete confidence is that there exists a severe institutional deficit in many regions and for the globe as a whole and that only the United States has the influence to organize support for addressing it.

By virtue of the attitudes that help define their place on the political spectrum—chauvinism, suspicion of the foreign, a rigid conception of sovereignty, the masculinization of honor,[62] and the related valorization of force—the constituencies and elites occupying the Right are disabled from multilateral institutional building. Liberalism, conversely, by virtue of its cosmopolitanism, that is its commitment to the idea of rights shared by all peoples and its corresponding dictation of limits on privileging one's own community, and its related view of coercion as at best a lesser evil, inspires a search for cooperative mechanisms. After all, dominating power unrestrained by norms and institutionalized obligations to consult is bound to be coercive, is bound to make claims for itself that it will deny to others, is bound, that is, to reject the Kantian dictum to take only such actions as you are prepared to generalize into rules for all.[63]

A second operational implication of a liberal grand strategy is the large-scale use of public resources to create environments relatively inhospitable to advocates of transgressive violence. Kilcullen, the counter-terror strategist, speaks favorably of a Marshall Plan for impoverished parts of the Islamic world presumably to identify the United States with the dramatic expansion of economic and social opportunity for their exponentially expanding youth cohorts and to empower religious leaders, teachers, and institutions open to dialogue with the West or at least unsympathetic to terrorist violence. Certainly there are grounds for believing that the intelligent deployment of financial resources can affect public sentiment in Muslim societies.

In this connection Louise Richardson cites the case of Indonesia. Before 9/11 polling data showed approximately 70 per cent of Indonesians had a favorable attitude toward the United States. Two years later, following the invasion of Iraq and new rivers of blood in Gaza and the West Bank, favorable opinion was down to 15 per cent and, according to Richardson, the country had become a hotbed of Al Qaeda enthusiasts: polling showed 58 per cent of the Indonesian public

---

[62] See generally, Leo Braudy, *From Chivalry to Terrorism* (New York: Vintage Books, 2005); compare Tahira Khan, *Beyond Honor* (New York: Oxford University Press, 2006).
[63] See Arnold Brecht, *Political Theory* (Princeton: Princeton University Press, 1959), 375–7.

had confidence in bin Laden as a world leader. Then in December 2004 came the devastating tsunami. The United States responded quickly and generously, rapidly upping an initial offer of $35 million in aid to $950 million pledged by the President himself. And with assistance from the US military, aid began actually flowing openly and at speed. In the wake of this response, a new public opinion poll taken in 2005 found (a) that 79 per cent of Indonesians had a more favorable view of the United States as a result of the aid, and (b) 35 per cent were generally positive in their view of the United States.[64] In addition, positive answers to the confidence-in-bin-Laden question fell to 35 per cent.

Although Paul Berman, relying on sources he does not bother to cite, paints Muslim schools, the "Madrassas," as seedbeds of terrorist organizations, a study of ones in India and Pakistan, where they are numerous, concludes that only a small minority preach *jihad*.[65] But while many are attempting in good faith to provide children generally from the lower classes with the rudiments of a practical education while deepening their commitment to and understanding of Islam, they are hardly centers of Enlightenment thought and many lack the resources to prepare students for professional success. Suppose President Bush had envisioned the half-trillion dollar cost of the war[66] (never mind the human and political costs) and had decided, therefore, to skip the war and instead to offer 20 per cent of that amount in a match (whether one-to-one or some other proportion) with funds from the governments of Saudi Arabia, Kuwait, and the United Arab Emirates to endow Madrassas initially in Afghanistan, Pakistan, India (one hundred million Muslims), and Bangladesh and to establish a number of associated teachers' colleges. The resulting educational system could be administered by a body of leading intellectuals from all over the Islamic World, people like the brilliant Indian (Muslim) writer, MJ Akbar,[67] perhaps selected by a special educational committee of the Organization of the Islamic Conference, an institution in which Indonesia and Malaysia, centers of moderate Islamic thought, play an increasingly prominent role.[68] Its core curriculum and textbooks relating to history in particular could be developed by the administering body in conjunction with intellectuals from other religious and philosophical traditions under the aegis of UNESCO so that the project would have an ecumenical character, would be a symbol of dialogue rather than conflict between civilizations.

Suppose that, in addition, the President proposed to spend, in conjunction with other wealthy states, 4 per cent of the $500 billion to endow centers for peace and poverty-reduction research and inter-communal dialogue to be located

---

[64] Richardson, 223.

[65] Alexander Evans, "Understanding Madrasahs," *Foreign Affairs*, 85(1) (January/February 2006), 9–16.

[66] Joel Havemann, "The Conflict in Iraq: Footing the Bill," *The Los Angeles Times*, 14 January 2007, A9.

[67] See, among many other works, *The Shade of Swords: Jihad and the Conflict Between Islam and Christianity* (London: Routledge, 2002).

[68] See Robert R Bianchi, *Guests of God* (Oxford: Oxford University Press, 2004).

perhaps in India and Pakistan, with a third planned for Jerusalem following a settlement of the Israeli-Palestinian conflict which will have to include, he would say, either a division of sovereignty in that city or shared sovereignty. The Centers, which would also be governed by intellectuals (in this case from all parts of the world) would train PhDs, hold workshops and symposia, publish policy papers, and develop adult and child educational programs for distribution through a satellite network and through interested private and public media like PBS, the BBC, and Al Jazeera.

I am confident that counter-terrorist strategists like US Government-connected Kilcullen define themselves as "pragmatists," not as "liberals," that species being anathema to the Bush Administration for its imagined contributions to the terrorist threat, a view that Paul Berman schizophrenically channels, as I noted earlier. I construe Kilkullen's "Marshall Plan" for helping address the terrorist threat as a synonym for very large-scale investment of public funds in non-military projects overseas designed to further certain strategic aims.

My heuristic proposal has five such aims. One is dramatically signaling respect for the great body of Islamic believers, signaling a sense of common humanity and shared concern for the fate of our children. The second is actually enhancing the life chances of a substantial slice of Islamic youth in a volatile subcontinent occupied by polarized nuclear states. A third is empowering mainstream Islamic thinkers in their implicit struggle with those Muslims who are unable or unwilling to envision benign relations with the non-Islamic peoples. The fourth is fostering among young Muslims and their teachers, particularly through the history and current affairs curriculum of the schools and the programs of the centers, a growing capacity for empirically based critical thought not about religious belief as such, but rather about the complex and shifting historical relationship among Islamic peoples and between the Islamic and the non-Islamic nations and civilizations; about the basic international normative structure (including human rights) to which all of the civilizations have contributed, and about the global experience of trying to build responsible governments, to spread affluence, to increase life chances and to eliminate extreme poverty. The fifth, finally, is to provide an educational model for all countries with large Muslim populations. (Ideally the curriculum would insinuate itself into all countries, including the United States, as an antidote to communal chauvinism.) I offer this hypothesis: that had the President chosen the alternative expenditure of funds I hypothesize, today we could all rest rather more securely in our beds[69] and more than 3,000 young Americans and anywhere from 50,000 to 600,000 Iraqi civilians estimated to have died in the last three years would now be alive.[70]

---

[69] Even the Central Intelligence Agency credits the widespread belief that the Iraq war has been an accelerator for terrorist recruitment; see, eg, Karen De Young, "Spy Agencies Say Iraq War Hurting US Terror Fight," *The Washington Post*, 24 September 2006, A1.

[70] See the estimates summarized in Mark Danner, "Iraq: The War of the Imagination," *The New York Review of Books*, 21 December 2006, 81 at 84. The stated determination of the Bush

Any large-scale public investment for non-military purposes cuts sharply against the ideological and emotional grain of the American right-wing coalition: against its nativism, its exaltation of military means, its demand for "small government" and, coincidentally, for financially disabling the production of non-military public goods, and, finally, its faith-based commitment to the proposition that public programs for effecting social change are at best ineffective.[71] Conversely, it is entirely consistent with the political culture of modern liberalism. That does not preclude some idiosyncratic Republican from adopting this kind of strategic agenda. After all, the episodically triumphant Victorian Conservative leader, Benjamin Disraeli, sometimes expropriated pieces of the Liberal Party's program. But like Disraeli, my hypothesized Republican leader, precisely because he would be executing a strategy stemming from liberal thought, would inflict severe strains on the loyalty of his political base. It is, perhaps, suggestive that even where President George W Bush proposed some sort of public investment program—his "no-child-left-behind" initiative being a rare case in point, the Republican-controlled Congress left it gasping for lack of funds.[72]

The usual right-wing riposte to proposals for ameliorating social and economic conditions as a counter-terrorist strategy is to invoke the middle or occasionally even privileged-class background of some of the more notorious terrorists, bin Laden, scion of a mega-rich family, prominent among them. It follows logically, rightists claim, that terrorism is unrelated to poverty or, though this is generally not mentioned, to the humiliations and denials of elementary justice which compound the misery of the poor.

If sincerely made, the argument is merely fatuous. Obviously the desperately poor are too sick, exhausted, uninformed, and absorbed in quotidian survival to serve in much less to lead terrorist networks. As all fact-based people know, with rare exceptions insurgent and terrorist leaders and even more uniformly the intellectuals who often shape their political projects have come from the more leisured and literate classes. Marx was a middle-class chap and Engels was

---

Administration not to keep track of Iraqi civilian deaths and the difficulty whatever the will of tracking deaths in such a violent and chaotic environment have collectively produced this immense range of estimates.

[71] It is true, as Peter Beinart has noted, that the first generation of neo-conservatives, having separated themselves from the Democratic Party ostensibly, in part, because they had lost faith in large-scale social engineering, generated ideological successors who beat the drums for an essay in social engineering—namely the forced-draft democratization of the middle East—that dwarfed in resources and complexity the social programs their elders noisily repudiated. See Beinart's *The Good Fight: Why Liberals—and Only Liberals—Can Win the War on Terror and Make America Great Again* (New York: Harper Collins, 2006). Though a fact, it is not really an ironic one, since the intent to produce democracy first in Iraq by imposing at the point of a bayonet a President, Ahmad Chalabi, chosen by neo-conservatives sitting in Washington rather than the people of Iraq, could hardly be said to spring naturally from the ethos of liberalism. See James Risen, *State of War: The Secret History of the CIA and the Bush Administration* (New York: Free Press, 2006). Moreover, for them, as for the rest of the Right, force was the means of first choice, not last.

[72] See "Bait-and-Switch on Public Education," *The New York Times*, 21 October 2003, 26.

positively wealthy; but unlike many of their class, they were unable to look down with indifference into the nineteenth-century pit of Dickensian misery. Instead of seeing the working out of iron Malthusian laws or a different and inferior species, they saw broken human lives. Louise Richardson makes precisely this point when surveying the extensive literature on the terrorist mind: what the psychological profiles reveal is that "terrorists tend to act not out of a desire for personal gratification but on behalf of a group with which they identify (though the two motives can of course coexist). Islamic terrorists, for example, regularly invoke the suffering of Palestinians and other Muslims."[73] Empathy can produce a Mother Teresa; it can also produce an Osama bin Laden.

C. Words and Deeds

A principal theme of the counter-terror empiricists is the public communications dimension of the struggle. This dimension is something much larger than "propaganda" with its now conventional connotation of indoctrination by deception and distortion. The multiple sources of information in global civil society and the multiple means now available to individuals for accessing them even from remote corners of the globe have radically reduced the capacity of governments, other than a few peculiarly isolated totalitarian ones like North Korea's, to propagate successfully grossly distorted if not utterly false narratives. Of course all advocates tell only one part of a story. When bin Laden accuses the United States of complicity in the death of thousands of Muslims (citing among other cases the post Gulf-War sanctions against Iraq which sharply increased child mortality in that country[74]), he does not stop to note the American-led interventions in Bosnia and Kosovo on behalf of their Muslim populations any more than President Bush, when declaring the unswerving[75] American commitment to democracy, feels the necessity of regretting the American hand in the overthrow of elected governments in Brazil, Chile, Iran, and Guatemala. Still, in their selective accounts, today's propagators of favorable narratives cannot simply invent facts and hope to be effective or make claims which conflict conspicuously with widely known facts.

There seems to exist even in right-wing policy circles agreement about the pitiable state of the country's so-called "public diplomacy" particularly in relation to the Islamic World. President Bush was sufficiently sensitive to its decrepitude to dispatch one of his closest political operators, the never-off-the-right-wing-message Karen Hughes, to the exotic precincts of the State Department presumably with

---

[73] Richardson, 41.

[74] *See* "Health and Human Rights Consequences of War in Iraq: A Briefing Paper." *Physicians for Human Rights*, 14 February 2002; available at <http://www.physiciansforhumanrights.org/library/documents/reports/health-and-human-rights.pdf>. See also "The Situation of Children in Iraq," *United Nations Children's Fund*, February 2002, available at <http://www.casi.org.uk/info/unicef0202.pdf>.

[75] See Packer, above, note 16, at 67.

the objective of reanimating the convalescent who, to be sure, has been sickly for a very long time. To that end, shortly after her arrival in the Department, she went off to the Middle East where, according to news reports, she sought to bond with Muslim women of the privileged class as fellow "moms" and religious believers. In other words, she appealed for mutual understanding on the only grounds available to an emissary of the American Right determined to stay on message. The result, again according to reports, was dismal, a conversation of the deaf.[76]

What would be the measure of a successful public diplomacy program? Presumably it is its capacity to help reduce the appeal of terrorist politics for target audiences. Thus it must be able to speak to their grievances and their dreams. It must persuade them that America is not the source of their grievances, nor the enemy of their dreams.

A country like a single human being communicates principally by what it does, not what it says. When the United States claims to be an honest broker in the Israeli-Palestinian conflict, it does not pass the laugh test and even if we invested half of the Pentagon budget in promoting that claim, if US policy remains the same, every cent would be wasted. No communications program no matter how lavishly funded and artfully designed could hide the reality of Abu Ghraib or the museums and libraries we consigned to the looters at the beginning of our Marx Brothers occupation of Iraq. The implicit message to Muslims had to be that we did not care enough about the patrimony of the Iraqi people to save it. At the time of the US invasion of Afghanistan, senior American officials assured the world that in contrast to our abandonment of the country after the Soviet withdrawal, this time we would stay the course; we would rebuild this shattered place. Yet within months the resources and attention shifted to Iraq and Afghanistan was left largely to rot. There are few propositions you can utter with absolute certainty about their truth, but there is at least one: public diplomacy cannot conceal the real substance of public policy.

In the series of lectures that became this book, I have tried to explain how policies inspired by liberal beliefs and values rather than those of the Right are far more likely to mitigate the felt grievances of the Muslim world in relation to the United States. In doing so they will help isolate true believers in politics by terror and reduce the biographical triggers that propel youth from mere disaffection to violent action. I am under no illusion that this would happen all at once. And not merely because the sense of grievance is sticky. There will be an inevitable lag between changes in policy, should they occur, and changes in perception. Memory, particularly remembered grievances, can be fiercely tenacious. It is not only in the Bible that people dream of revenge unto the fourth generation.

Beyond that difficulty, there is the tattered condition of norms governing the use of force for political ends. Terrorism is violence that transgresses moral limits. I believe that at the heart of those limits is the belief that violence, if it is justified

---

[76] Ibid.

at all, must be directed against violators of basic rights, whether the violators be individuals, private groups, or states. What is above all forbidden is violence deliberately employed against the innocent, those who have not violated the rights of others. The human rights conventions express this taboo by prohibiting brutal treatment and punishment without fair process even in times of emergency. The humanitarian laws of war do the same by prohibiting retaliatory brutality; one country cannot, for instance, torture its prisoners to retaliate for torture of prisoners by its enemy.

But since, even in the course of conducting a just war, the innocent will suffer, moralists had either to embrace pacifism or rationalize the non-deliberate but entirely predictable killing of the innocent. As I pointed out earlier, most chose to rationalize by constructing the theory of the double effect, that is the intended effect (ie destroy a legitimate target) and the incidental albeit envisioned effect which is the death of the innocent. And as long as the incidental effect is not entirely out of proportion to the military benefit of the intended effect, the moral norm is notionally respected. Even as the core moral principle was crystallizing into a legal one during the sanguinary years of the twentieth century, two world wars and many smaller ones loosened passions that certainly during the Second War often burst through the thin wall of normative restraint. The United States and its allies like their ruthless nihilistic opponents were, at the day's end, prepared to pulverize citizen and soldier alike.

In the joyful, optimistic wake of victory, restraints were reaffirmed, at the Nuremburg Trials and also in the Geneva Conventions of 1949, which also happened to be year one of the Korean War in the course of which the United States bombed so heavily that after a time strategic bombing could do little more than make North Korea's rubble bounce. It is arguable that in subsequent conflicts, even Vietnam, and more recently in Kosovo and Serbia,[77] Afghanistan and Iraq, and with the benefit of far superior targeting capability and guidable weapons, discrimination in the use of force is far greater than in the past. But thanks to the revolution in communications, images of the results of firepower, however discriminating, the images of broken places and people, sweep through the world and sweep along with them, I fear, the remnants of belief that such restraint as is practiced has moral importance. The Israeli policy of retaliating with great disproportion to any injury suffered, in the understandable hope of deterring a campaign of endless small cuts, and the policy of preemptive killing too, may have contributed to what I fear is a growing sense among peoples of living in a normless universe.

In such a universe there is no transgressive violence. There is just violence. So one of the ends of a liberal grand strategy for confronting terrorism must be the reaffirmation of limits on violence, a reaffirmation by deeds, since words will surely not suffice.

---

[77] For an account of the use of air power to force Serbian armed forces out of Kosovo, see Michael Ignatieff, *Virtual War* (New York: Picador, 2000).

In October 2002, virtually on the eve of the invasion of Iraq, Karen Hughes came to the University of Denver to participate in a debate on liberal and conservative approaches to civic values.[78] Before we went on stage, I stood listening to Karen responding to a question from a television reporter about the purposes of the approaching war. As always, she was voluble and on message. I had no incentive to recall her exact phrasing; but what remains indelible is her invocation in so many words of the freedom and democracy the blessings of which we intended to bring to the Iraqi people. And I still recall thinking that any government of the American Right, much less the one for which she spoke, was, by its nature, an improbable vehicle for delivering to those people what she promised.

Well, it was indeed improbable. And now, after all that has passed, peering back over the mountain of corpses in Iraq, imagining all of the biographical triggers the images of this war must have built, remembering that day on the eve of the occupation, I find myself obsessively recalling some lines from the First World War novel of that most American of modern novelists, Ernest Hemingway:

We had heard them [the words sacred, glorious, hallowed and the expression in vain], sometimes standing in the rain out of earshot, so that only the shouted words came through…and the things that were glorious had no glory and the sacrifices were like the stockyards in Chicago, if nothing was done with the meat except to bury it. There were many words that you could not stand to hear and finally only the names of places had dignity…. [They] were all you could say and have them mean anything. Abstract words…were obscene beside the concrete names of villages, the numbers of roads, the names of rivers, the numbers of regiments and the dates.[79]

But, as I said earlier, liberals are by their nature optimists. Abstract words like freedom and democracy and universal rights define us and point the way toward a grand strategy far more likely than the swaggering brutalism of the right to contain terrorism while preserving at home and advancing elsewhere by slow degrees and with caring hands those things that were once promised to the still living and to the dead people of Iraq.

---

[78] For an account of the event see <http://www.media-visions.com/colorado/greatdebate.html>.
[79] Ernest Hemingway, *A Farewell to Arms* (New York: Scribner, 1986), 185.

Index